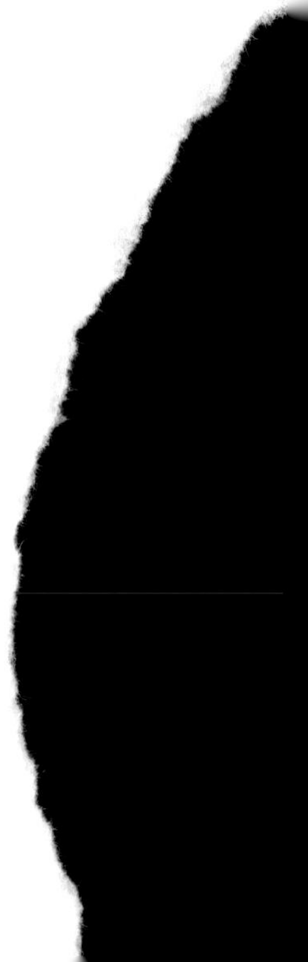

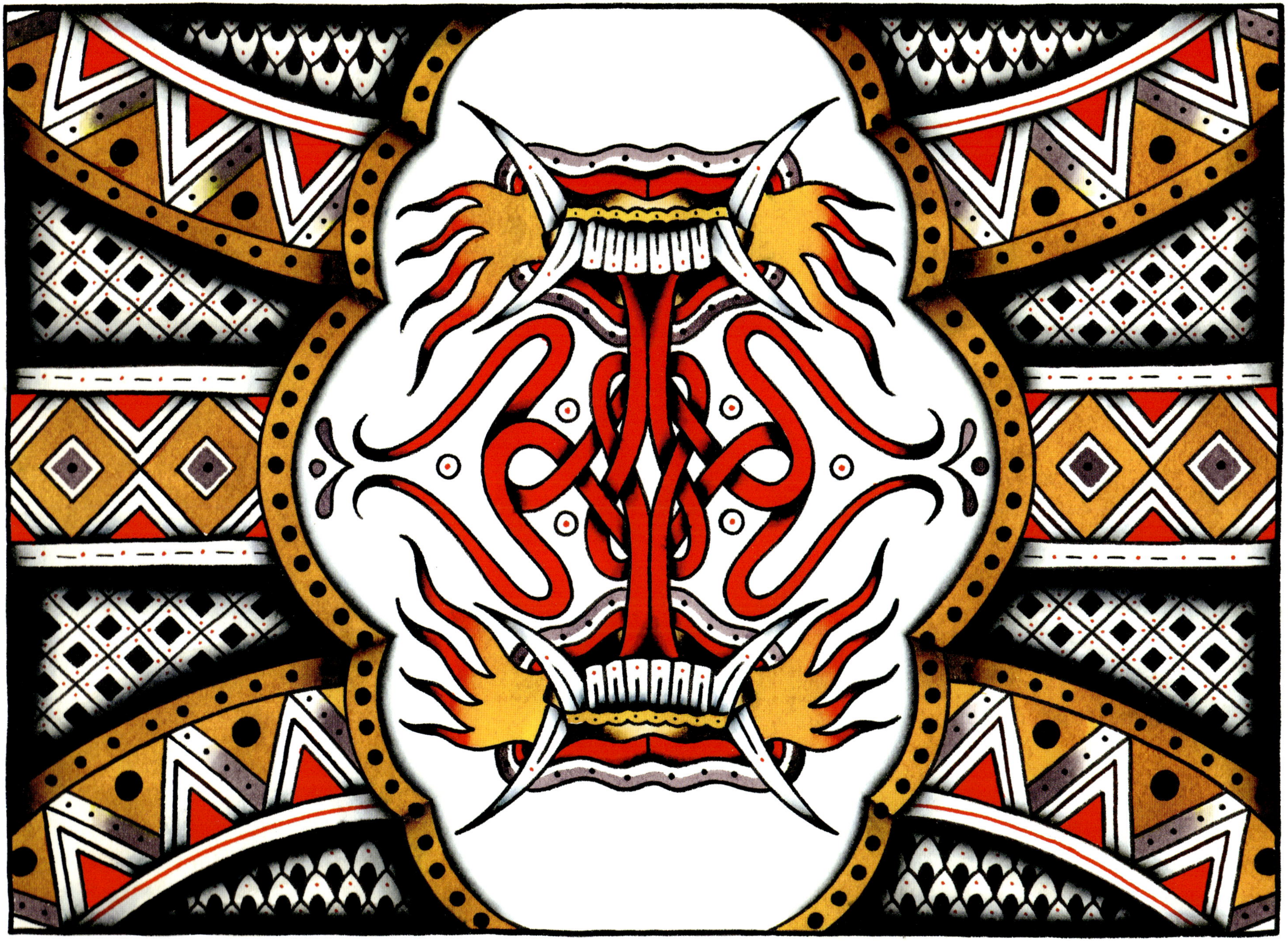

Other Schiffer Books on Related Subjects:

Classic Flash in Five Bold Colors, Jeromey "Tilt" McCulloh, 978-0-7643-3165-7
Classic Flash 2: In Five Bold Colors, Jeromey "Tilt" McCulloh, 978-0-7643-3867-0
Neoclassical Tattoo Flash, Stizzo, 978-0-7643-6397-9
Flash from the Bowery: Classic American Tattoos, 1900–1950,
Cliff White, 978-0-7643-3928-8

Originally published as *Tattoo Artists: French Kiss Project*, ©2022 by Éditions Place des Victoires, Paris

Translated from the French by Ordentop Agency

Library of Congress Control Number: 2025931519

Editorial manager: Marie Clavel
Layout: El Bent
Front cover and title page illustrations: © John Stone
Back cover illustration: © El Bent

Type set in Quicksand Book

ISBN: 978-0-7643-7035-9
ePub: 978-1-5073-0618-5
Printed in China

10 9 8 7 6 5 4 3 2 1

MIX
Paper | Supporting responsible forestry
FSC® C104723

Published by Schiffer Publishing, Ltd.
4880 Lower Valley Road
Atglen, PA 19310
Phone: (610) 593-1777; Fax: (610) 593-2002
Email: Info@schifferbooks.com
Web: www.schifferbooks.com

John Stone • Tiwan • El Bent

TATTOO FLASH

FROM THE FRENCH KISS PROJECT

Collaborative Flash Pairings by Tattoo Artists from Around the World

SCHIFFER PUBLISHING

4880 Lower Valley Road • Atglen, PA 19310

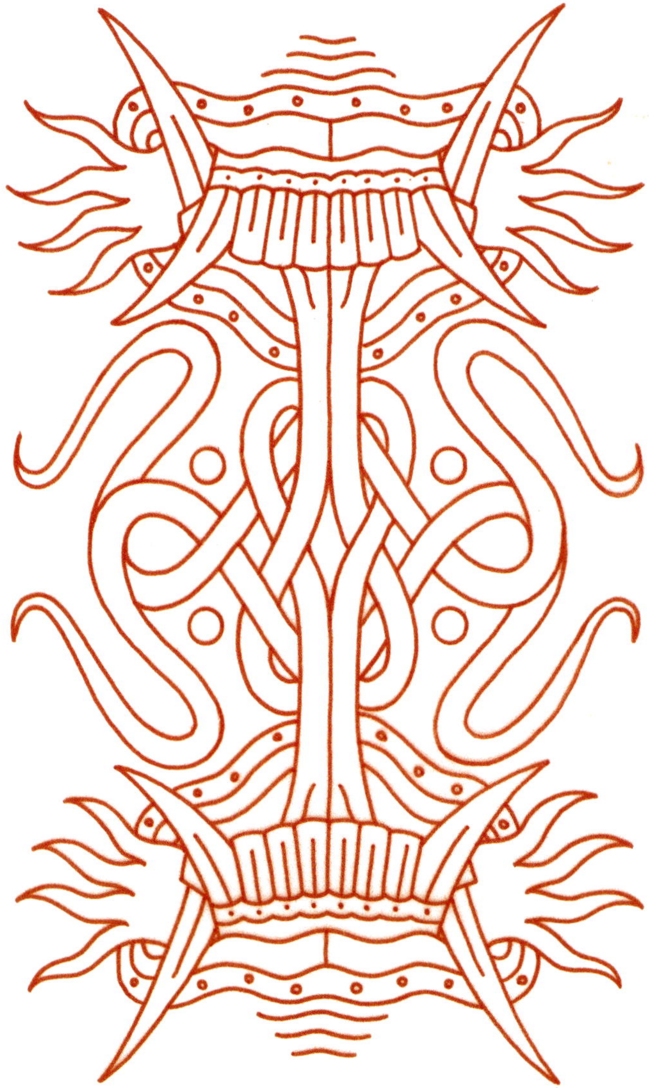

Tattoo Flash from the French Kiss Project

You've probably noticed that tattoos have become quite mainstream in recent years, appealing to an ever-growing and diverse clientele.

Above all, this book is our way of expressing our love for this art. We invited various artists to come together and work in pairs to create illustrations that blend the unique styles and universes of each artist. That's how we decided to name this the French Kiss Project.

We started thinking about this project awhile ago, without any specific idea, without even imagining that we could turn it into a book. We simply wanted to share our passion and celebrate the incredible evolution of what has become an art form in its own right.

We took care of the initial illustrations, then invited tattoo artists to join us. They in turn spread the word to other artists. Very quickly, the enthusiasm for the project exceeded all our expectations, and many new collaborations were born, each with their own inspiring style.

From the outset, we chose not to impose a theme, to avoid restricting the creativity of the artists. This allowed them to give free rein to their imagination, expressing their ideas to the full and producing some remarkable works that are presented here in the form of "flash" drawings. Often smaller in size than the original, flash drawings are created by the tattoo artists for anyone looking for a unique piece. Flash drawings come in the form of stencils, meaning that the design is copied onto transfer paper, a layer of carbon paper covered with a protective tissue. The design is then transferred to its final destination: the skin. Now, the tattoo artist must demonstrate his/her skills.

This book will introduce you to a hundred or so tattoo artists of all ages and backgrounds, who have agreed to mix their art and style in the name of their common passion: tattooing. We would like to thank them for their participation and commitment. Without them, none of this would have been possible.

All that's left for us to do now is to wish you a pleasant journey, discovering and drawing inspiration from their rich artistic worlds!

—John Stone, Tiwan, and El Bent

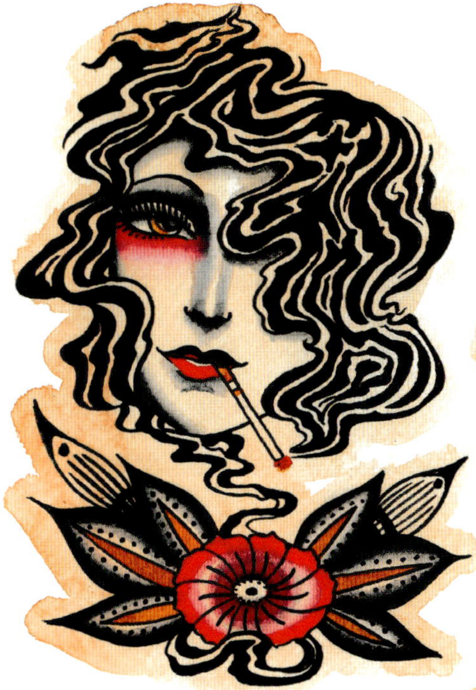
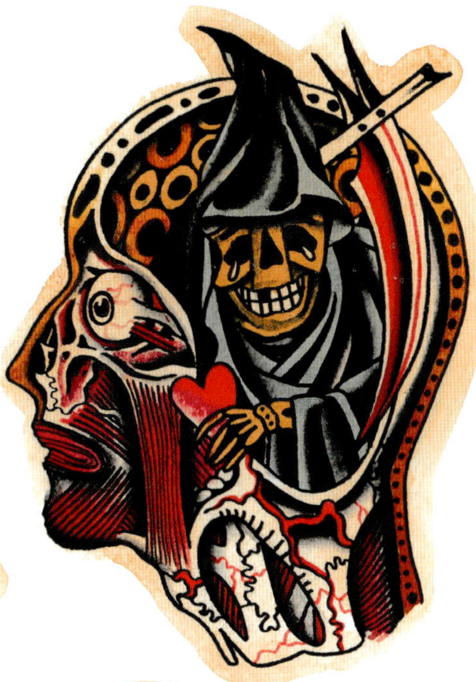
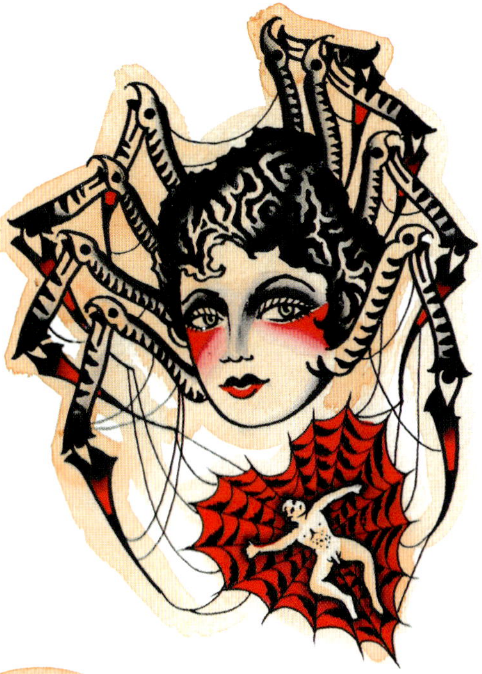

El Bent
@elbenttattoo
True Love / Paris / France

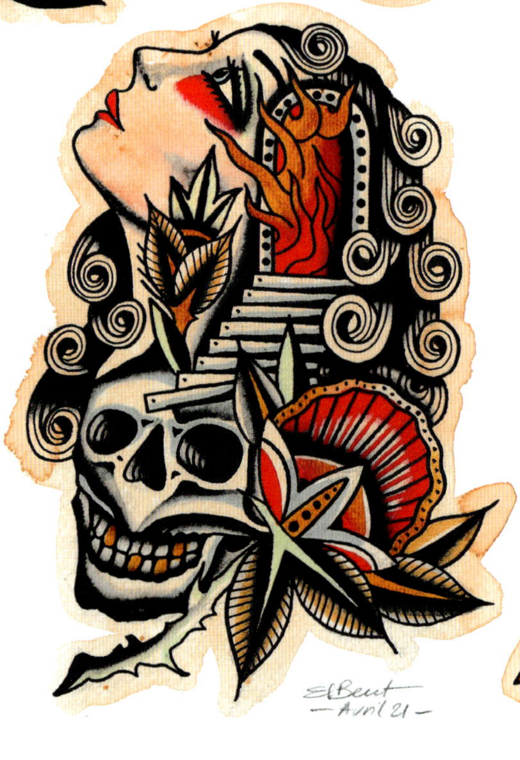
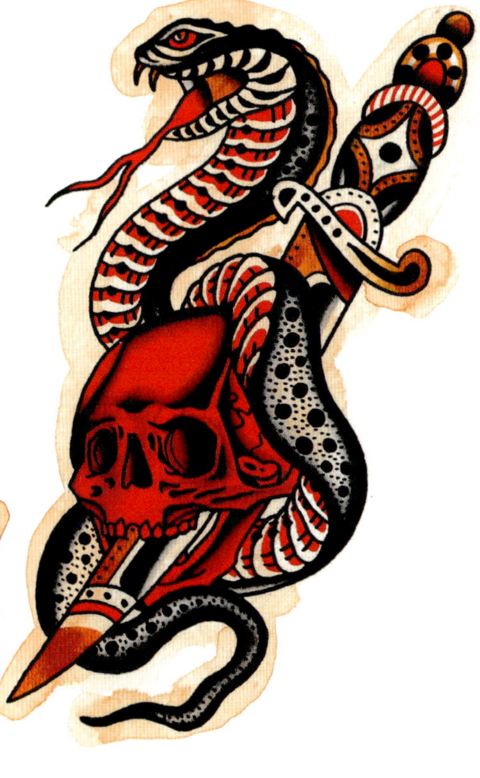

What Is Tattoo Flash?

Flash is an original drawing that reflects a tattooist's artistic world.

Traditionally associated with designs found in tattoo artists' portfolios or hung on the walls of tattoo parlors, flash could be reproduced repeatedly without requiring modifications. It was therefore not uncommon to find the same identical designs tattooed on different people around town.

But over the last few decades, flash has evolved from simple catalog designs to genuine works of art.

What clients are looking for in tattoo flash is the tattoo artist's style. With flash, artists can express all their creativity and know-how, without any constraints, except the size imposed by the client.

Getting a flash tattoo is like wearing a unique piece of art forever.

Left
Sylvester Boom
@sylvesterboom
Tribal Act / Paris / France

Right
xCYRx
@xCYRx
Chez Cyr Tatouages / Reims / France

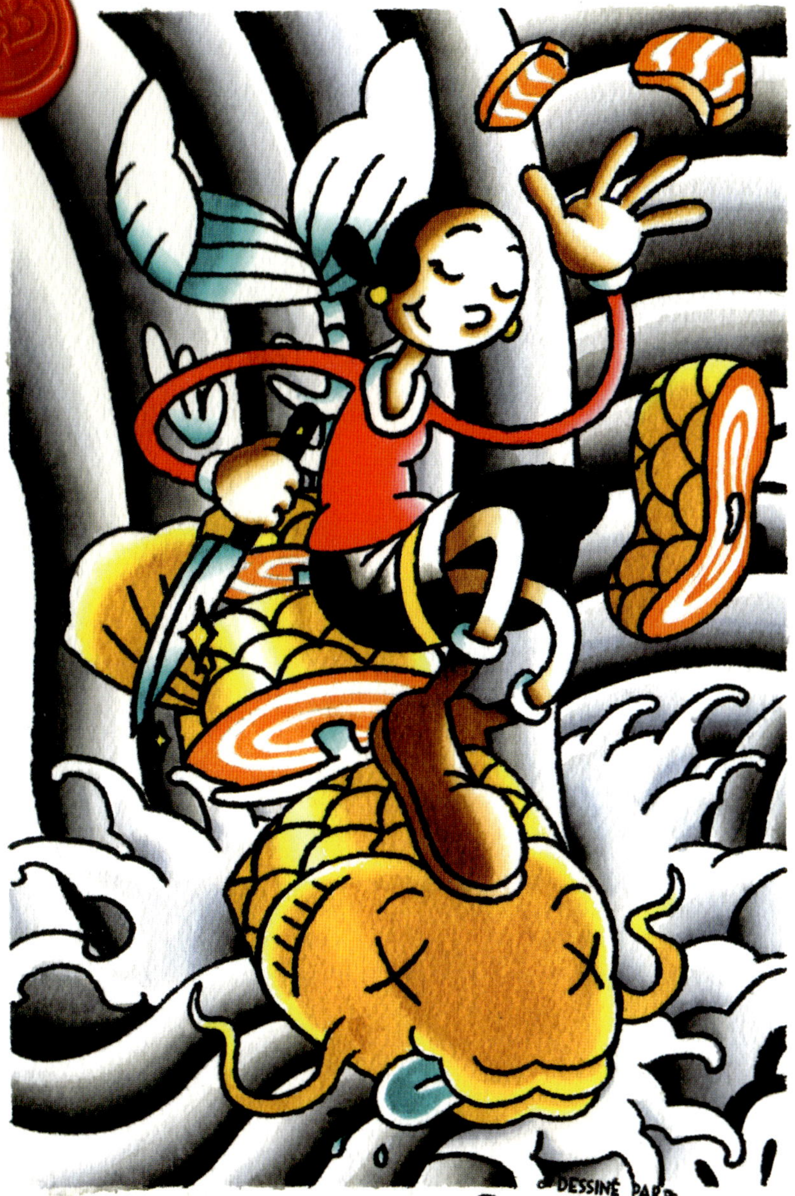

SYLVESTER BOOM * 2019

DESSINÉ PAR
SYLVESTER BOOM
☆TATOUAGE ÉLECTRIQUE☆

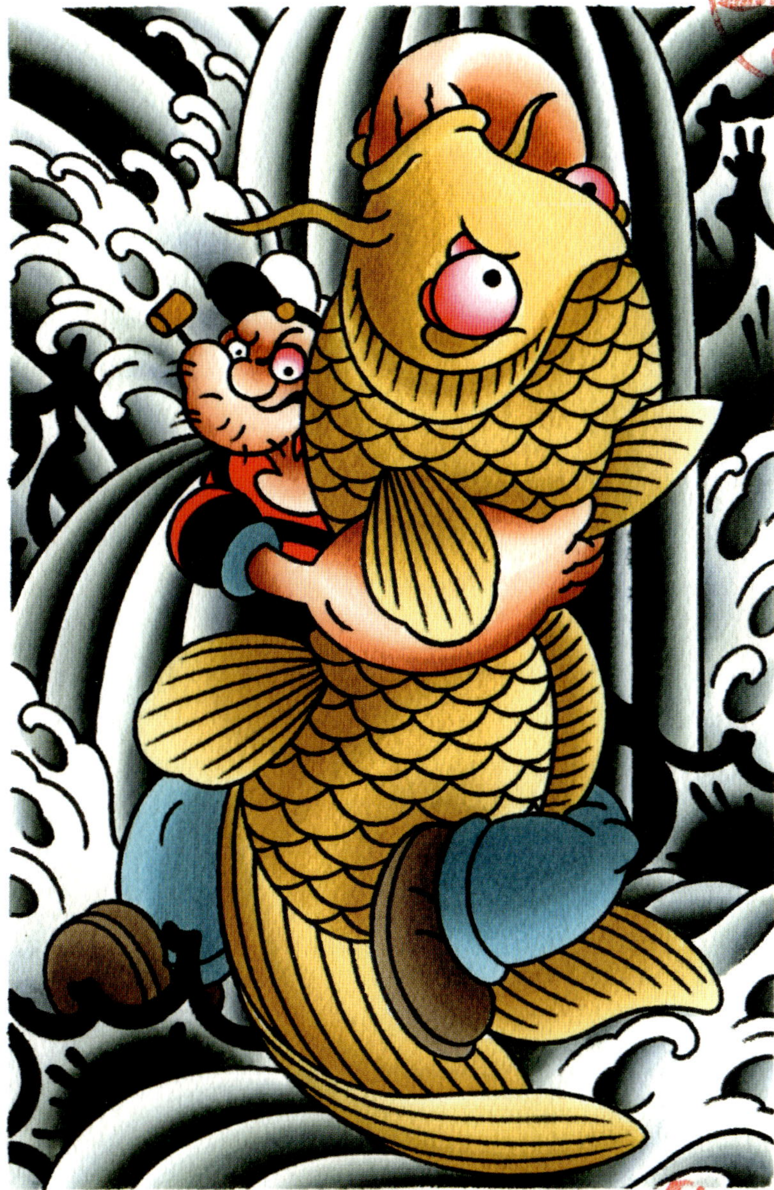

TATOUAGES TRADITIONNELS
FRANÇAIS

Left
Dino C'est Chiant
@dino_cestchiant_tattoo
Seven Eyes Tattoo / Montpellier / France

Right
Malflore
@malflore
Atelier Triptyque / Montpellier / France

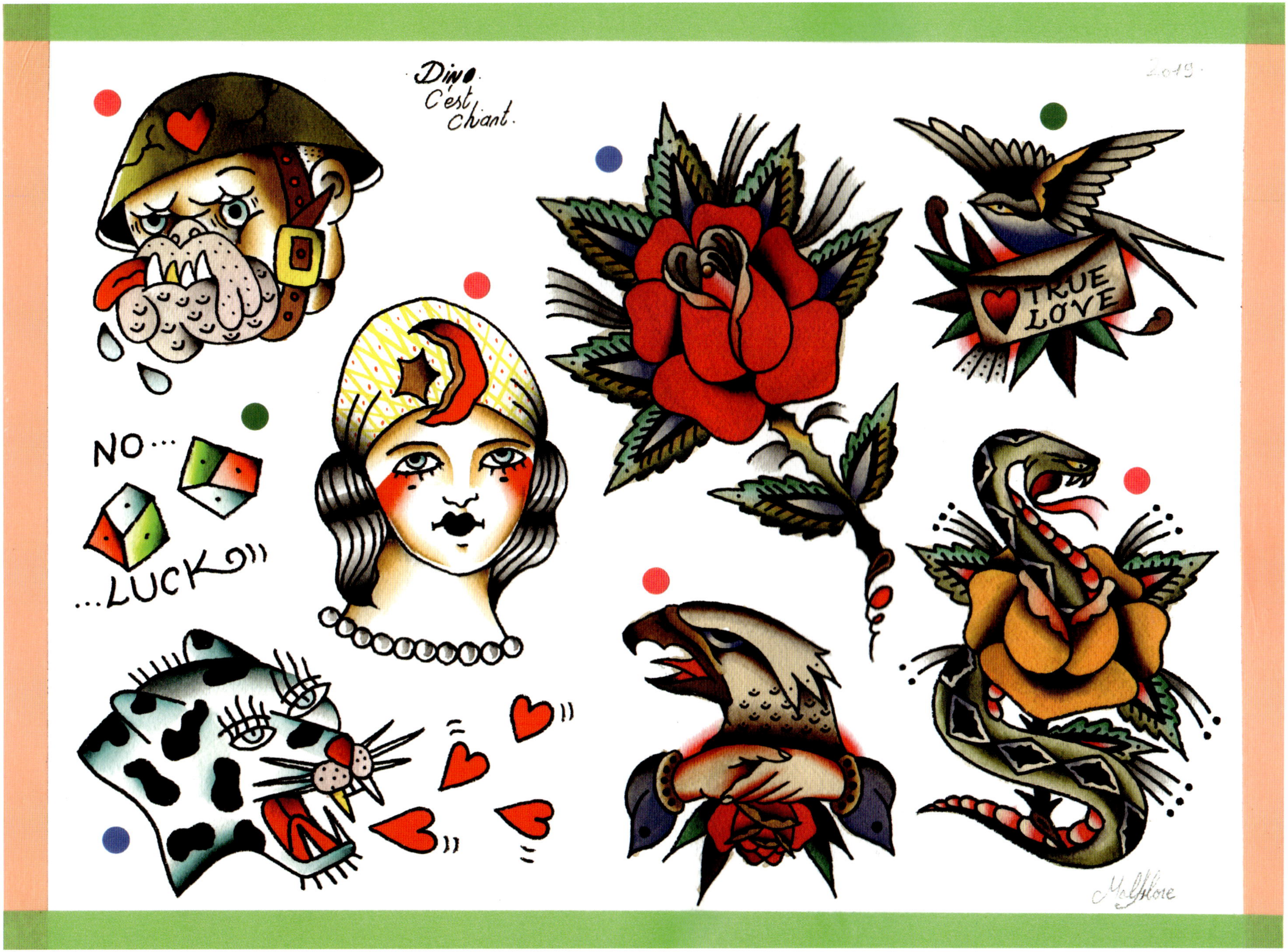
Dino.
C'est chiant.
2019
NO...
...LUCK
TRUE LOVE

Left
John Stone
@john_stone_tatouage
L'Astrolabe / Dinard / France

Right
Nacib T.
@nacib_t
On the road / Paris / France

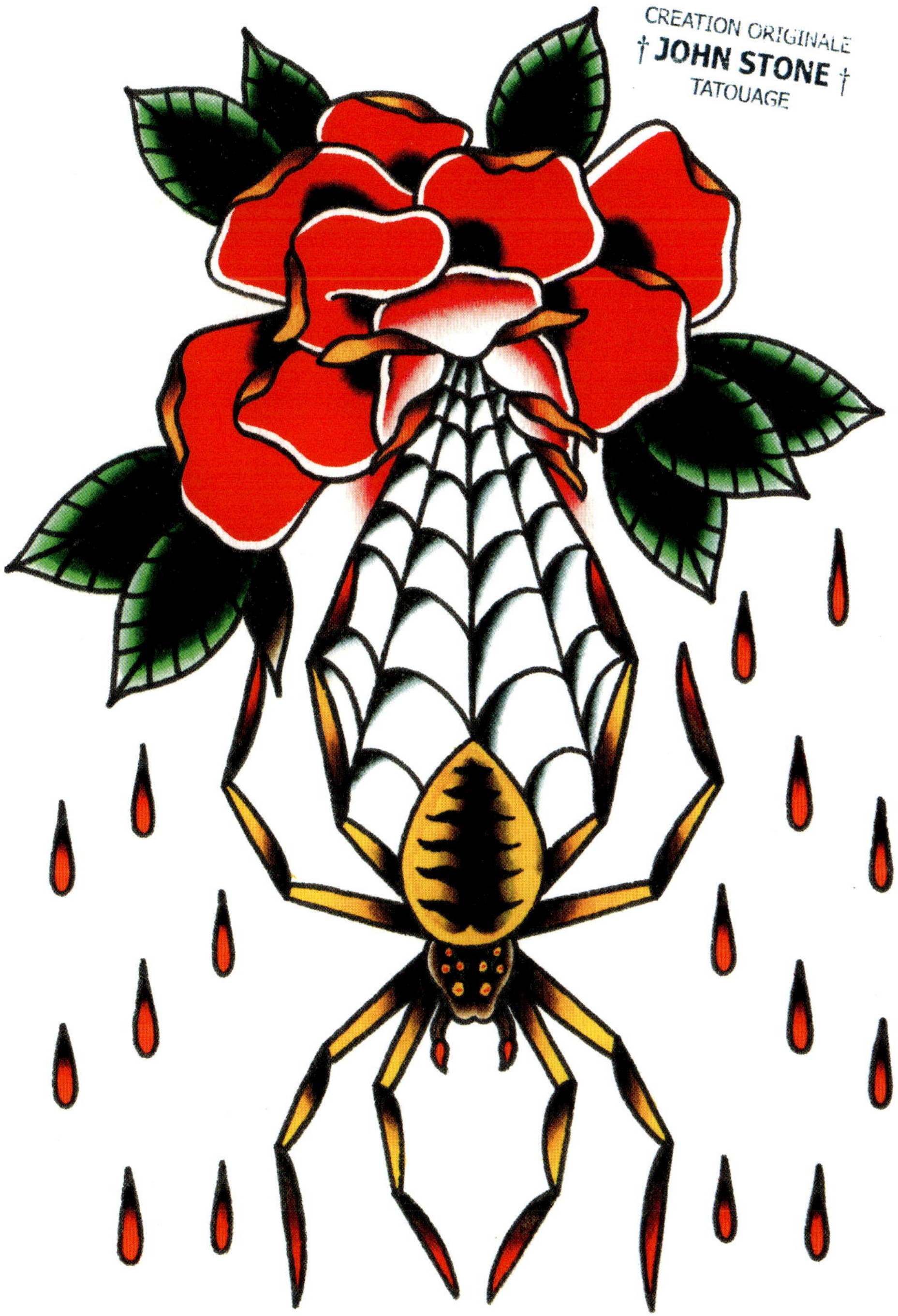
CREATION ORIGINALE
† JOHN STONE †
TATOUAGE

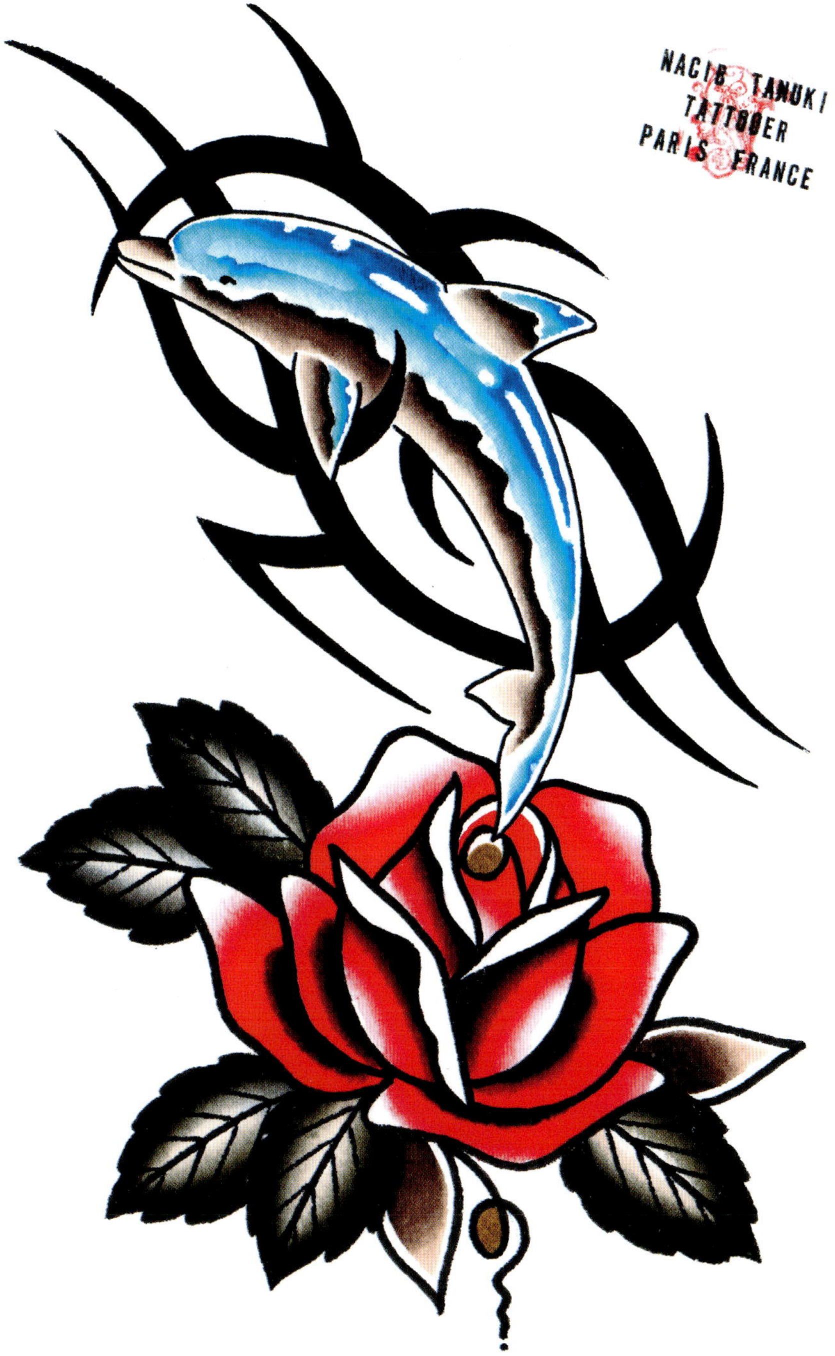
NACIB TANUKI
TATTOOER
PARIS FRANCE

Left
Ben Fessetaud
@benfessetaud
Le Tigre / Annecy / France

Right
Iannis Le Tigre
@iannis_letigre
Le Tigre / Annecy / France

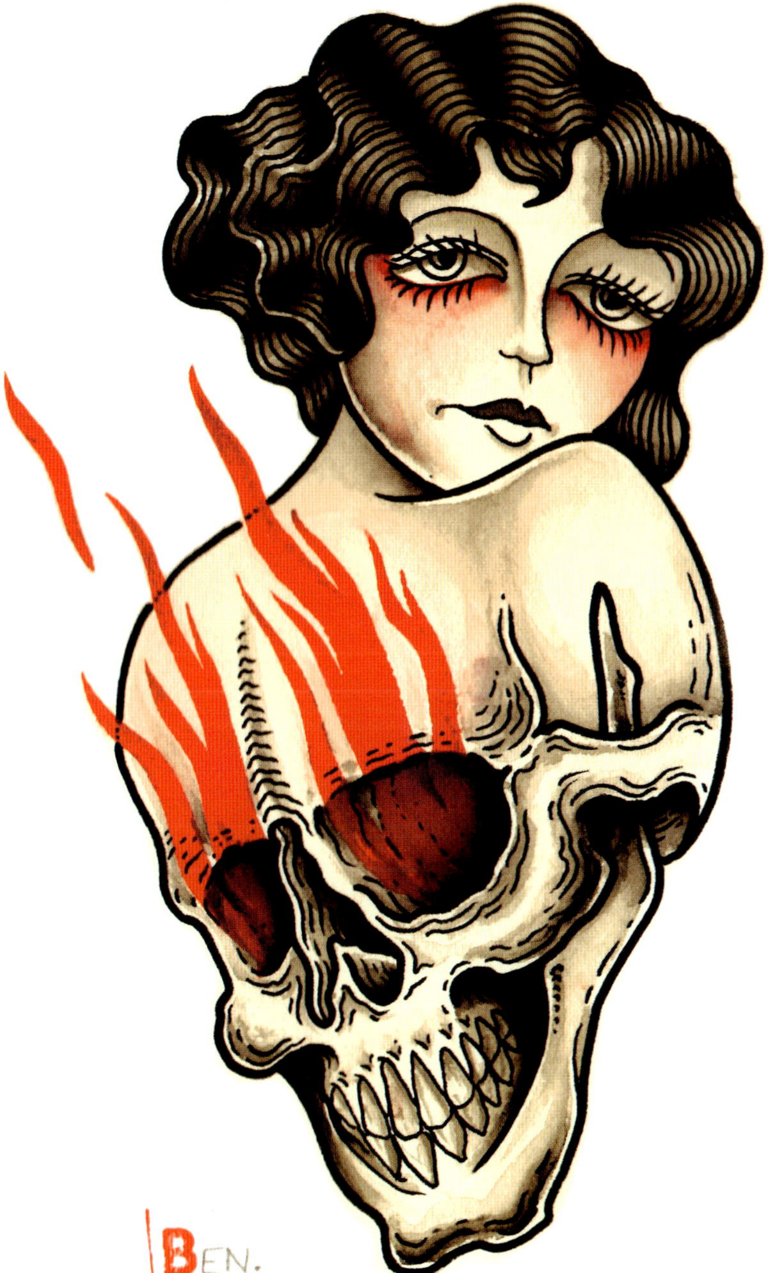

BEN.

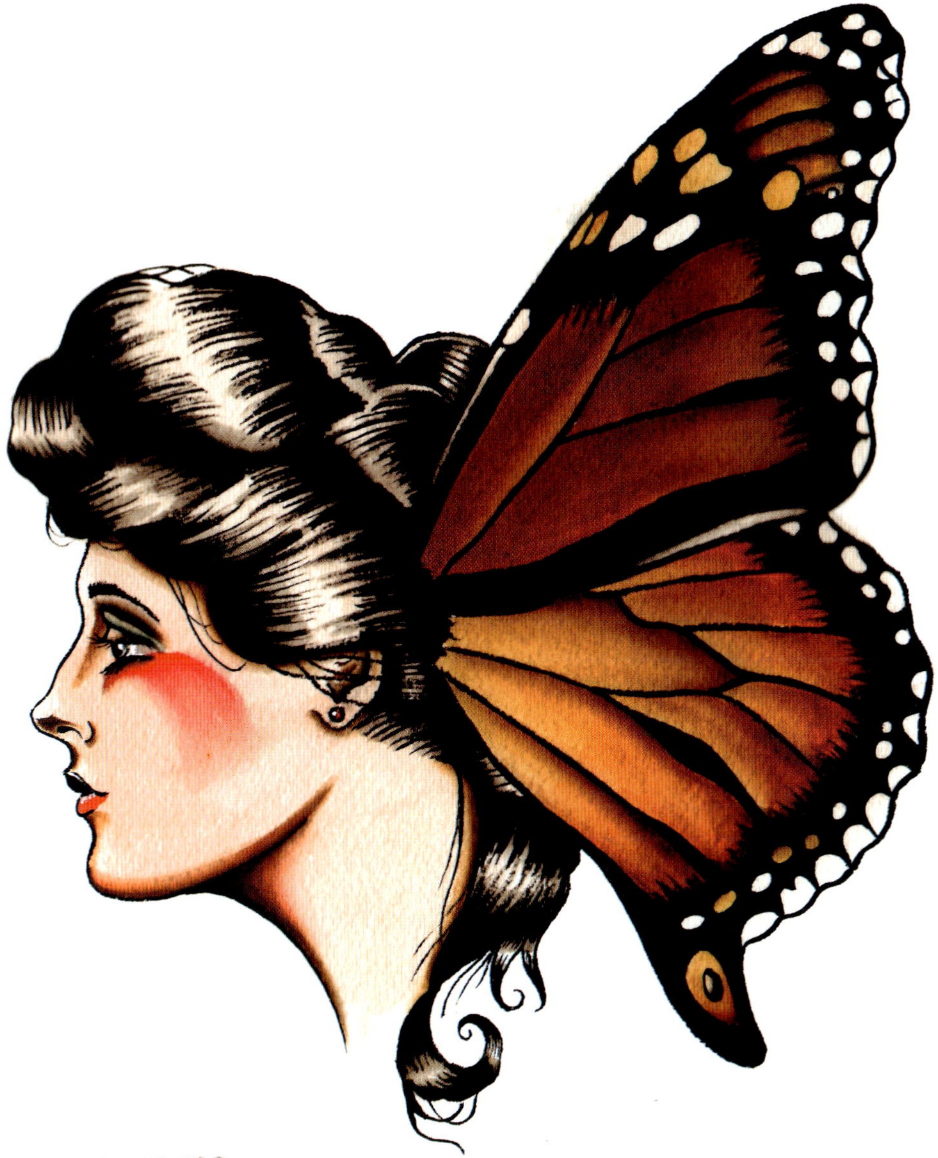

LE TIGRE
2019

IANNIS
·SR·

Bottom left and right
Uncle Ho
@uncle_ho_mitchmalone
Iron Claw / Strasbourg / France

Top left and center
Loïc Mesot LMT
@loicmesotlmt
LM Tattoo Street Shop / Saint-Mihiel / France

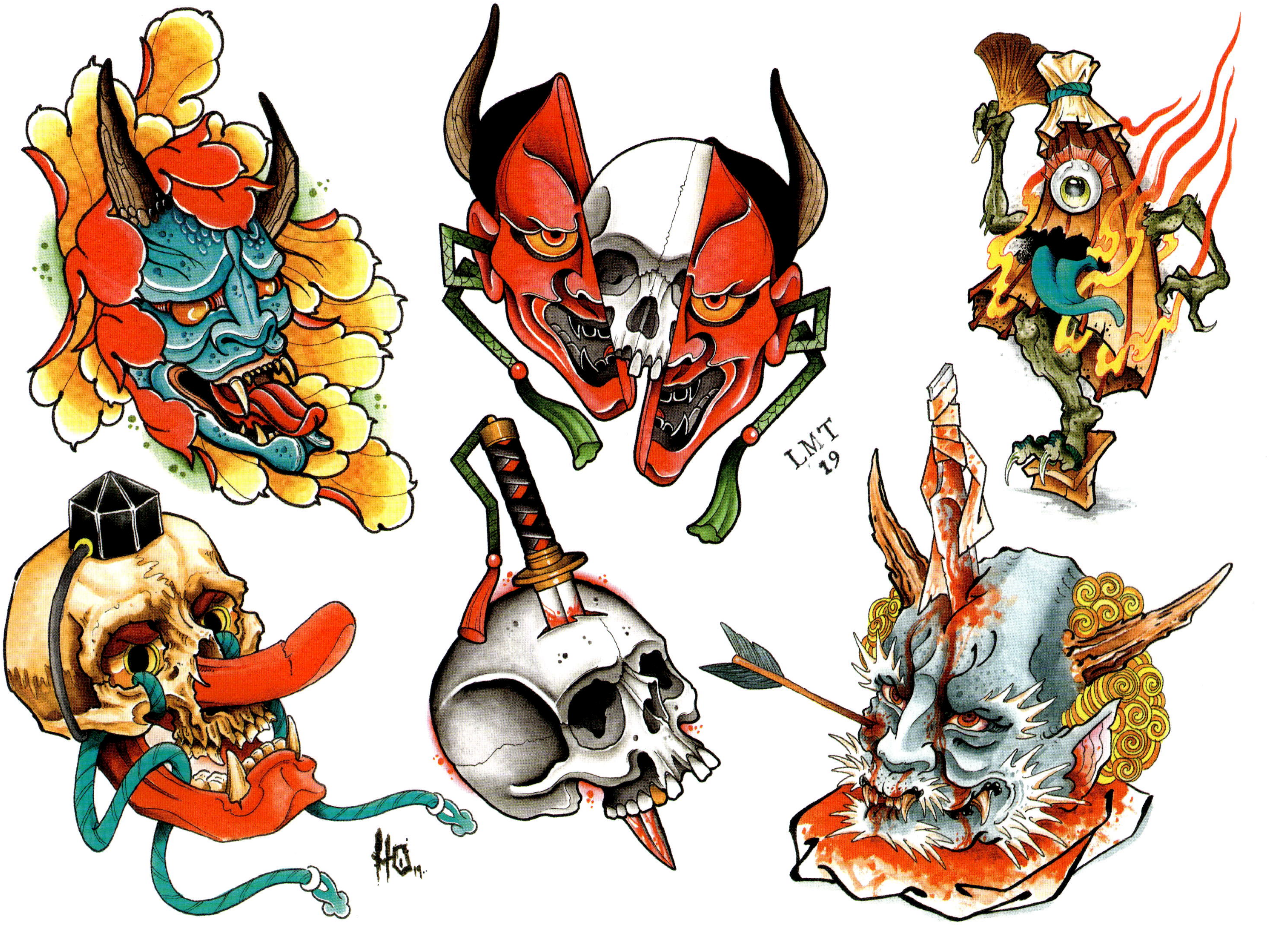
LMT
19

Left
El Bent
@elbenttattoo
True Love / Paris / France

Right
Julien Brunier
@julien.brunier
French Tattoo Connection / Marseille / France

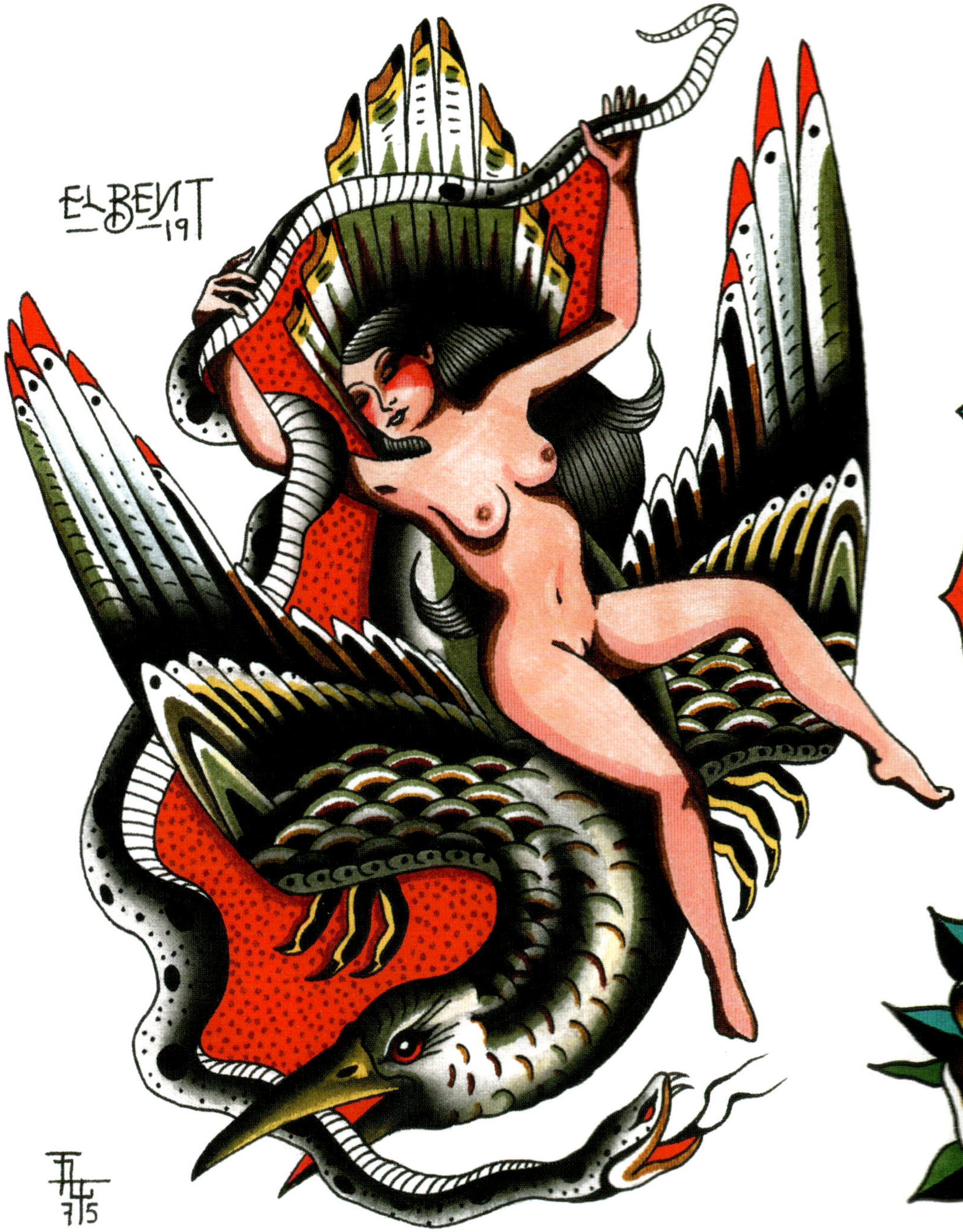

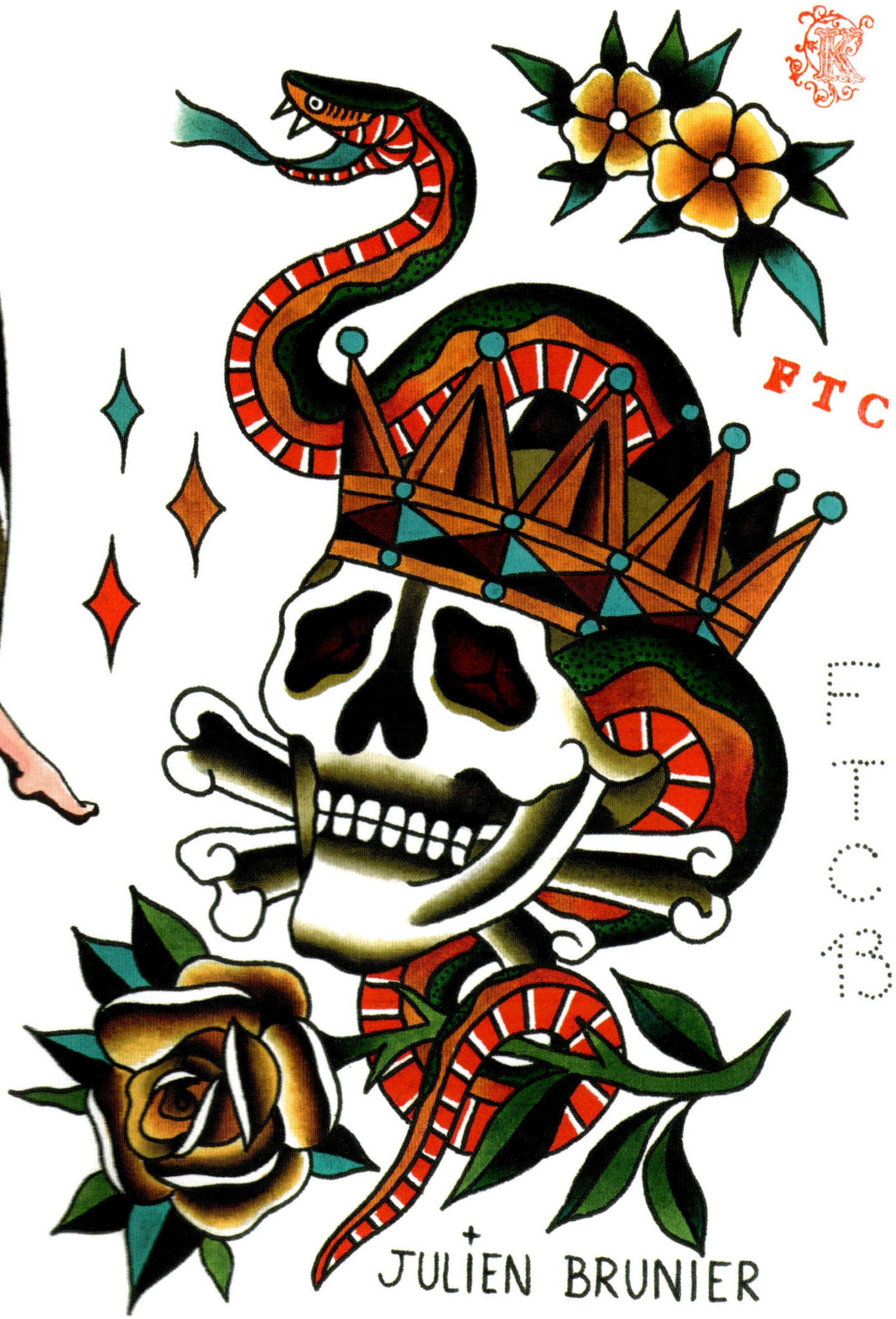
FTC
FTC 13
JULIEN BRUNIER

Left
Suzan Grimm
@suzangrimm
Private shop / Lille / France

Right
Virgulovic
@virgulovic
Artax Tattoo / Lille / France

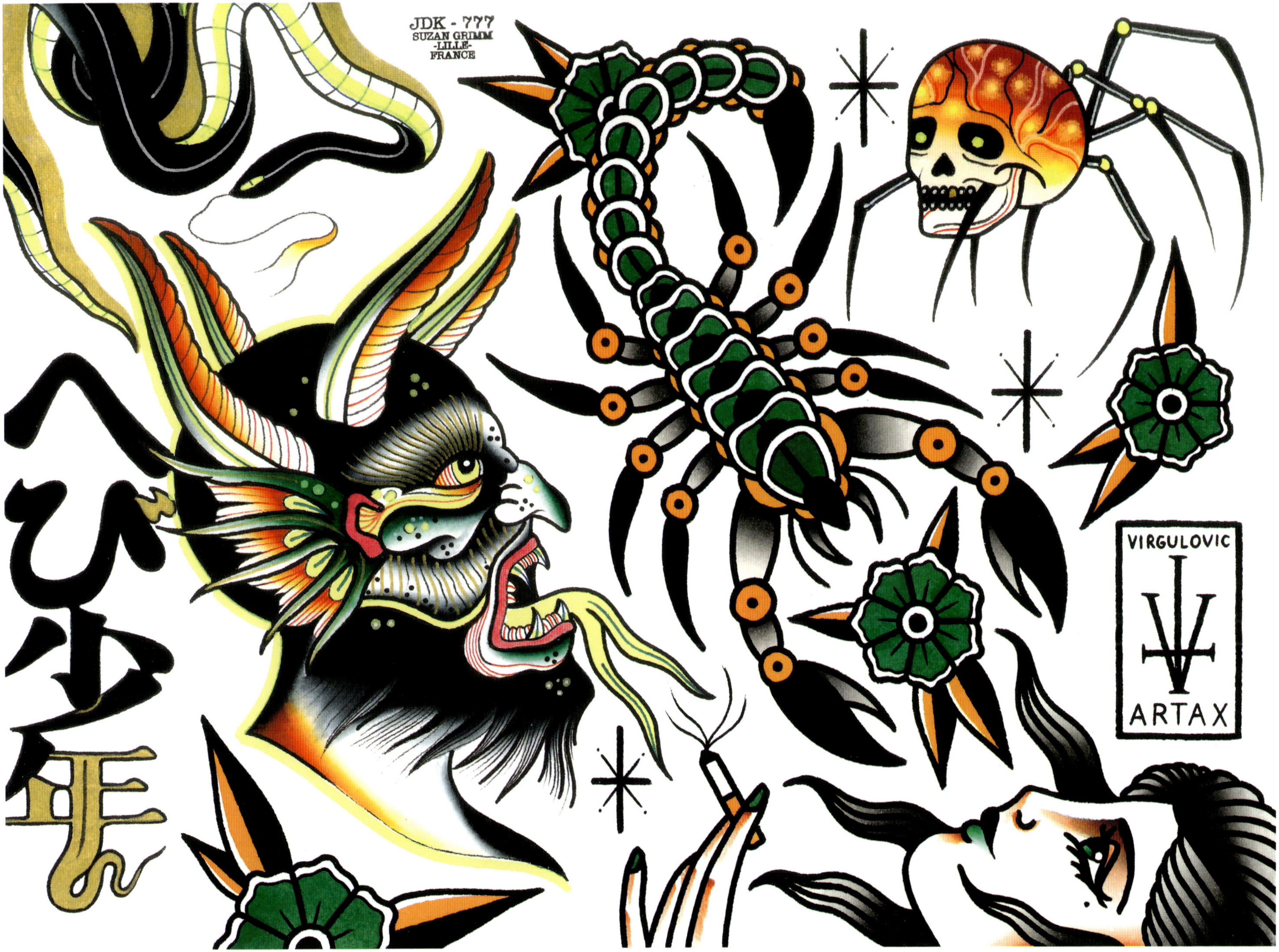
JDK - 777
SUZAN GRIMM
-LILLE-
FRANCE
VIRGULOVIC
ARTAX

Left
Alex 290
@alex290_tattoo
Biribi Tattoo / Lyon / France

Right
Malflore
@malflore
Atelier Triptyque / Montpellier / France

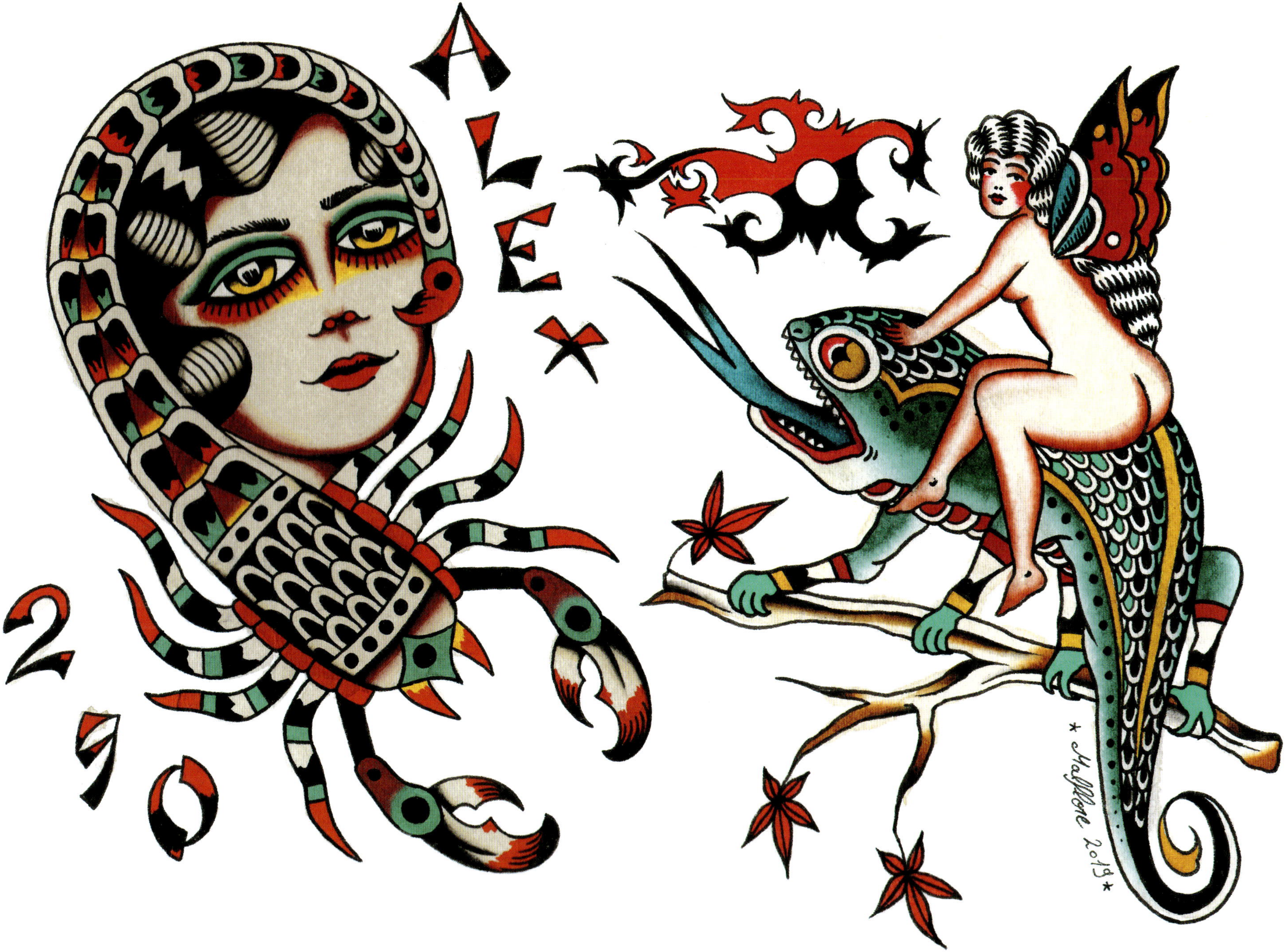
ALEX

Left
Carlito
@carlito__tattoo
Black Leaf Tattoo / Saint-Alban-de-Roche / France

Right
Grom Tattooer
@gromtattooer G.Rom
Tattoo Shop / Lyon / France

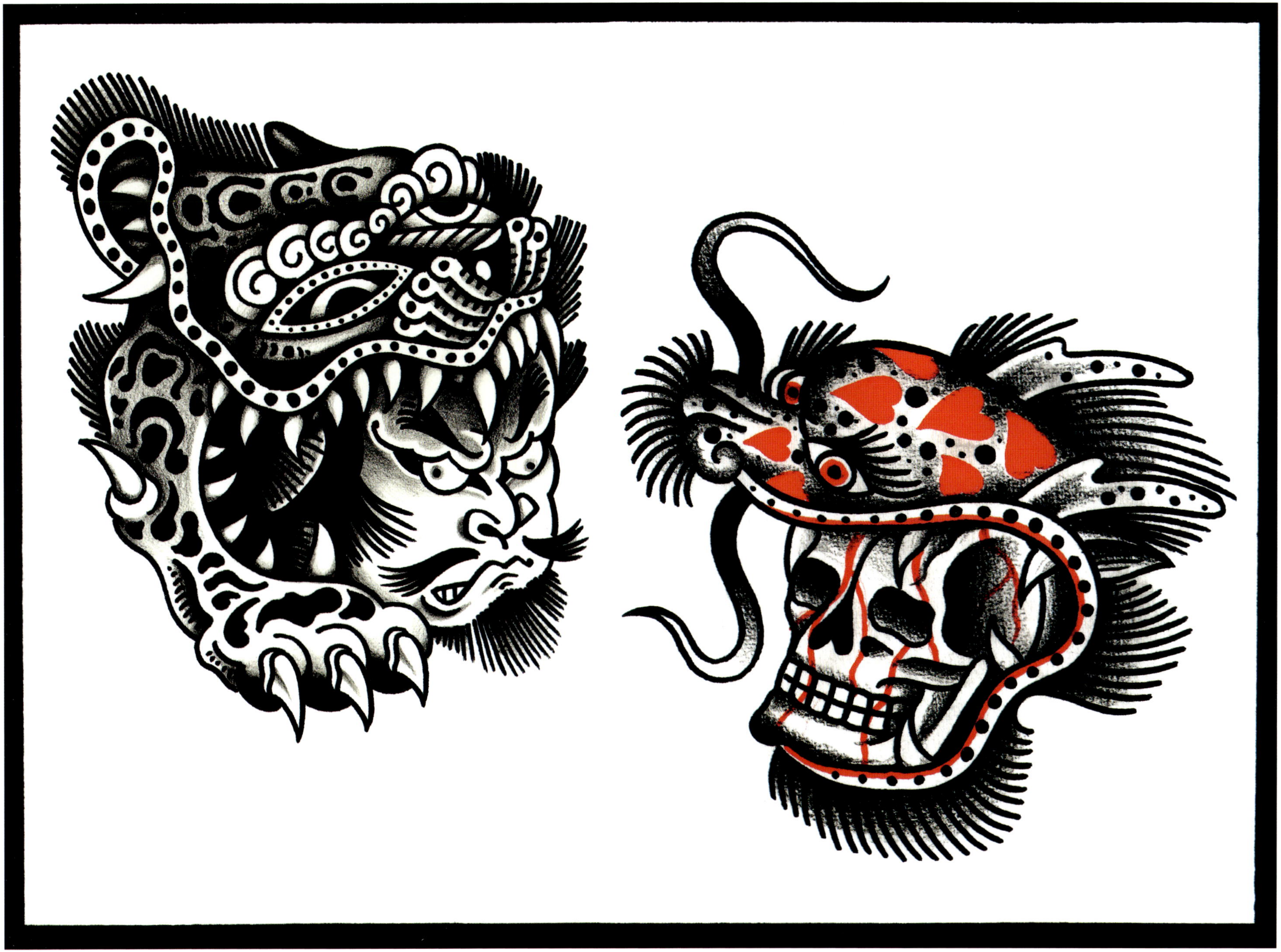

Left
Tony Grande Truandise
@tonygrandetruandise
L'Ogre Rouge / Pont-Péan / France

Right
Charles
@charlestattoorennes
L'Ogre Rouge / Rennes / France

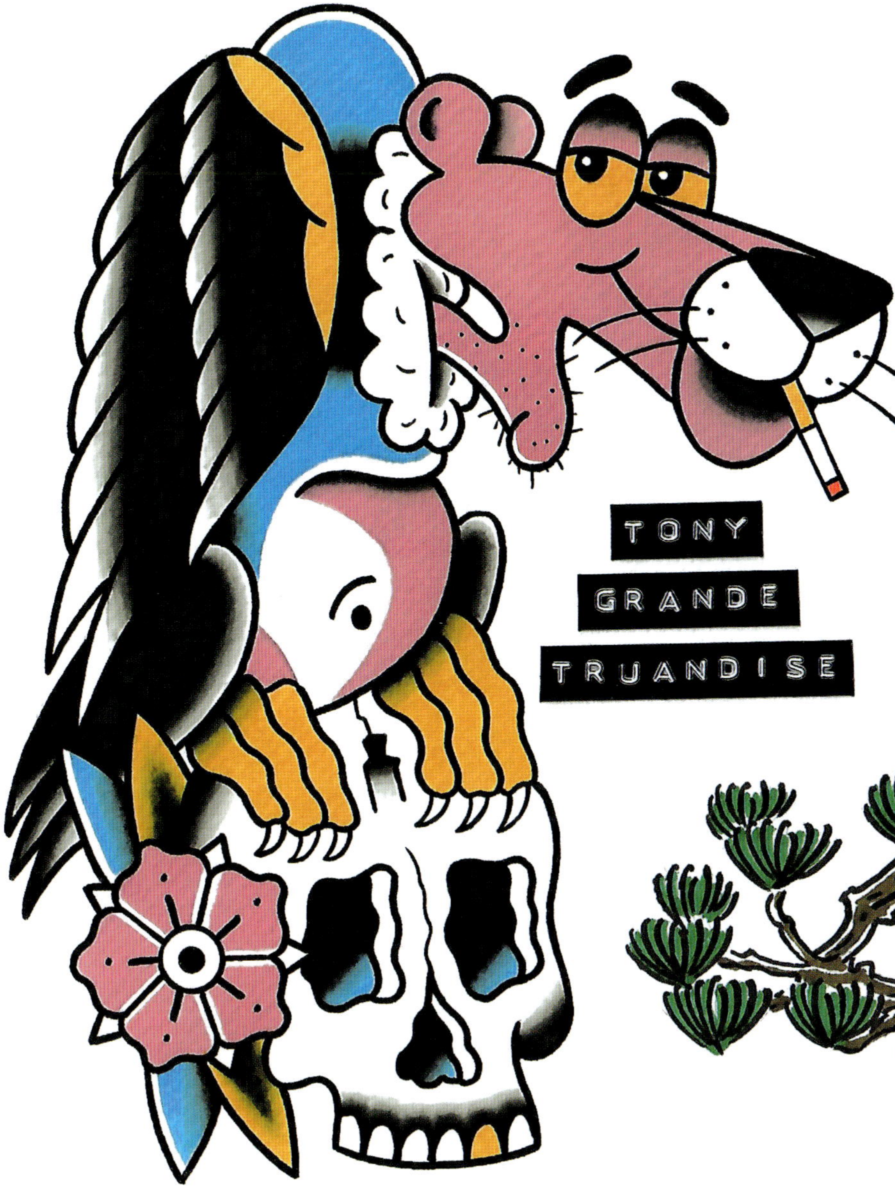

TONY
GRANDE
TRUANDISE

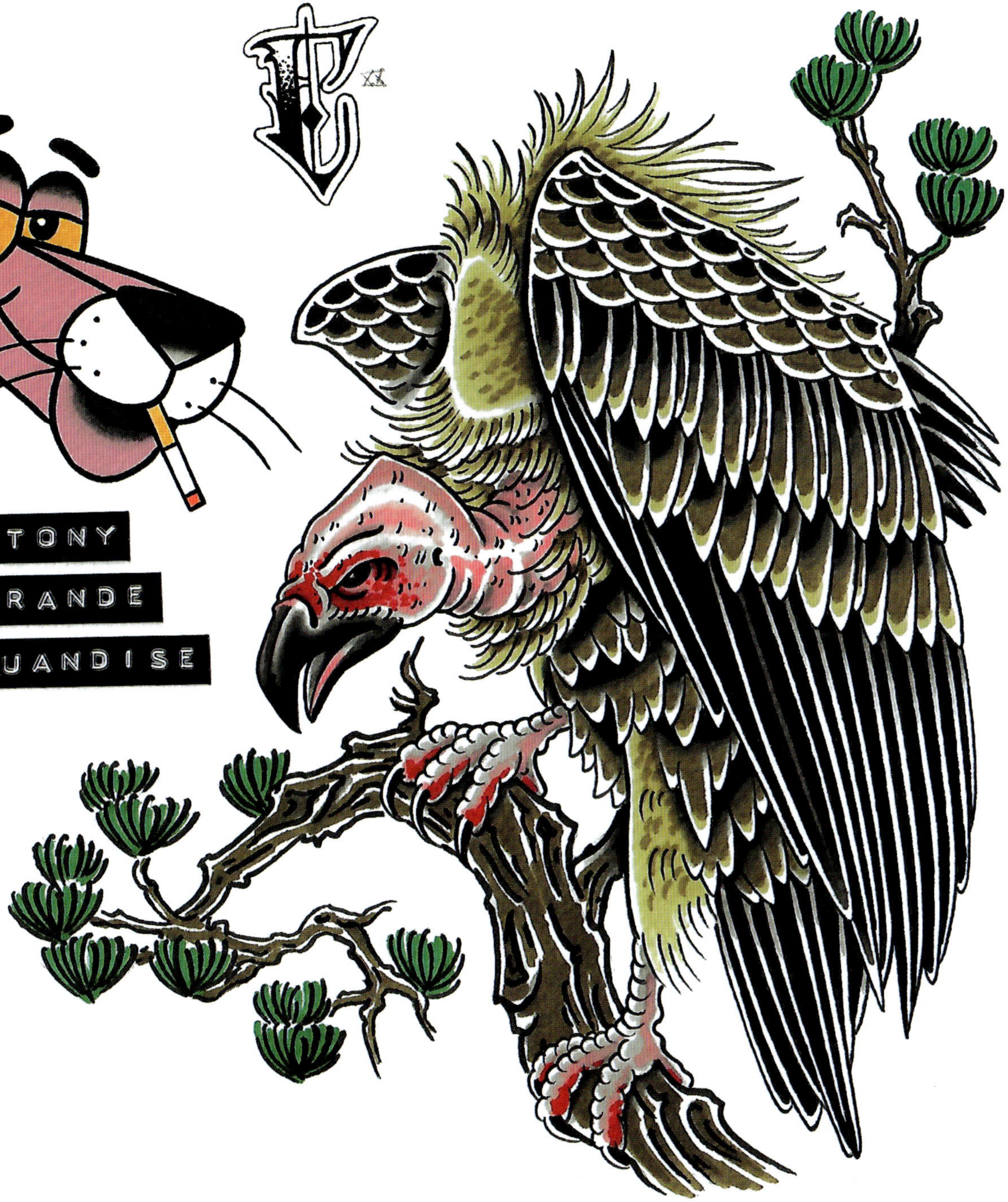

Left
Iannis Le Tigre
@iannis_letigre
Le Tigre / Annecy / France

Right
El Bent
@elbenttattoo
True Love / Paris / France

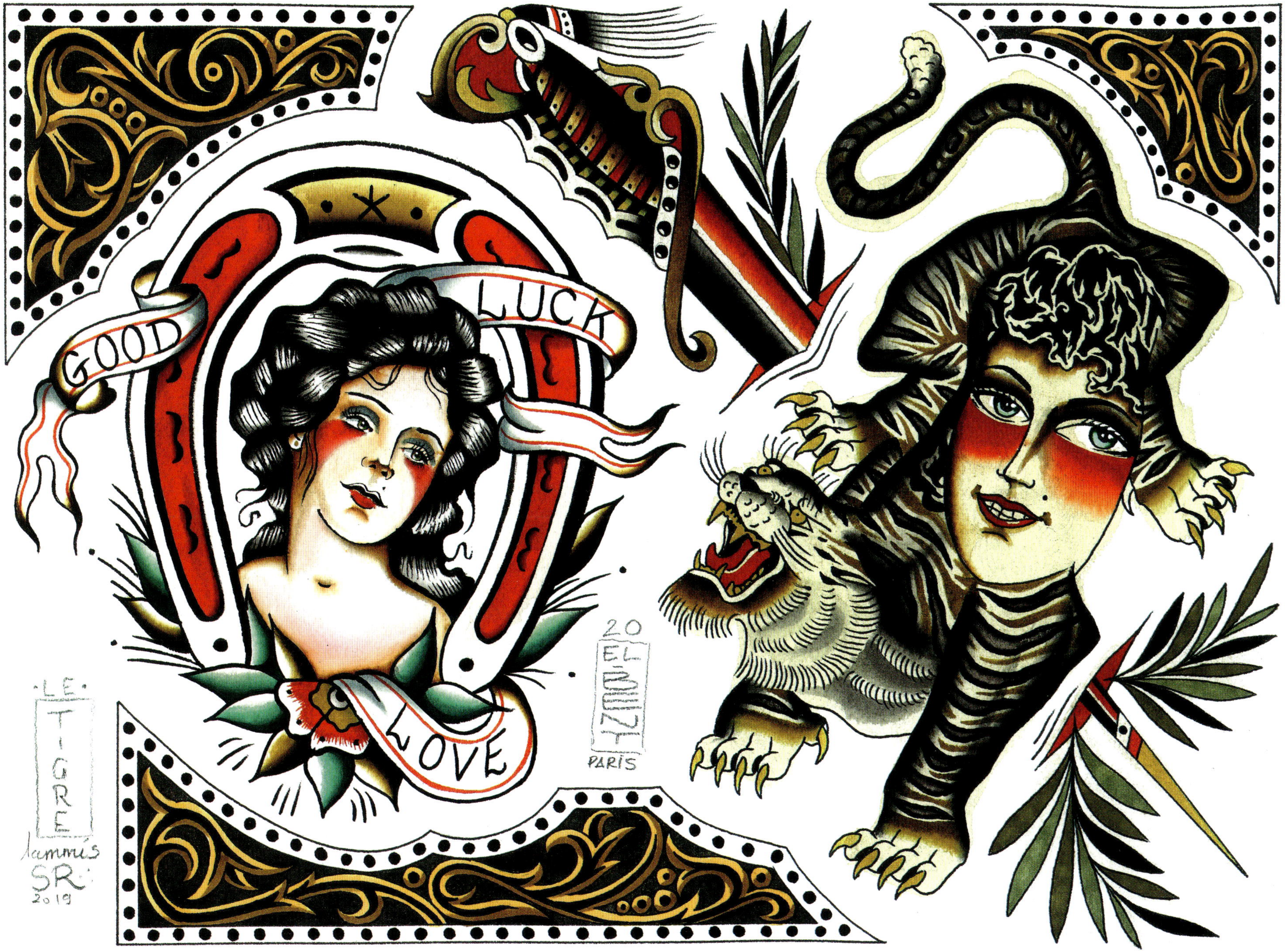
GOOD
LUCK
LOVE
LE TIGRE
SR
2019
PARIS

Top
Peter Panther
@peter.panther_
Perdu d'Avance Tattoo Club / Paris / France

Bottom
Dr. Djee
@dr.djee
Perdu d'Avance Tattoo Club / Paris / France

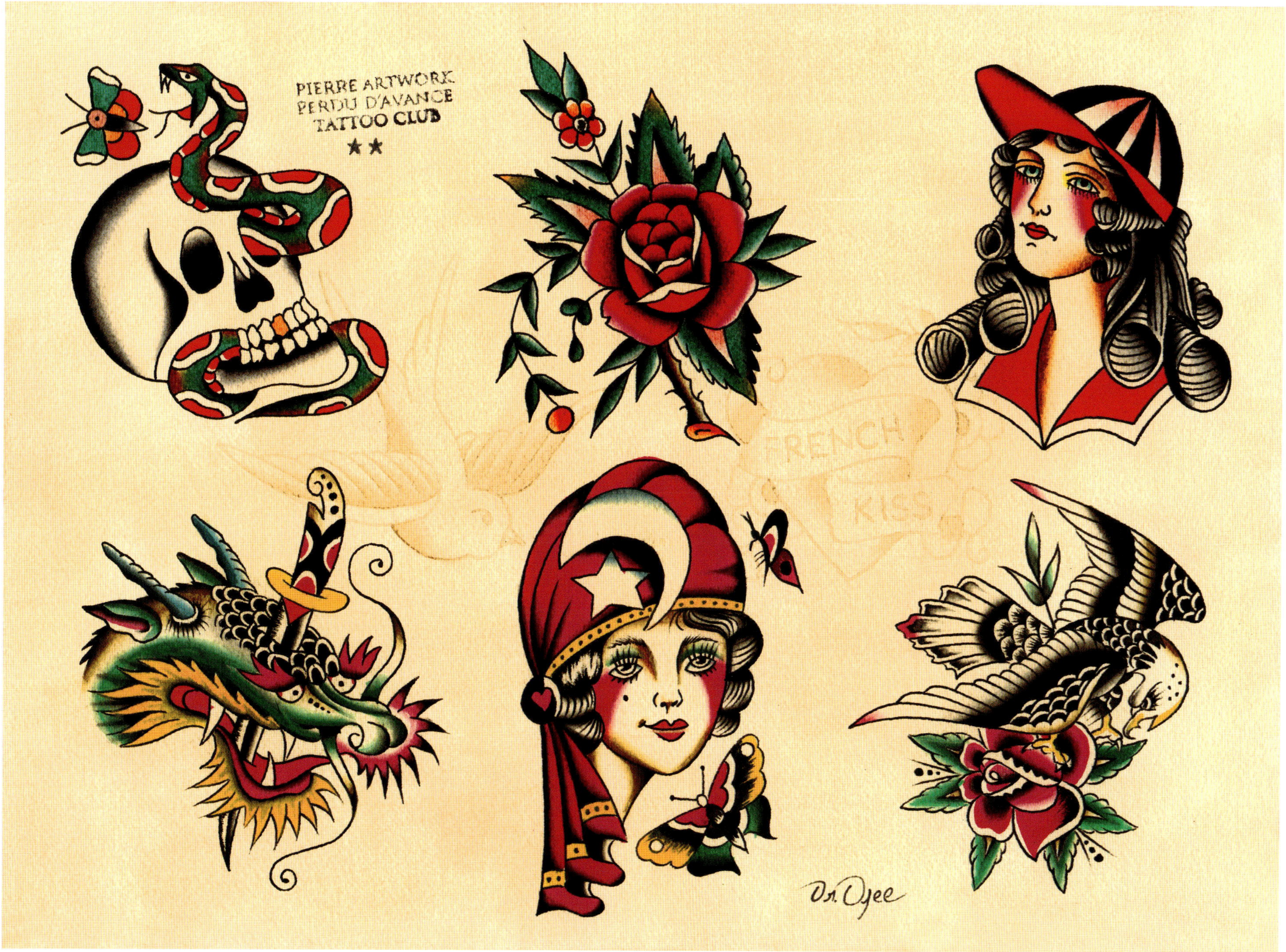
PIERRE ARTWORK
PERDU D'AVANCE
TATTOO CLUB
FRENCH
KISS

Left
Toy-Arthur
@toy_arthur_tatouage
FTC Bordeaux / Bordeaux / France

Right
Cécile Pages
@cecilepagestats
Triple Dragon Tattoo / Réunion / France

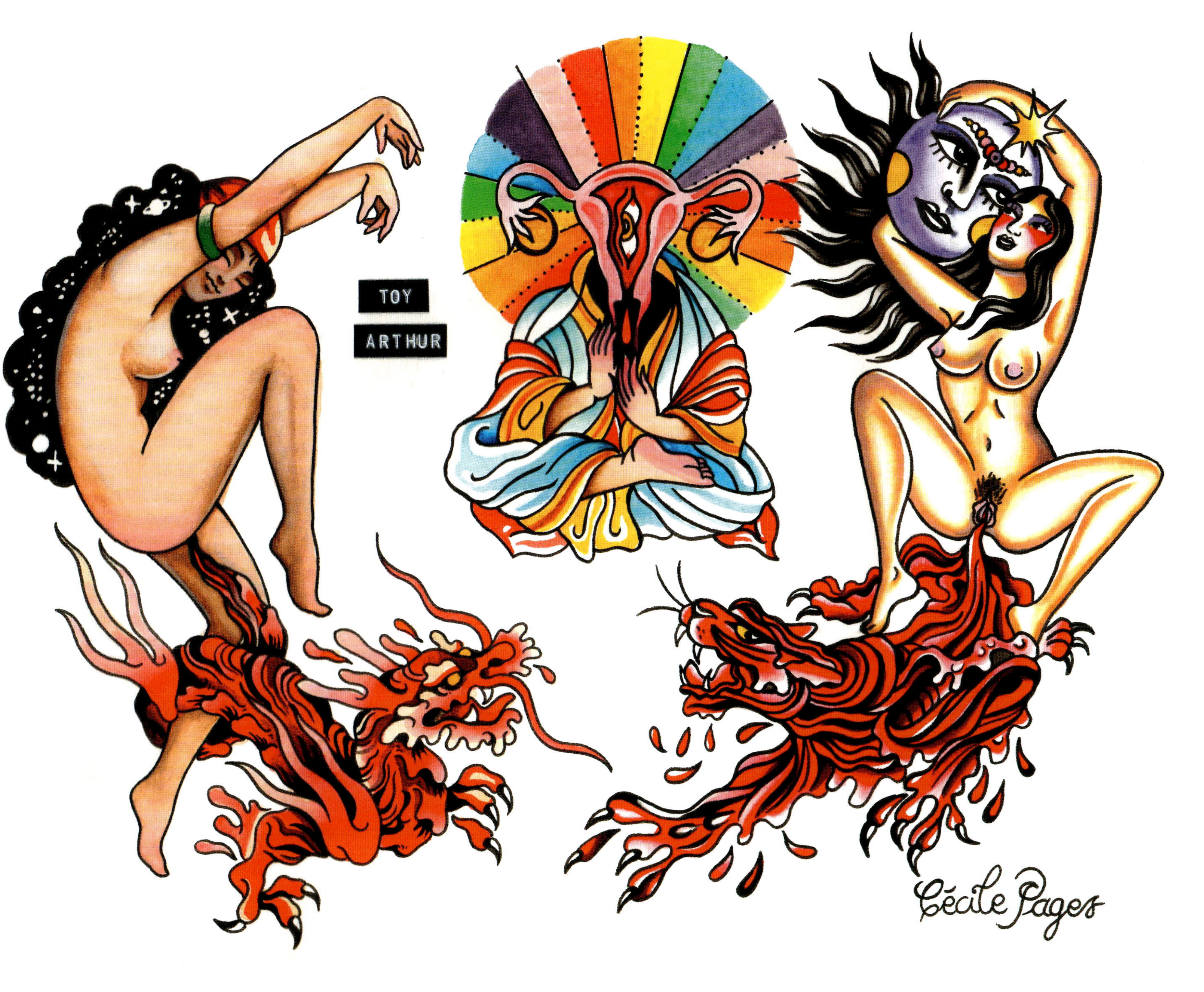
TOY
ARTHUR
Cécile Pages

Left
Clément Tarsia
@clement.tarsia
Melrose Market / Annecy / France

Right
Valentin Blasterz
@valentin_blasterz
Shaut Crying Tattoo Shop / Grenoble / Franc

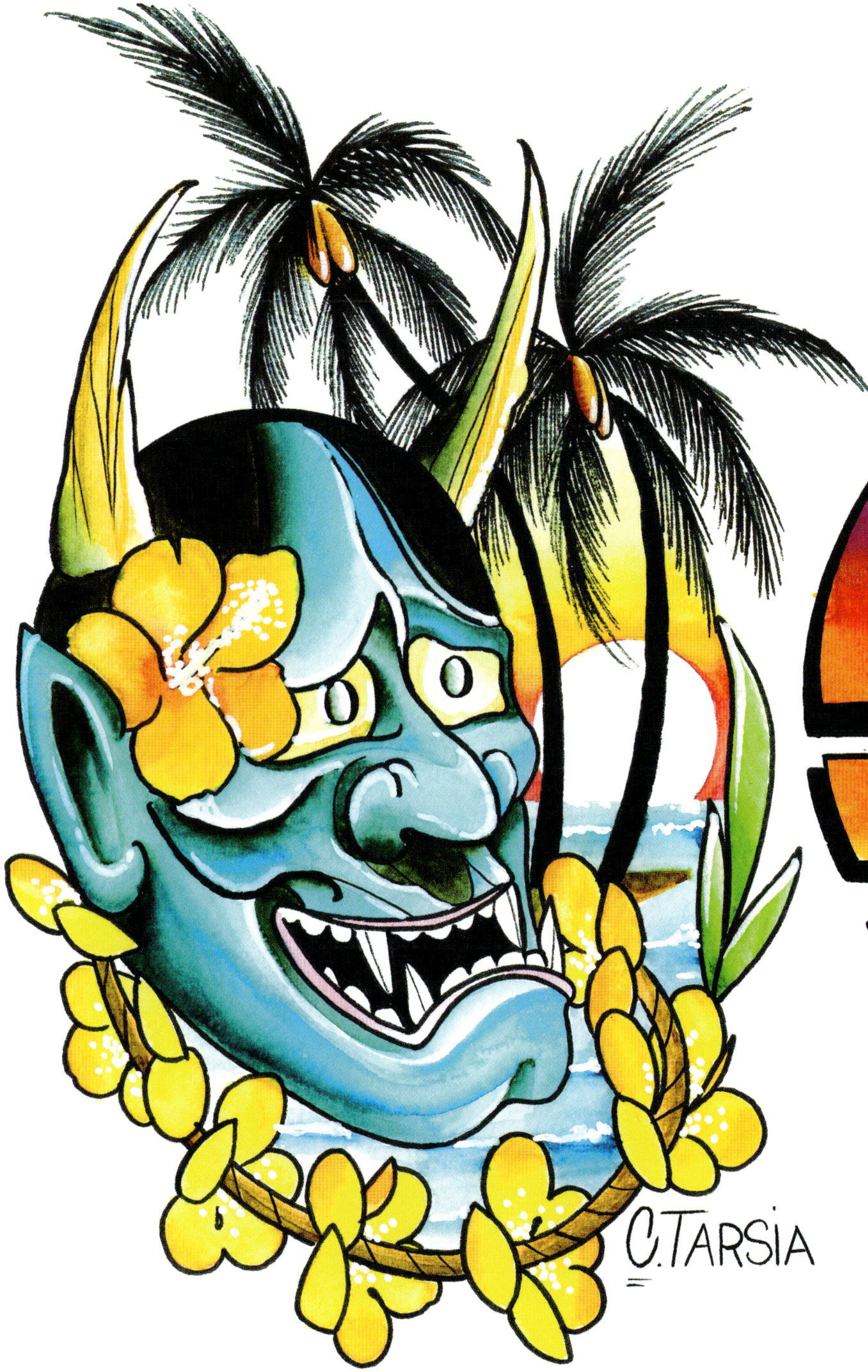
C.TARSIA

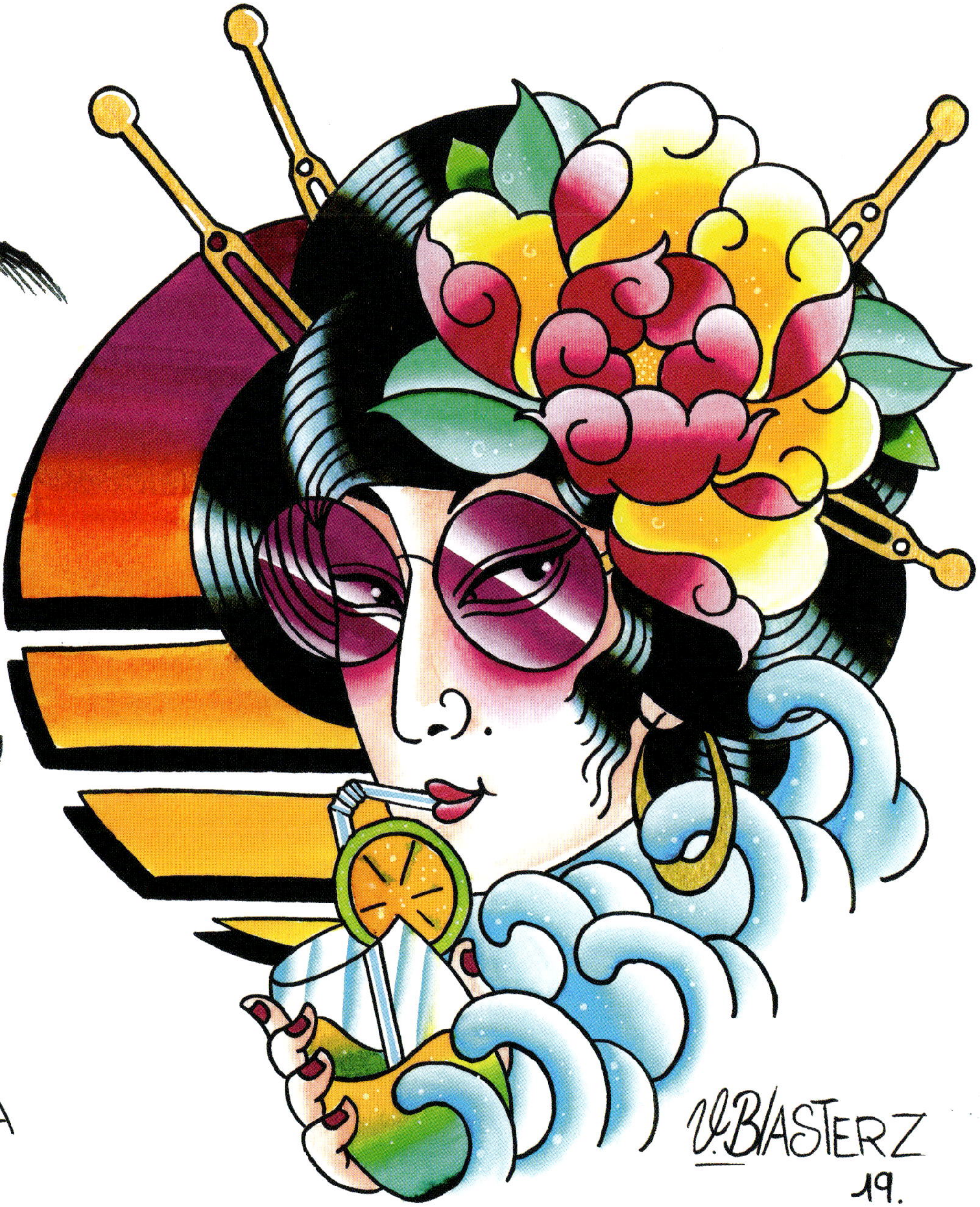
V.BLASTERZ
19.

Center
Damien Tello
@damien_tello_tattoo
Timeless Tattoo Montpellier / Montpellier / France

Dragon
Lautaro
@lautaroyatusabes
Triple Cobra Tattoo / Oslo / Norway

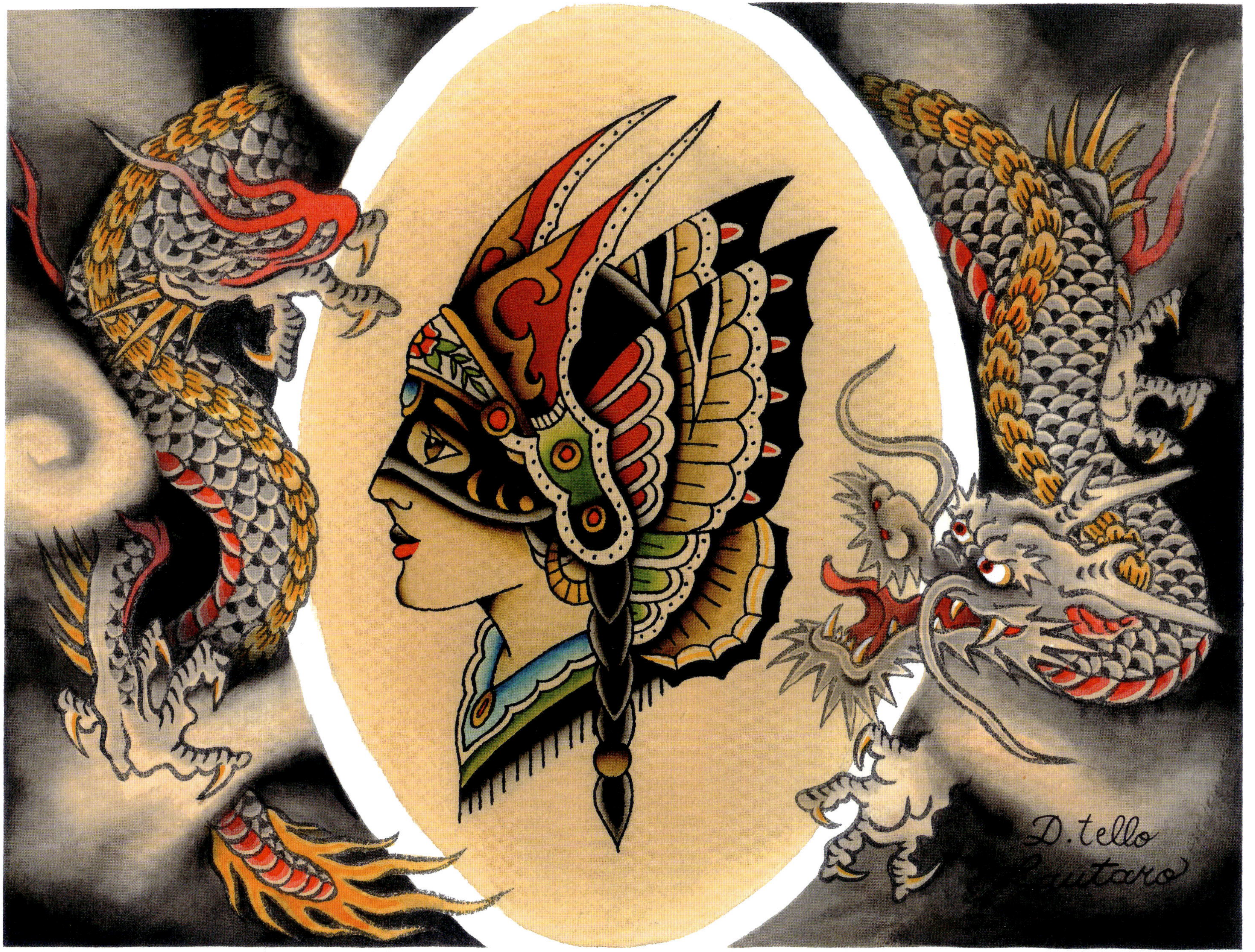
D.tello

Left
John Stone
@john_stone_tatouage
L'Astrolabe / Dinard / France

Right
Jonathan Perle
@jonathan_perle
Turbo Zéro / Nantes / France

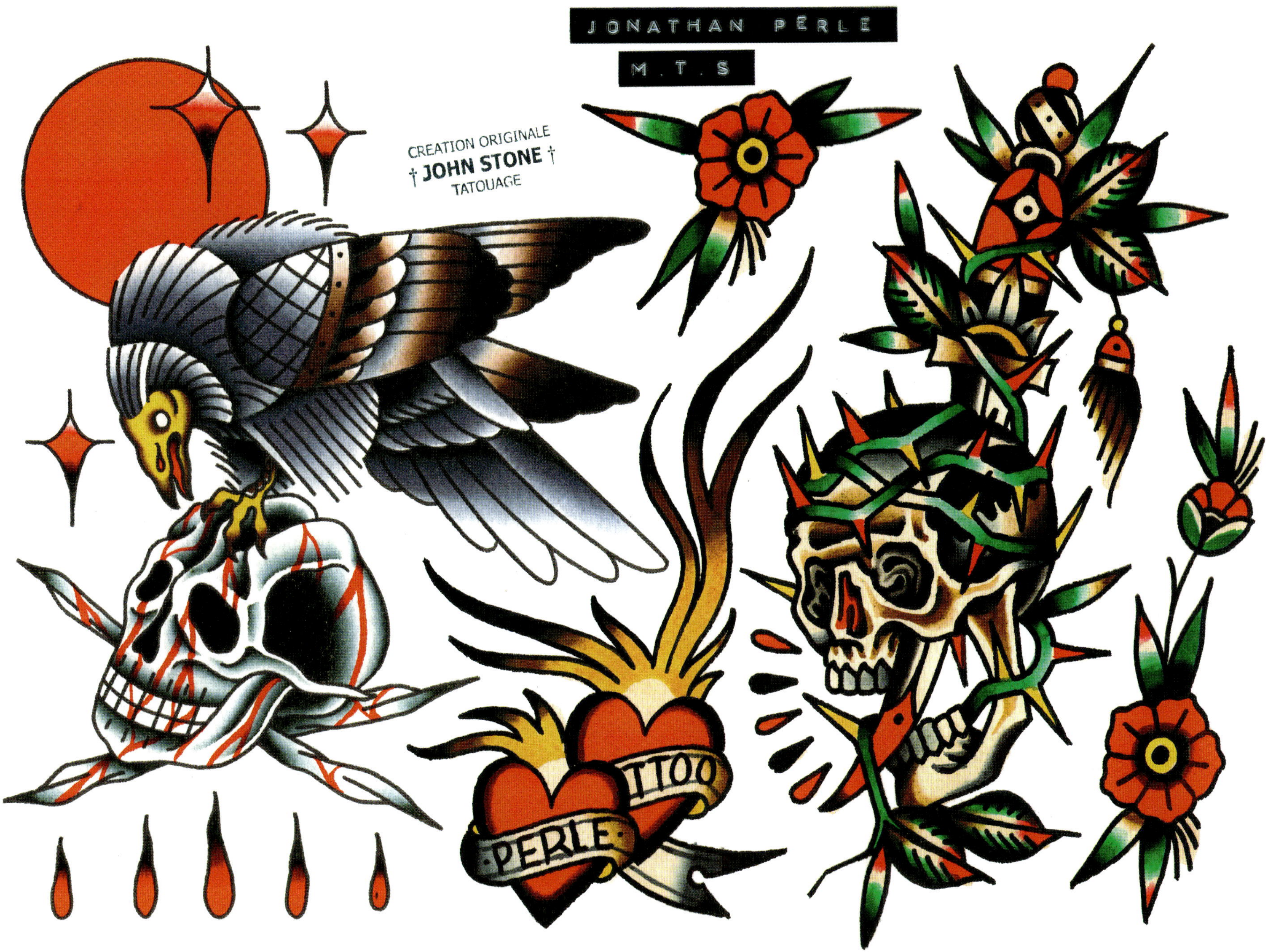
JONATHAN PERLE
M.T.S
CREATION ORIGINALE
† JOHN STONE †
TATOUAGE
TTOO
PERLE

Left
Frandries
@fr_andries
Private shop / Lille / France

Right
Manue BST
@manue_bst
Velvet Studio Grenoble / Grenoble / France

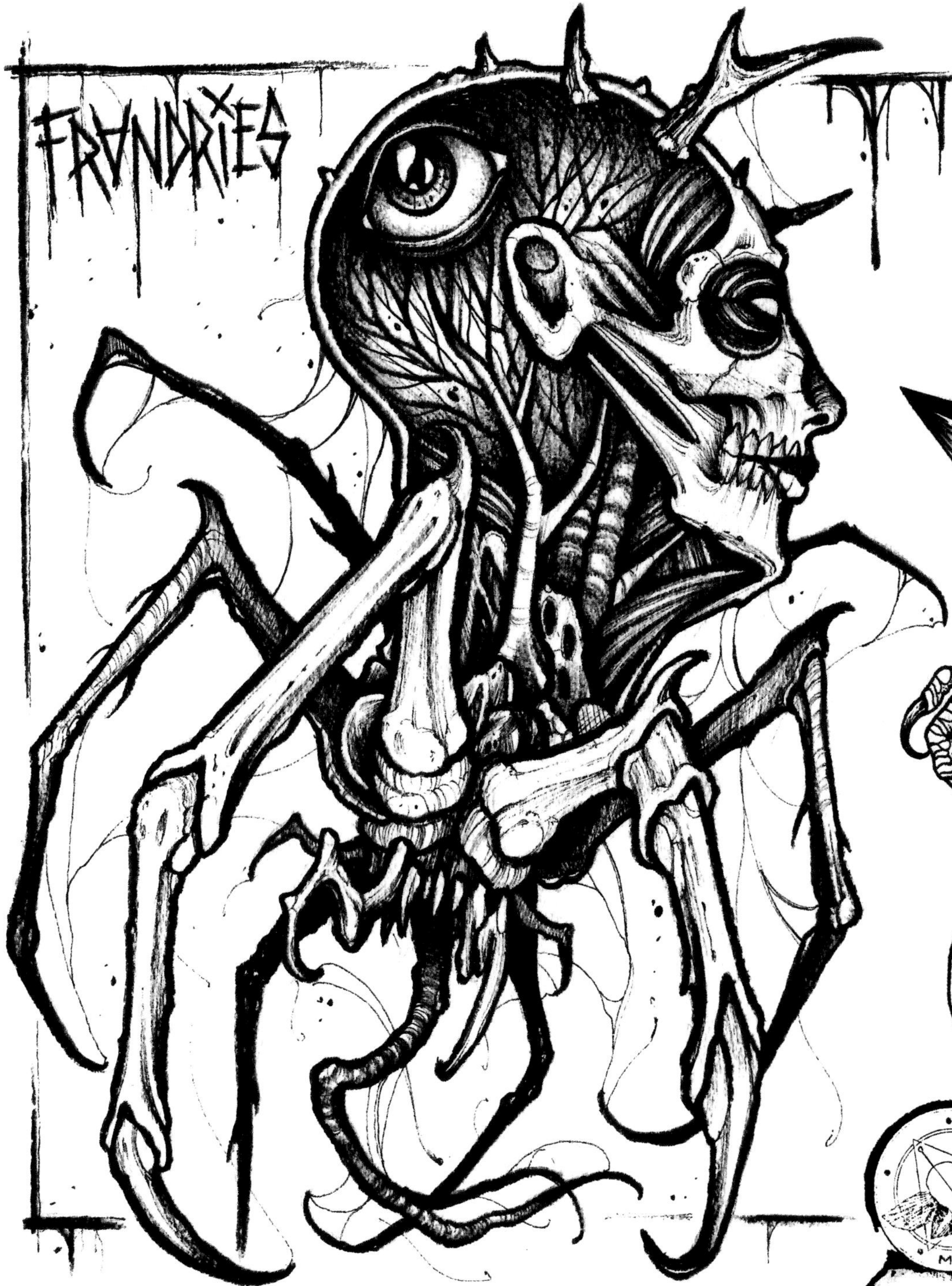
FRANDRIES

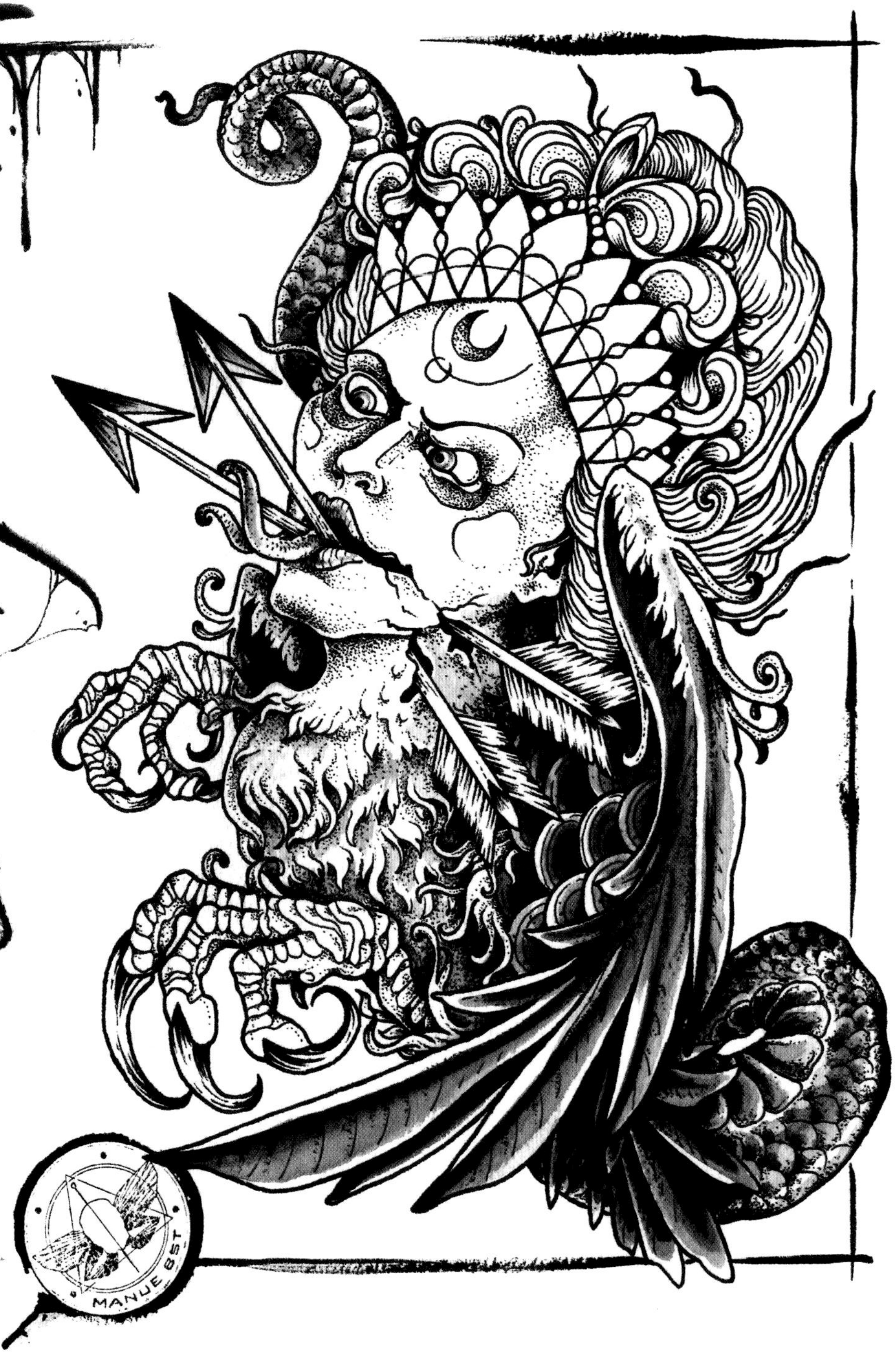
MANJE BST

Left
xCYRx
@xCYRx
Chez Cyr Tatouages / Reims / France

Right
Sylvester Boom
@sylvesterboom
Tribal Act / Paris / France

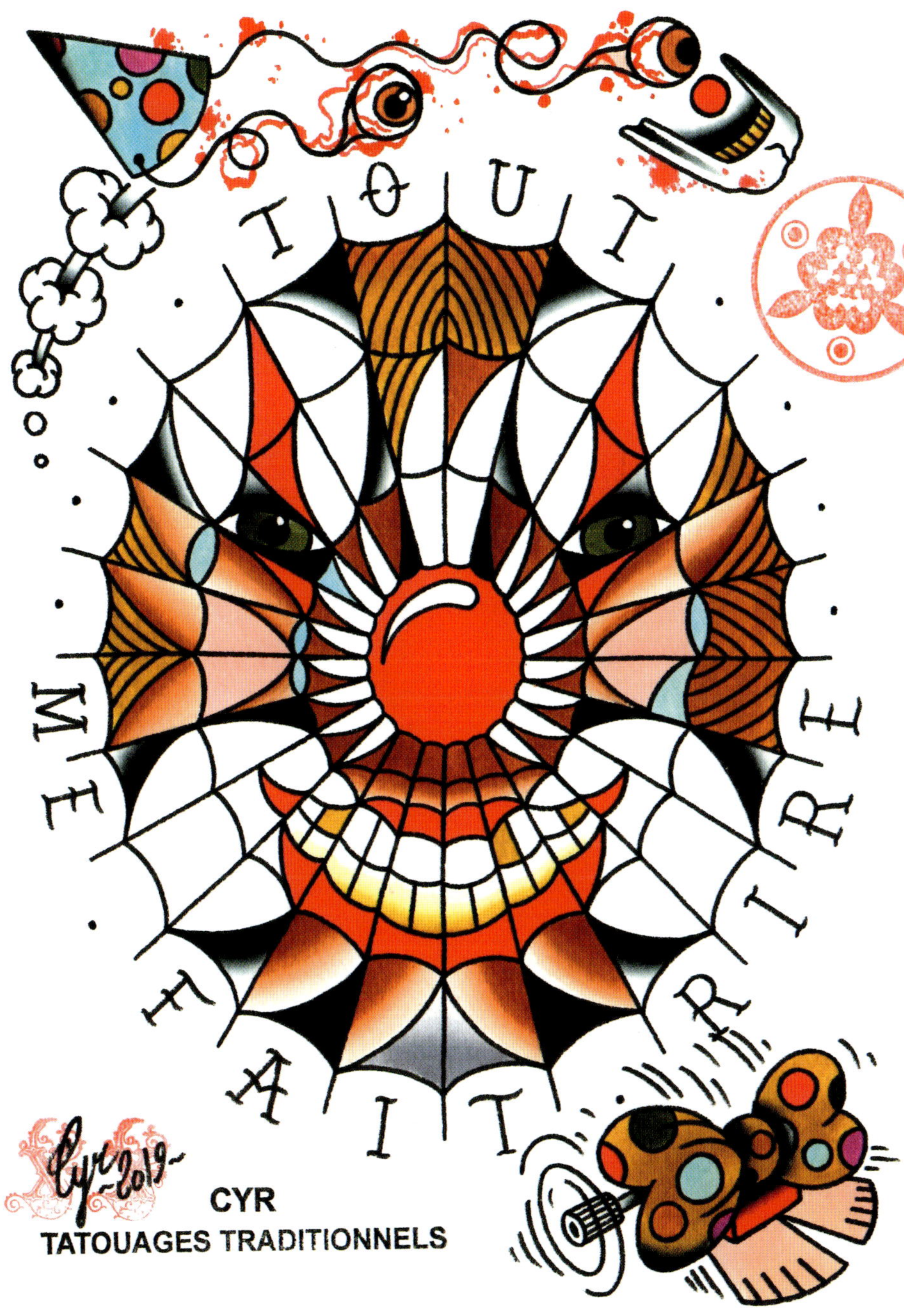

CYR
TATOUAGES TRADITIONNELS

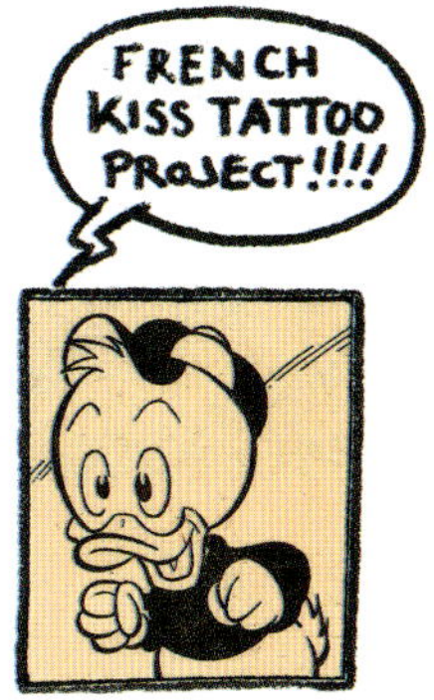

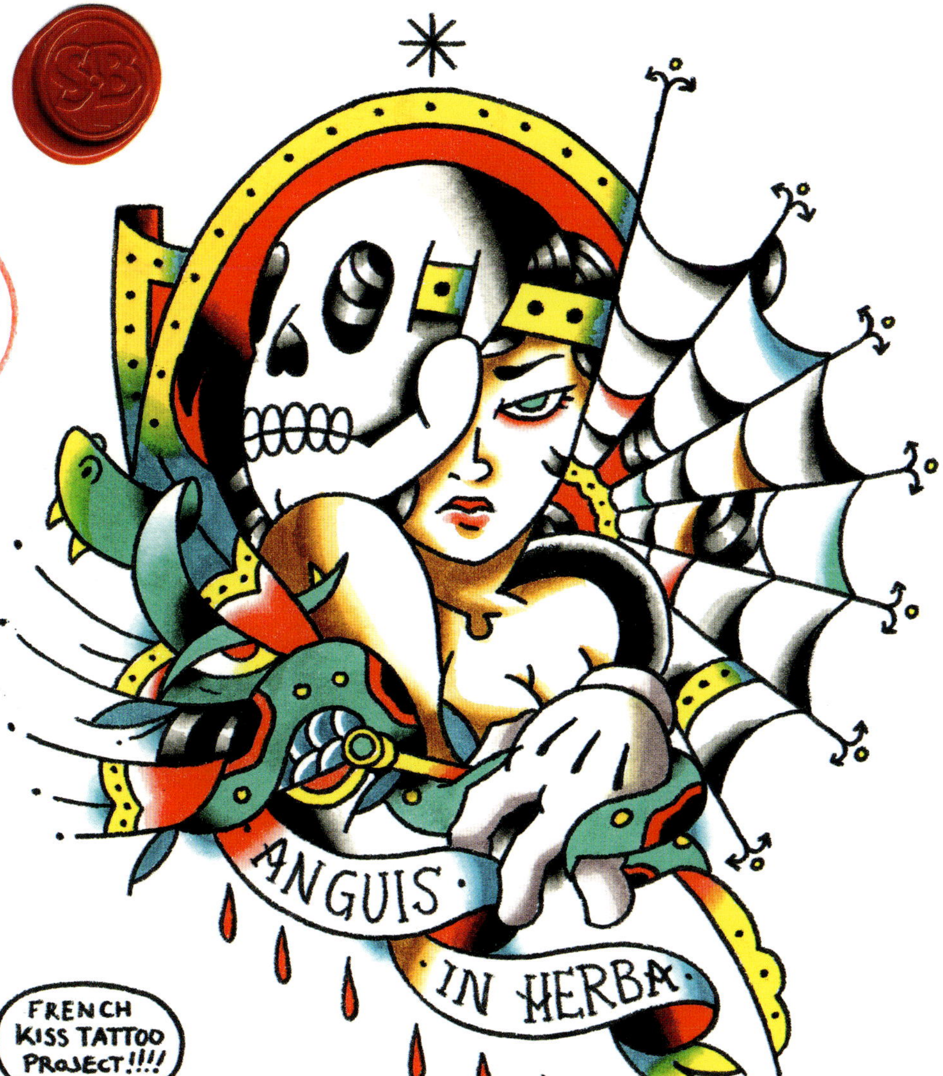

DESSINÉ PAR
SYLVESTER BOOM
☆TATOUAGE ÉLECTRIQUE☆
SLYBOOM2019 *

Left
Tiwan
@tiwan_tattoo
Spirit Tattoo Rennes / Rennes / France

Right
George Geary
@george_geary
Life and death / Shrewsbury / UK

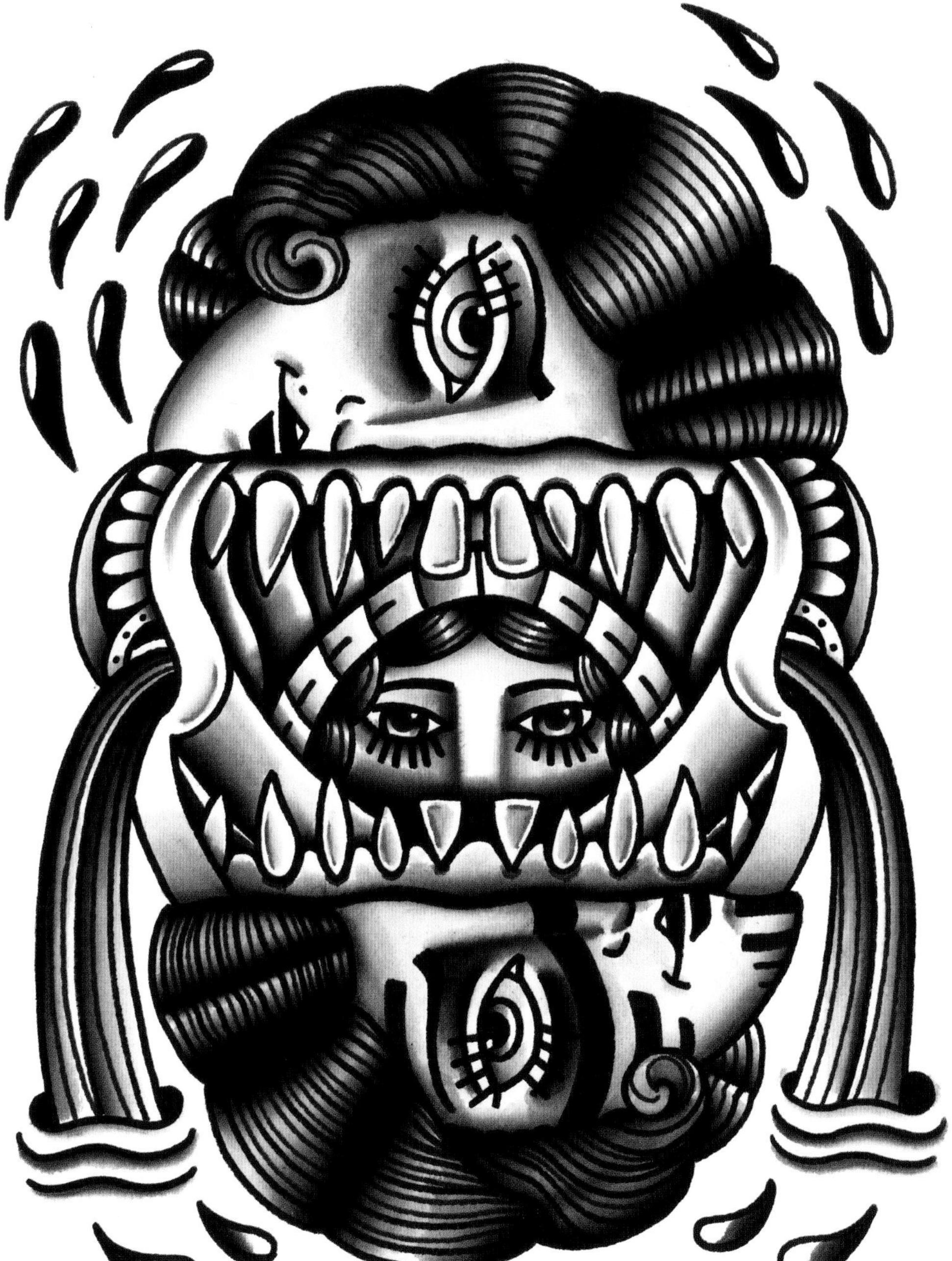
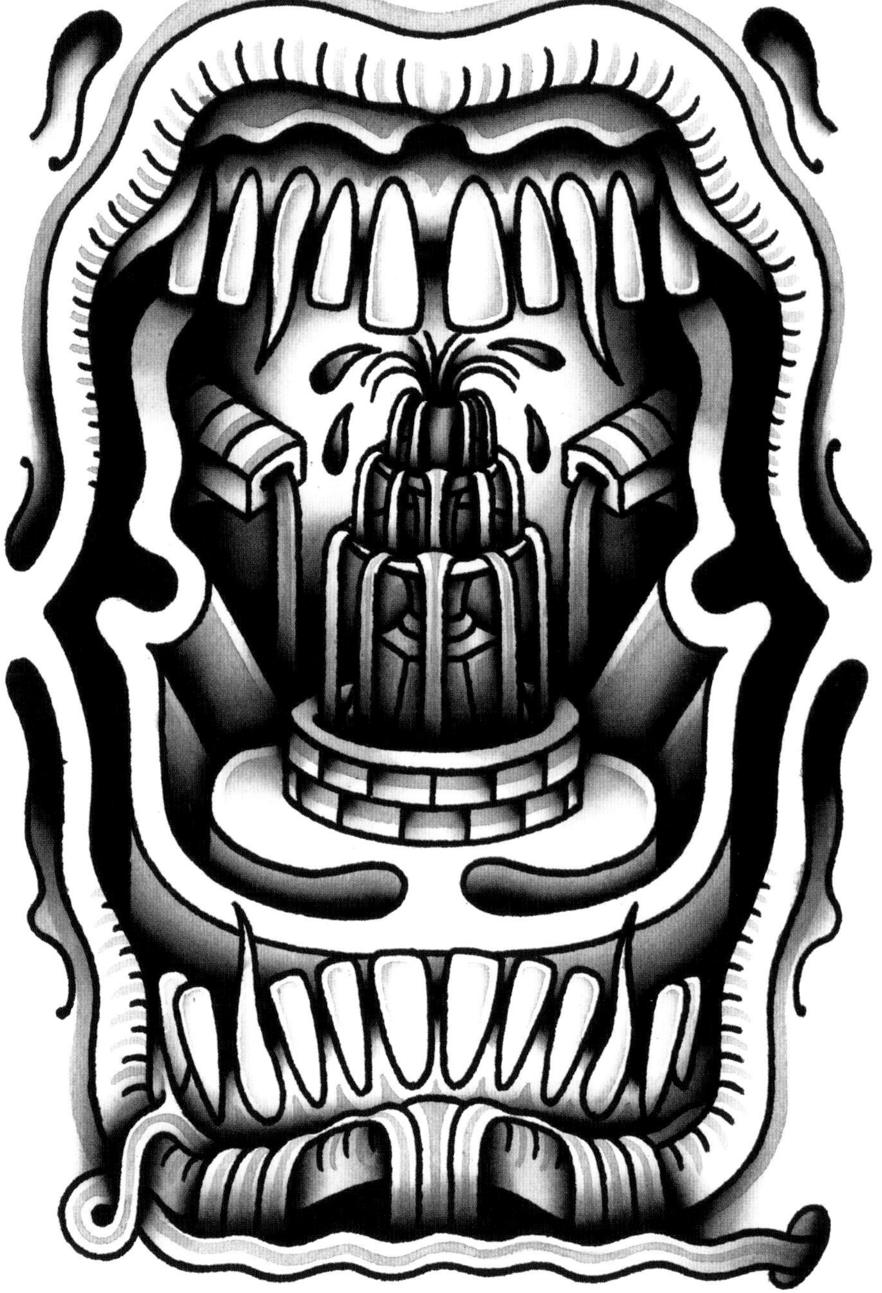

Left

El Bent

@elbenttattoo

True Love / Paris / France

Right

Clément Doineau (Dague Rouge)

@clementdoineau

Grey Bronco Tattoo / Nantes / France

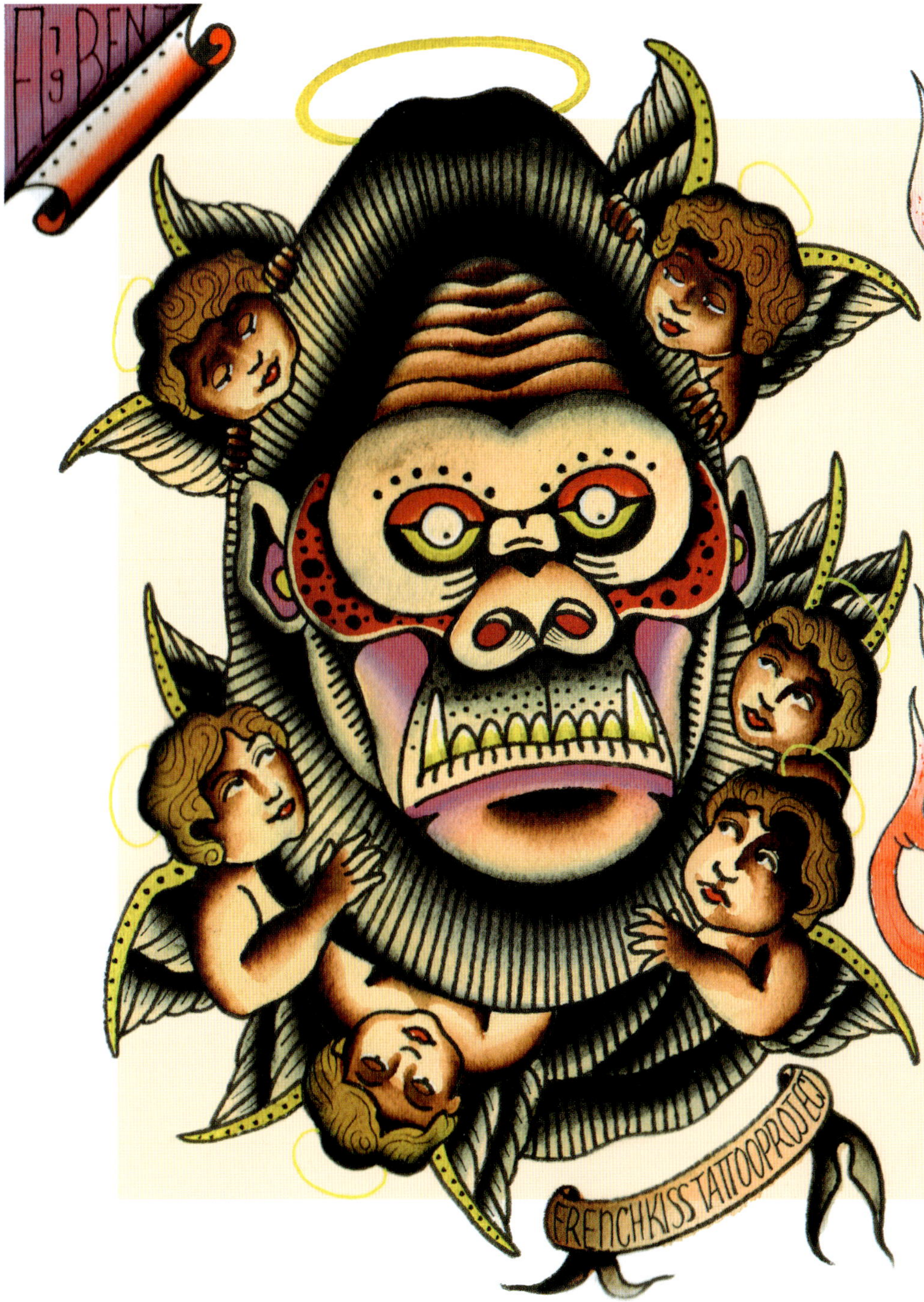
EL 19 BENT
FRENCHKISSTATTOOPROJECT

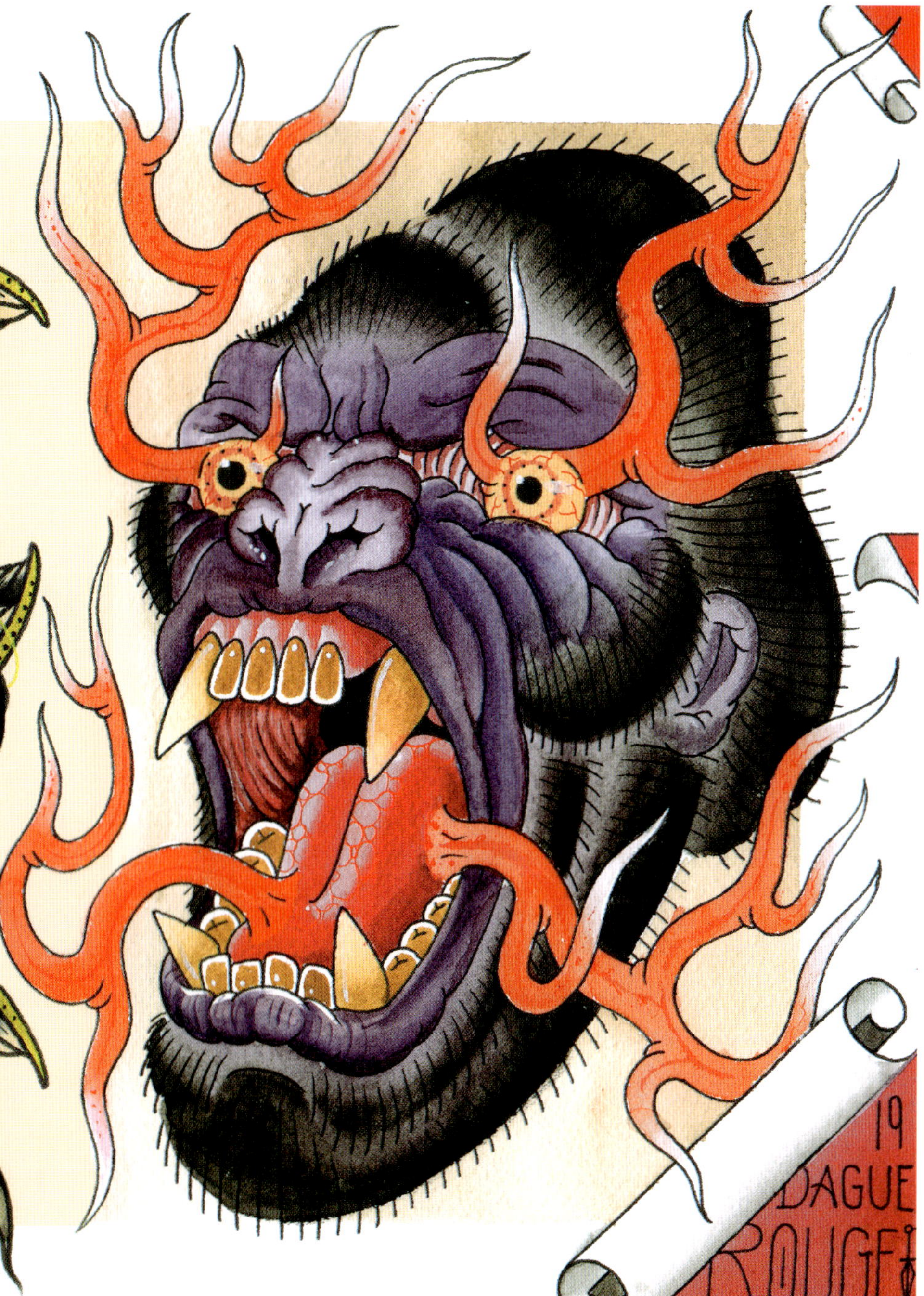
19
DAGUE
ROUGE

Left
Fred Inkvader
@fredinkvader
Inkvader / Sète / France

Right
Toy-Arthur
@toy_arthur_tatouage
FTC Bordeaux / Bordeaux / France

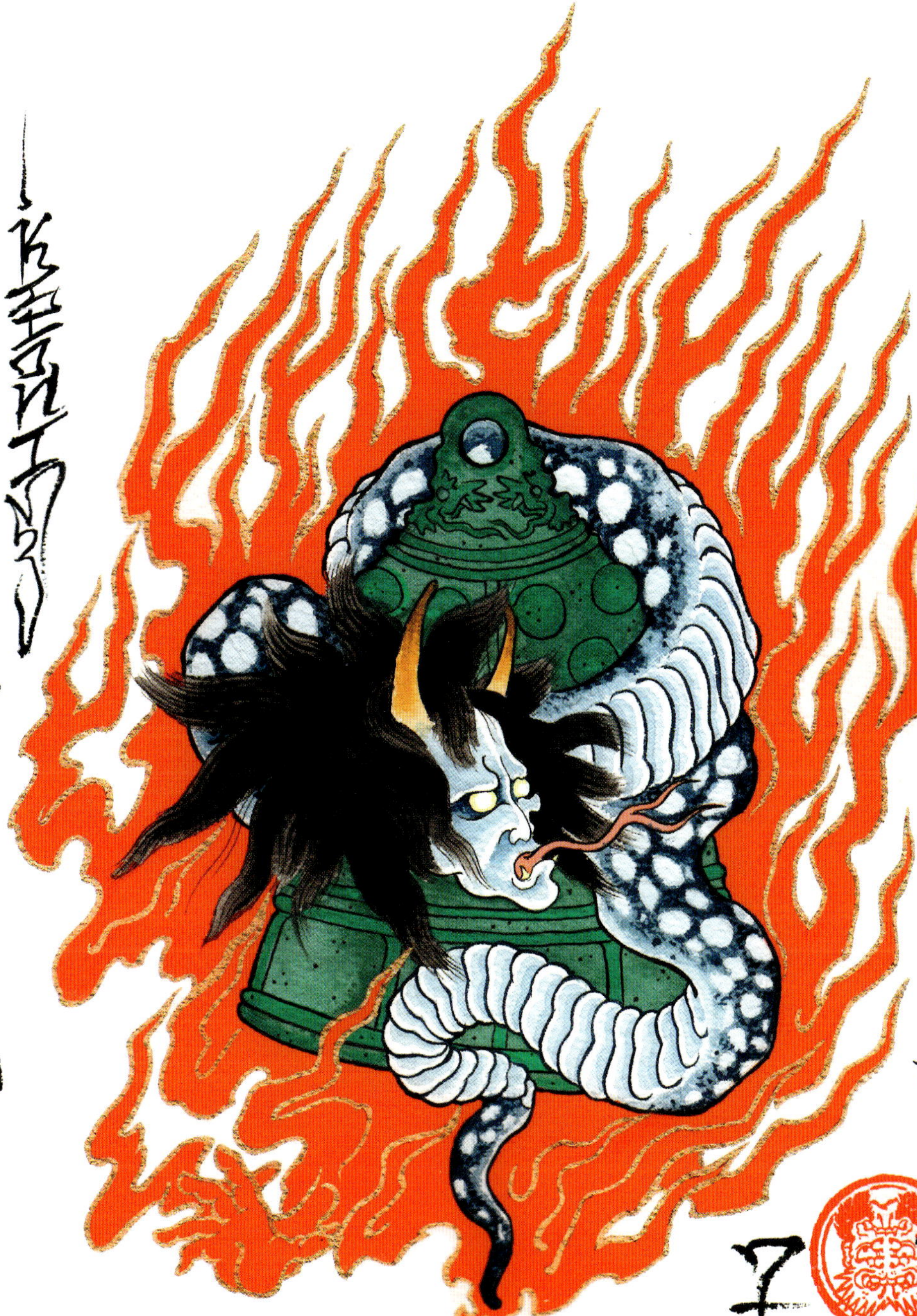

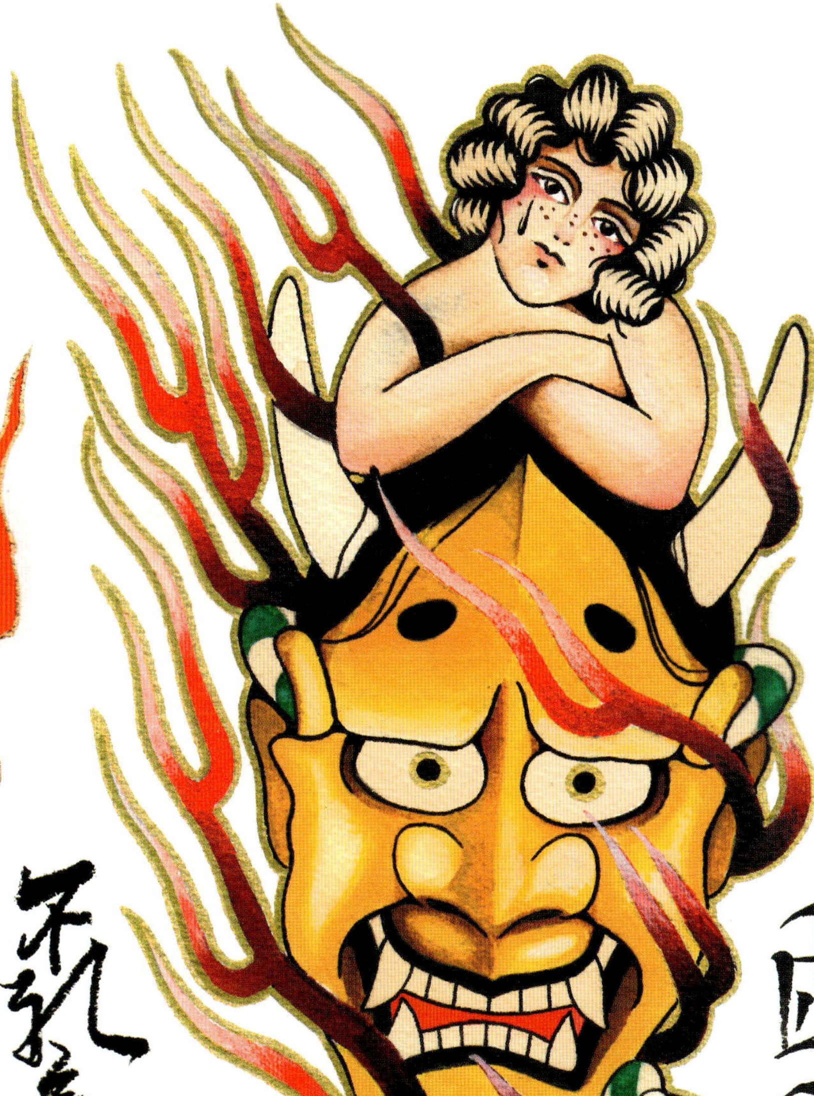

Left
Tattoobyjo
@tattoobyjo
Le Parloir Tattoo / Lausanne / Switzerland

Right
Iannis Le Tigre
@iannis_letigre
Le Tigre / Annecy / France

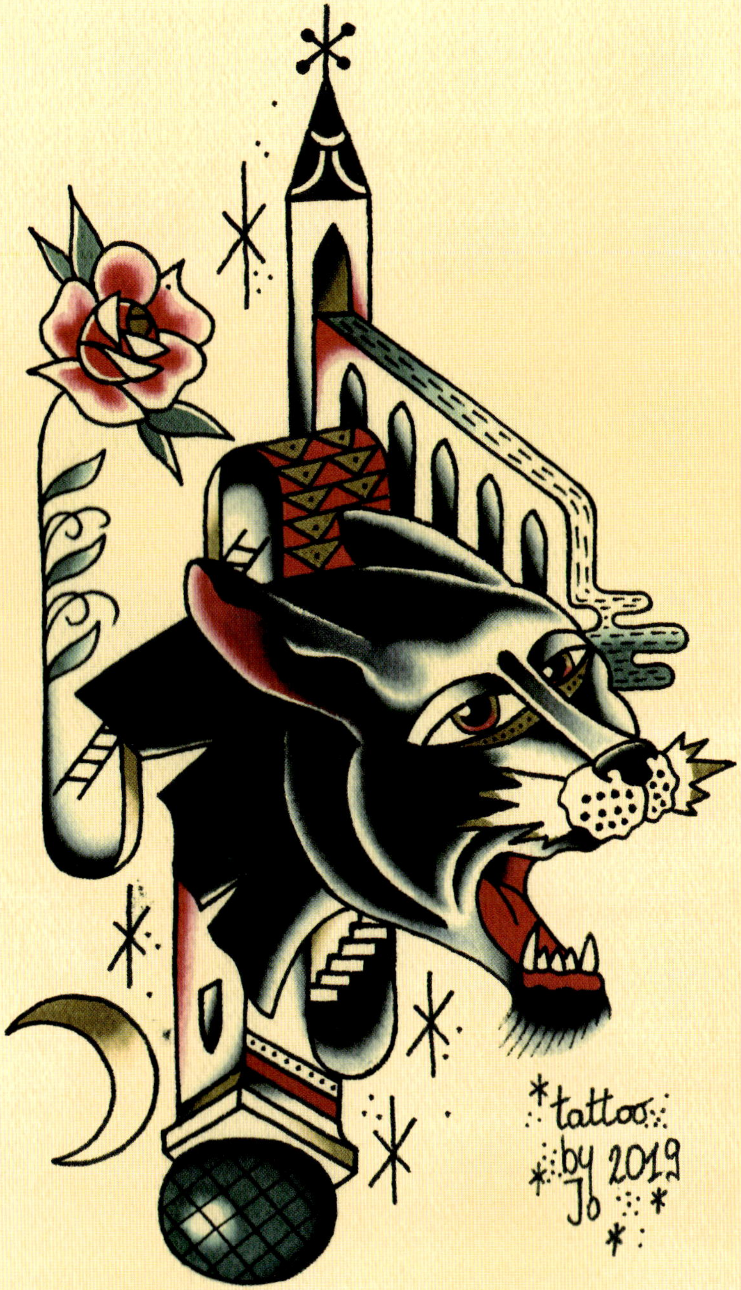
tattoo
by 2019
Jo

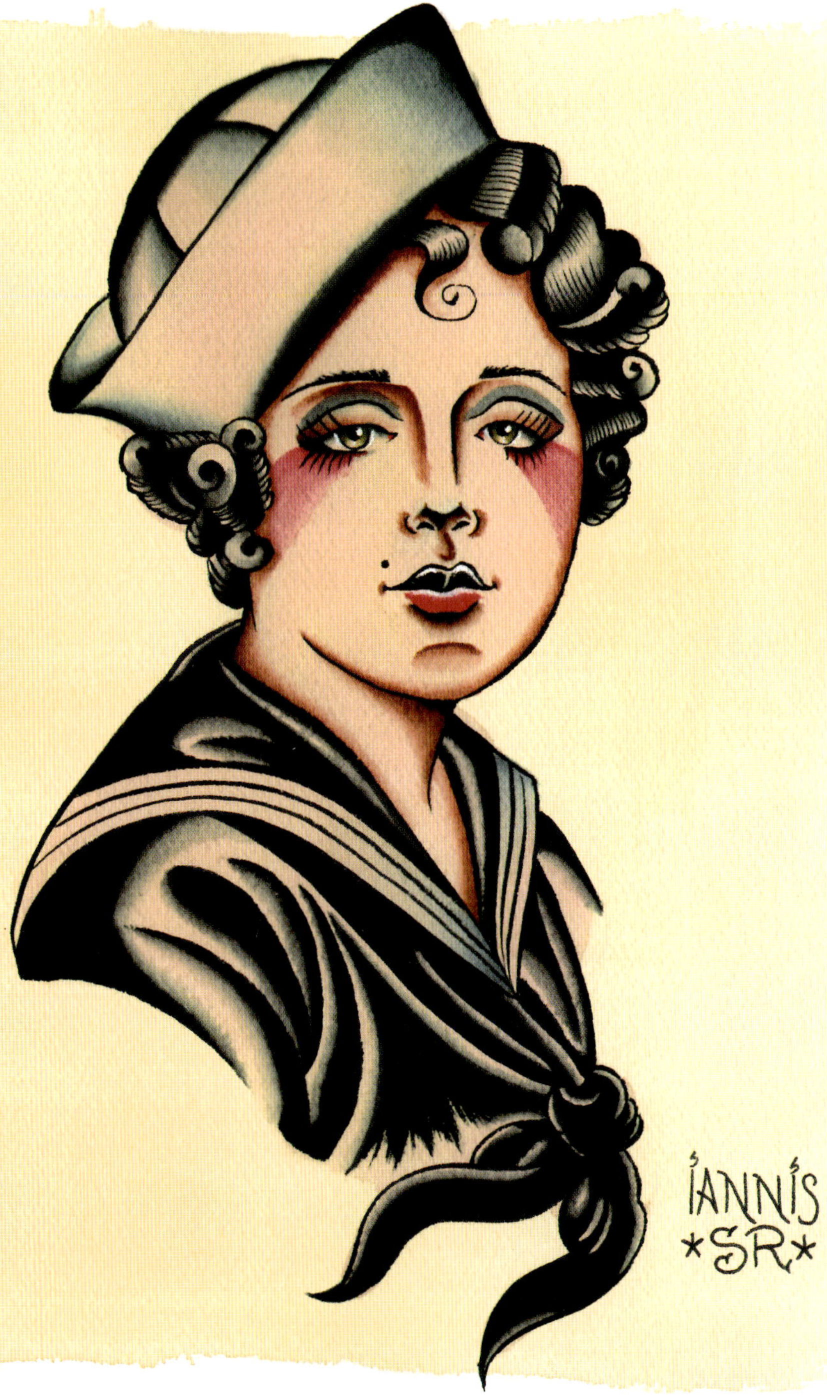
IANNIS
SR

Left
Emma Rouquette
@emmarouqtte
Tattoo Factory / Maisons Alfort / France

Right
Jimi Jugio
@jimijugio
Matière Noire / Paris / France

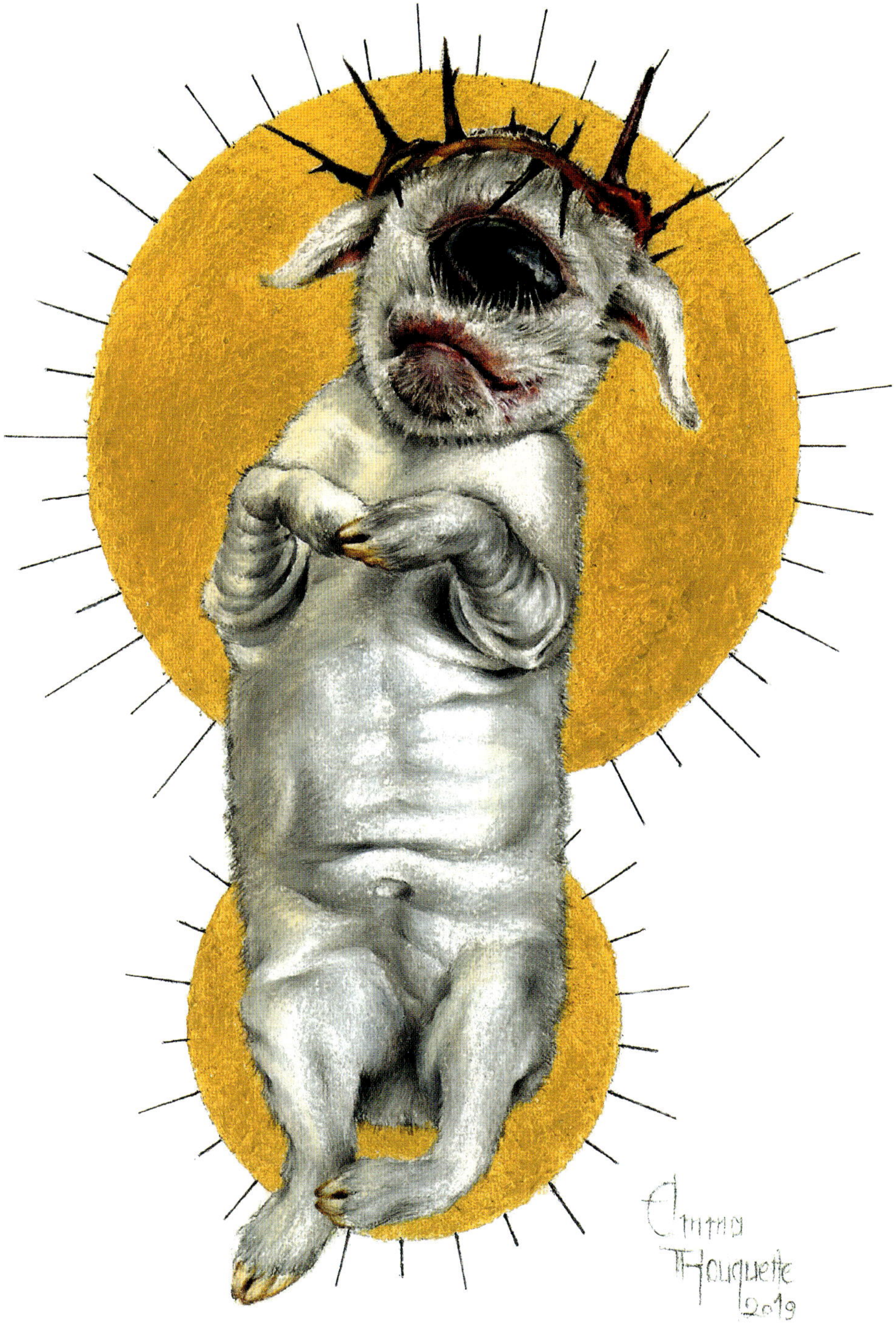

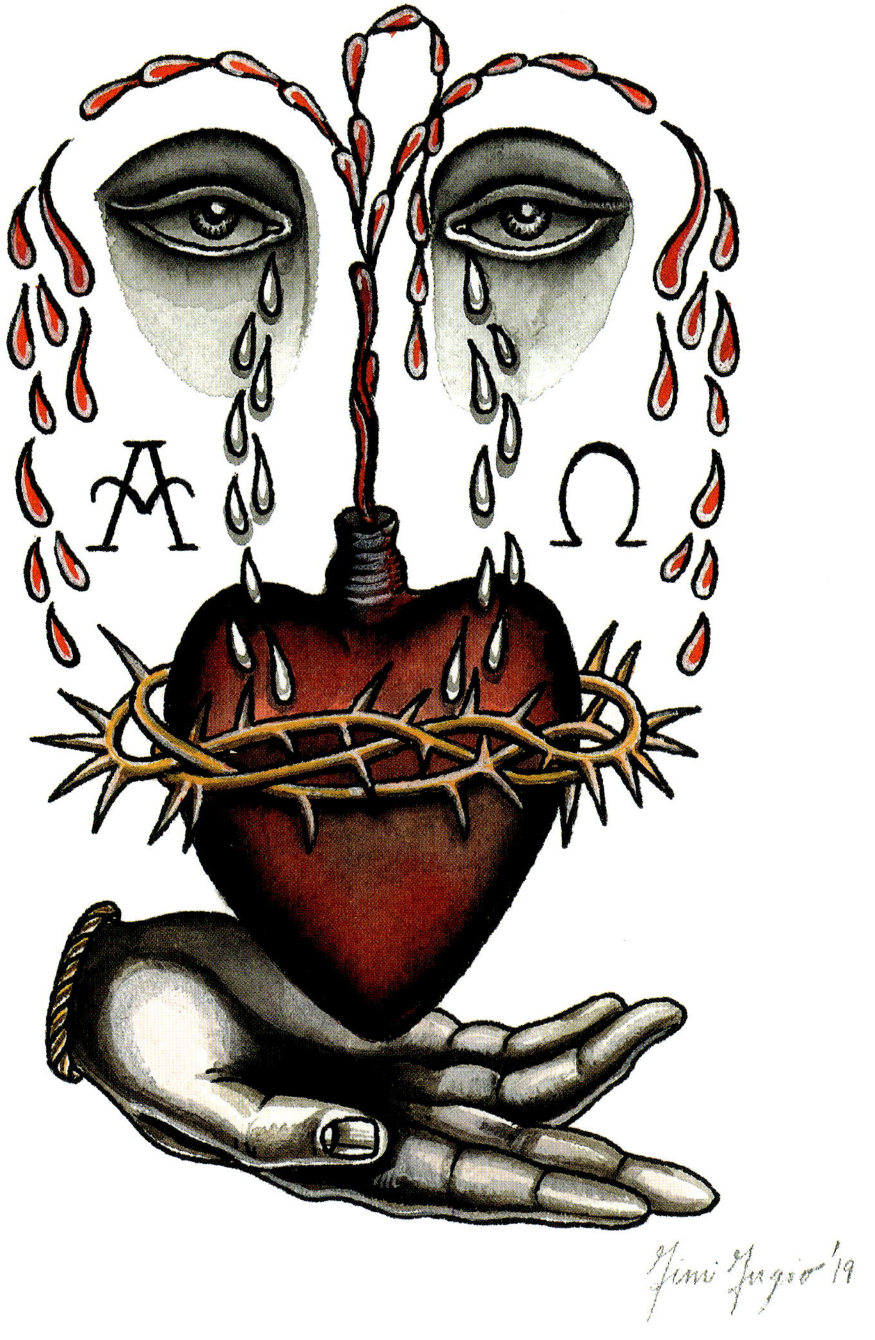

Left
Dr. Djee
@dr.djee
Perdu d'Avance Tattoo Club / Paris / France

Right
Pierre Panther
@peter.panther_
Perdu d'Avance Tattoo Club / Paris / France

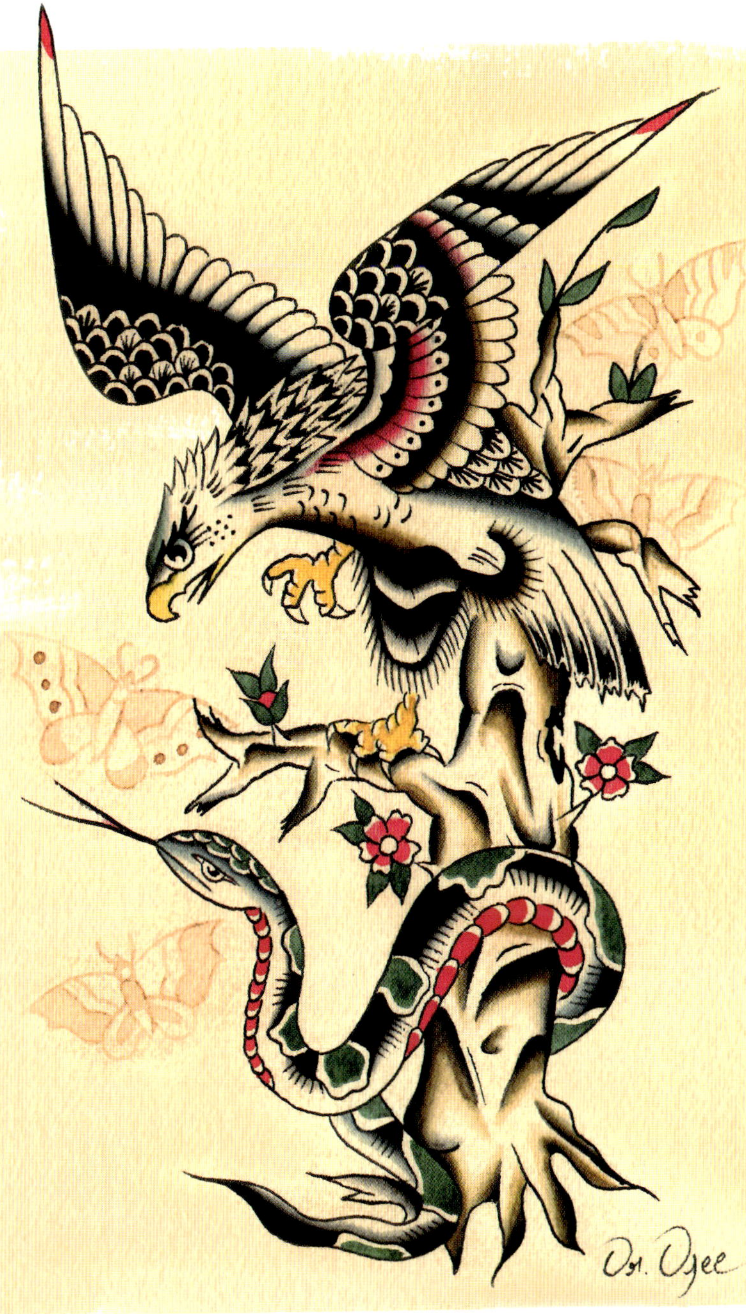

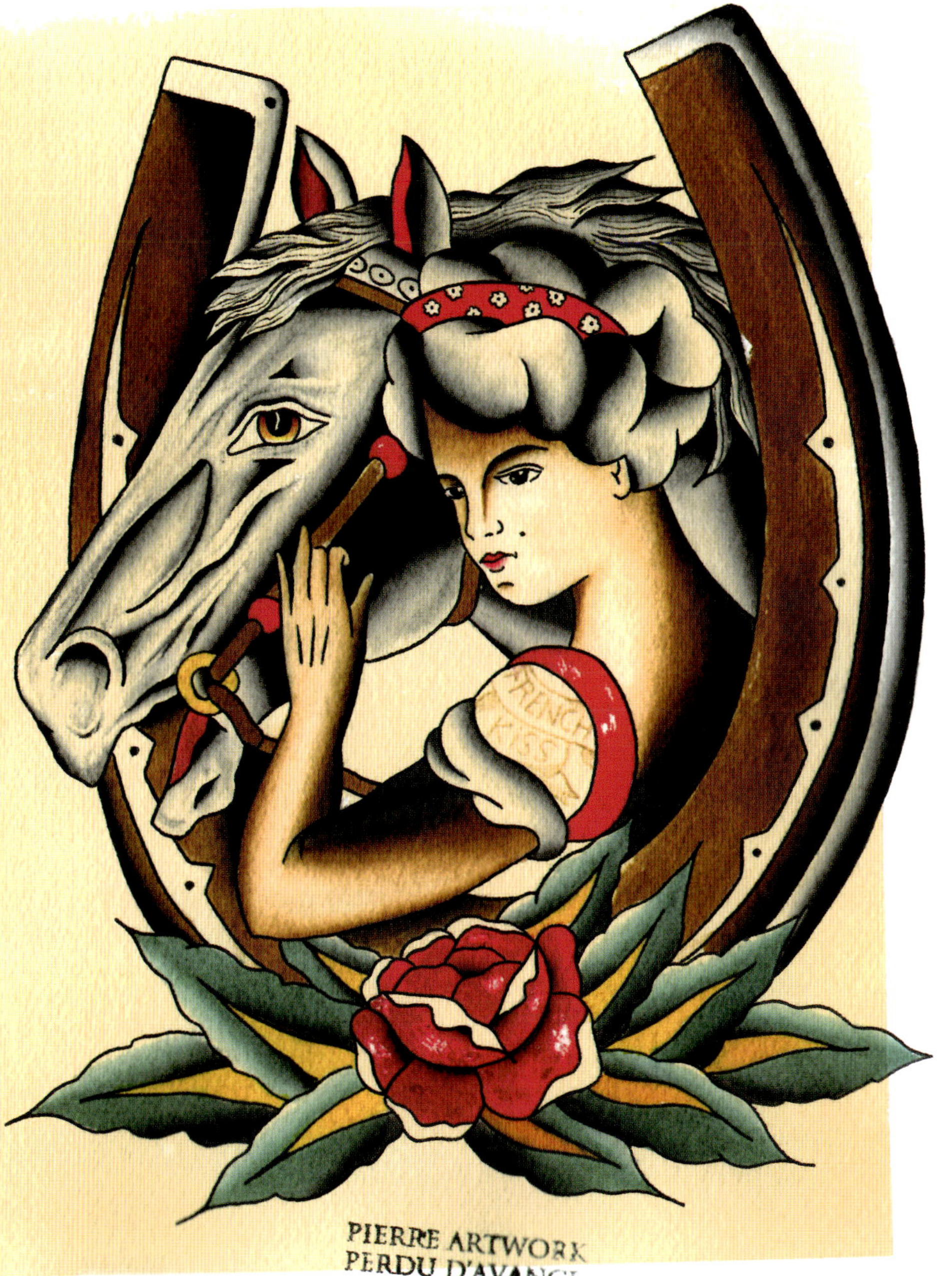

PIERRE ARTWORK
PERDU D'AVANCE
TATTOO CLUB

Left
Mélodie Walt
@melodiewalt
Popink Marseille / Marseille / France

Right
Monsieur Biz
@lionelmonsieurbiz
Monsieur Biz Tatouage / Aix-en-Provence / France

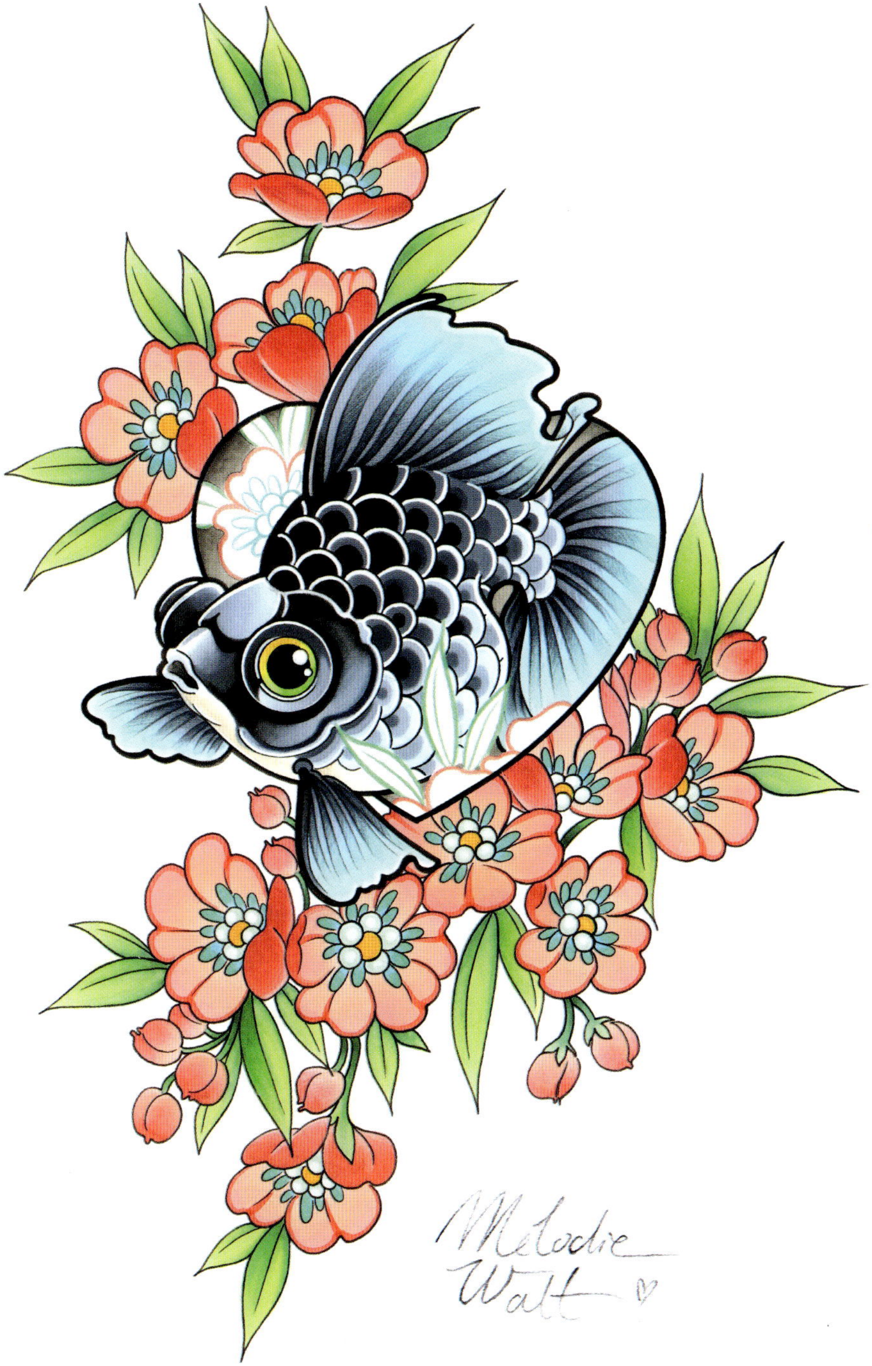
Mélodie
Walt

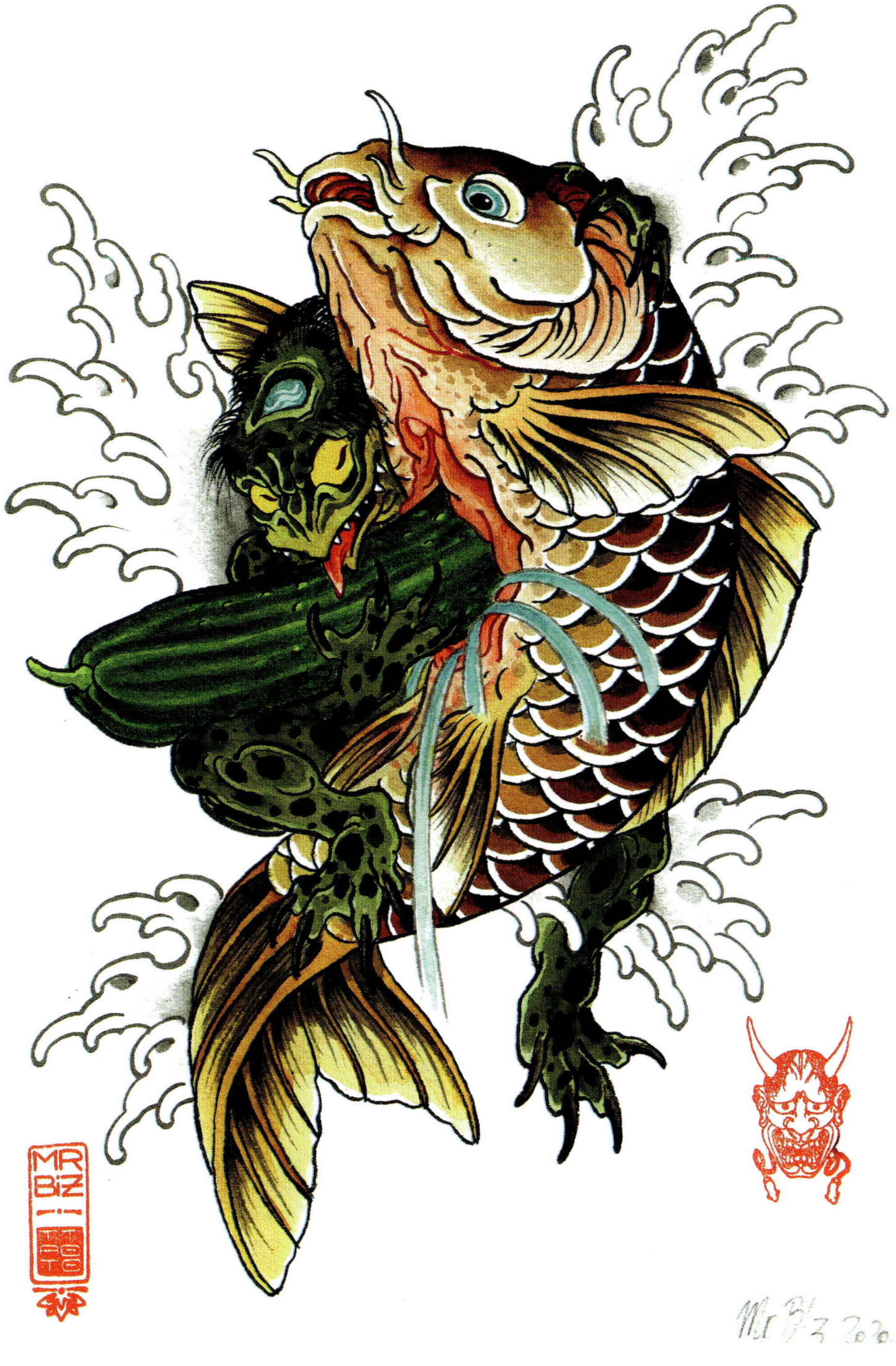
MR
BiZ

Left
John Stone
@john_stone_tatouage
L'Astrolabe / Dinard / France

Right
Malflore
@malflore
Atelier Triptyque / Montpellier / France

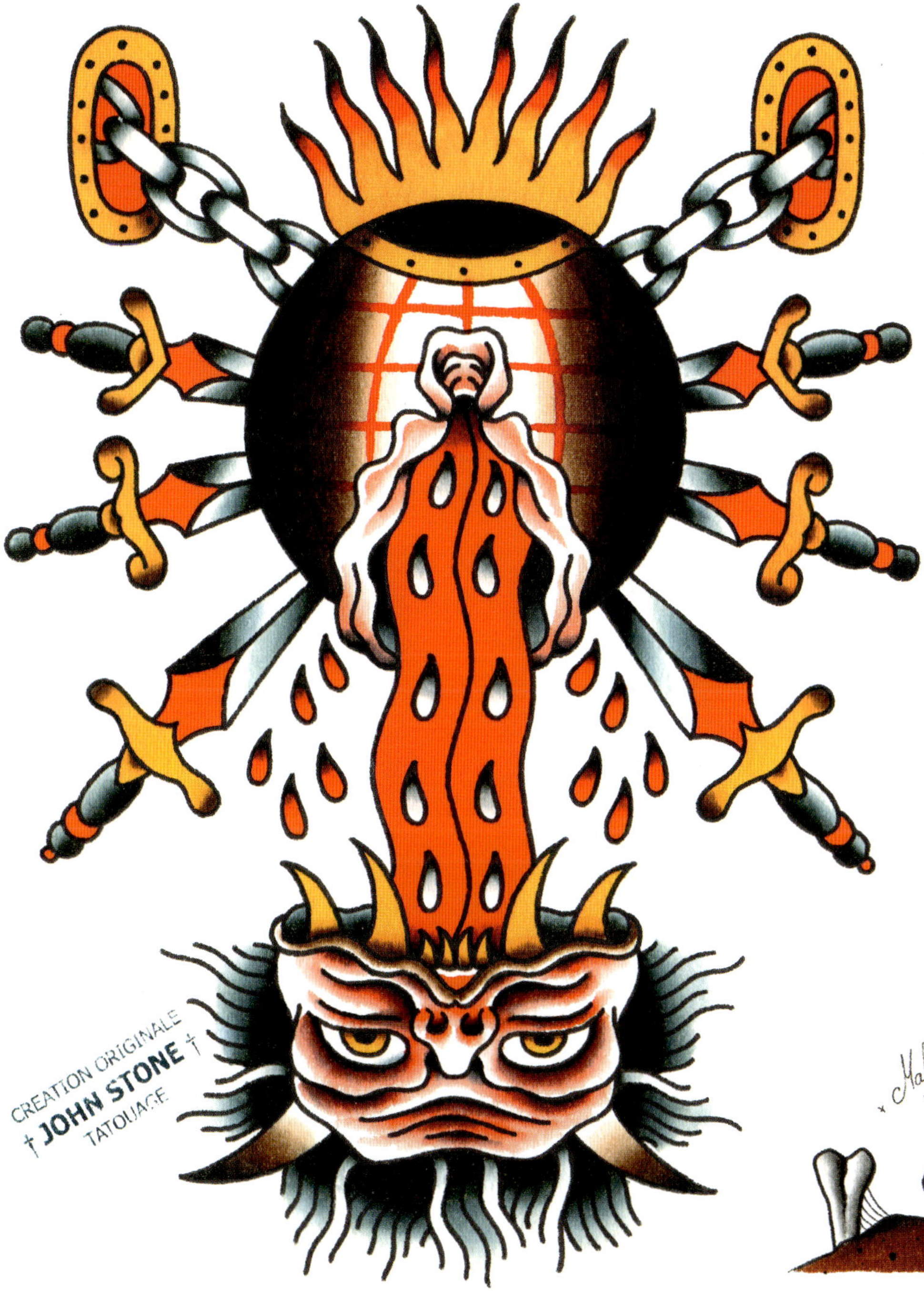
CREATION ORIGINALE
† JOHN STONE †
TATOUAGE

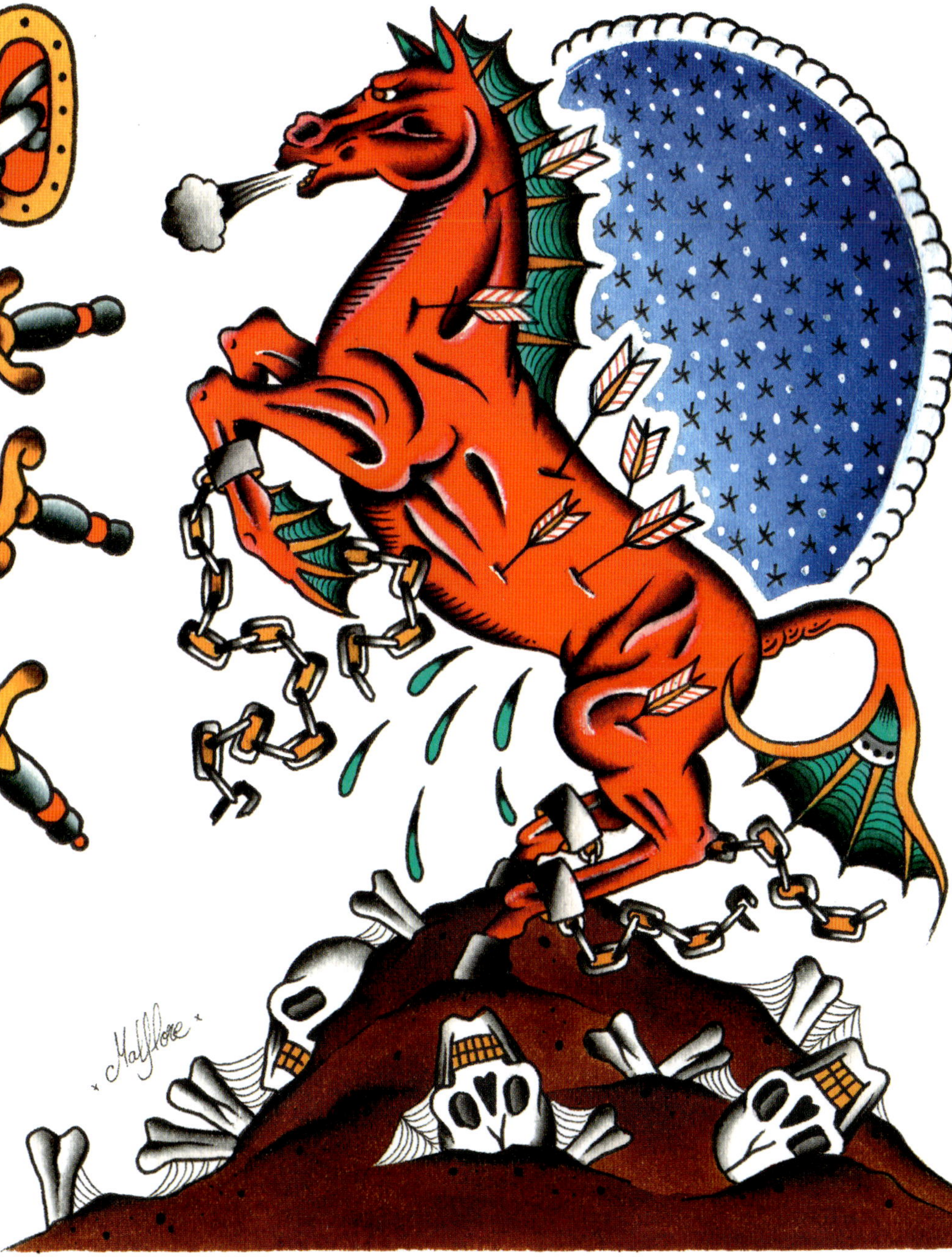
Malflore

Left
Leòn Weidle
@leonweidle
Private shop / Fellbach / Germany

Right
Kelu
@_kelu_
Crying Panther Tattoo / Stuttgart / Germany

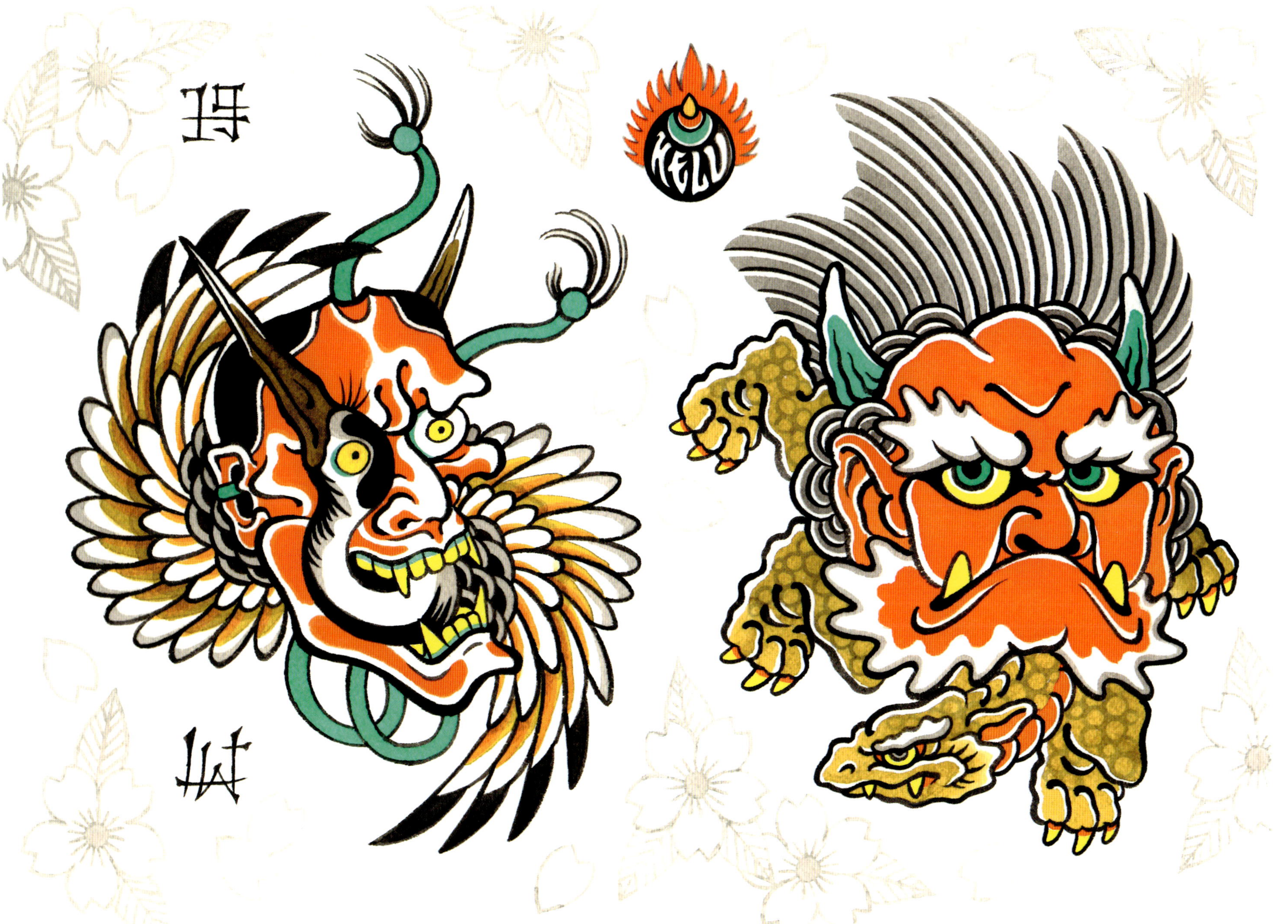

Left
Loïc Mesot LMT
@loicmesotlmt
LM-Tattoo Street Shop / Saint-Mihiel / France

Right
Vincent Simon
@vincentsimontattooer
Story Tellers Tattoo / Amnéville / France

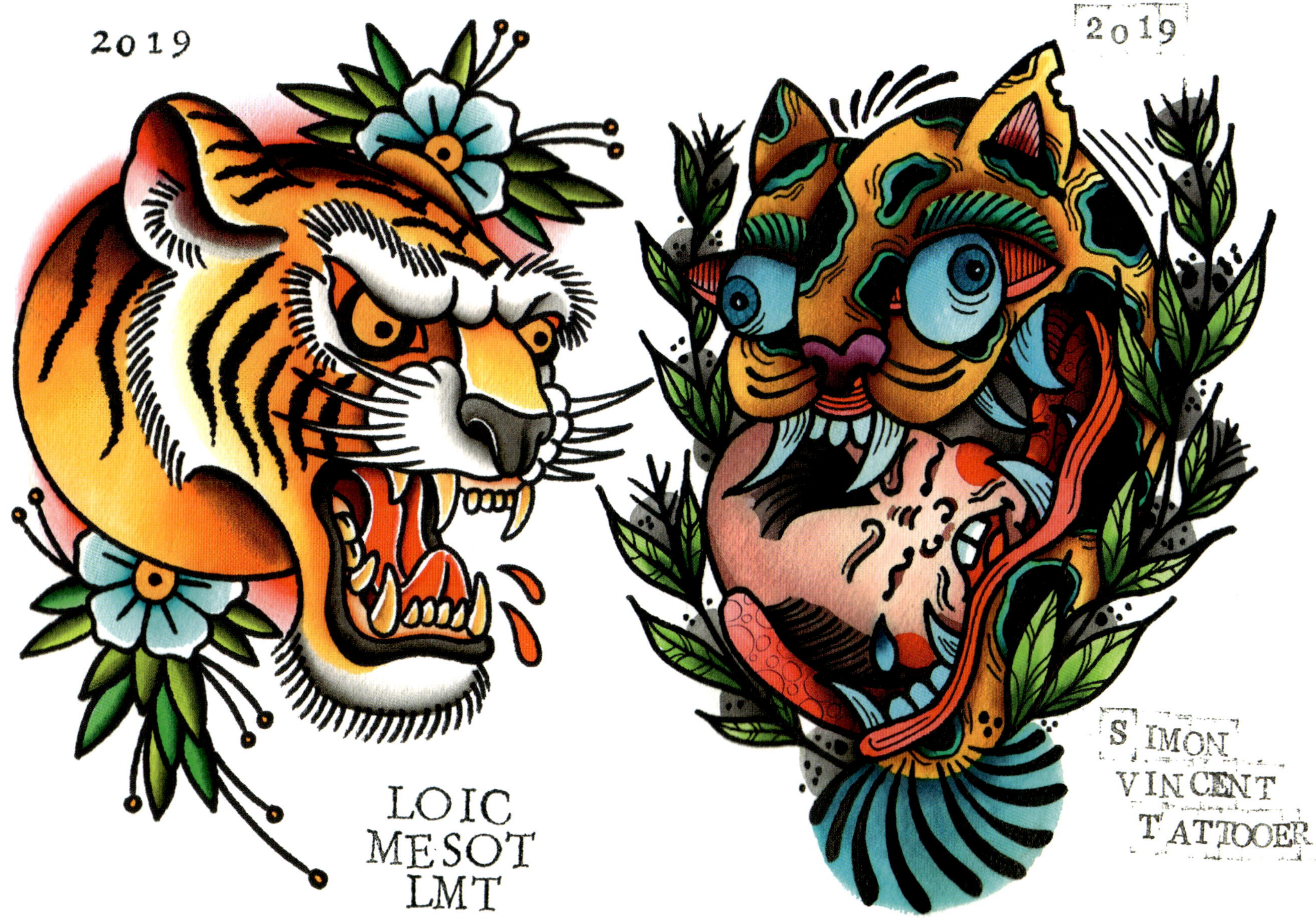
2019
LOIC
MESOT
LMT
2019
SIMON
VINCENT
TATTOOER

Left
Loïc Mesot LMT
@loicmesotlmt
LM Tattoo Street Shop / Saint-Mihiel / France

Right
Uncle Ho
@uncle_ho_mitchmalone
Iron Claw / Strasbourg / France

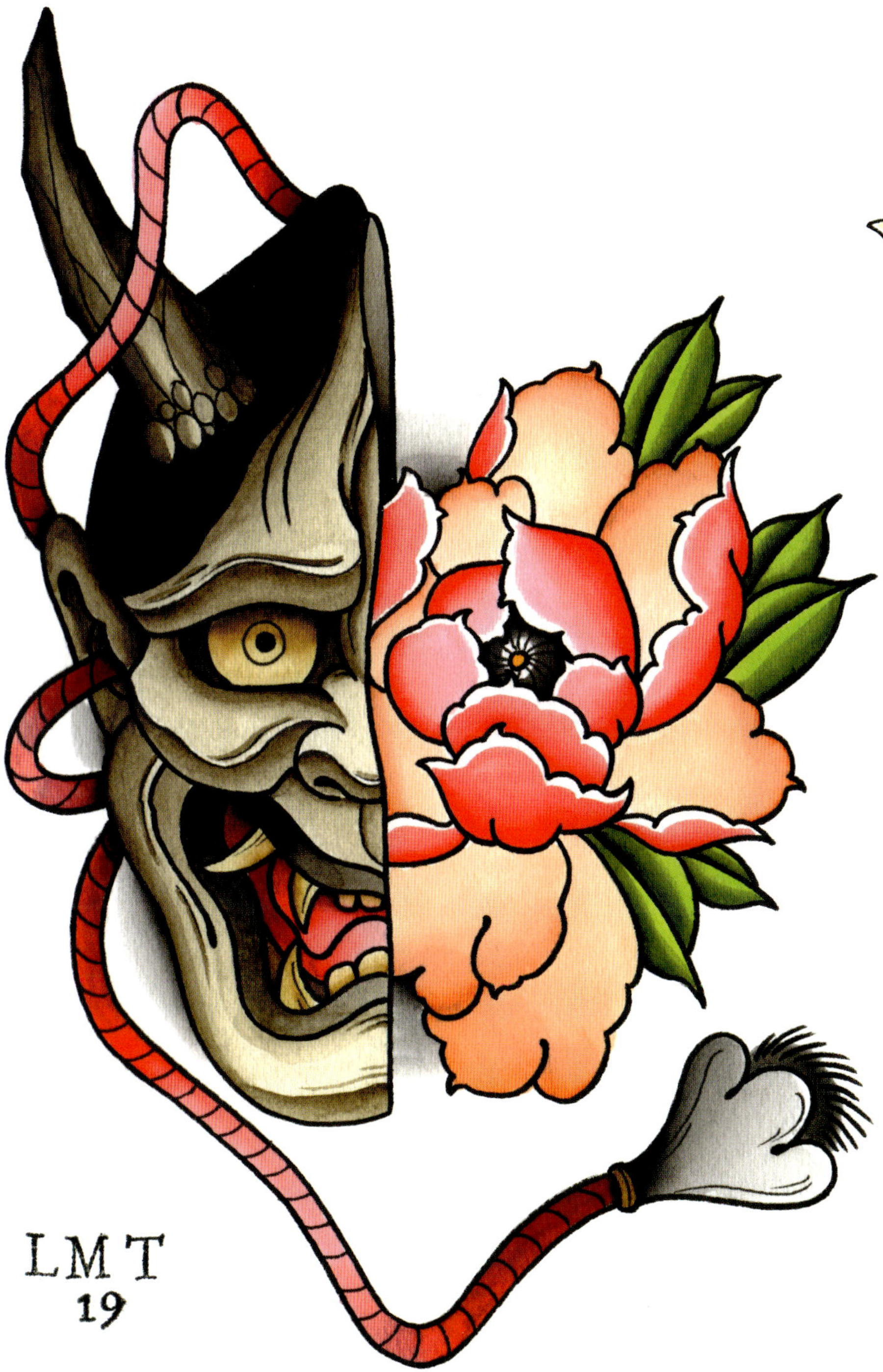
LMT
19
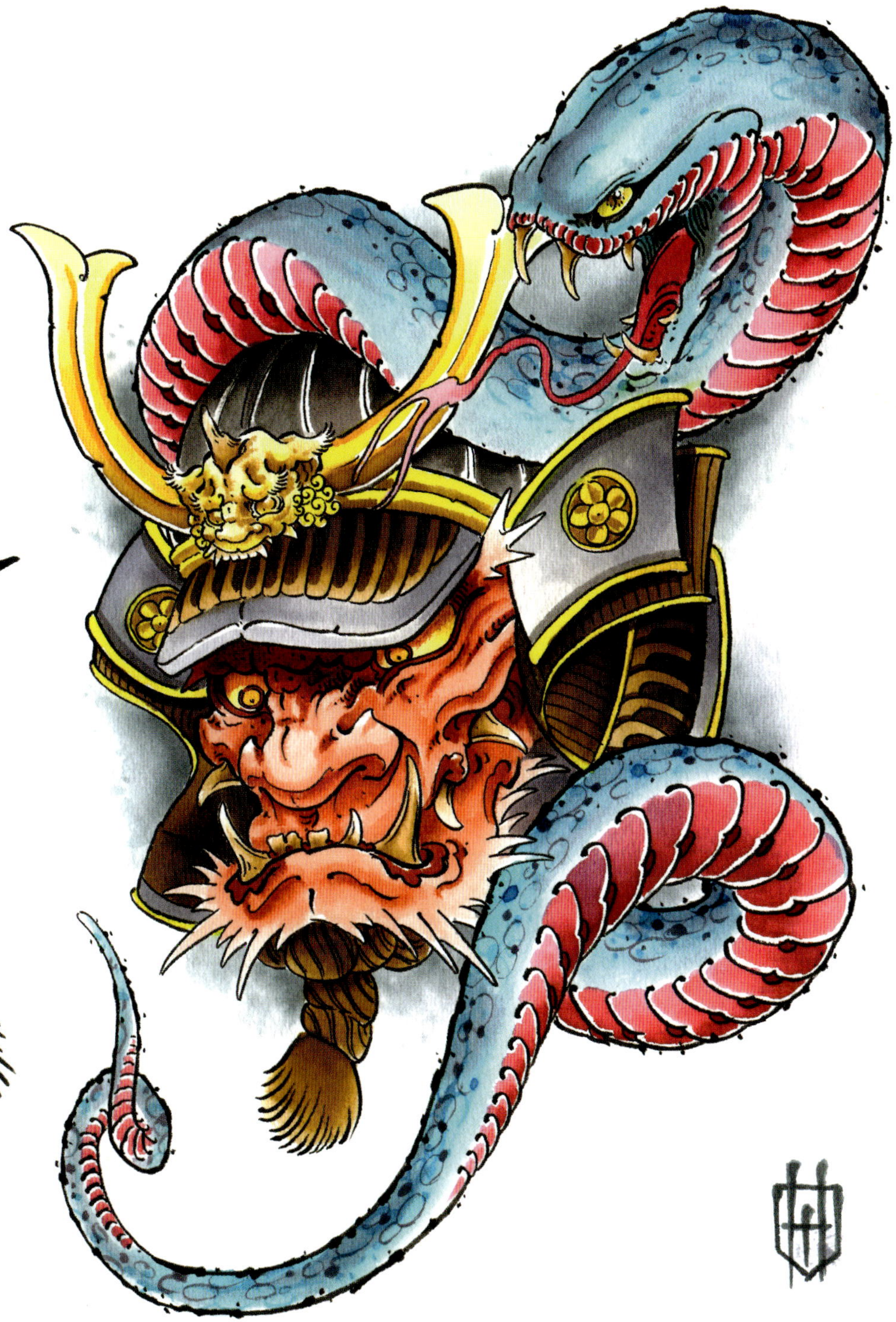

Left
Leni FTC
@leni.f.tatouage
FTC Bordeaux / Bordeaux / France

Right
Toy-Arthur
@toy_arthur_tatouage
FTC Bordeaux / Bordeaux / France

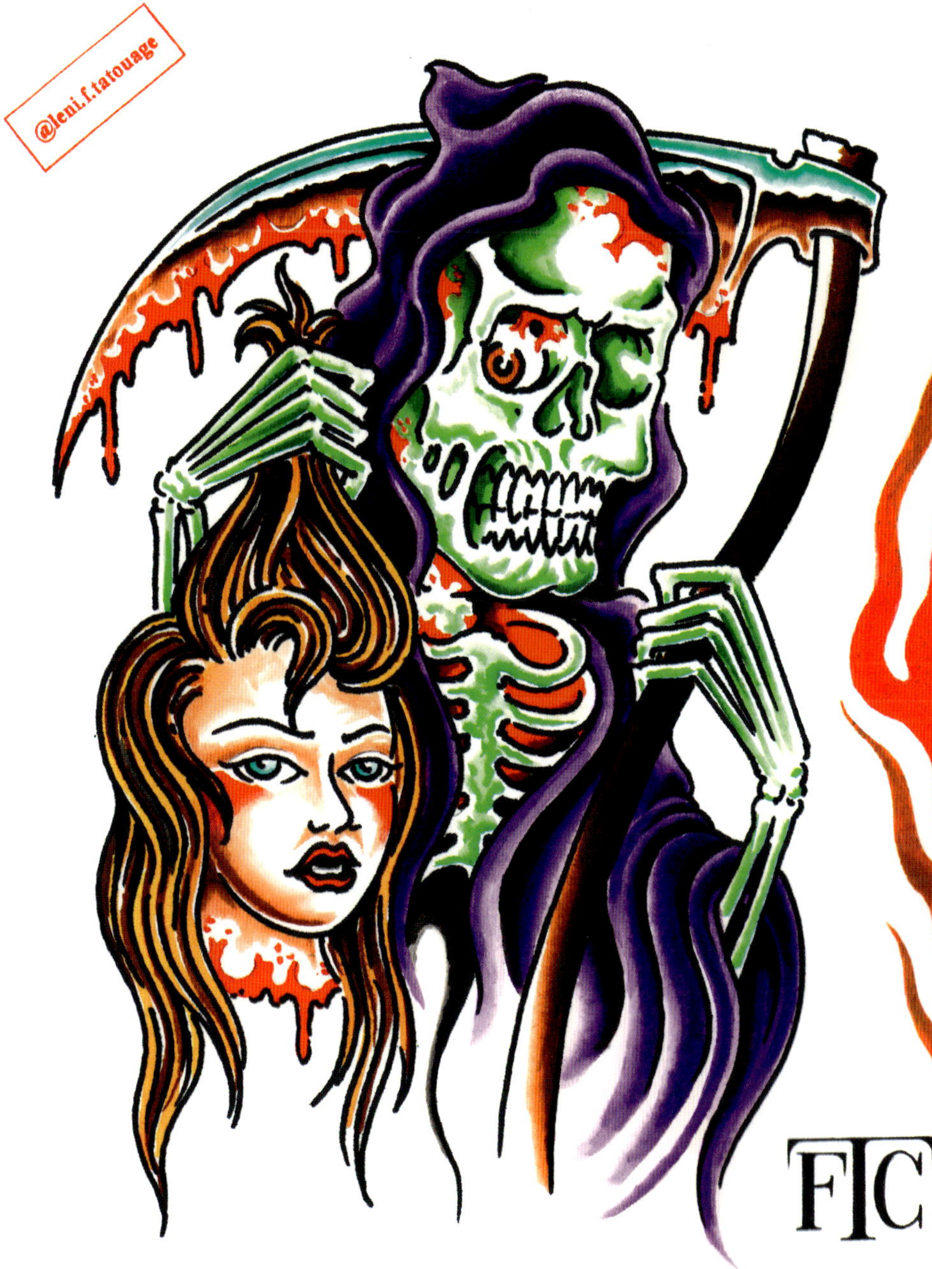
@leni.f.tatouage
FTC

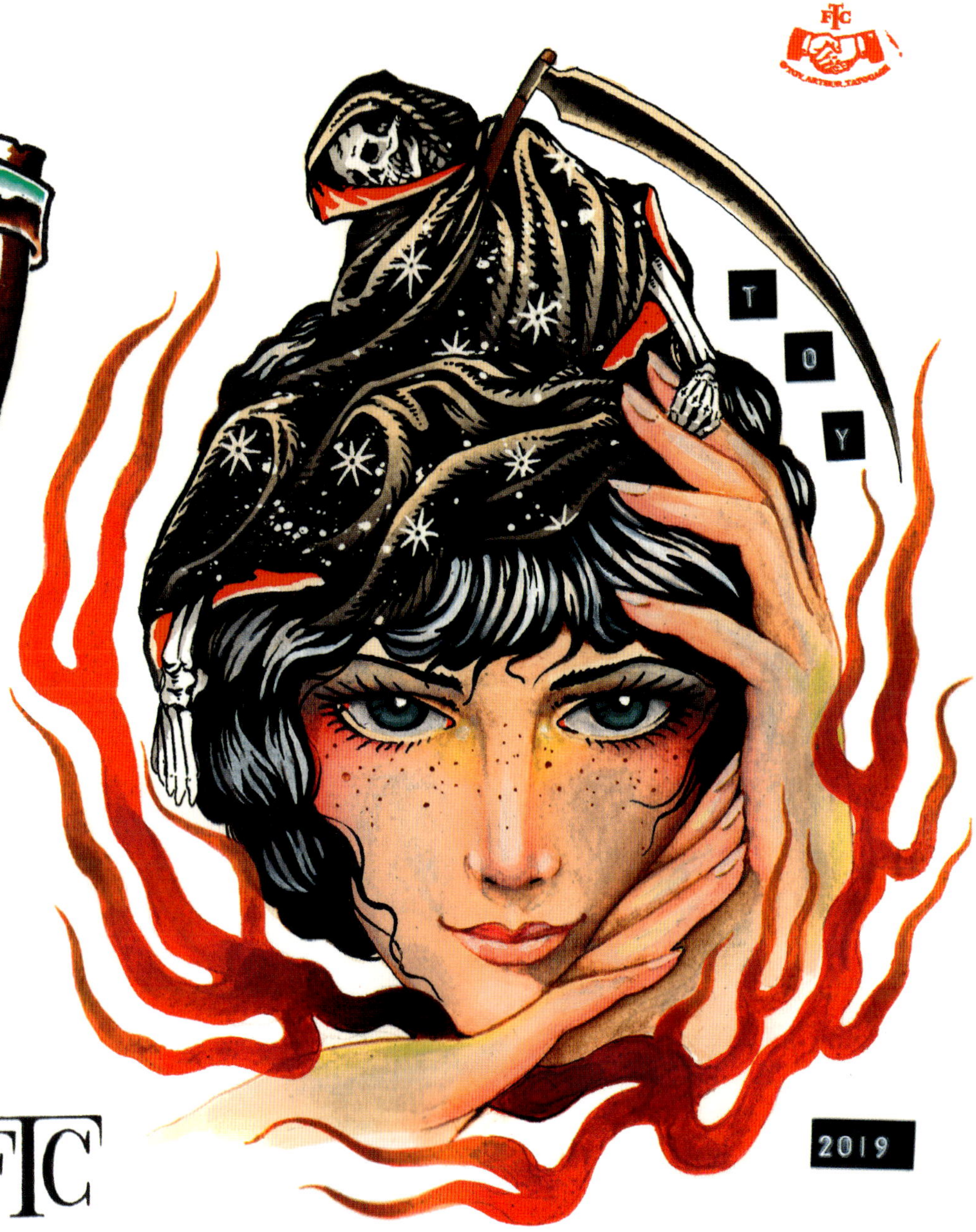
FTC
T O Y
2019

Left
La Mauvaise
@lamauvaisetattoo
La Sauvagerie / Sélestat / France

Right
El Bent
@elbenttattoo
True Love / Paris / France

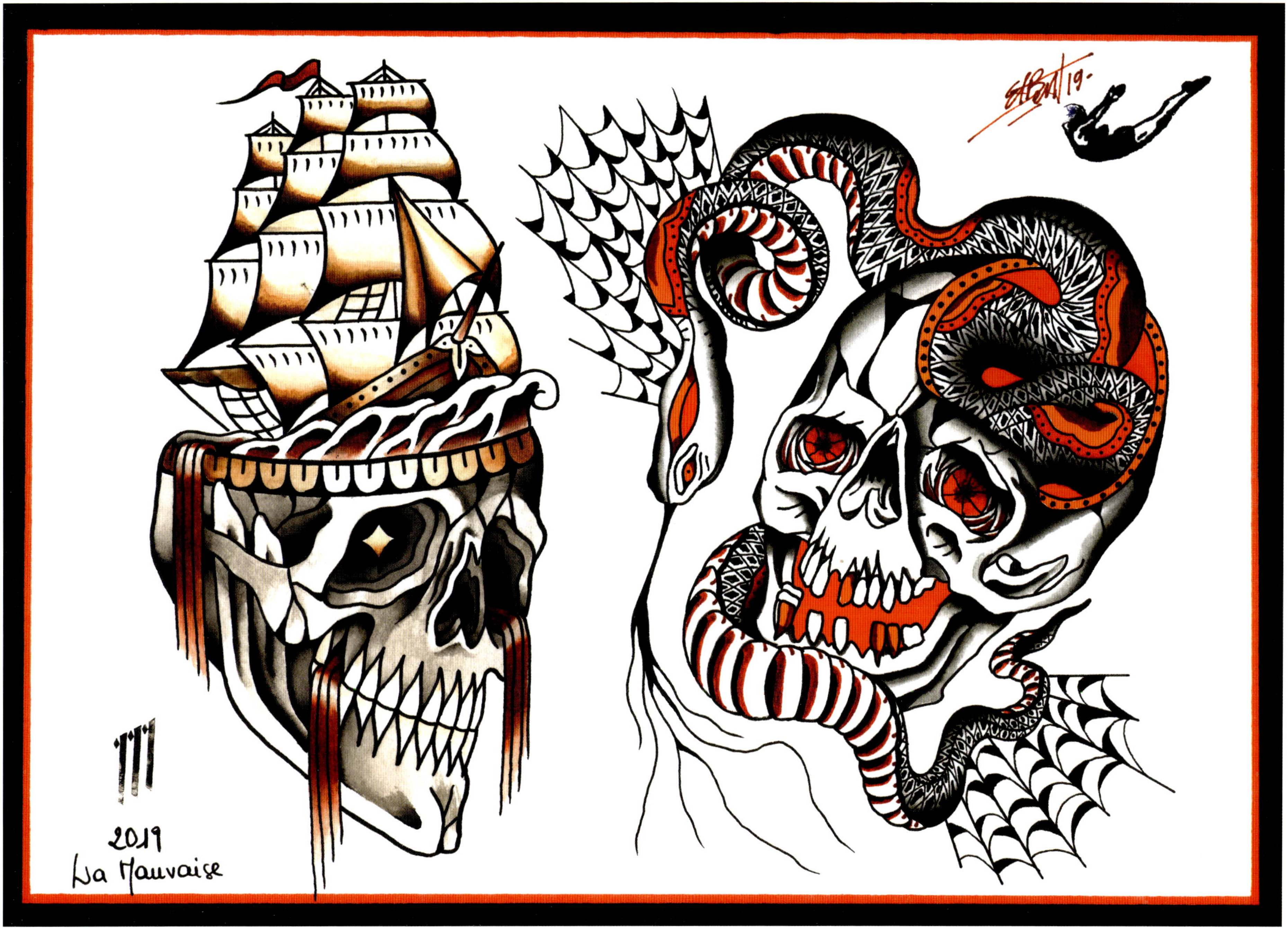
2019
La Mauvaise

Left
Komar Inkshot
@komarinkshot
Café Ink / Le Havre / France

Right
Uncle Ho
@uncle_ho_mitchmalone
Iron Claw / Strasbourg / France

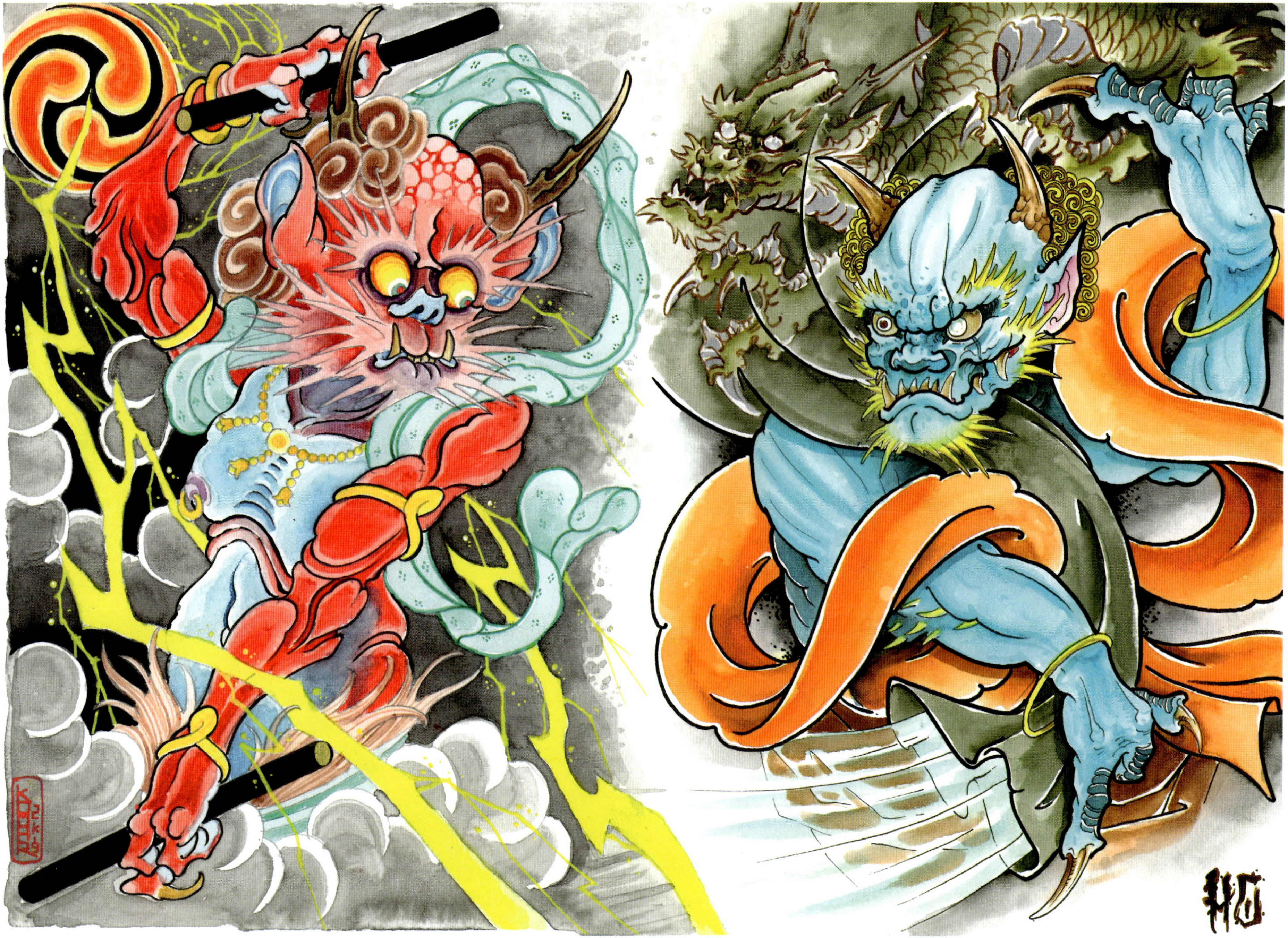

Left
Ento Noir
@ento.noir
Freaky Family / Lille / France

Right
Josh Dee
@joshdeetattoo
Black Ship Tattoo / Namur / Belgium

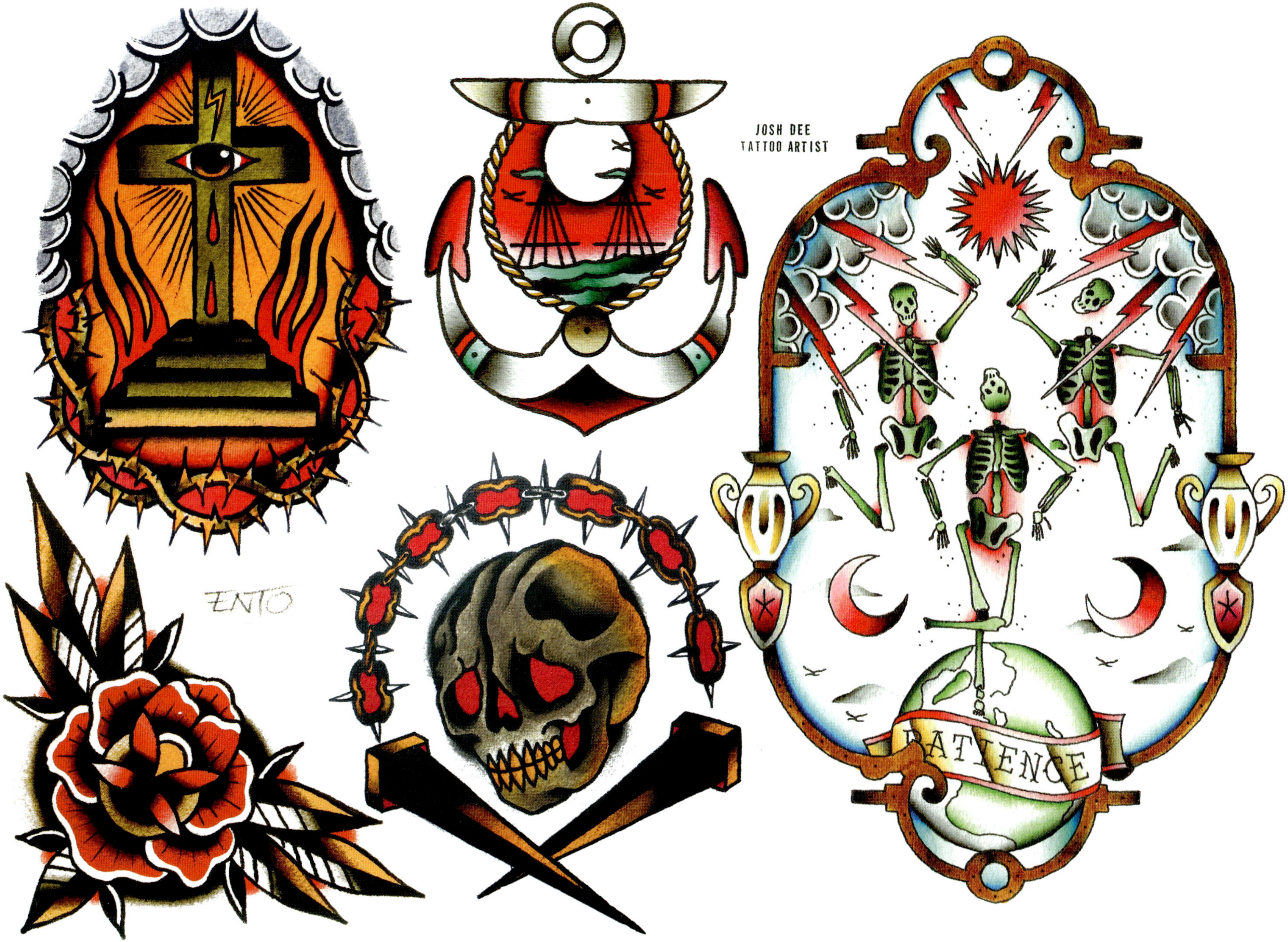

JOSH DEE
TATTOO ARTIST

Left
John Stone
@john_stone_tatouage
L'Astrolabe / Dinard / France

Right
Mosh
@moshtattooer
La Famille Tattoo Club / Grenoble / France

CREATION ORIGINALE
† JOHN STONE †
TATOUAGE

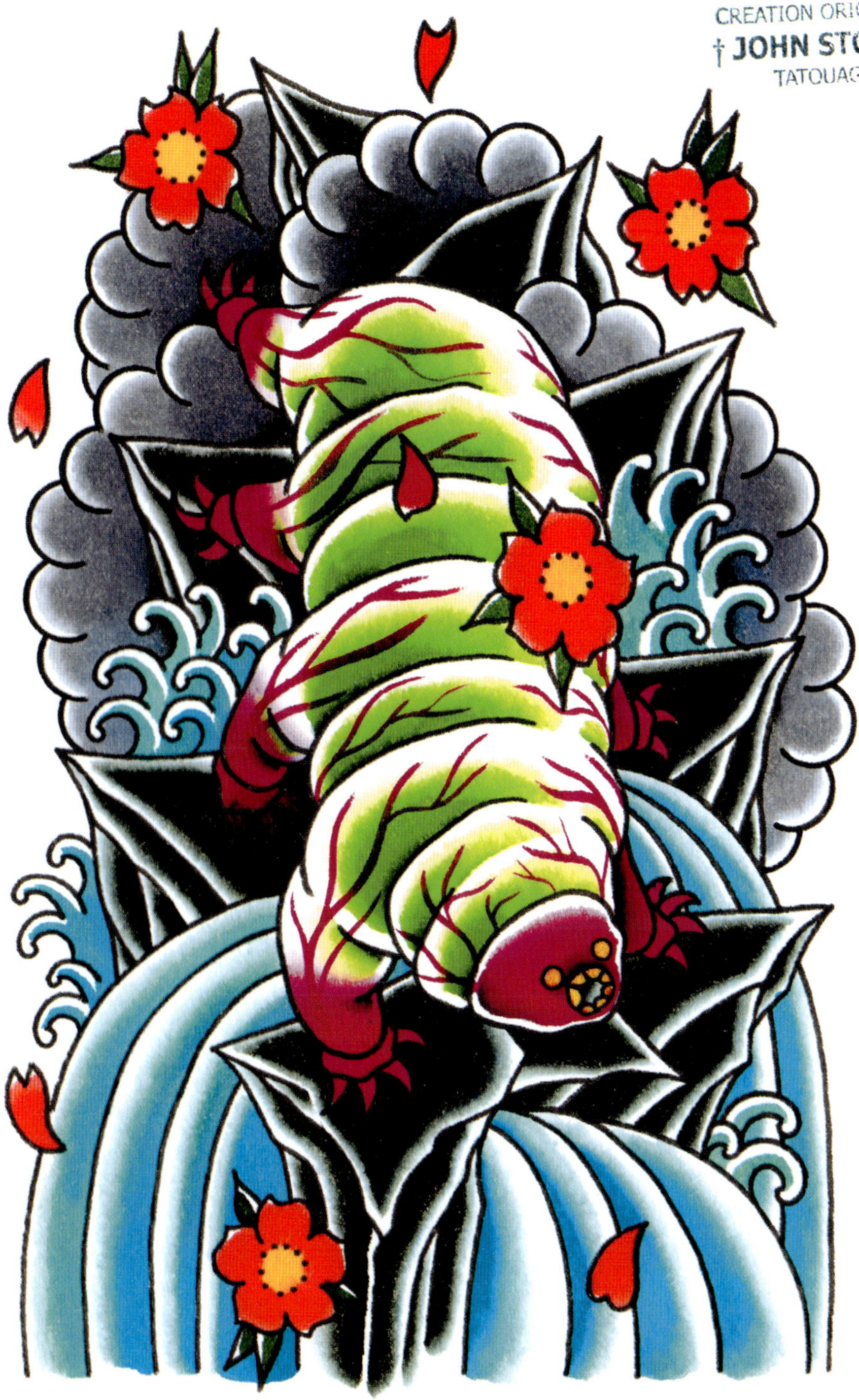

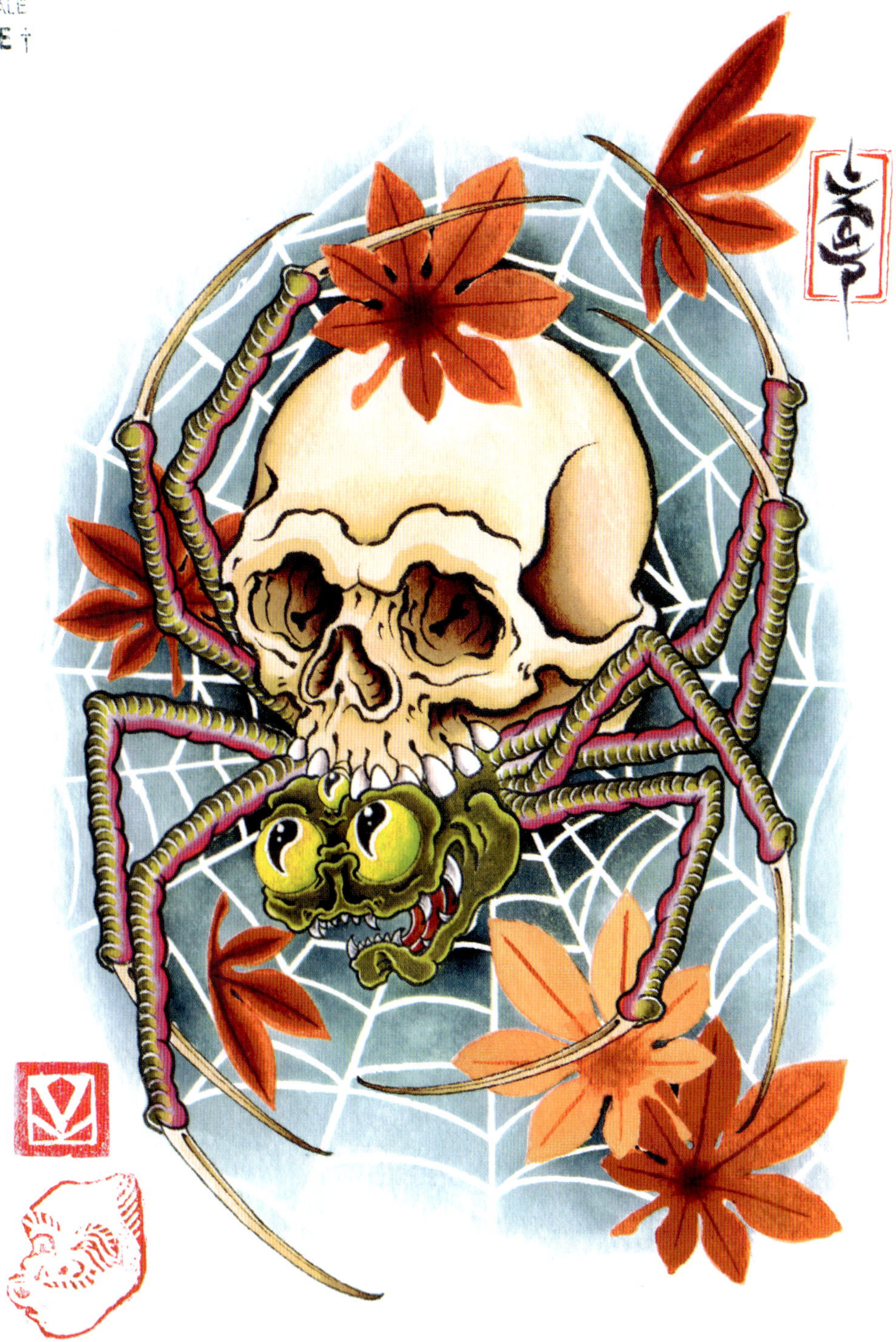

Left
Mitchsoos
@mitchgore_soos
Anderson Street Tattoo / Yarraville / Australia

Right
GroFab and Alice Rigal
@grofabtattoo / @alicetattooer
Matière Noire / Paris / France

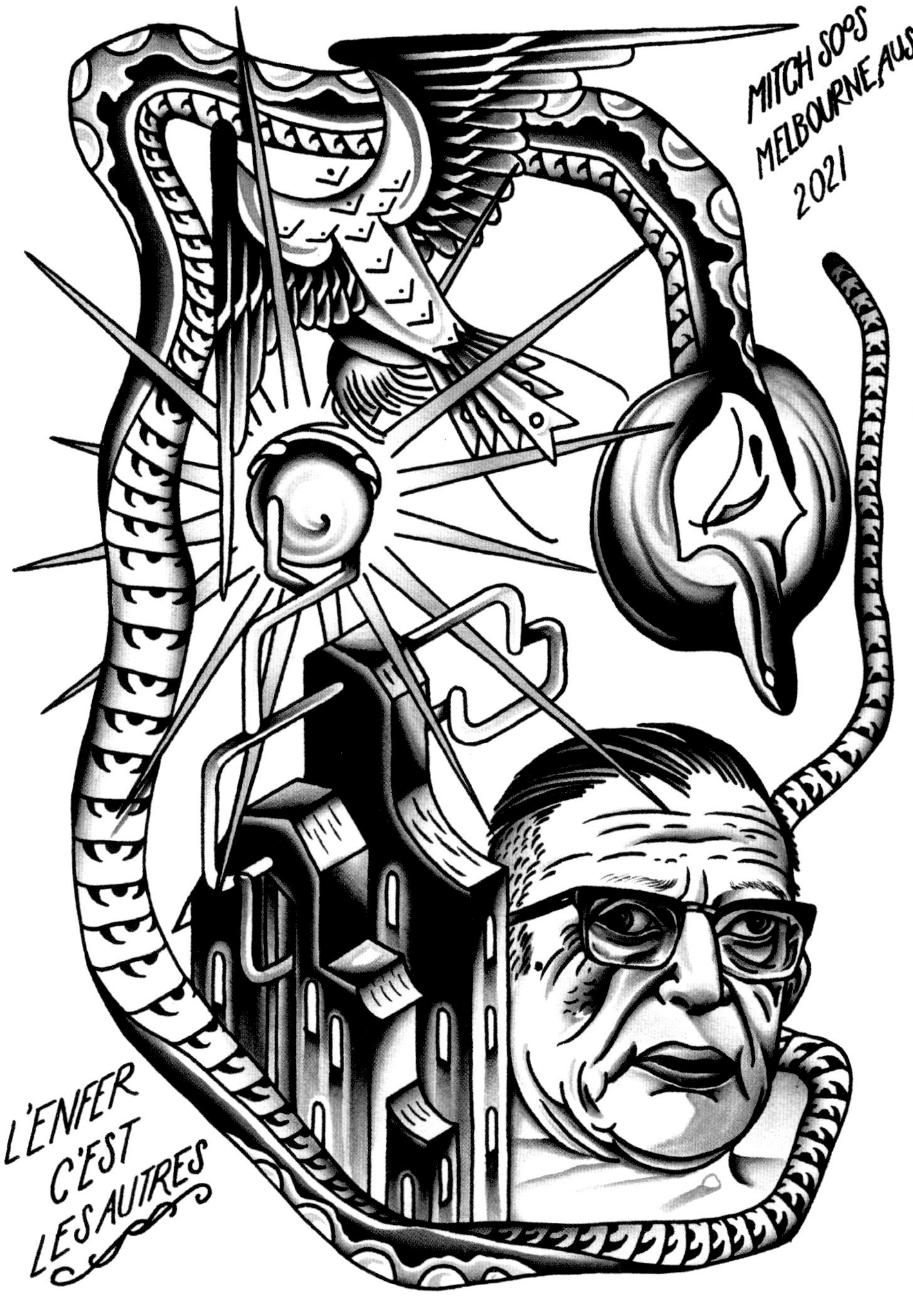
MITCH SOOS
MELBOURNE, AUS
2021
L'ENFER
C'EST
LES AUTRES

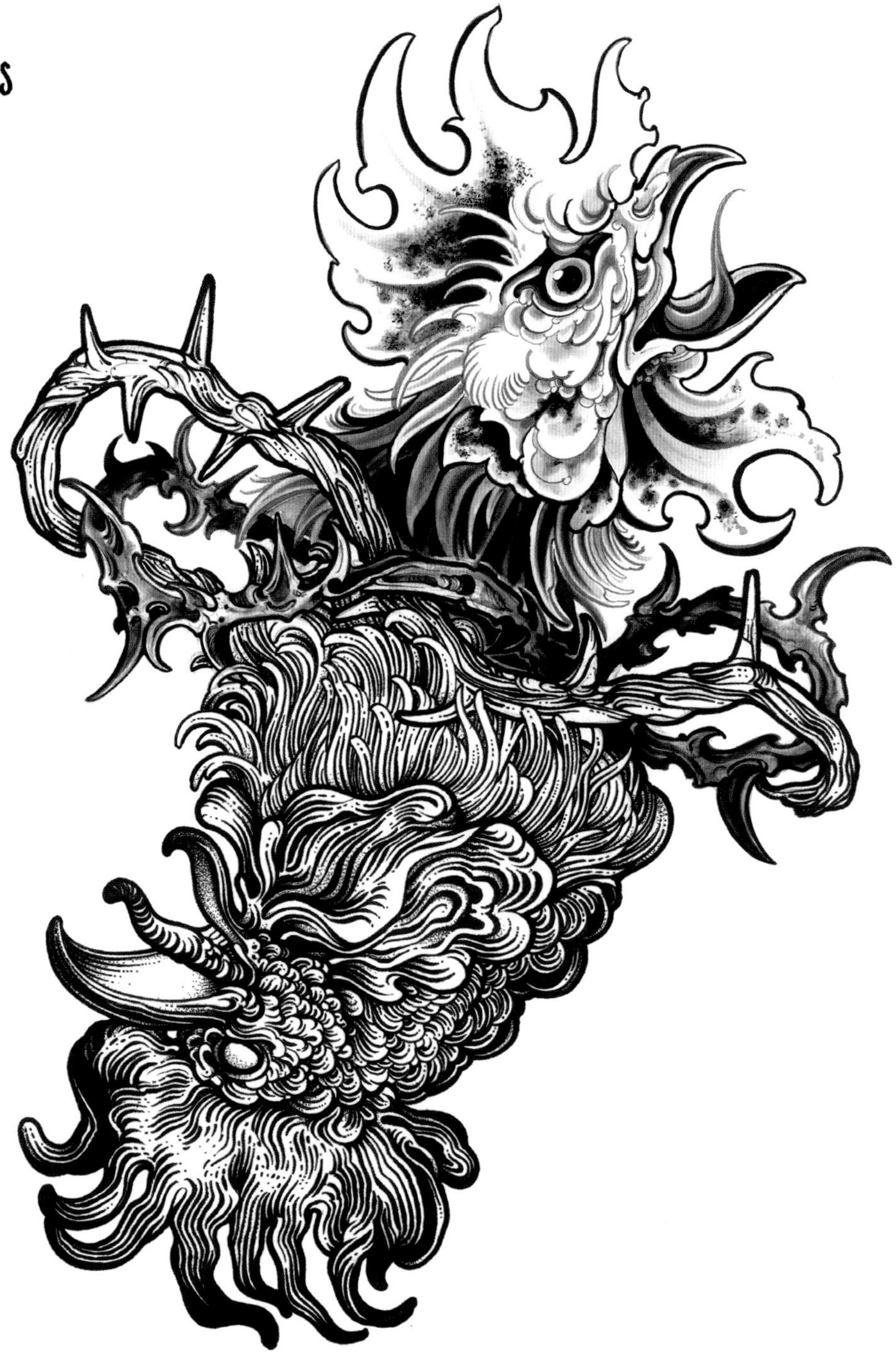

Left
JxB
@jxb_jamais_mal
Yfic Tatouages / Morlaix / France

Right
Clément Doineau (Dague Rouge)
@clementdoineau
Grey Bronco Tattoo / Nantes / France

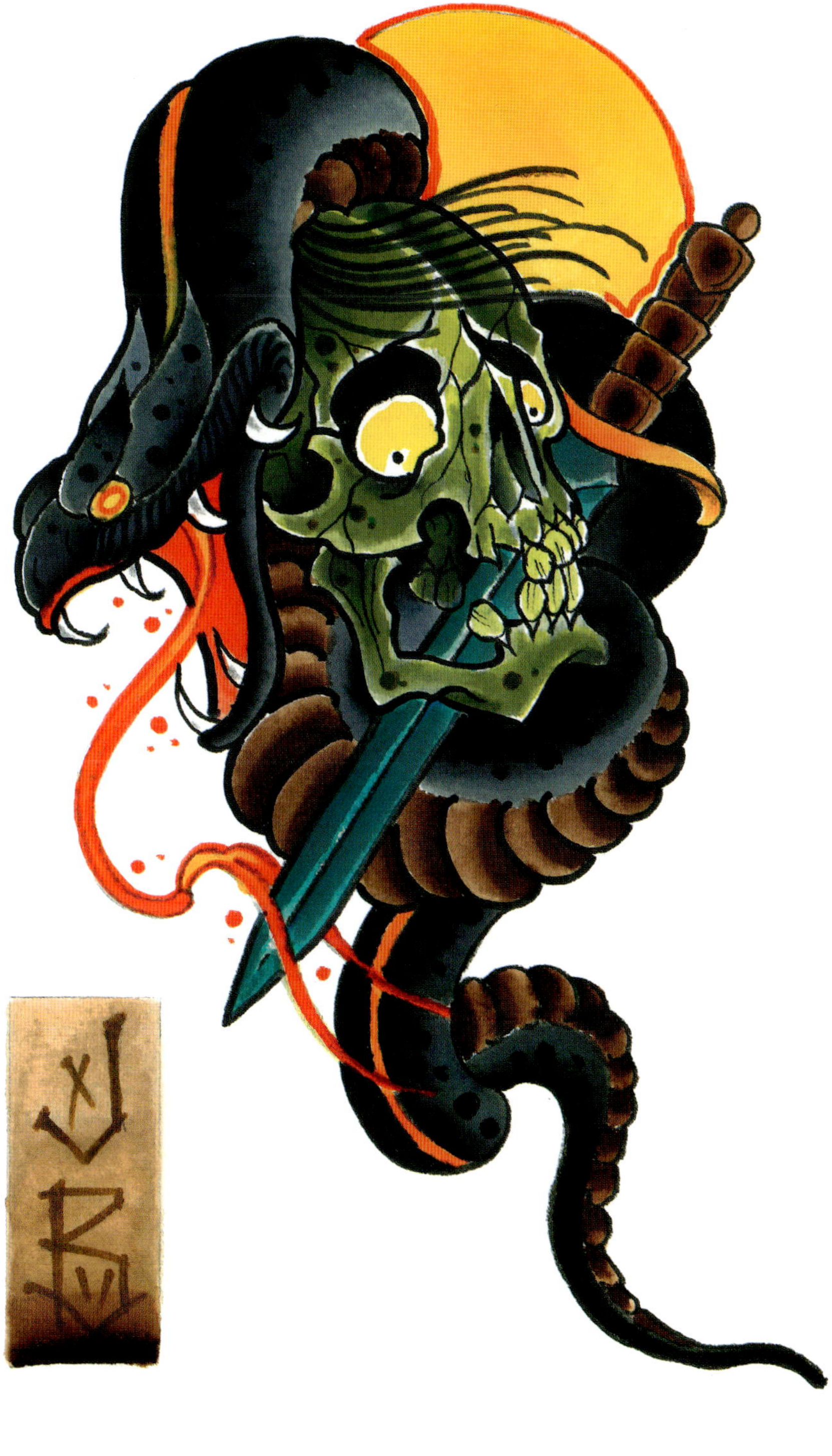

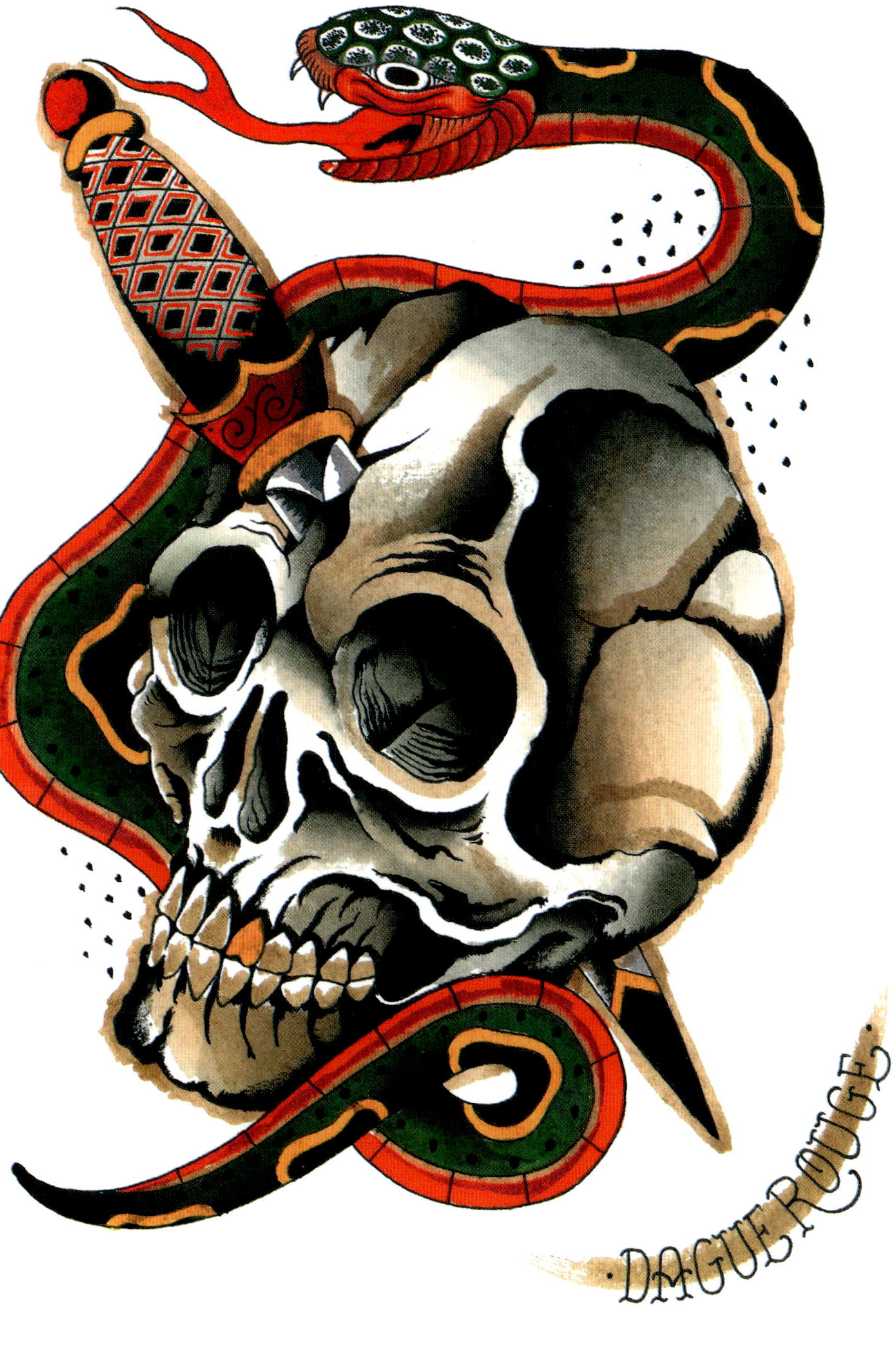
DAGUE ROUGE

Left
Ionno Tattooing
@ionno_tattooing
Mea Culpa Tattoo Studio / Bologna / Italy

Right
Swann
@swannlpx_lpx
The Good Place Tattoo / Toulouse / France

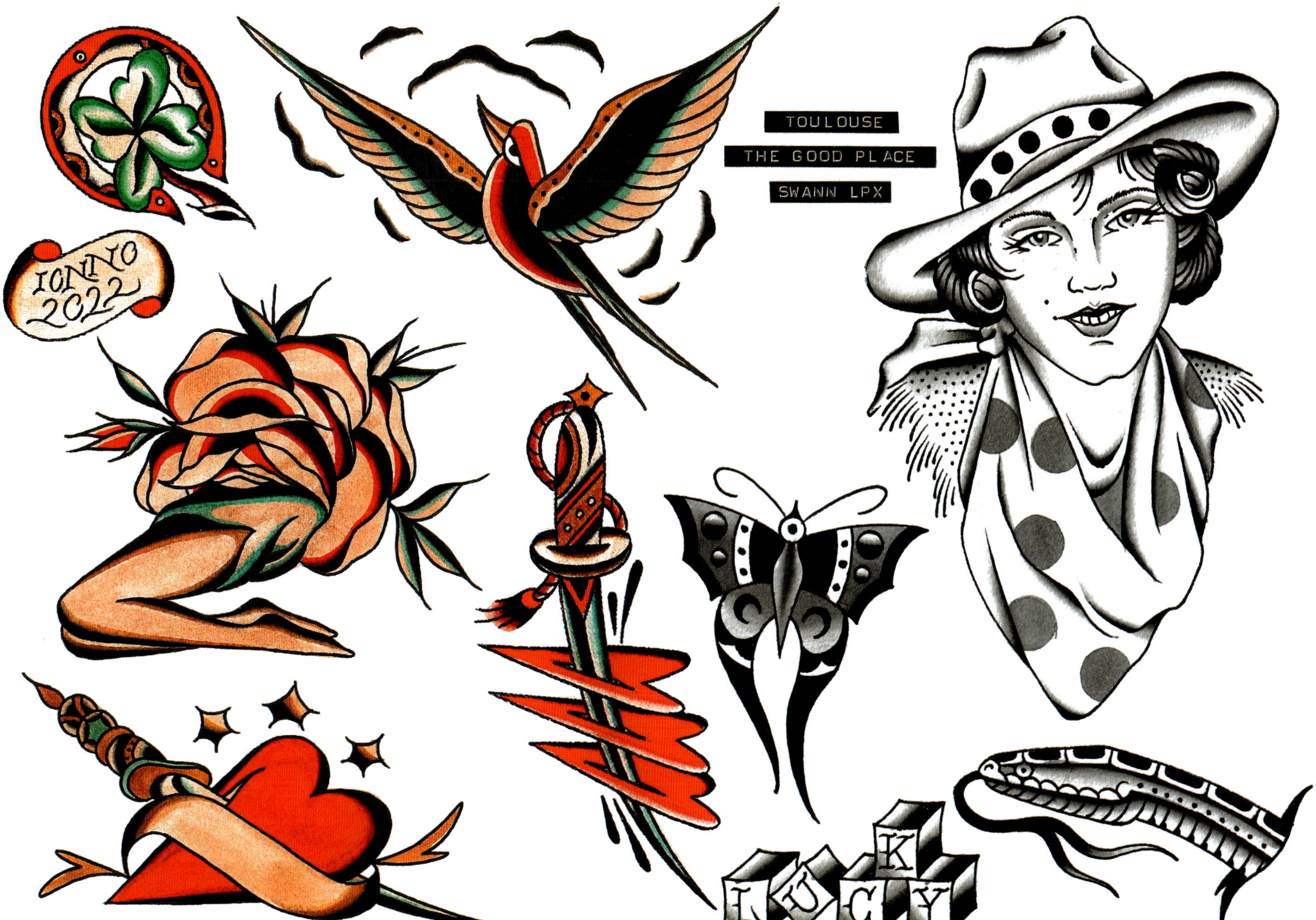
TOULOUSE
THE GOOD PLACE
SWANN LPX
IONNO
2022
LUCKY

Left
La Mauvaise
@lamauvaisetattoo
La Sauvagerie / Sélestat / France

Right
Tiwan
@tiwan_tattoo
Spirit Tattoo Rennes / Rennes / France

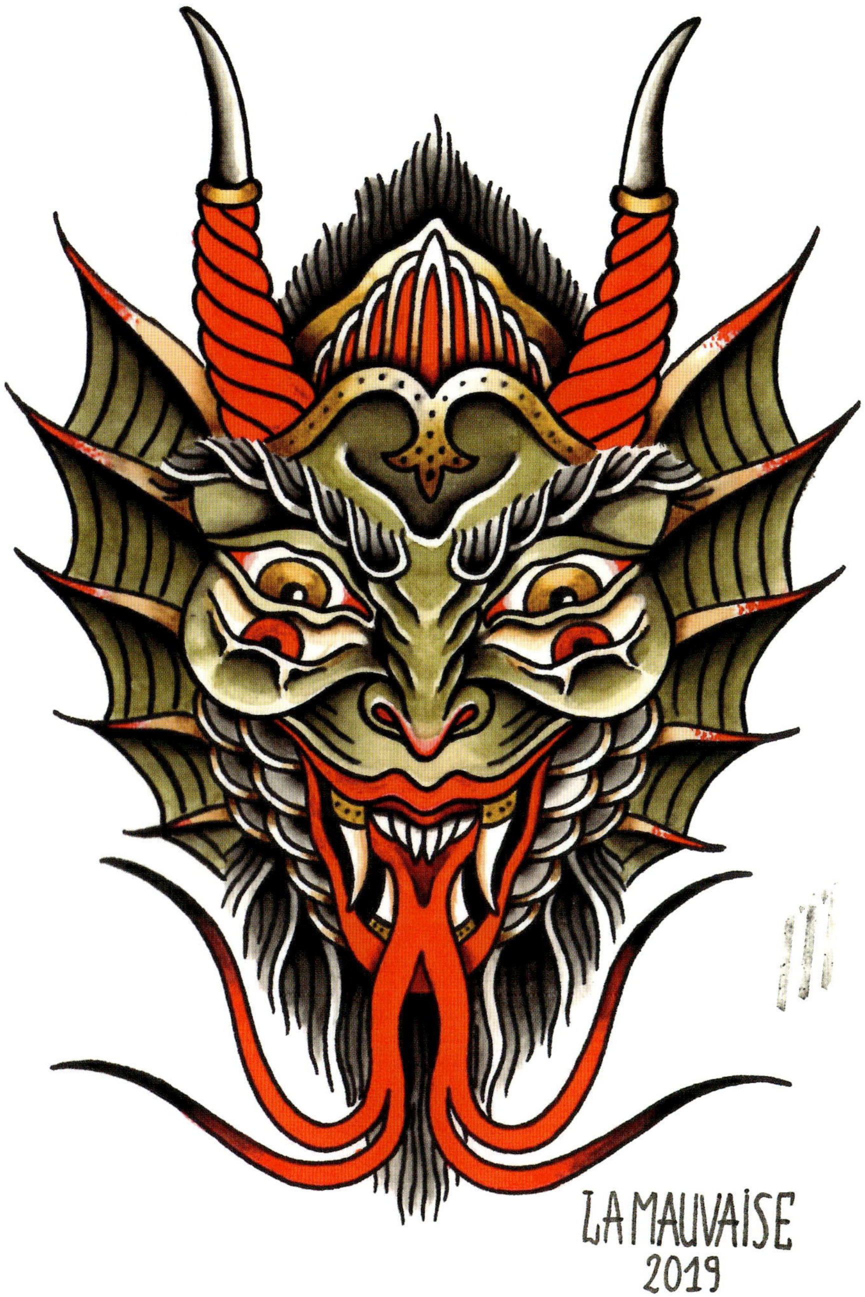
LA MAUVAISE
2019

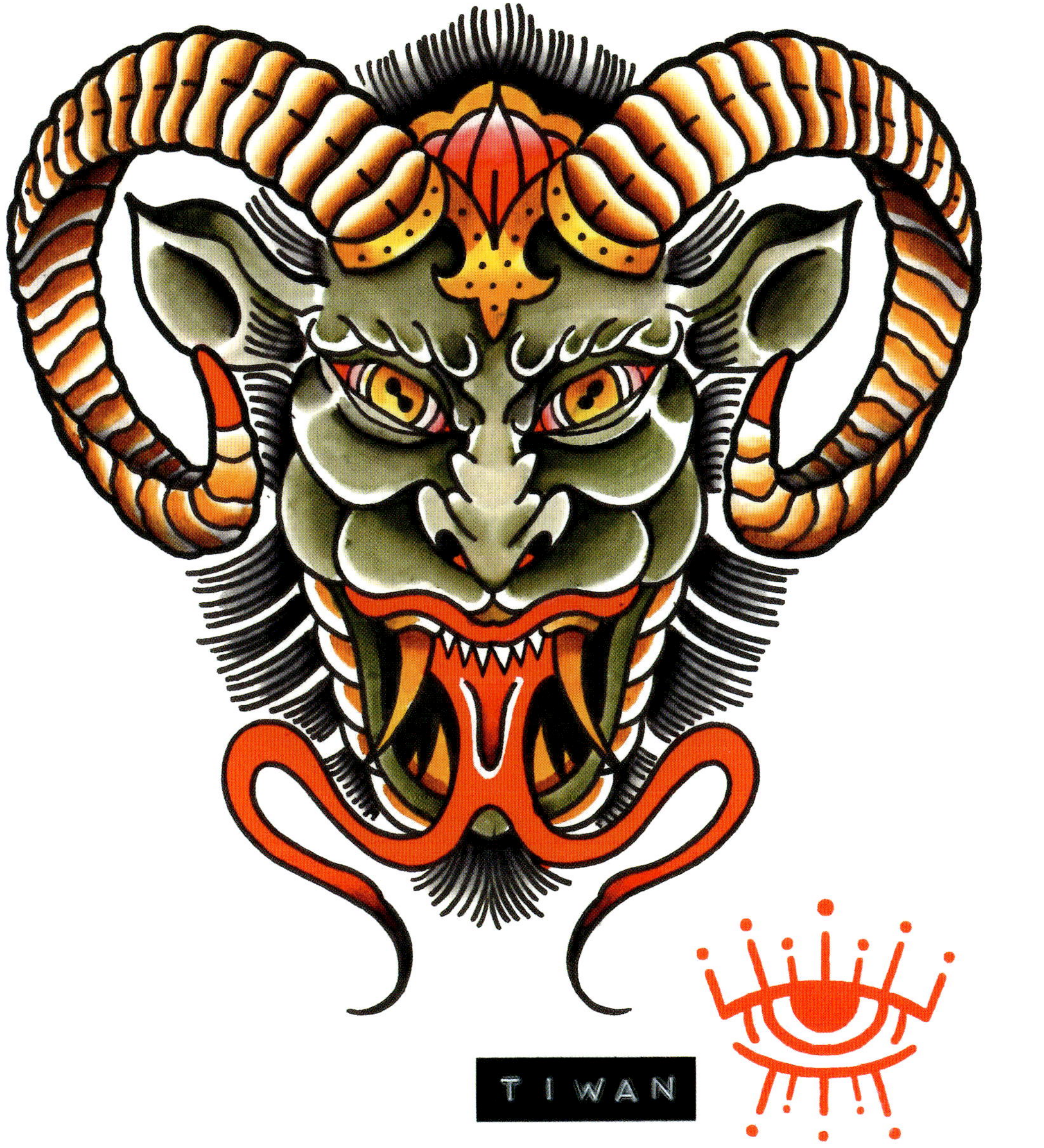
TIWAN

Left
Vincent JBS
@vincent_jbs_tattoo
Memento Tattoo / Oslo / Norway

Right
Alessio Errante
@alessio_errante
Studio Boreale / Cagliari / Italy

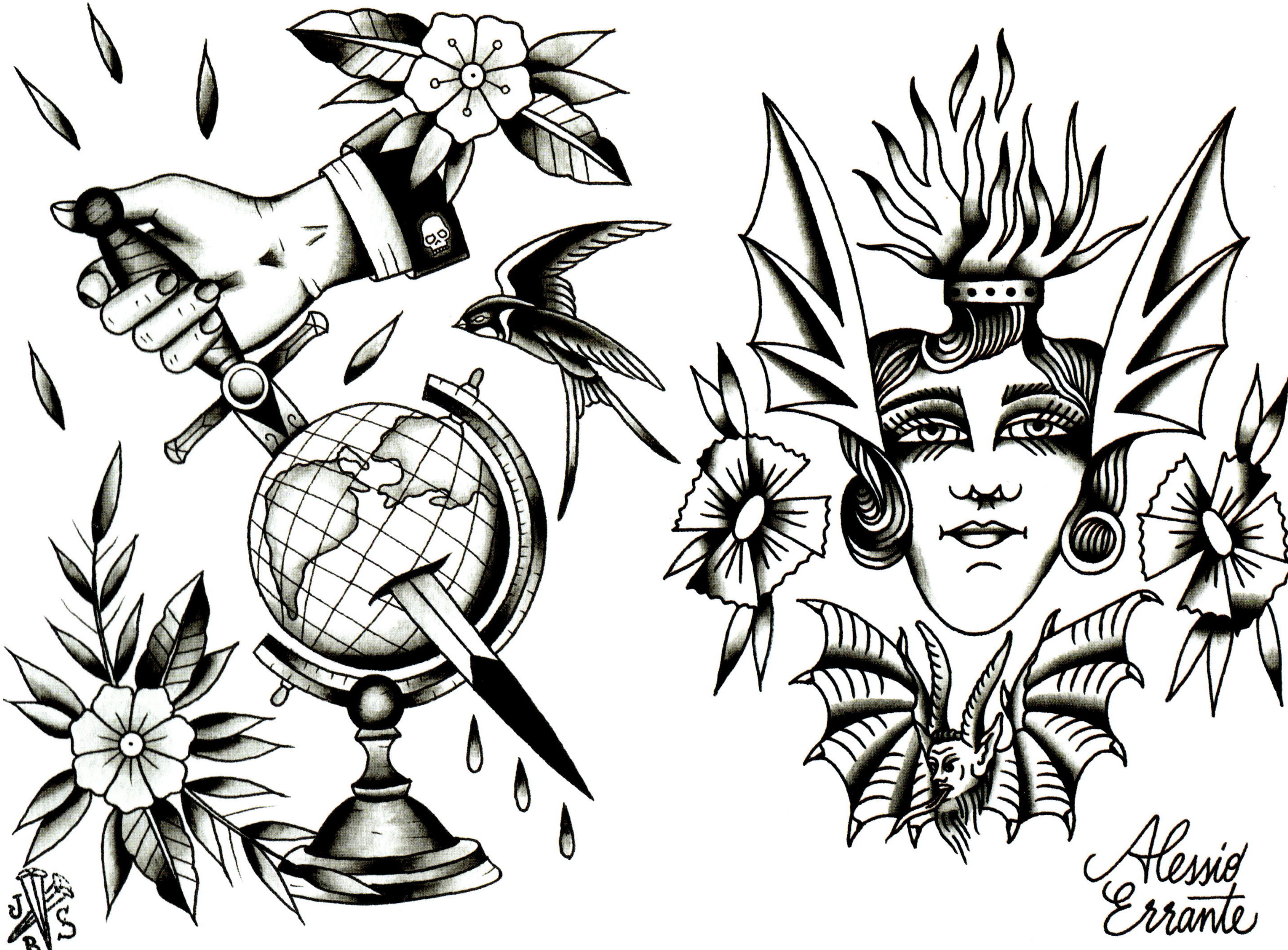
Alessio
Errante

Left
Lu.ky
@lu.ky_flsq
Atelier Triptyque / Montpellier / France

Right
Malflore
@malflore
Atelier Triptyque / Montpellier / France

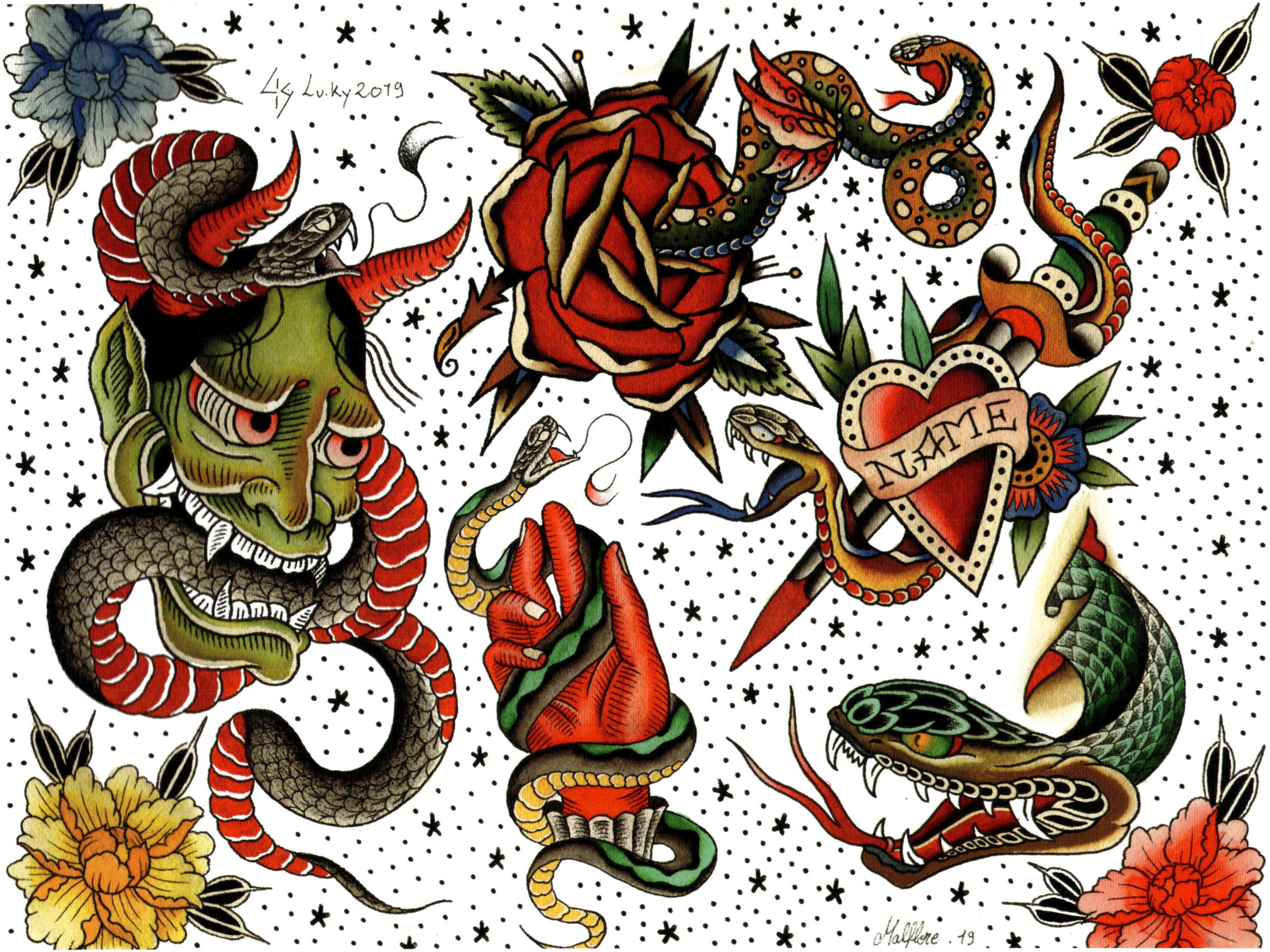
Lu.ky 2019
NAME
Malflore .19

Left
Salem Ink
@ink.salem
Minuit Soleil / Nantes / France

Right
Lucas
@lucasjustelucas
Arena Tattoo / Chartres de Bretagne / France

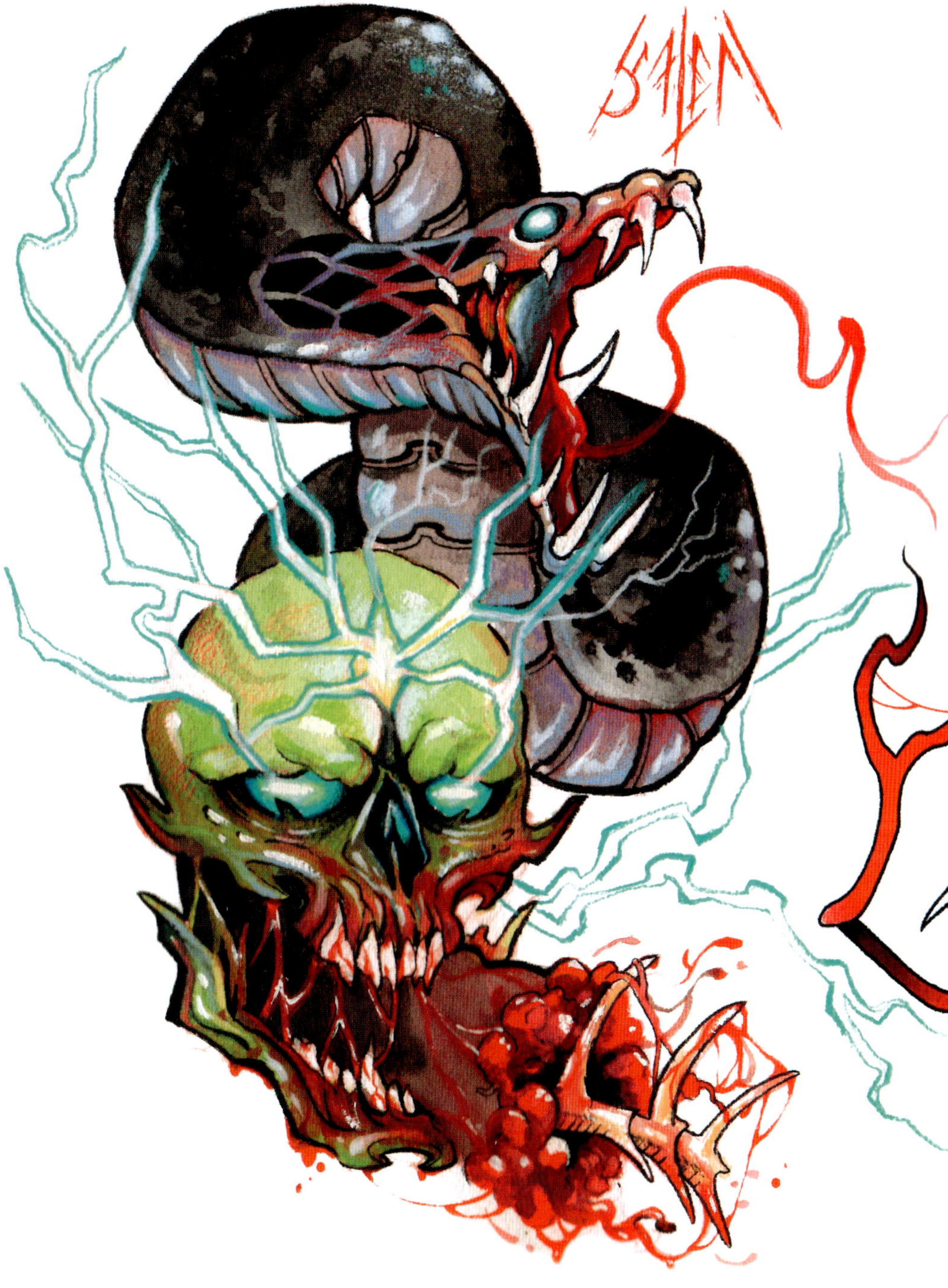

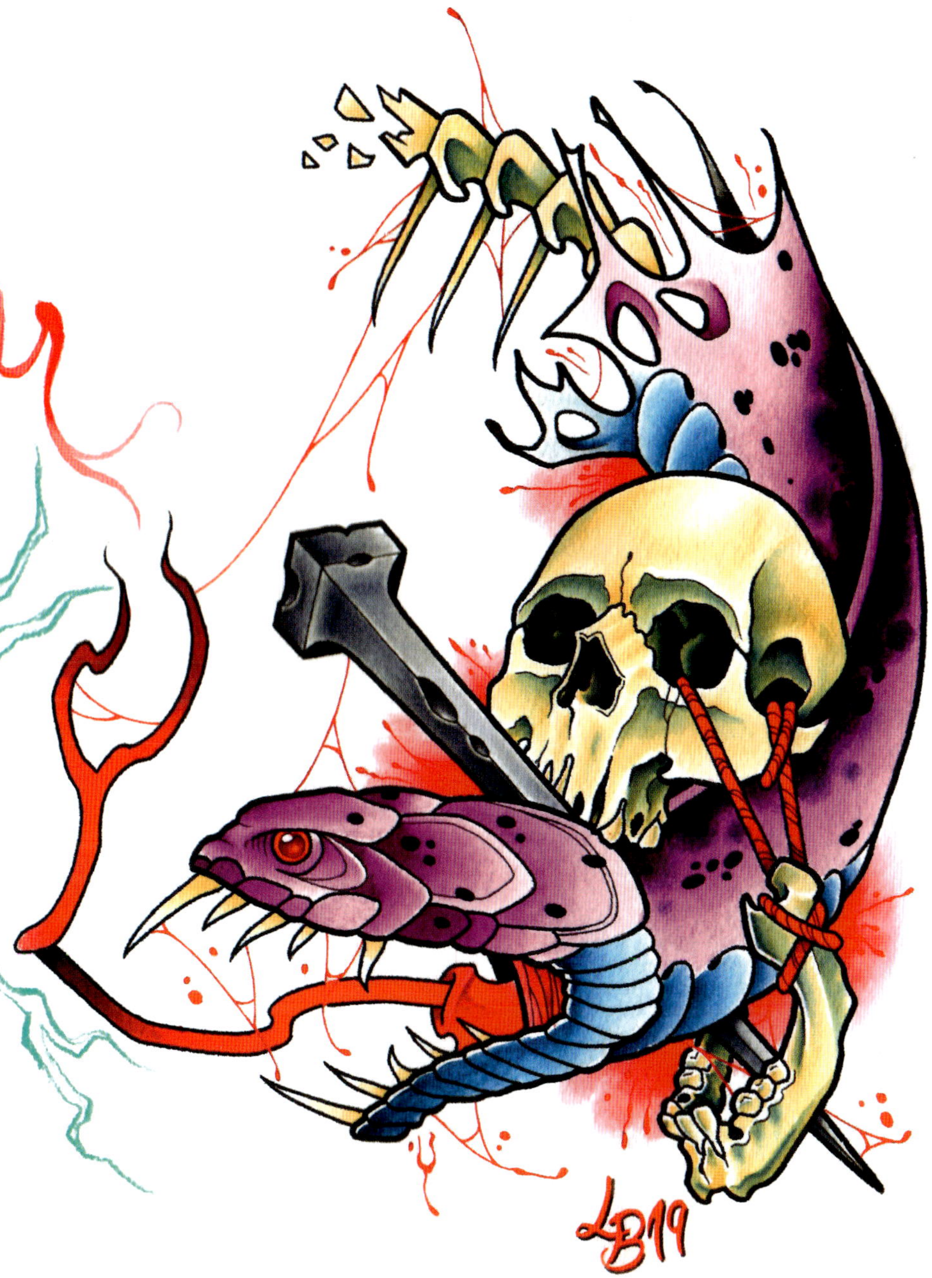

Left
Ento Noir
@ento.noir
Freaky Family / Lille / France

Right
El Bent
@elbenttattoo
True Love / Paris / France

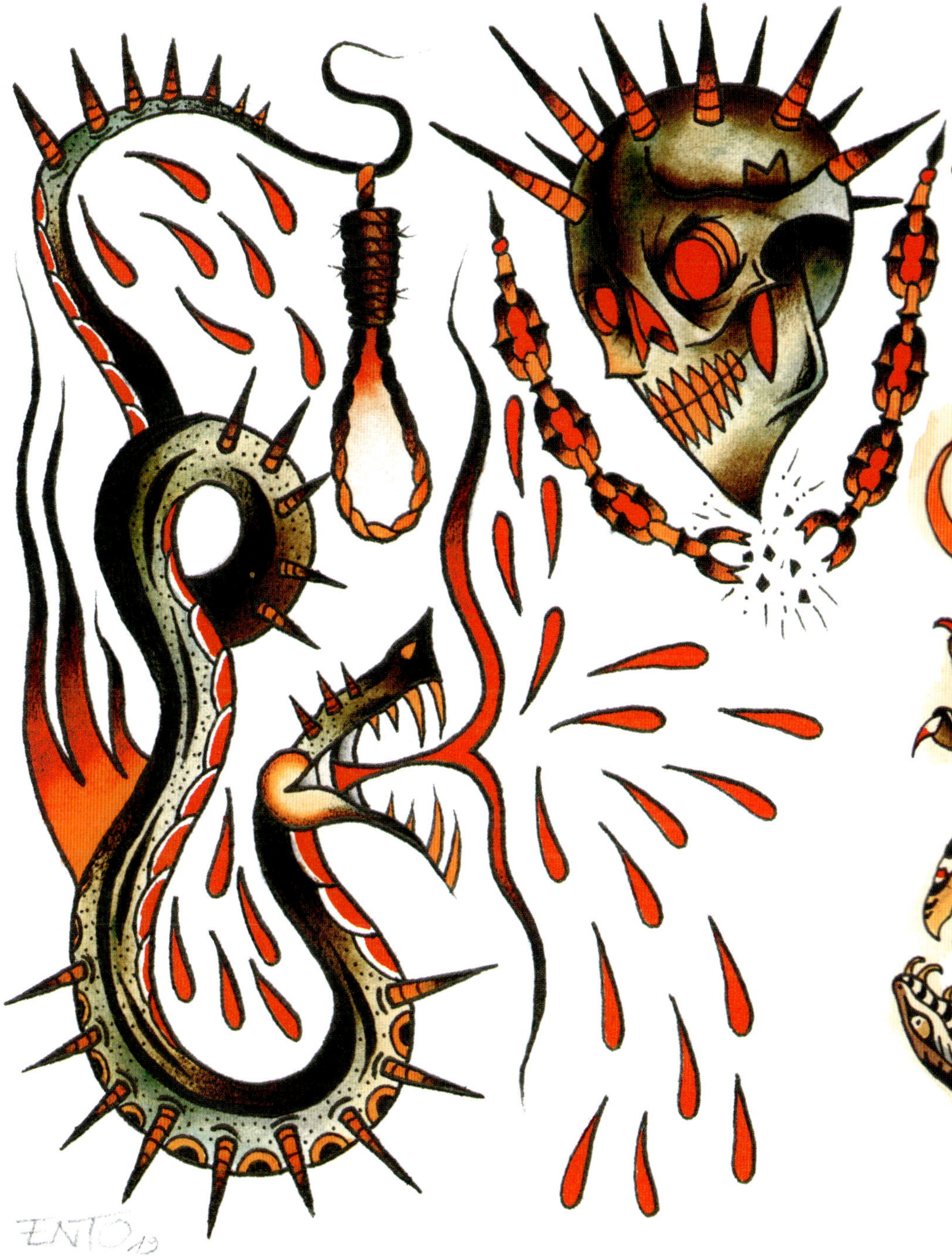

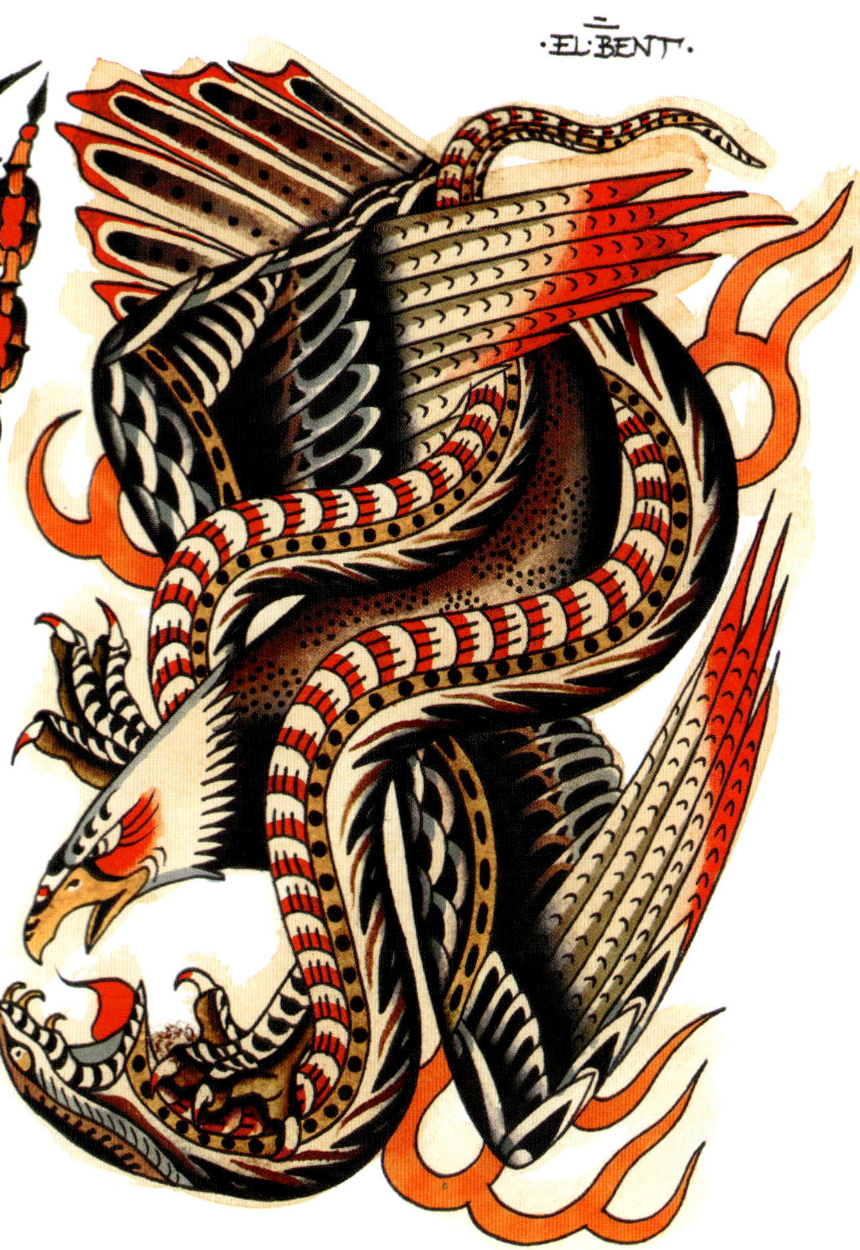
·EL·BENT·

Left
Polo Tattooer
@polotattooer_tgp
The Good Place Tattoo / Toulouse / France

Right
Swann
@swannlpx_tgp
The Good Place Tattoo / Toulouse / France

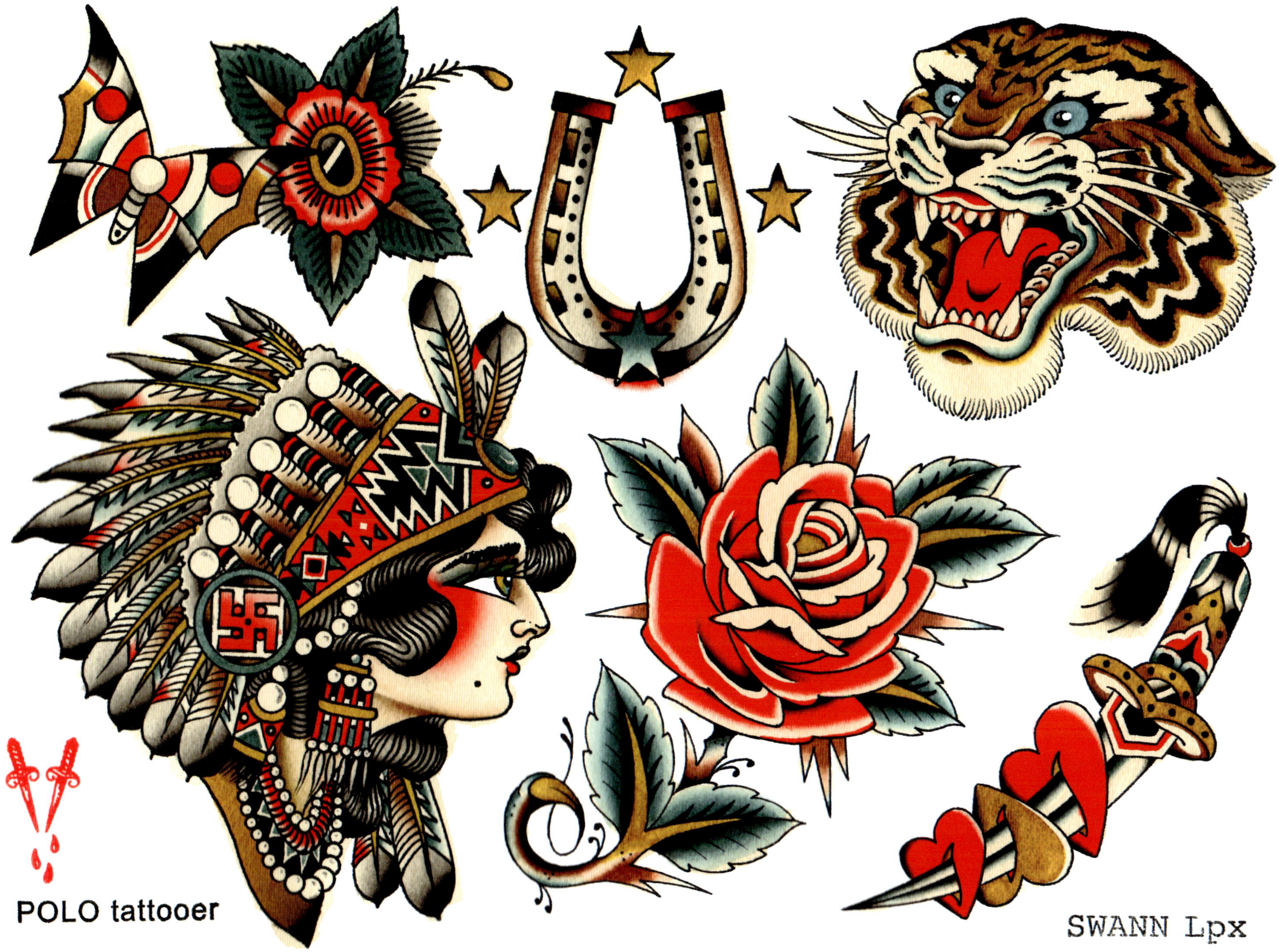
POLO tattooer
SWANN Lpx

Left
Mosh
@moshtattooer
La Famille Tattoo Club / Grenoble / France

Right
Geoff Horn
@geoffhorn_soos
Hole In The Sky Tattoo Parlor / Woodland Park / New Jersey / USA

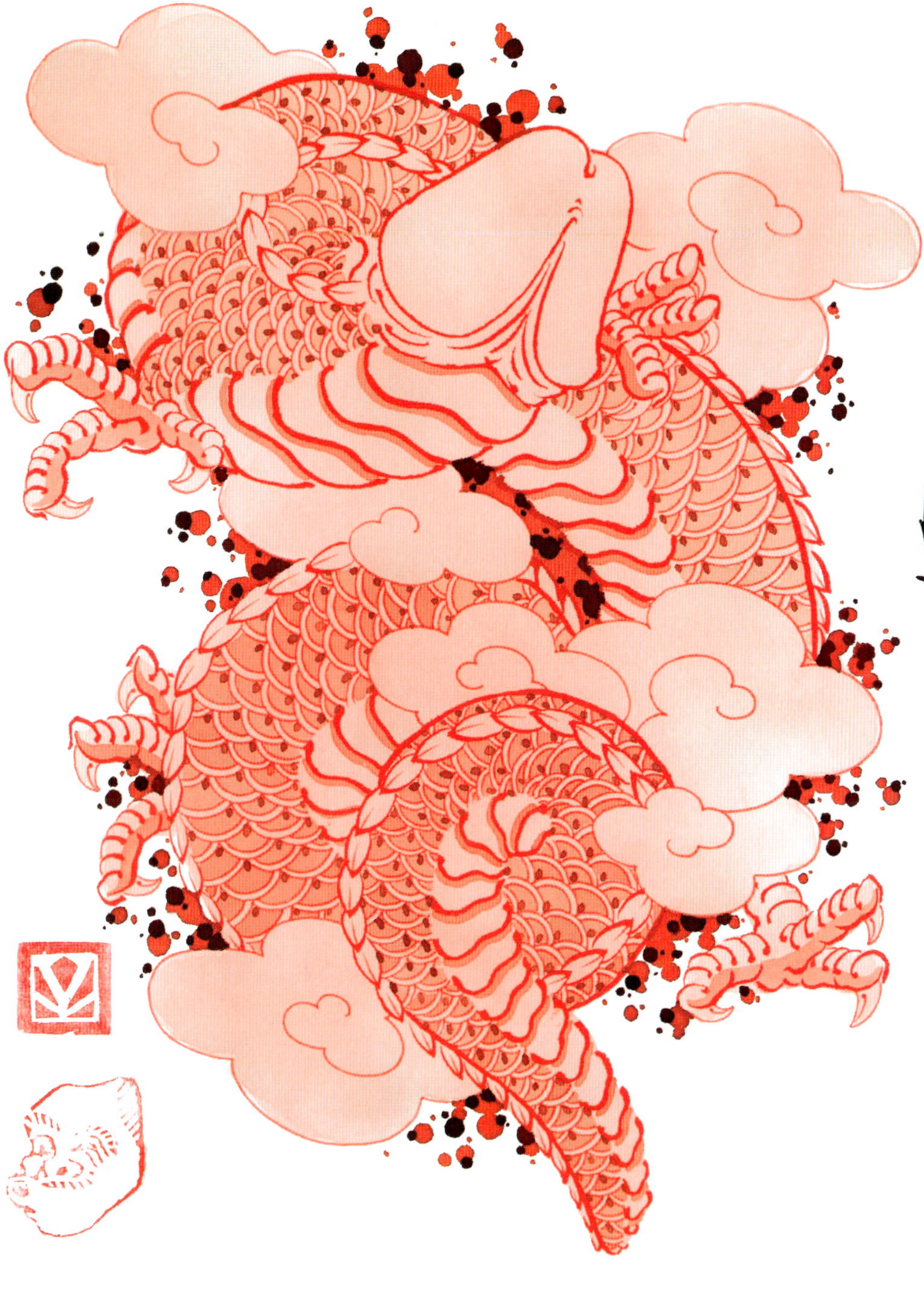

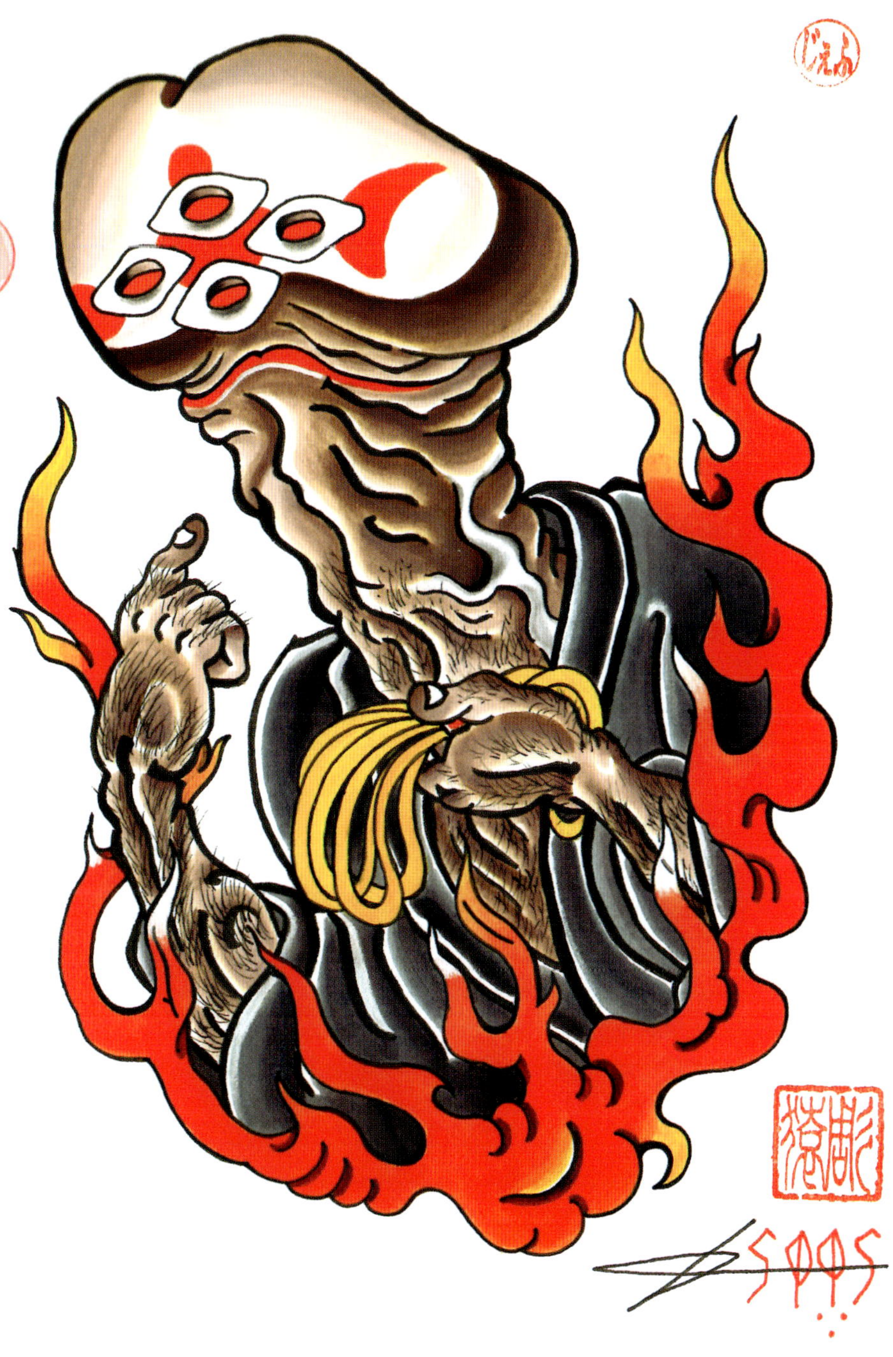

Left
Treiz
@xtreizx
Yoso / Paris / France

Right
Pauline Tabur
@paulinetabur
L'Ogre Rouge / Rennes / France

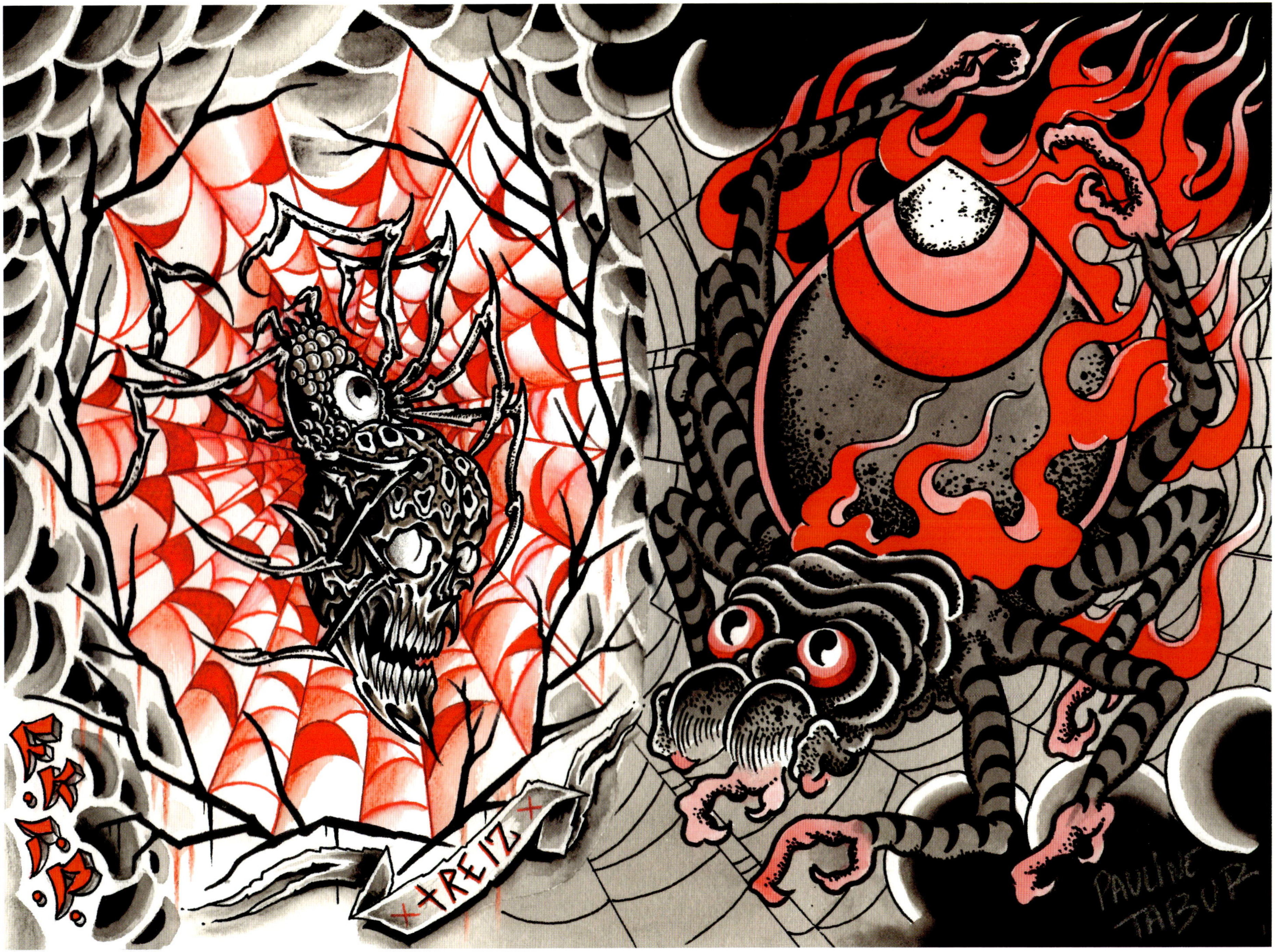

F.K.T.P.
TREIZ
PAULINE TABUR

Left
Antoine Paul
@antoinepaultatoueur
Dark Lines Tattoo Club / Bièvre / Belgium

Right
Romu
@romu.grn
Tattoo Lounge / Montreal / Canada

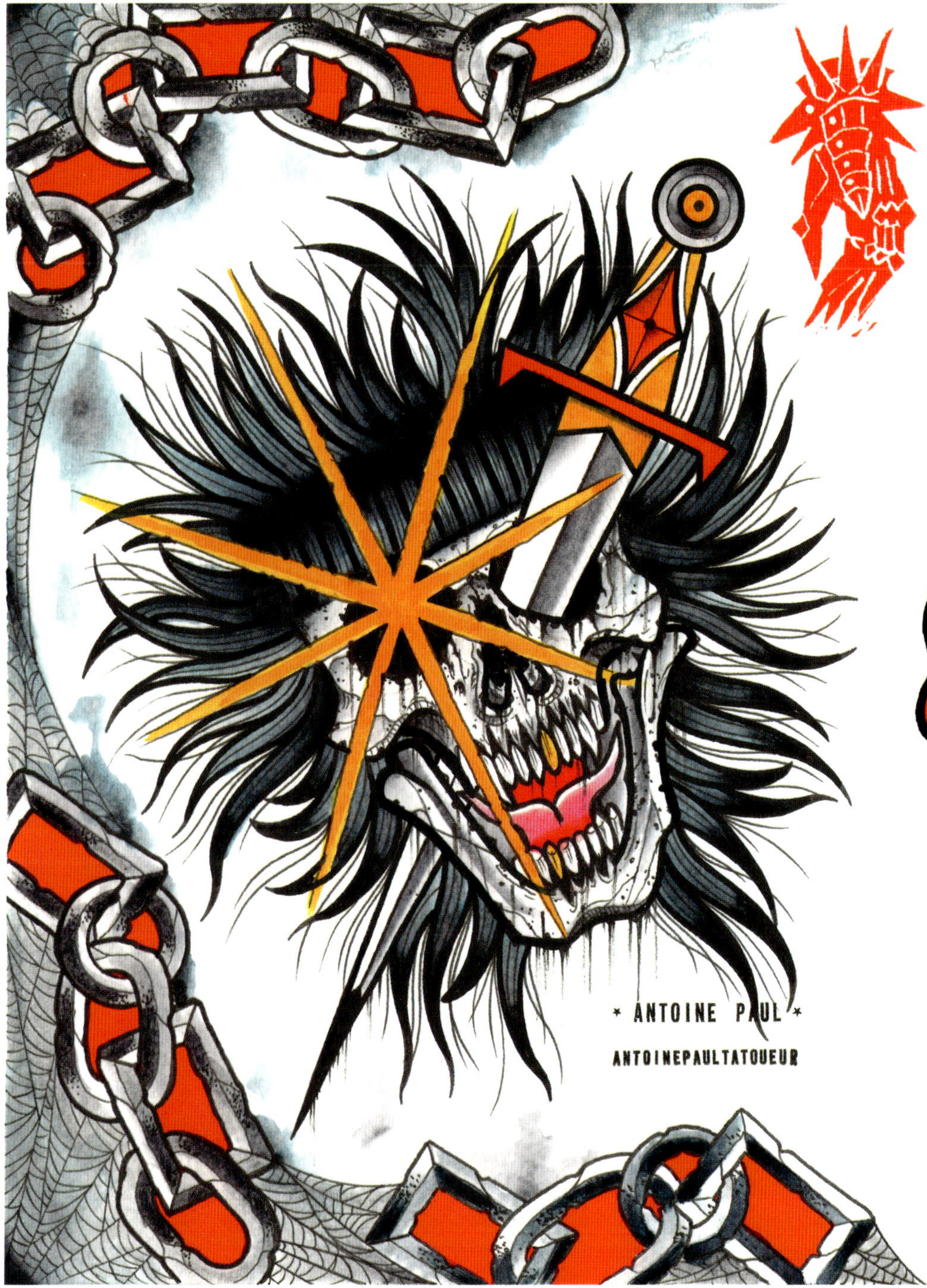
* ANTOINE PAUL *
ANTOINEPAULTATOUEUR

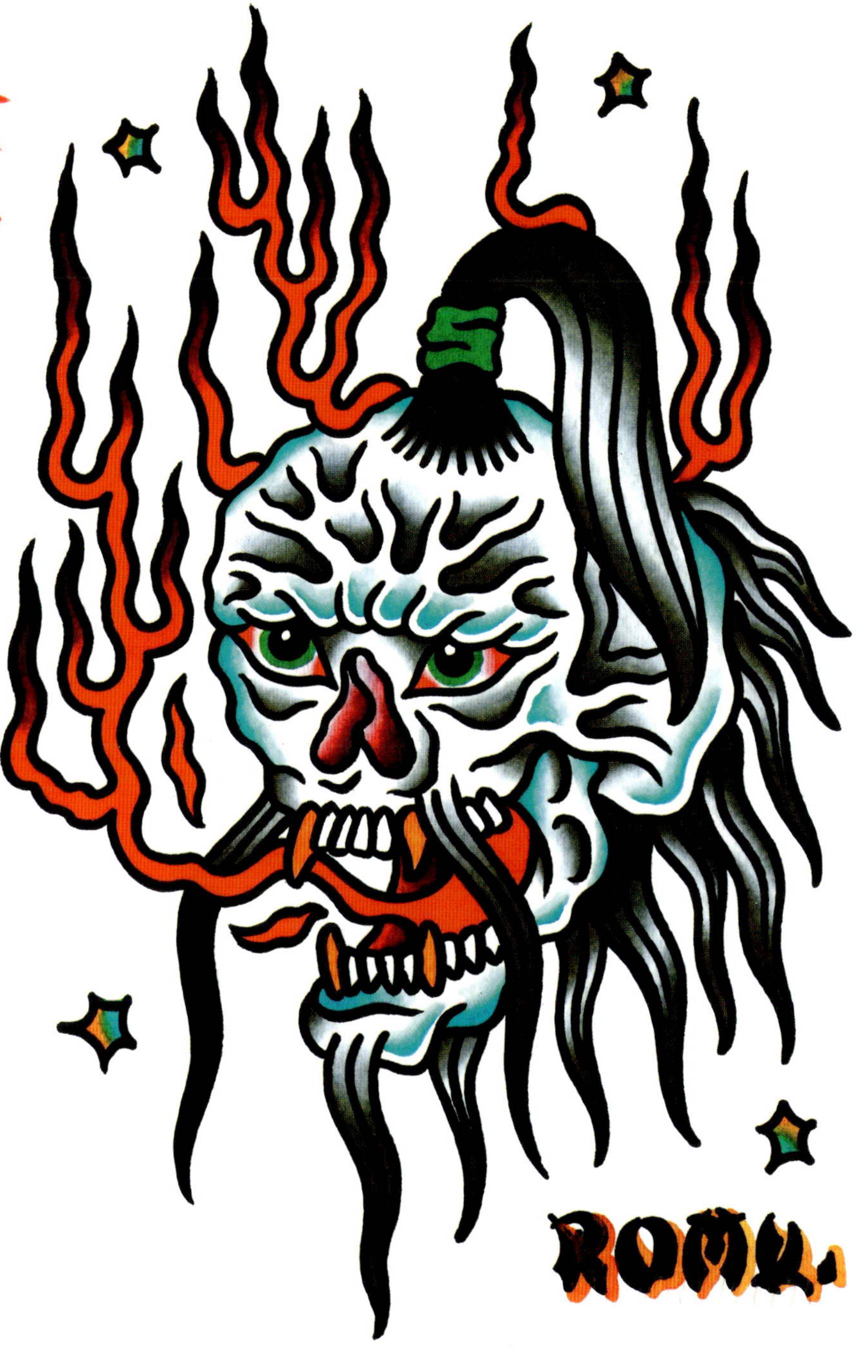
ROML.

Left
Phil Kyle
@philkyle
Magnum Opus Tattoo / Pleurtuit / France

Right
James Reuter
@james_reuter_tattoos
Remember Tomorrow / Neu-Anspach / Germany

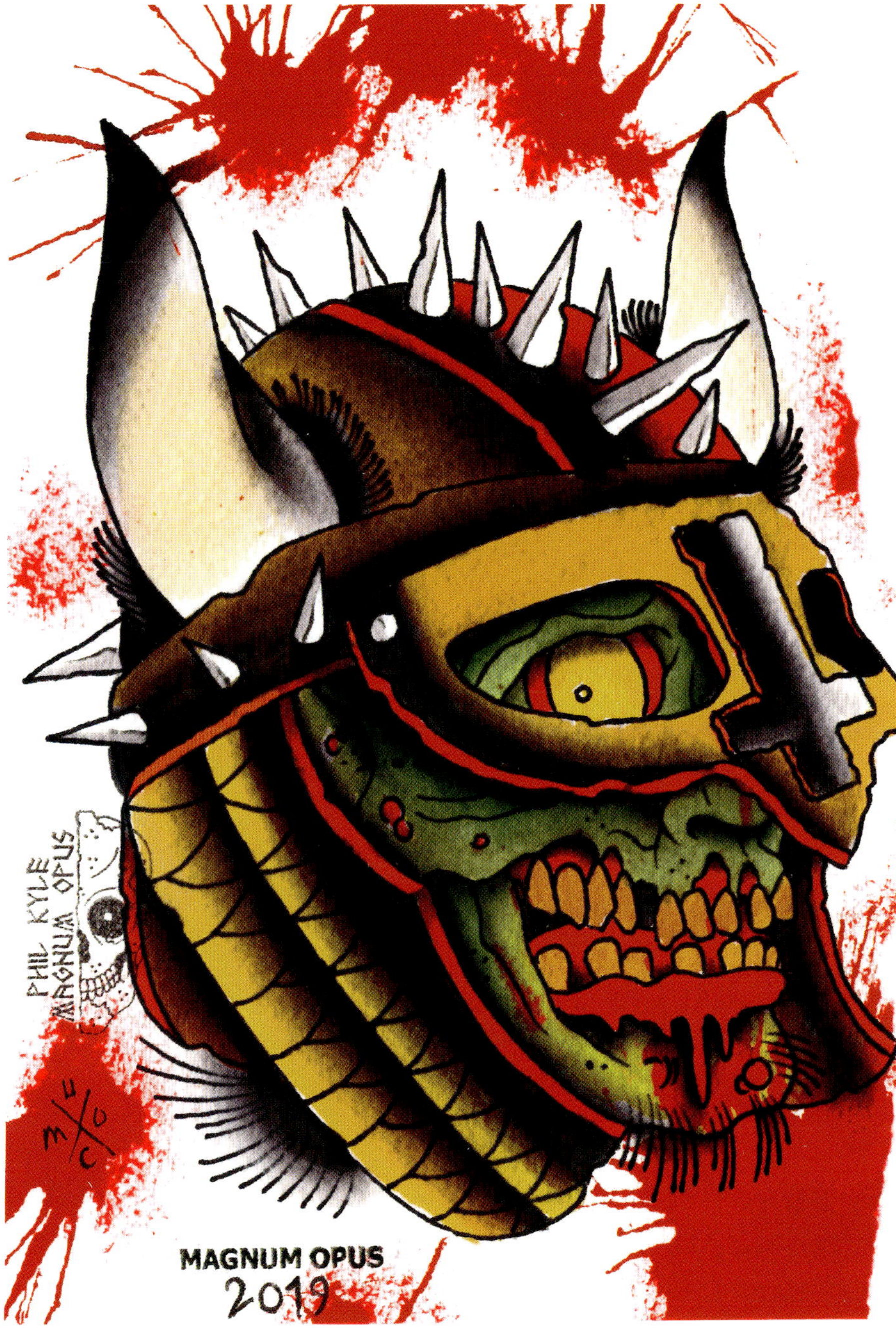
PHIL KYLE
MAGNUM OPUS
MAGNUM OPUS
2019

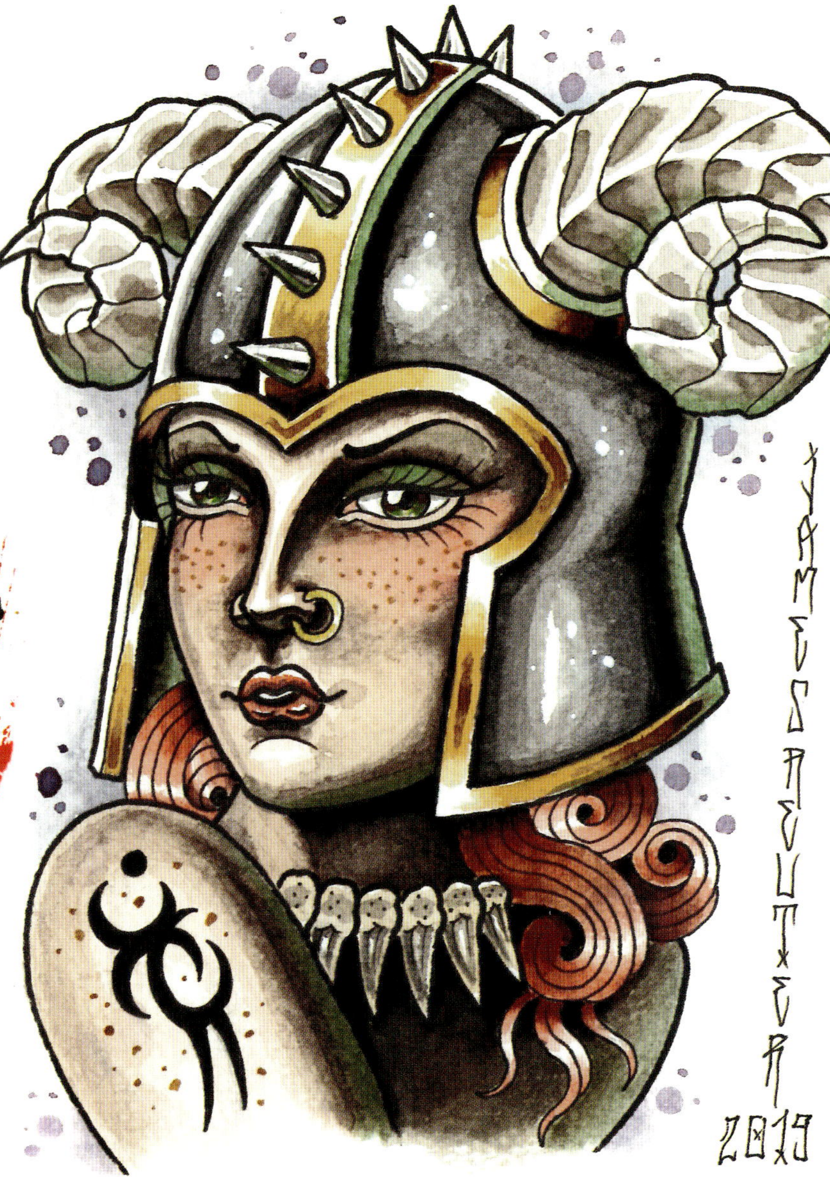
2019

Left
Tiwan
@tiwan_tattoo
Spirit Tattoo Rennes / Rennes / France

Right
Clément Doineau (Dague Rouge)
@clementdoineau
Grey Bronco Tattoo / Nantes / France

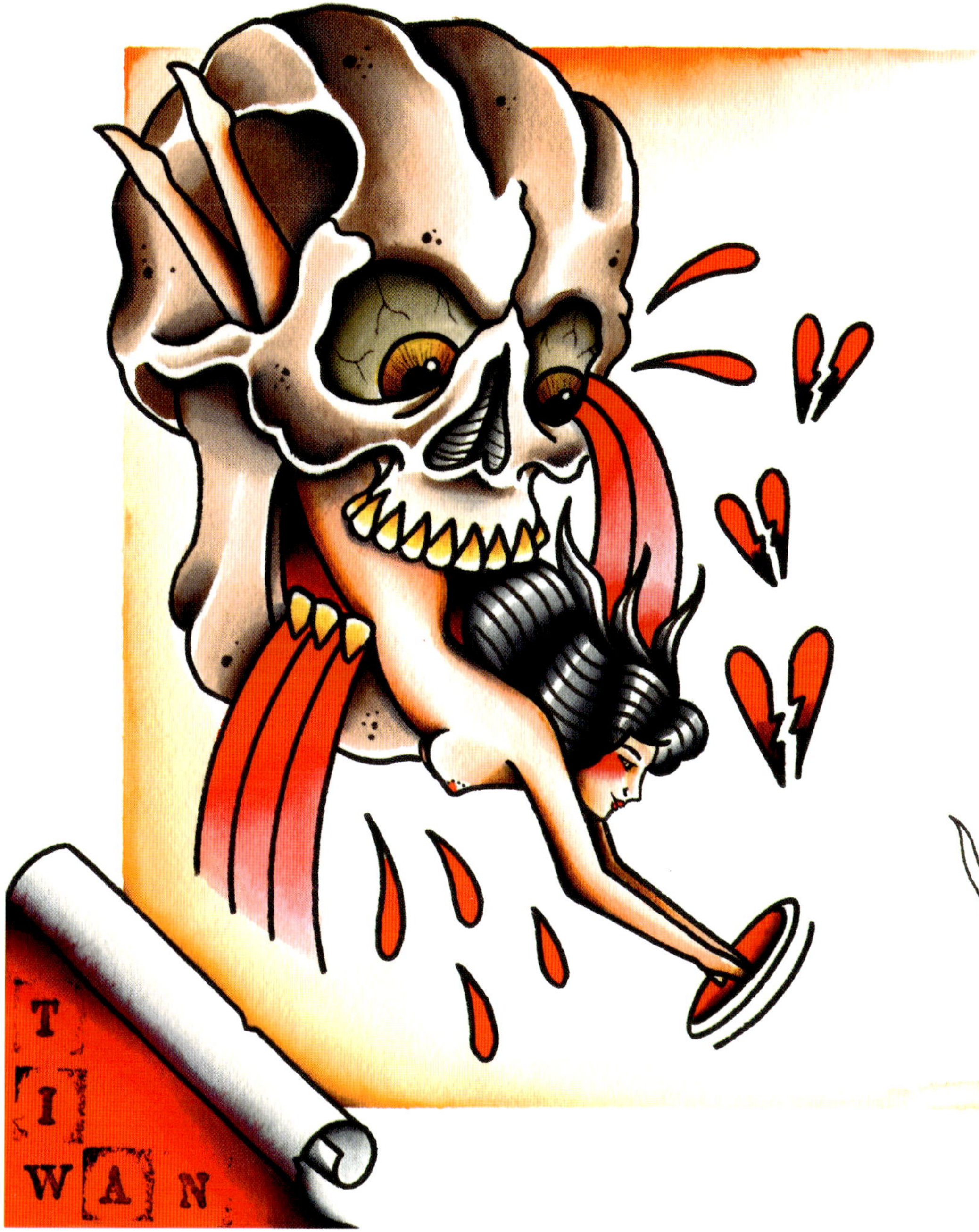
T
I
W A N

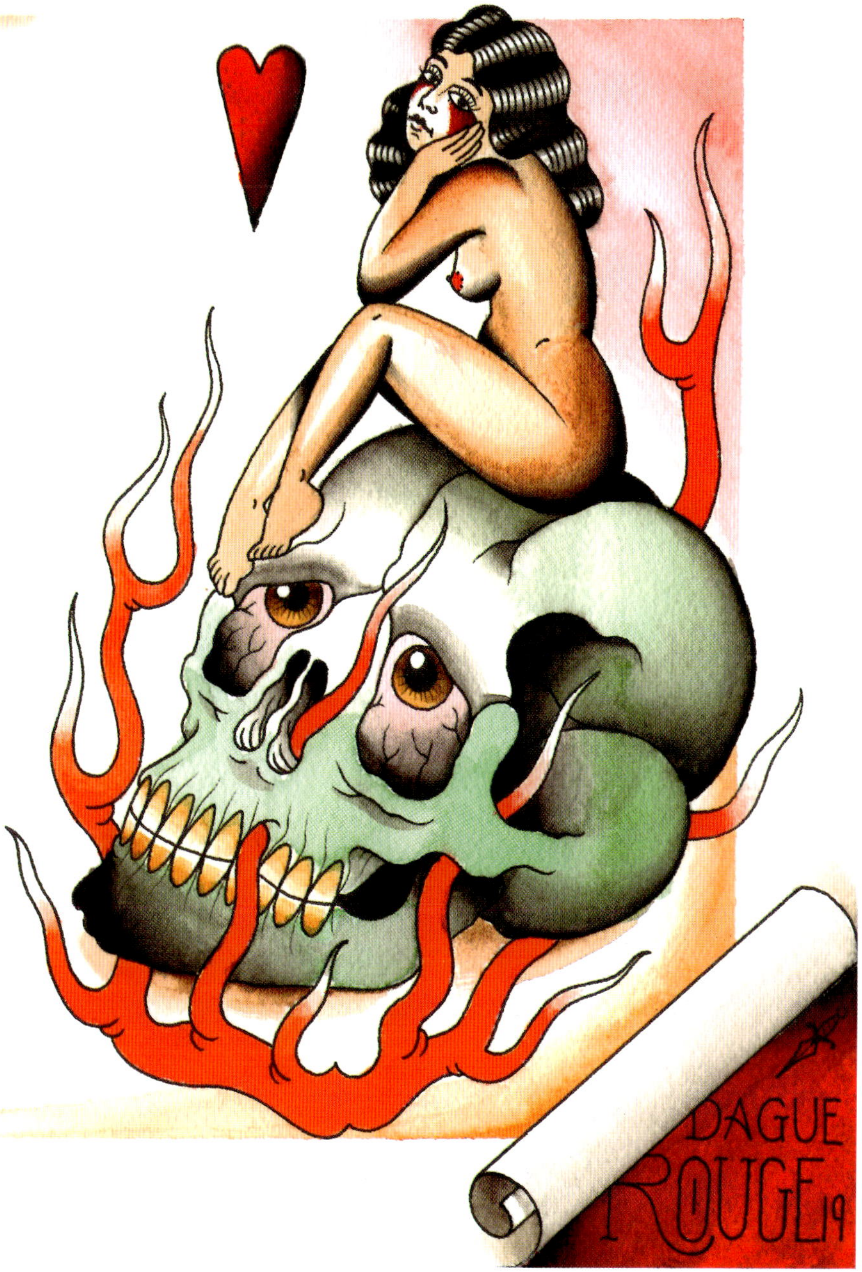
DAGUE
ROUGE 19

Left
Malflore
@malflore
Atelier Triptyque / Montpellier / France

Right
MaxNoname
@max_noname
On the road / Paris / France

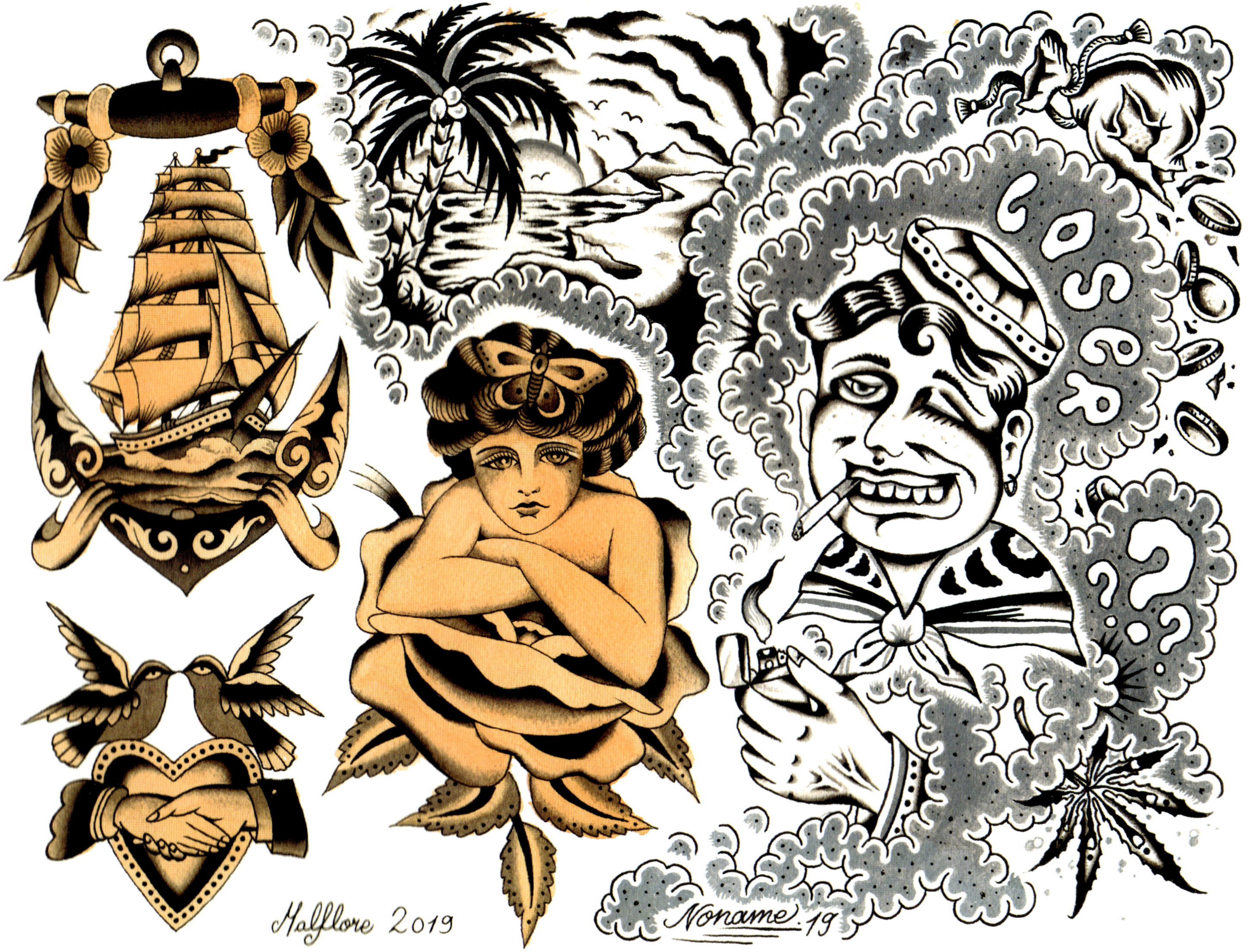
LOSER
Malflore 2019
Noname 19

Left
Cyril Bok Tattoo
@boktattoo
The Good Place Tattoo / Toulouse / France

Right
Polo Tattooer
@polotattooer_tgp
The Good Place Tattoo / Toulouse / France

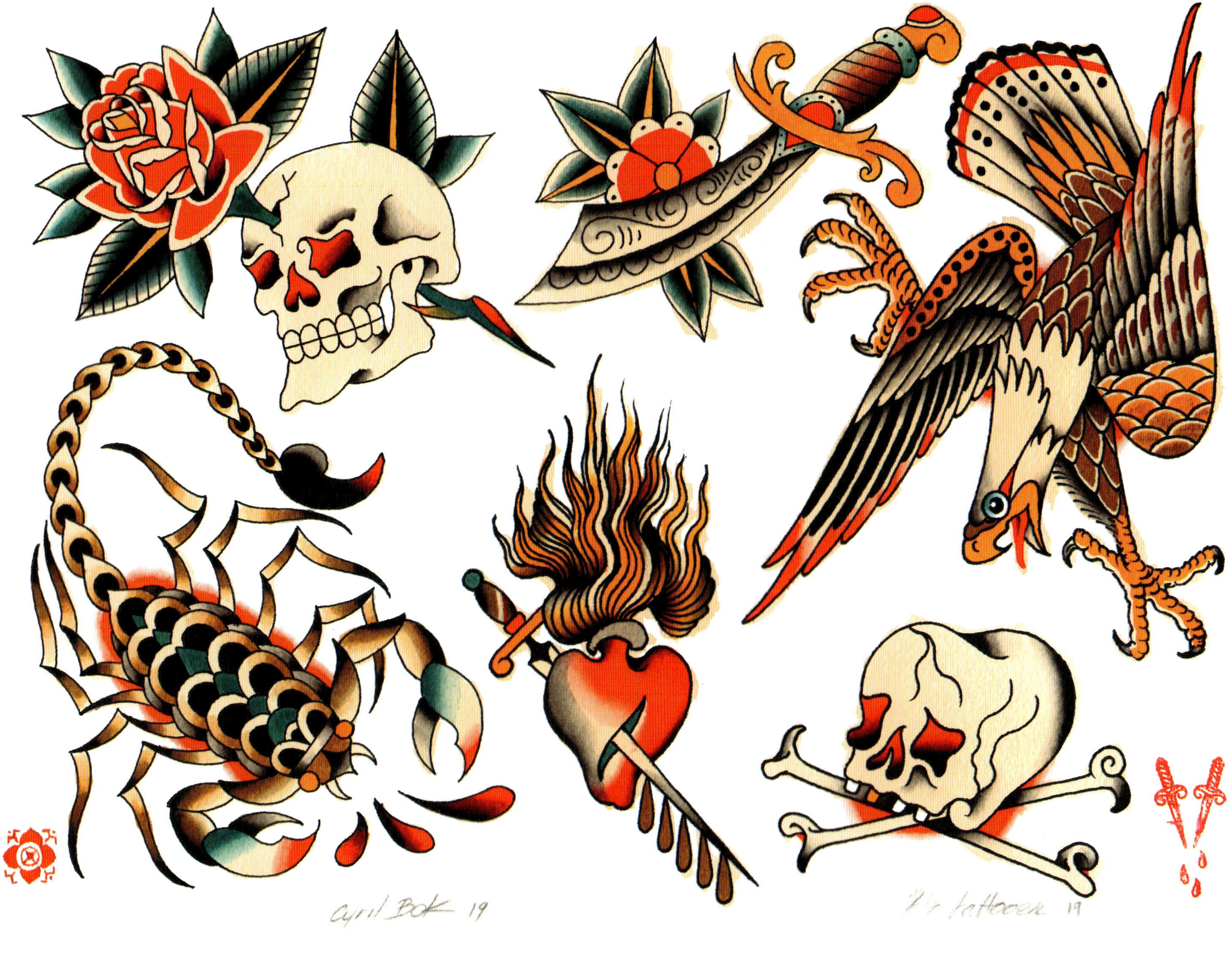
Cyril Bok 19

Left
Peter Panther
@peter.panther_
Perdu d'Avance Tattoo Club / Paris / France

Right
Toy-Arthur
@toy_arthur_tatouage
FTC Bordeaux / Bordeaux / France

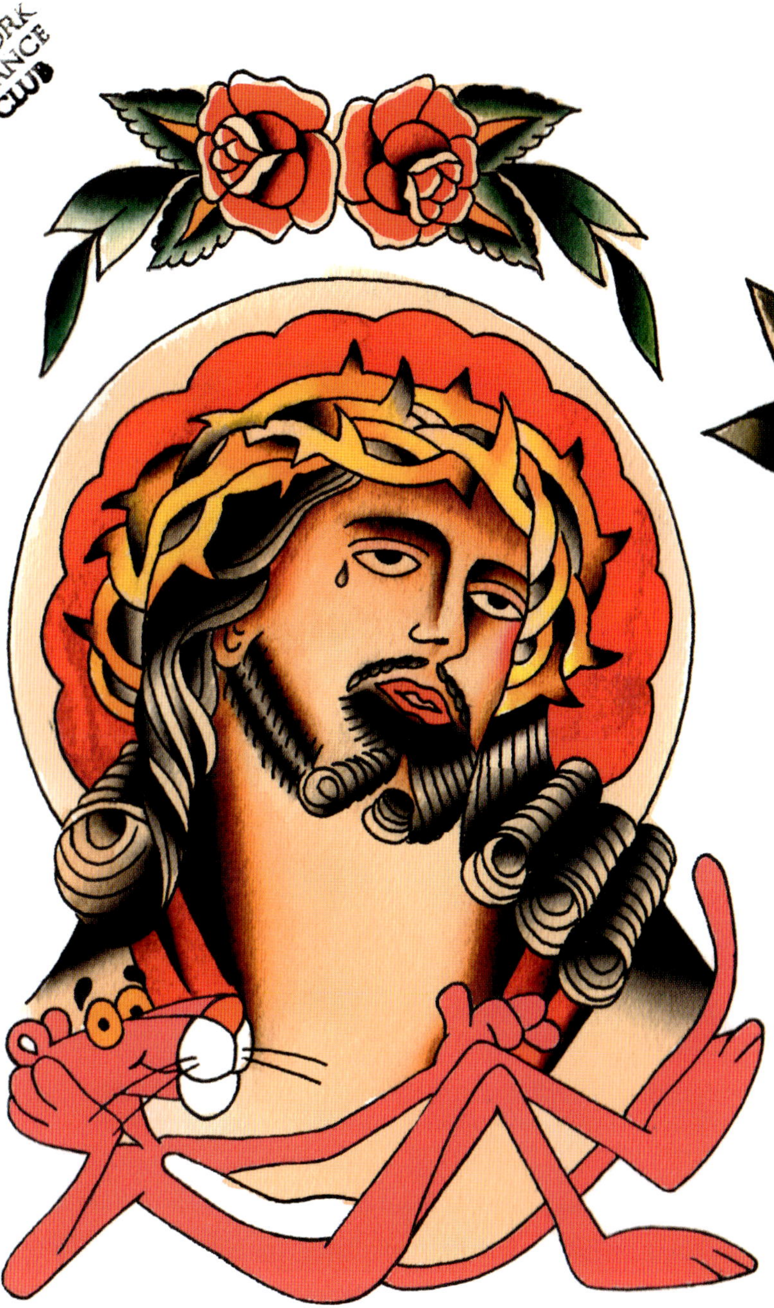
PIERRE ARTWORK
PERDU D'AVANCE
TATTOO CLUB

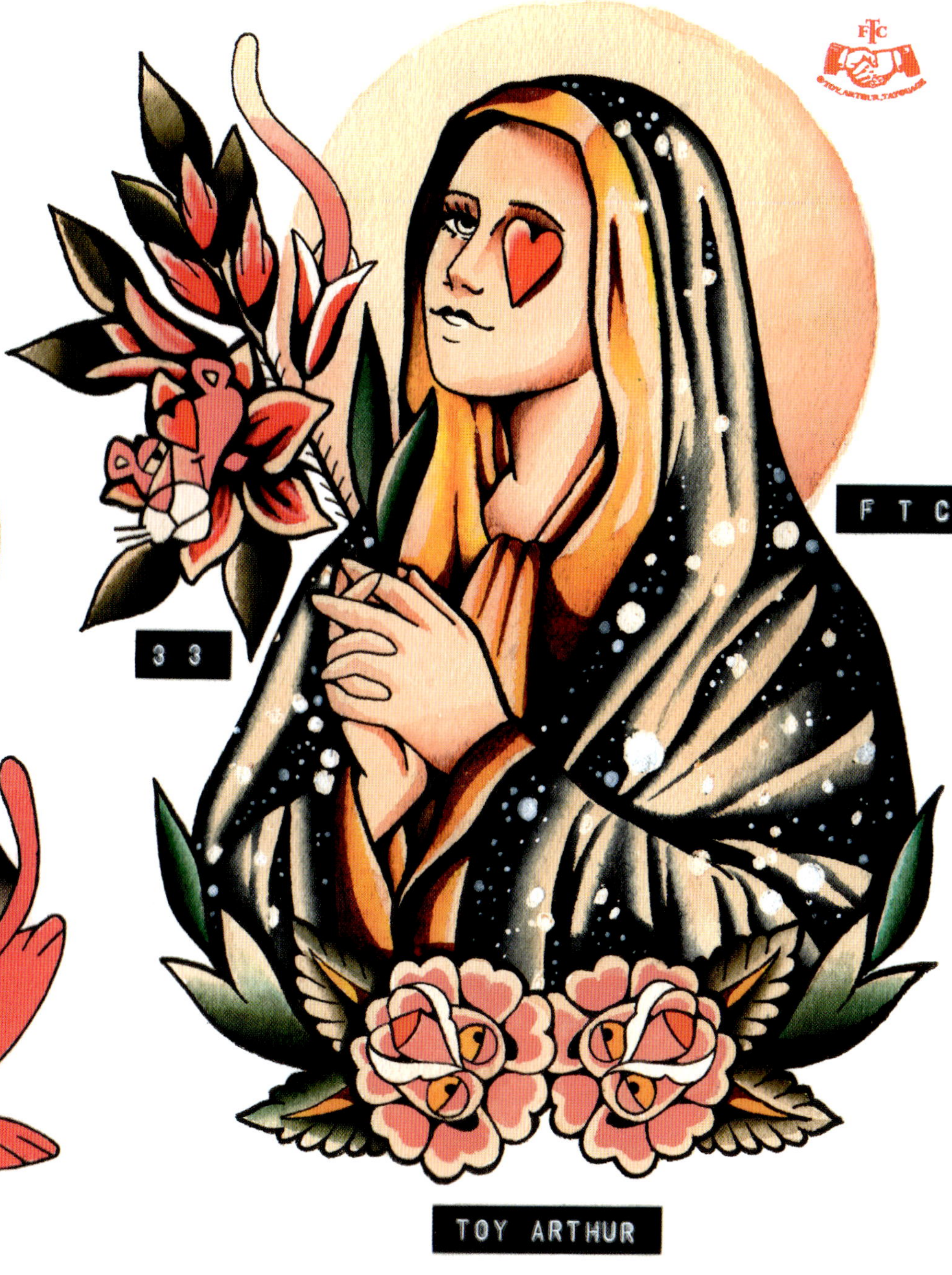
FTC
33
TOY ARTHUR

Left
Ben Manuarii
@benmanuarii
Bisous Bisous / Paris / France

Right
Pierre NBTatts
@pierrenbtatts
Nuevo Mundo / Strasbourg / France

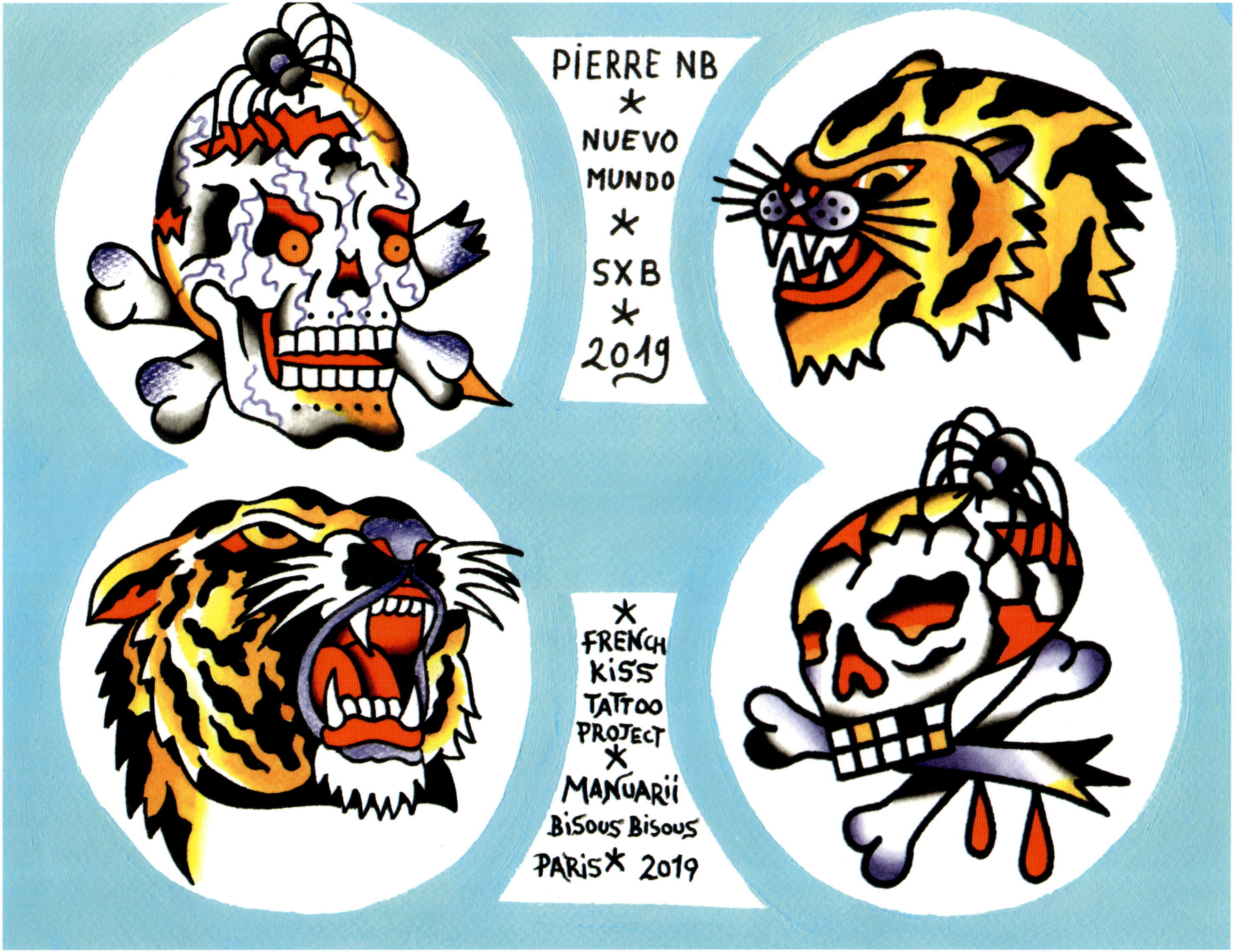
PIERRE NB
*
NUEVO
MUNDO
*
SXB
*
2019
*
FRENCH
KISS
TATTOO
PROJECT
*
MANUARII
BISOUS BISOUS
PARIS* 2019

Left
Chris Nero
@chrisnerotattoo
Nero Tattoo Shop / Rennes / France

Right
Tiwan
@tiwan_tattoo
Spirit Tattoo Rennes / Rennes / France

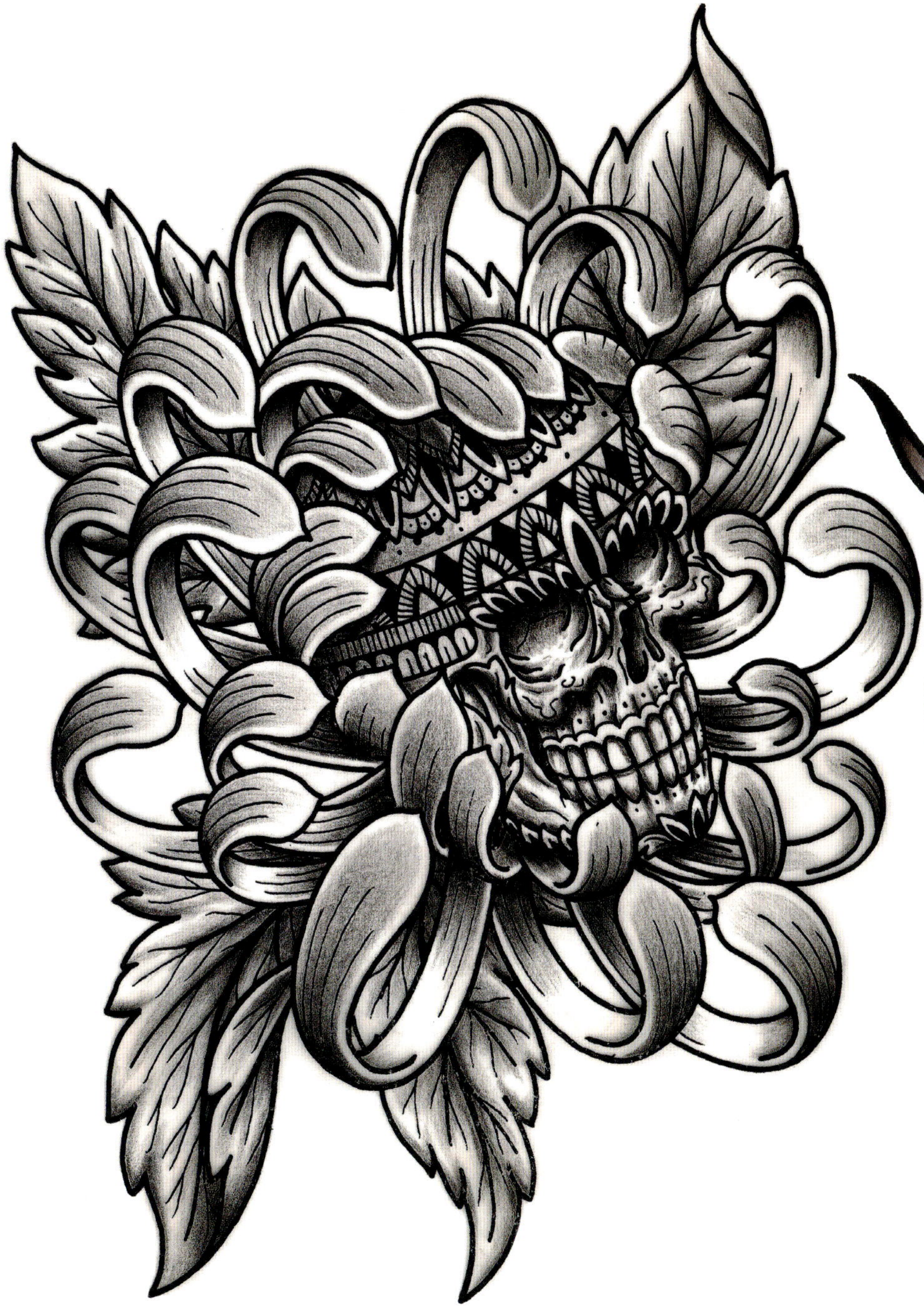

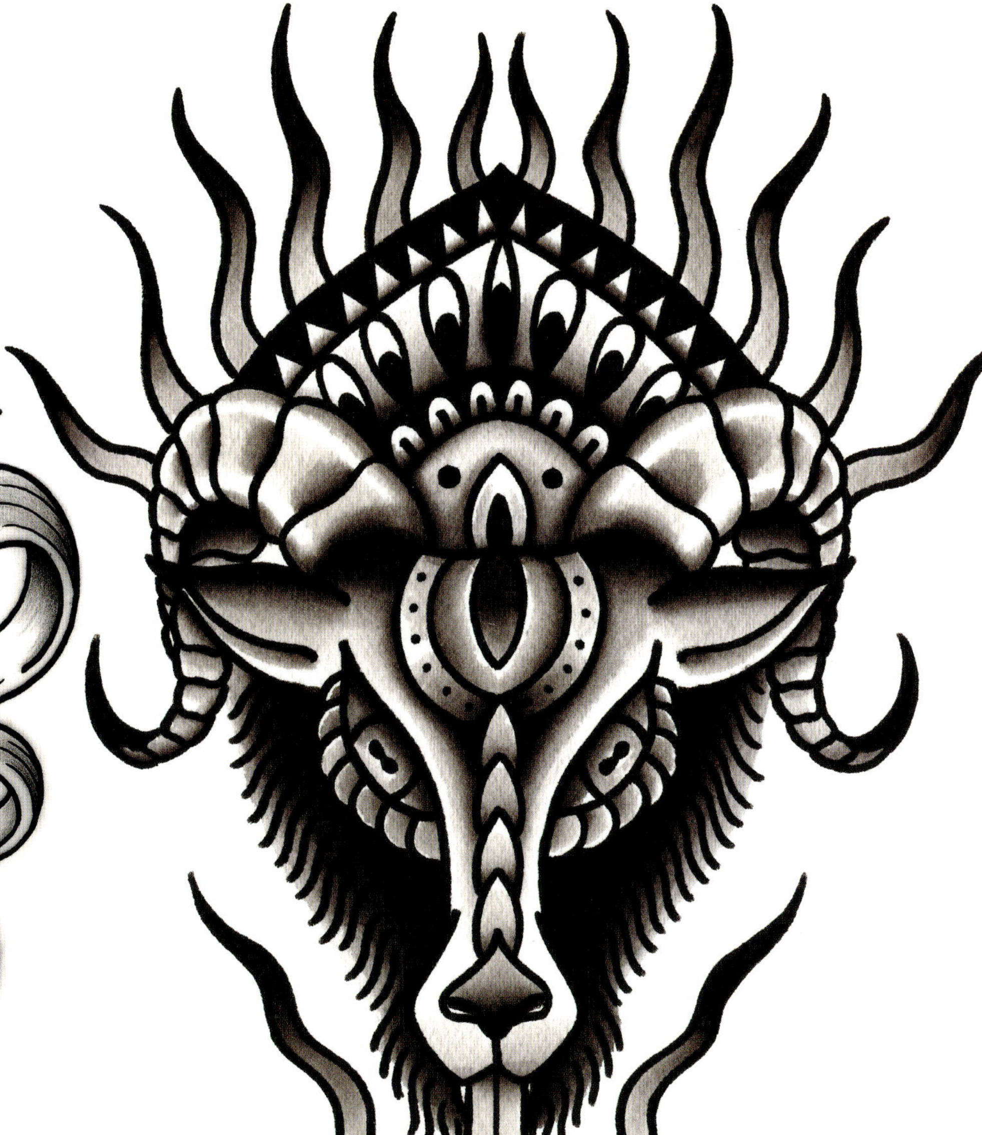

Left
Matt Colim
@mattcolim
Tribal Act / Paris / France

Right
Sylvester Boom
@sylvesterboom
Tribal Act / Paris / France

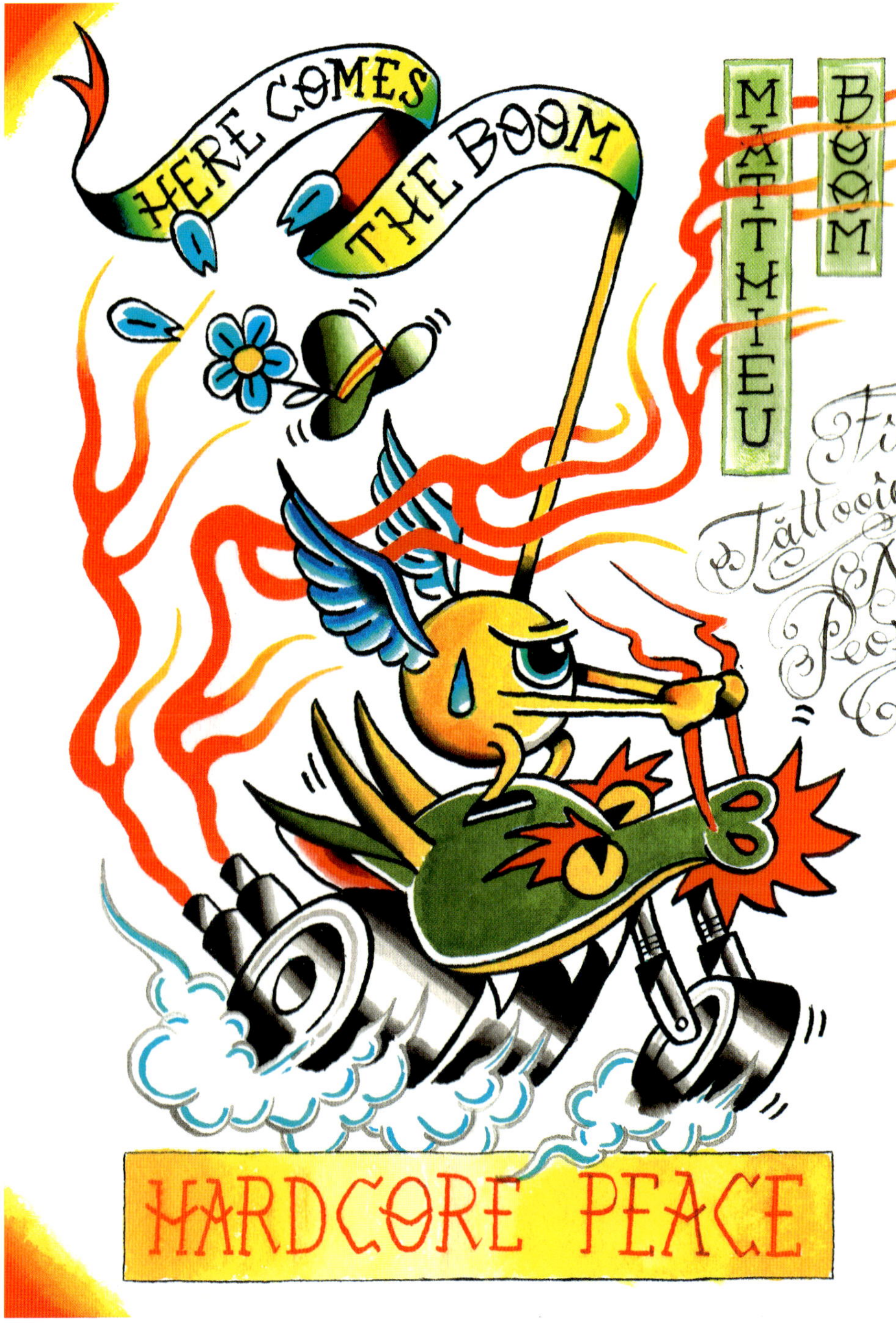
HERE COMES THE BOOM
MATTHIEU
BOOM
Fine Tattooing by Nice People
HARDCORE PEACE

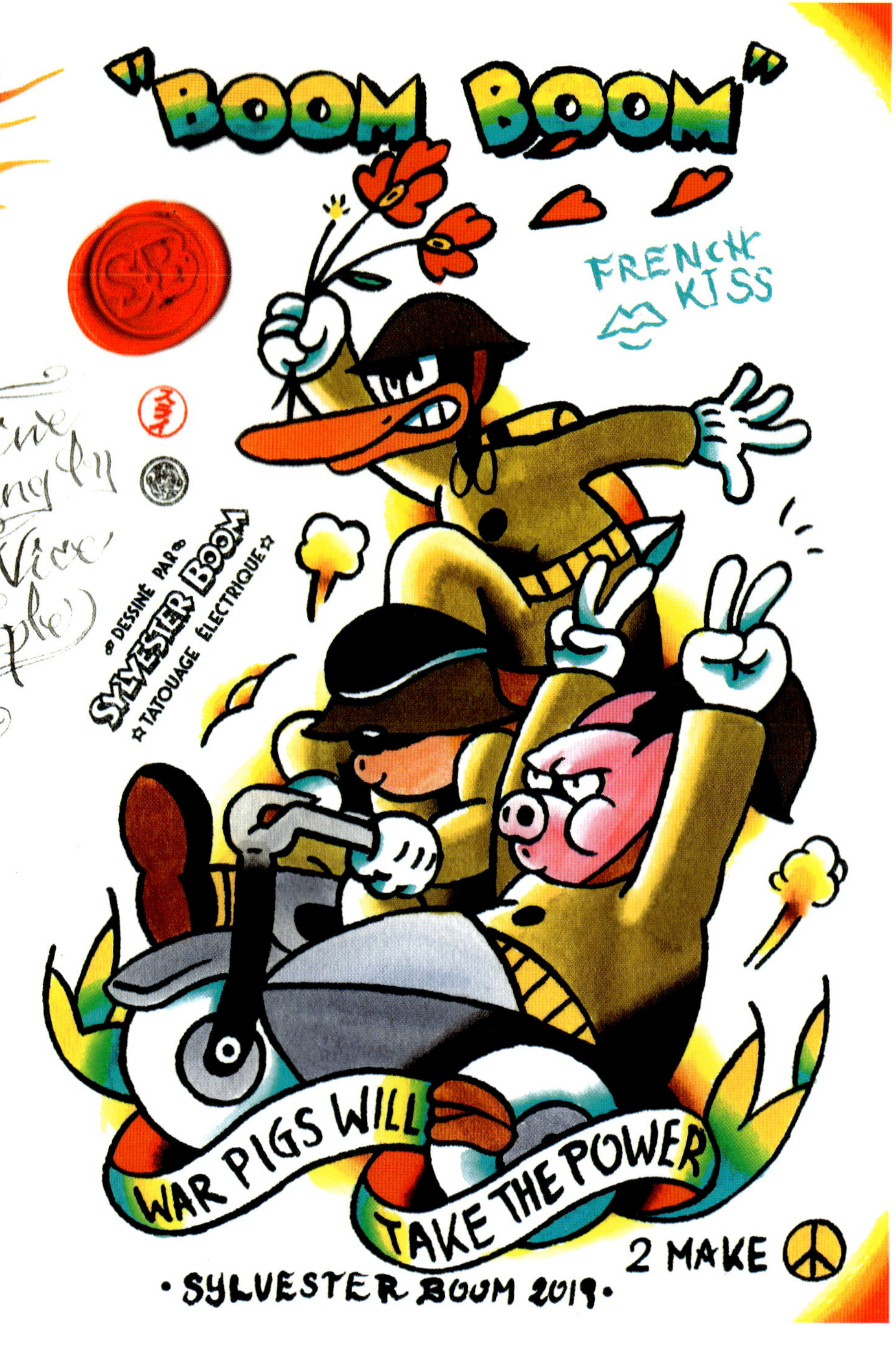
"BOOM BOOM"
FRENCH KISS
DESSINÉ PAR
SYLVESTER BOOM
TATOUAGE ÉLECTRIQUE
WAR PIGS WILL TAKE THE POWER
2 MAKE
SYLVESTER BOOM 2019

Center and bottom right
Florian Svaha
@florian.svaha
Tattoo Family / Bordeaux / France

Left and right
Enguerrand Bosco
@enguerrand.bosco
Electric Sun Tattoo / Saint-Raphaël / France

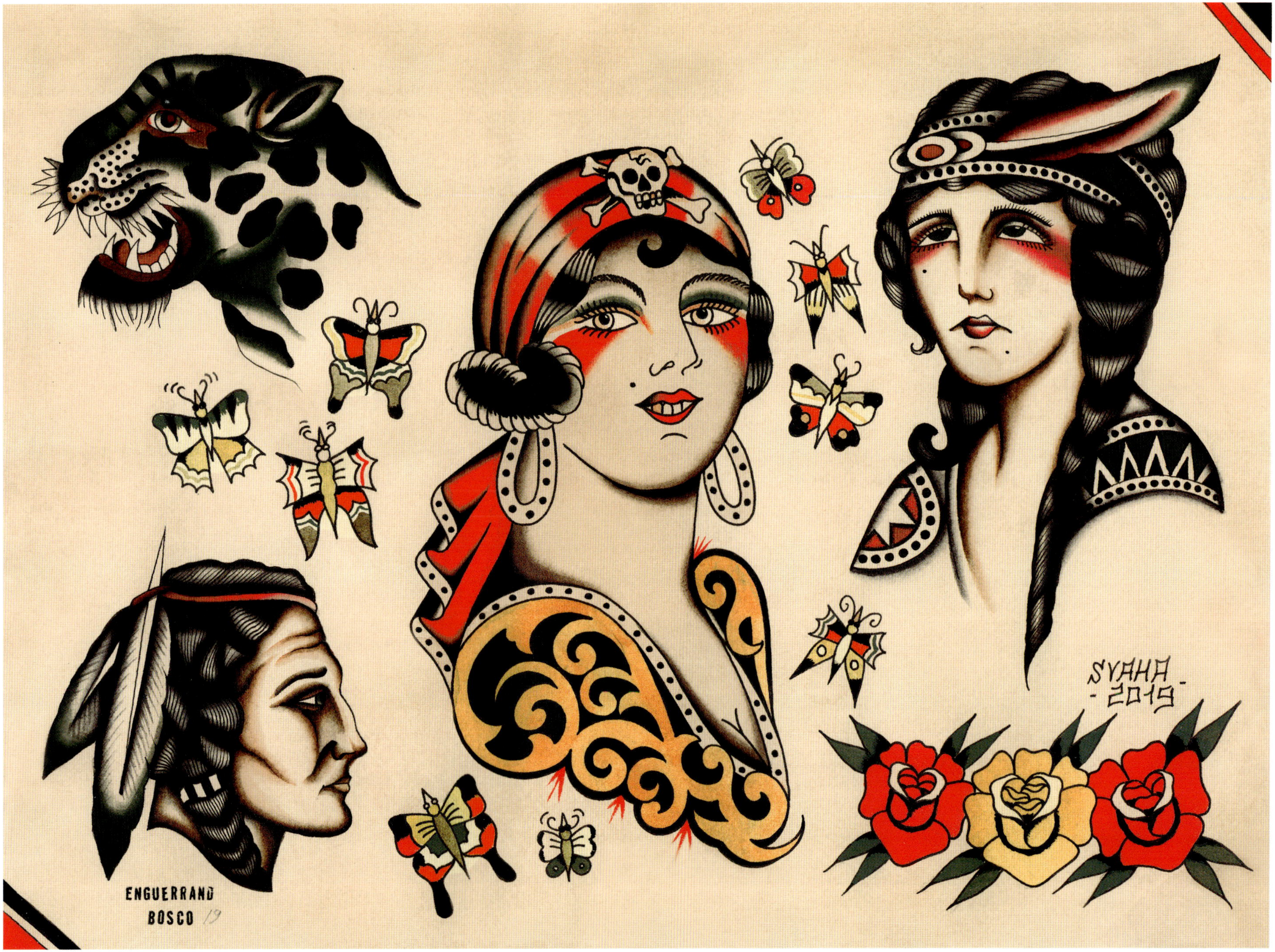
SVAHA
- 2019 -
ENGUERRAND
BOSCO 19

Left
Tiwan
@tiwan_tattoo
Spirit Tattoo Rennes / Rennes / France

Right
El Bent
@elbenttattoo
True Love / Paris / France

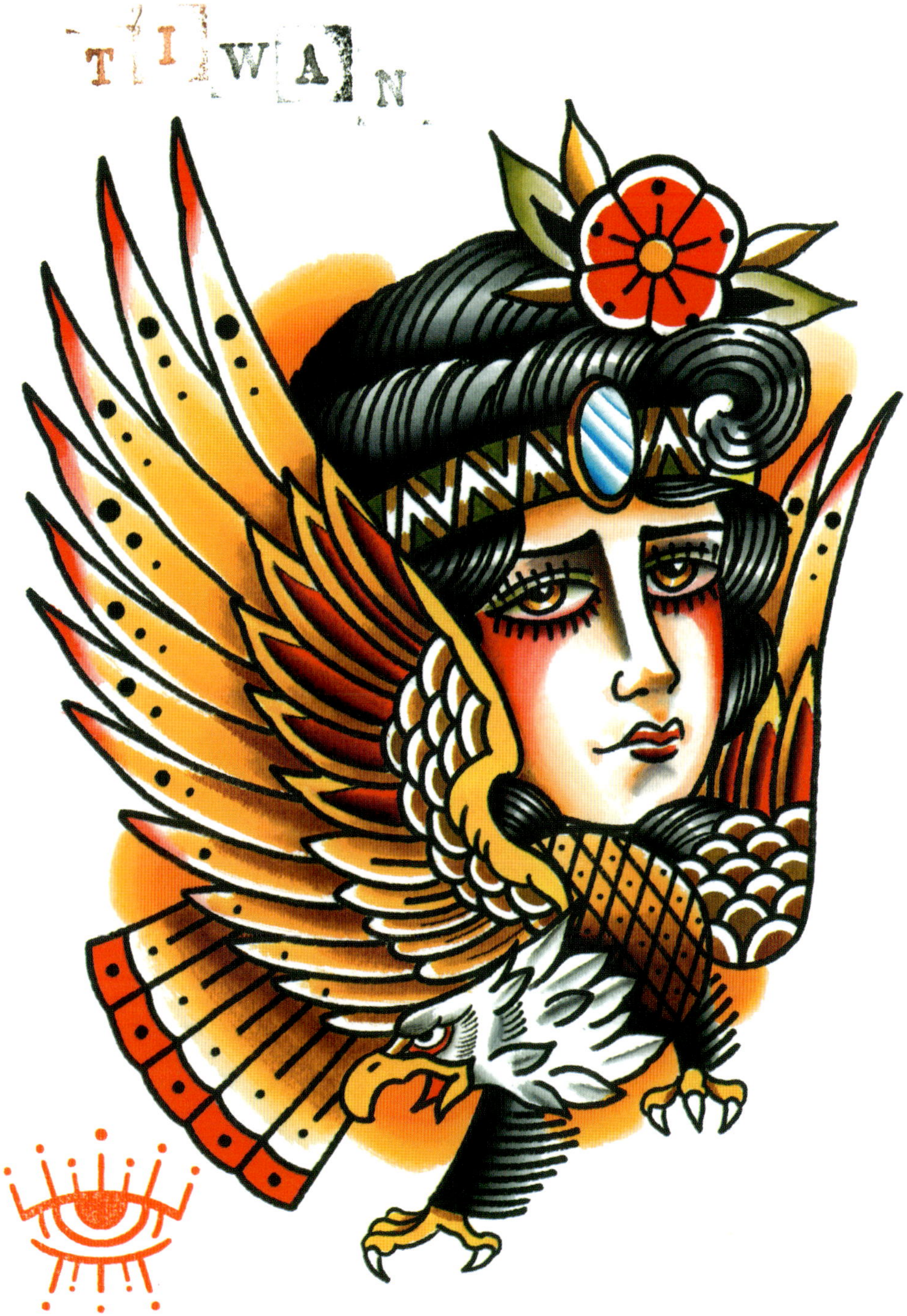
TIWAN

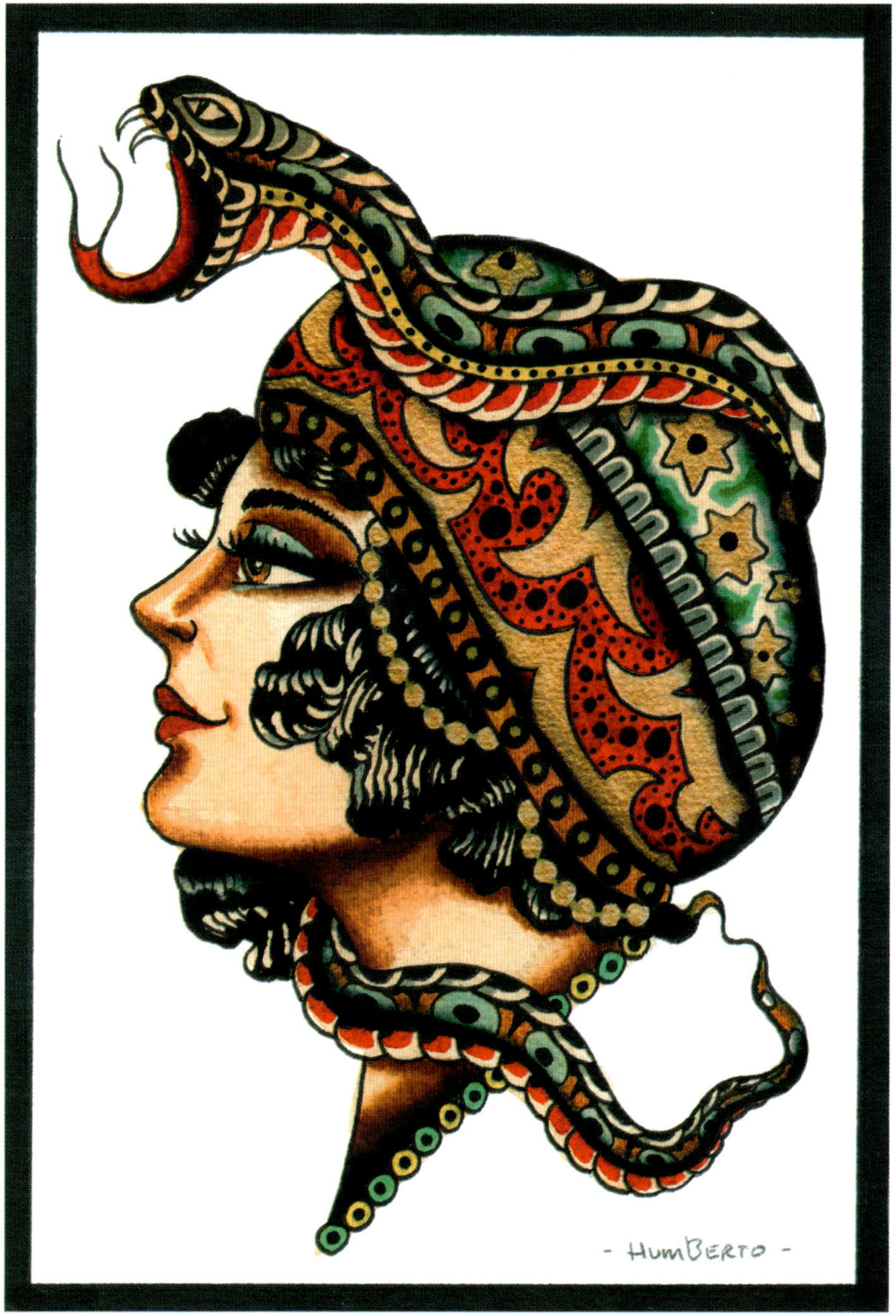
- HUMBERTO -

Left
John Stone
@john_stone_tatouage
L'Astrolabe / Dinard / France

Right
Fat Manu de Tours
@fatmanu_tattoo_de_tours
Coco Bongo Tattoo Club / Tours / France

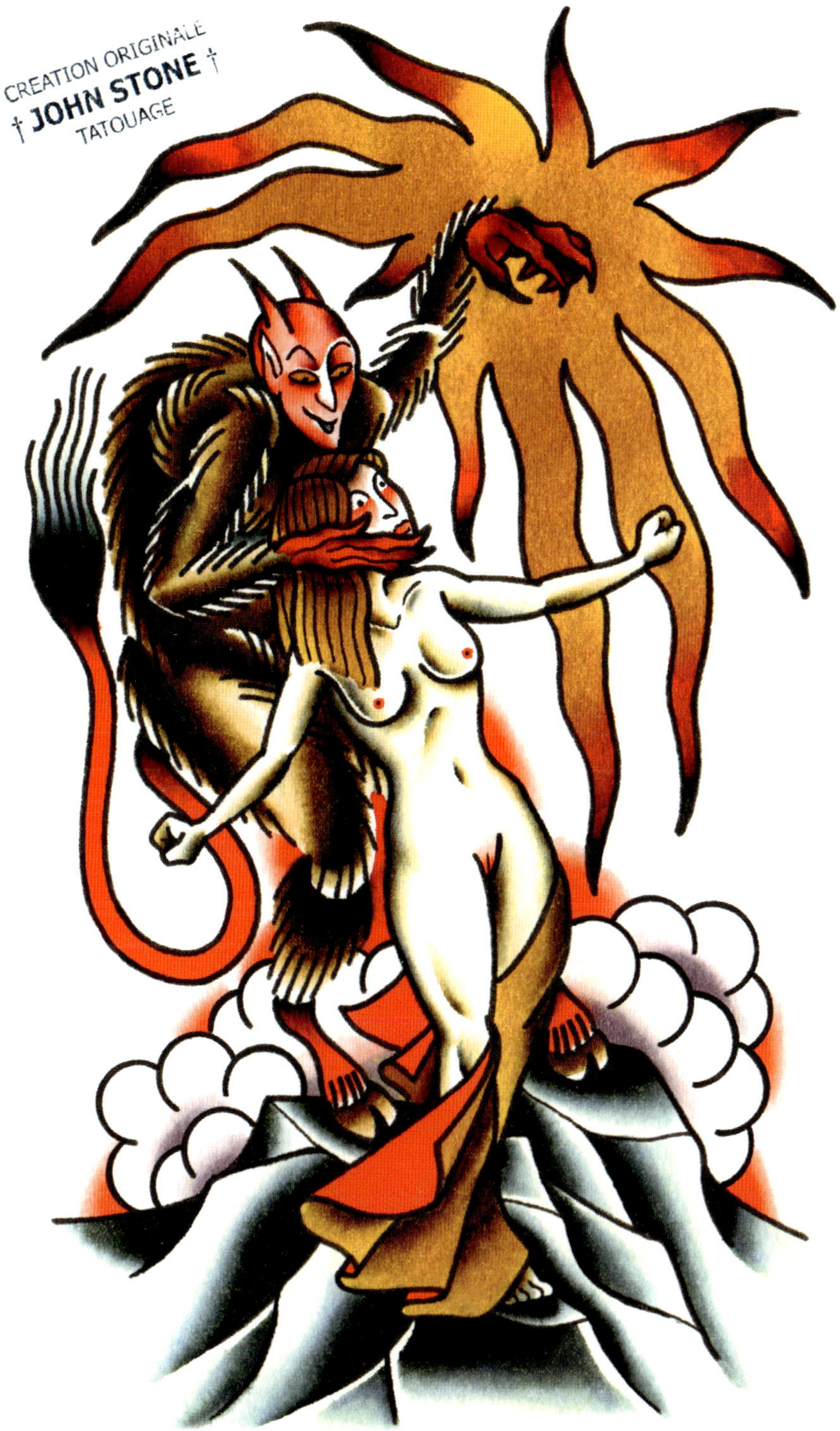
CREATION ORIGINALE
† JOHN STONE †
TATOUAGE

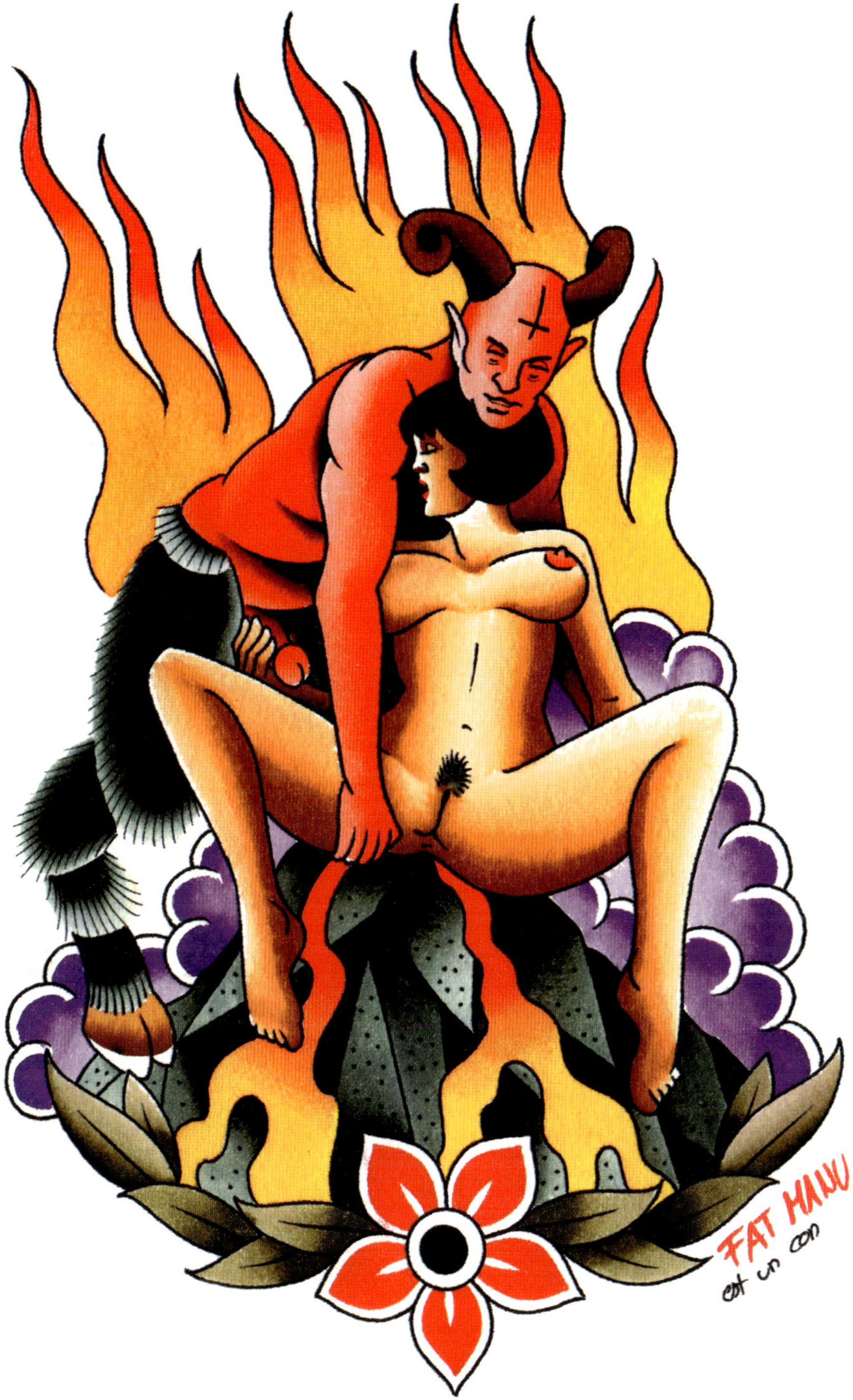
FAT MANU
est un con

Left
Sylvester Boom
@sylvesterboom
Tribal Act / Paris / France

Right
Tiwan
@tiwan_tattoo
Spirit Tattoo Rennes / Rennes / France

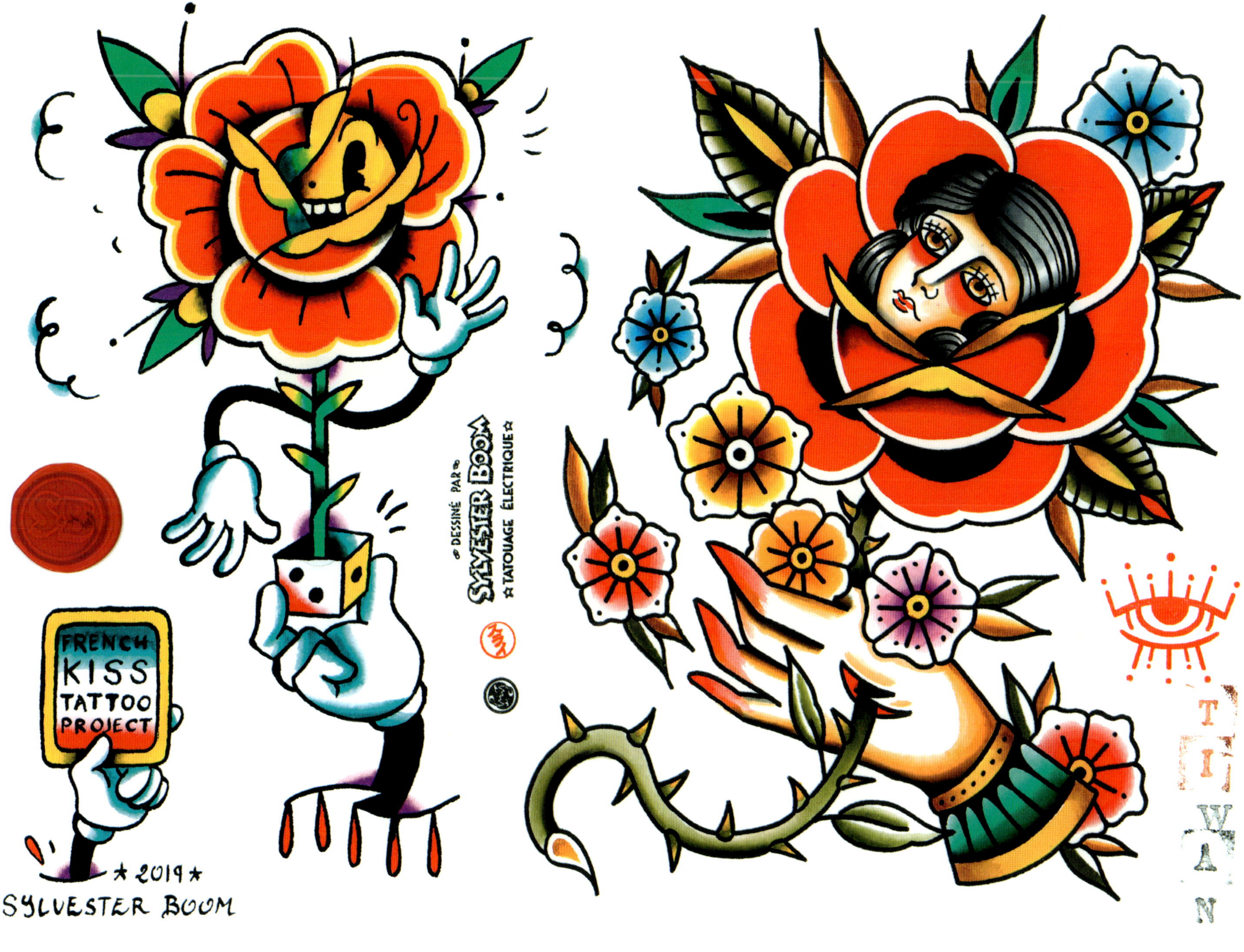
FRENCH KISS TATTOO PROJECT
DESSINÉ PAR
SYLVESTER BOOM
☆TATOUAGE ÉLECTRIQUE☆
★2019★
SYLVESTER BOOM

Left
Sombre d'Œil
@sombre_doeil
CopaBanana Club / Lille / France

Right
Malflore
@malflore
Atelier Triptyque / Montpellier / France

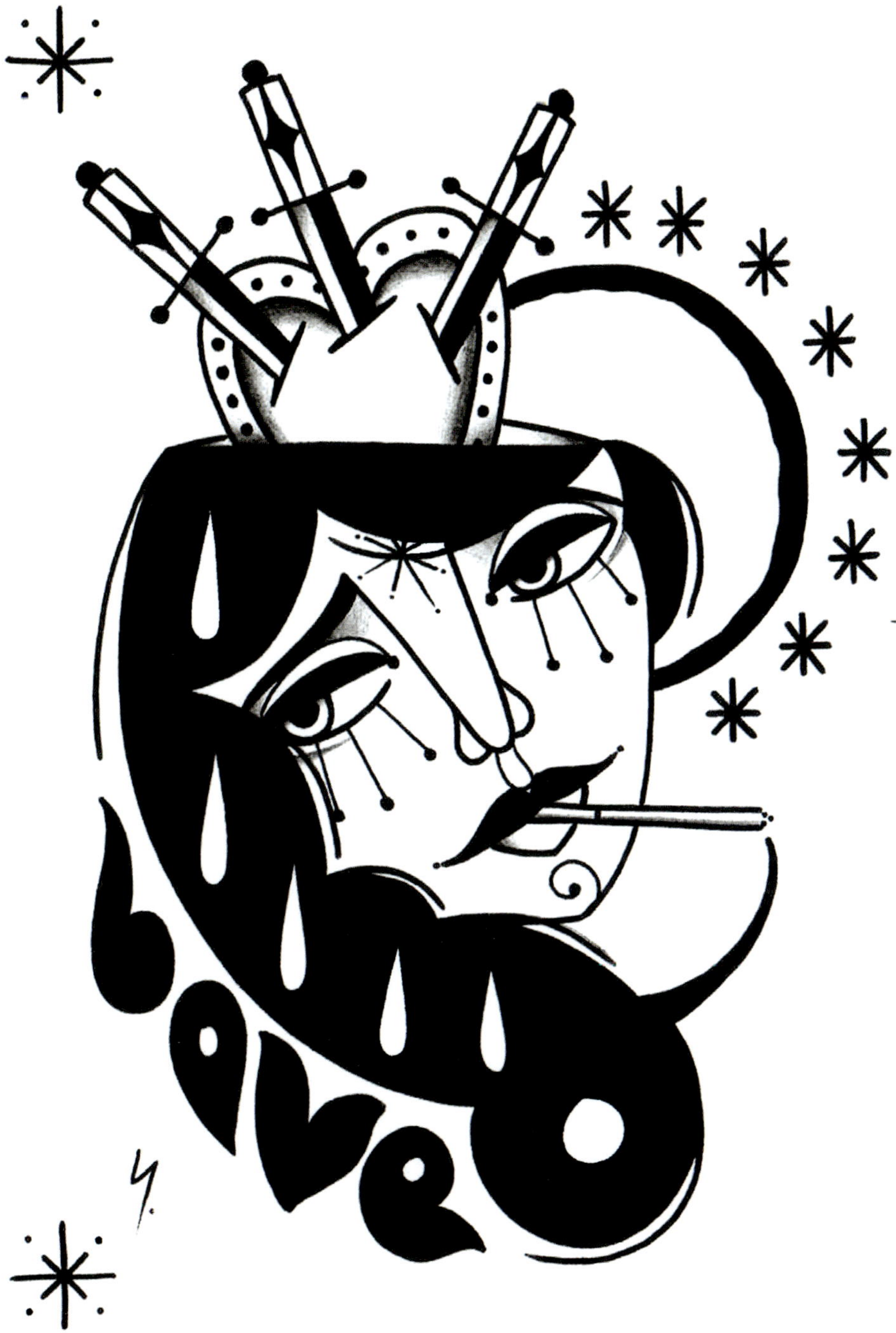

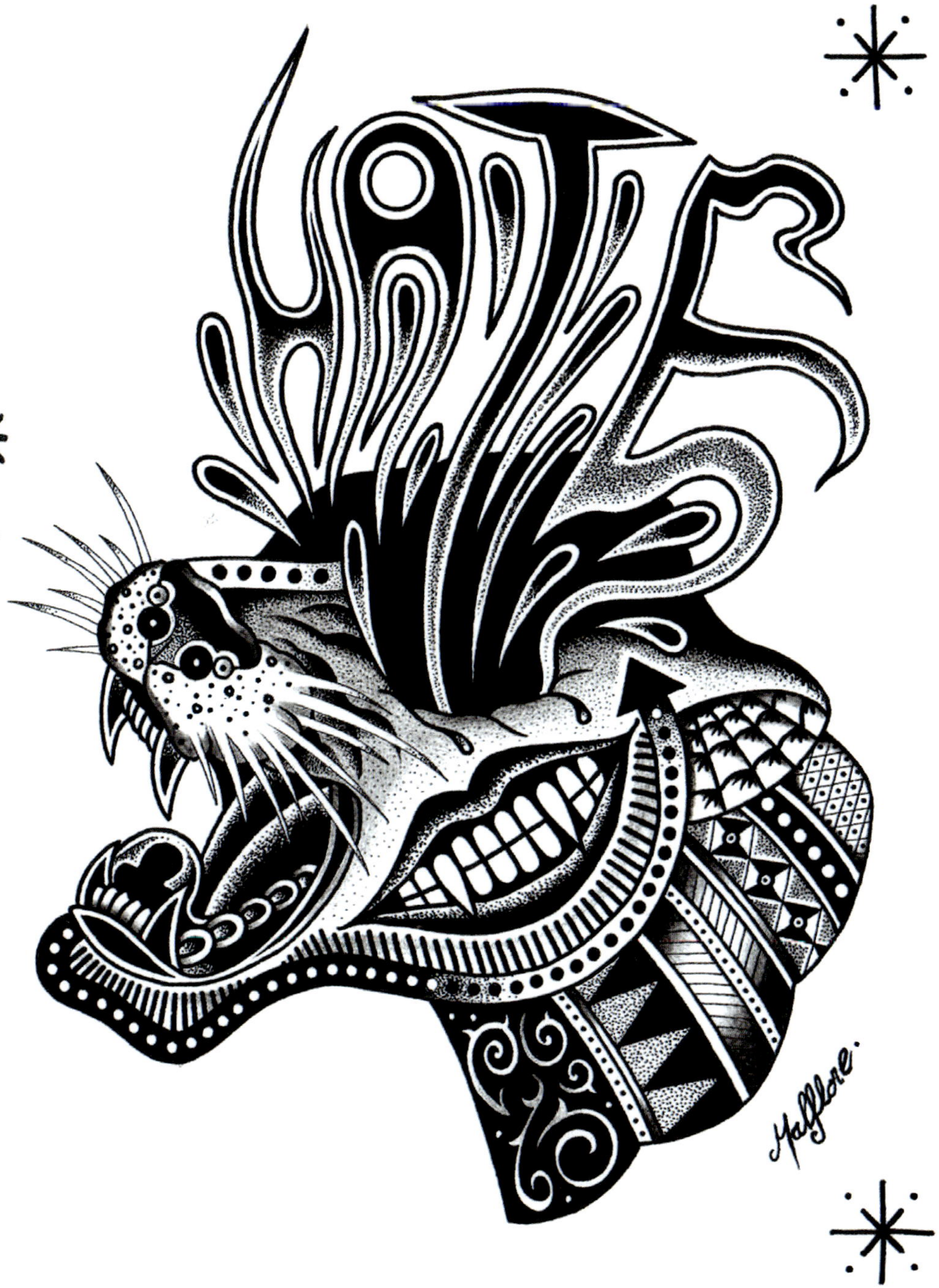

Left
Polo Tattooer
@polotattooer_tgp
The Good Place Tattoo / Toulouse / France

Right
Max Dem
@maxdemtattoo
Glorybound Tattoo / Antwerp / Belgium

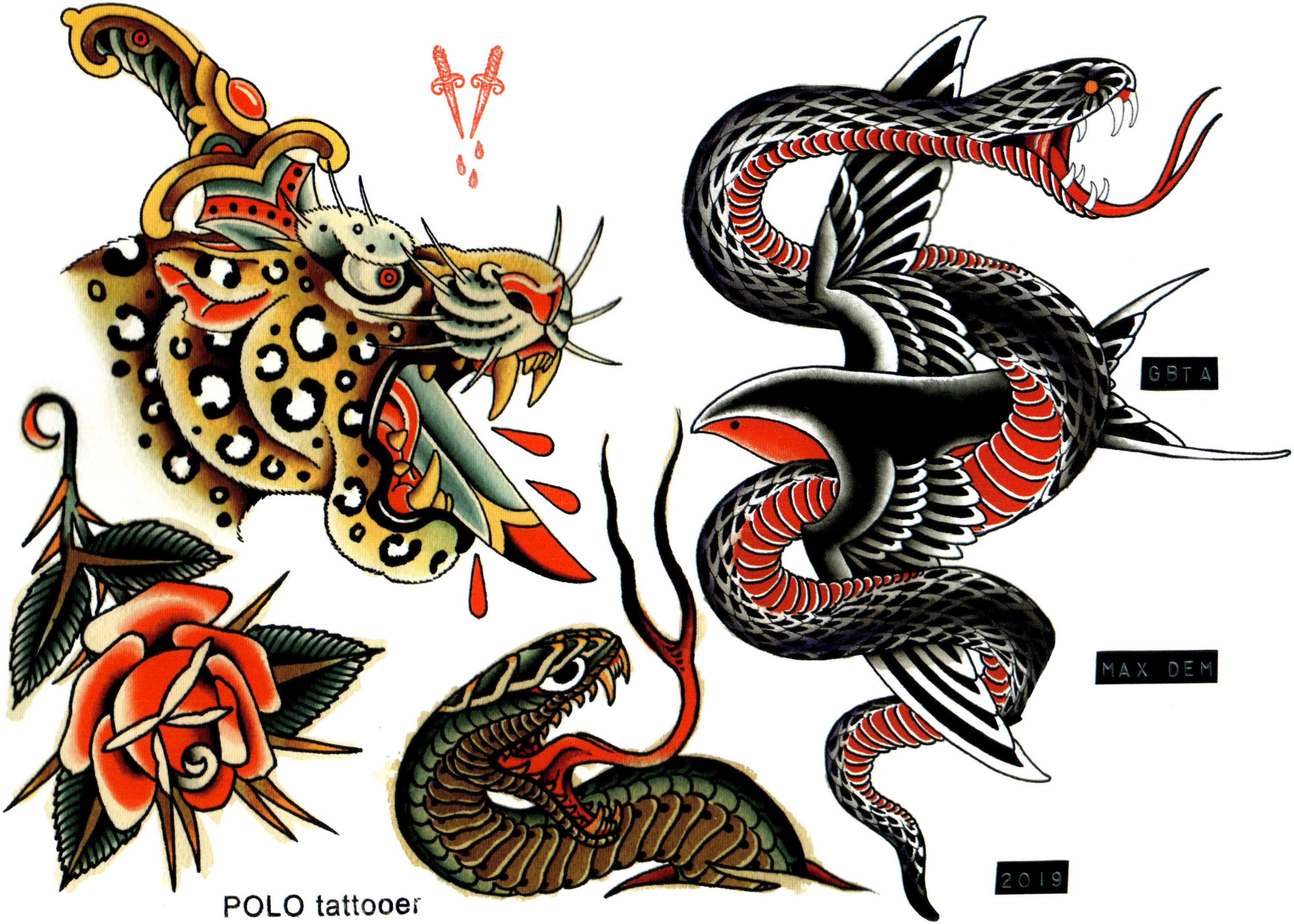
GBTA
MAX DEM
2019
POLO tattooer

Left
Alberto Solposto
@albertosolposto
Golden Mempo Private Studio / Barreiro / Portugal

Right
Alexxx
@studio22tattoo
Studio 22 Tattoo / Lousã / Portugal

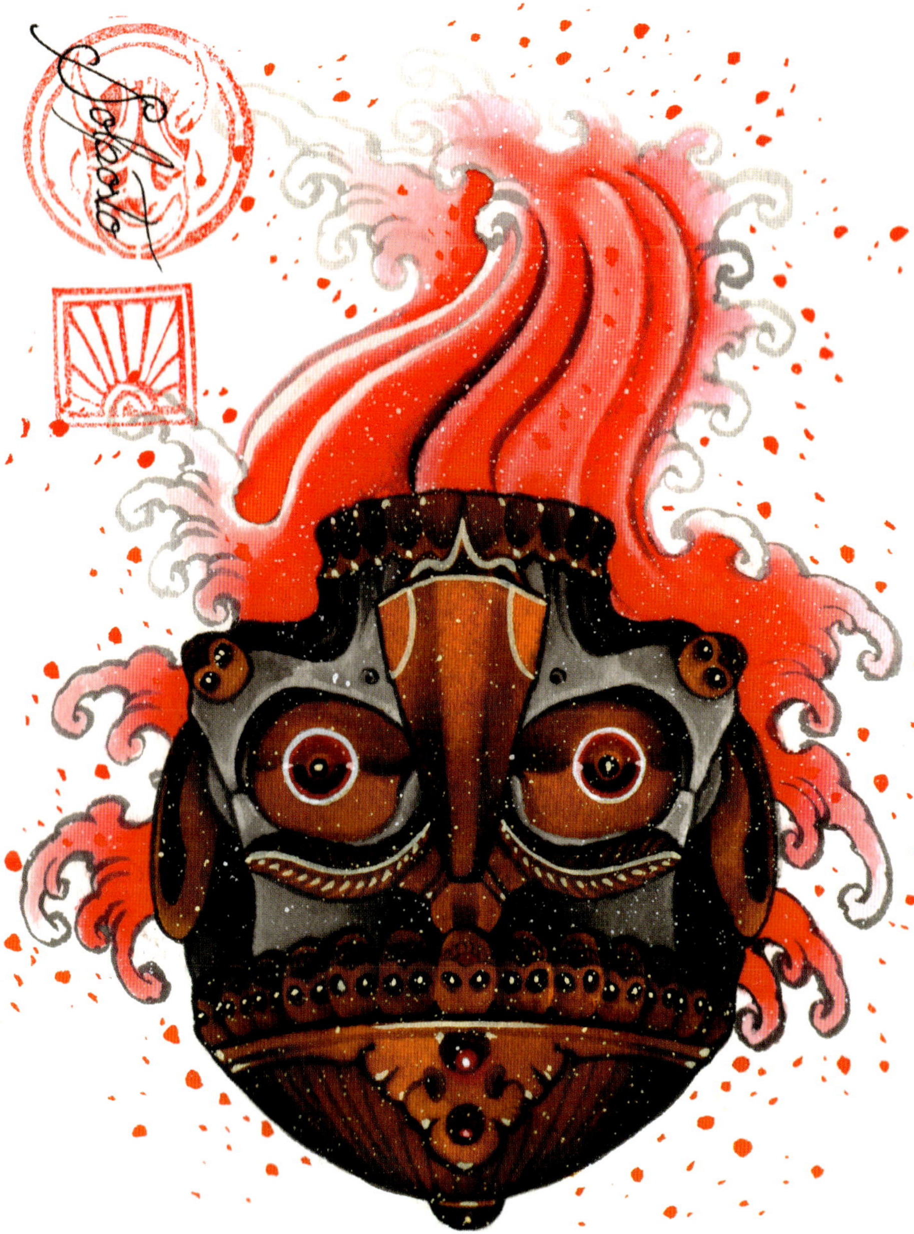

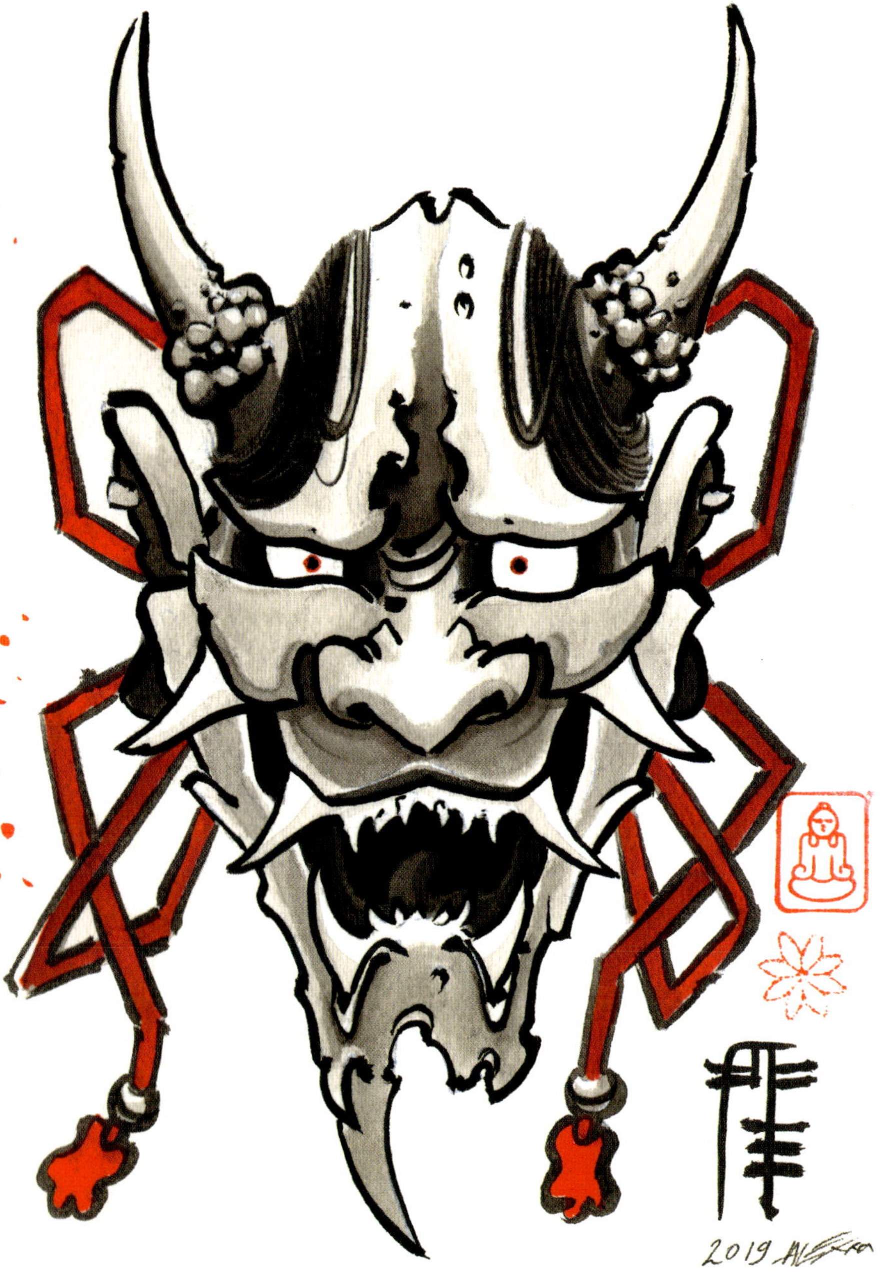
2019

Left
John Stone
@john_stone_tatouage
L'Astrolabe / Dinard / France

Right
Phil Kyle
@philkyle
Magnum Opus Tattoo / Pleurtuit / France

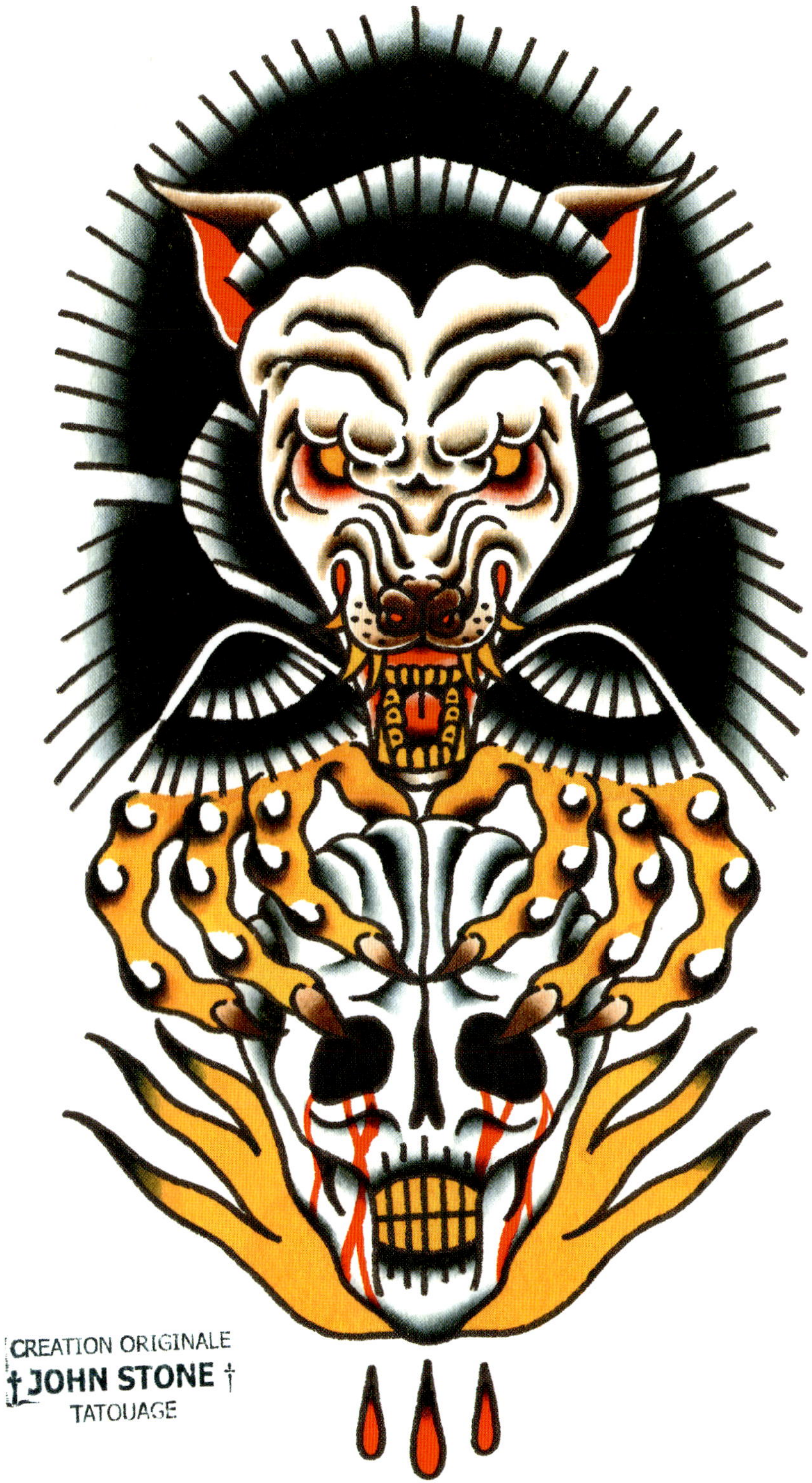
CREATION ORIGINALE
JOHN STONE
TATOUAGE

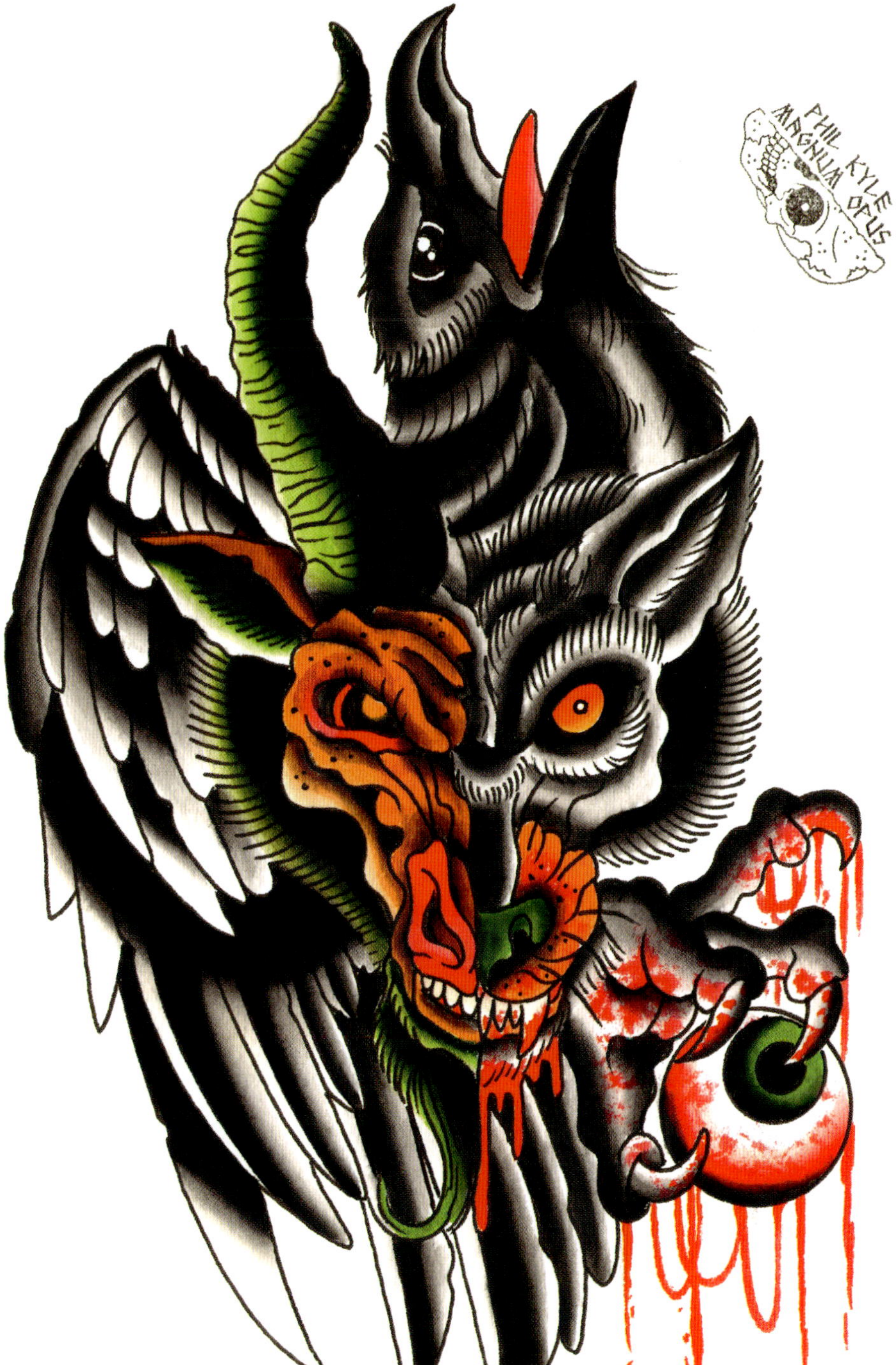
PHIL KYLE
MAGNUM OPUS

Left
Rou Bignol
@rou.bignol
Le Piment Tattoo / Nantes / France

Right
Clément Doineau (Dague Rouge)
@clementdoineau
Grey Bronco Tattoo / Nantes / France

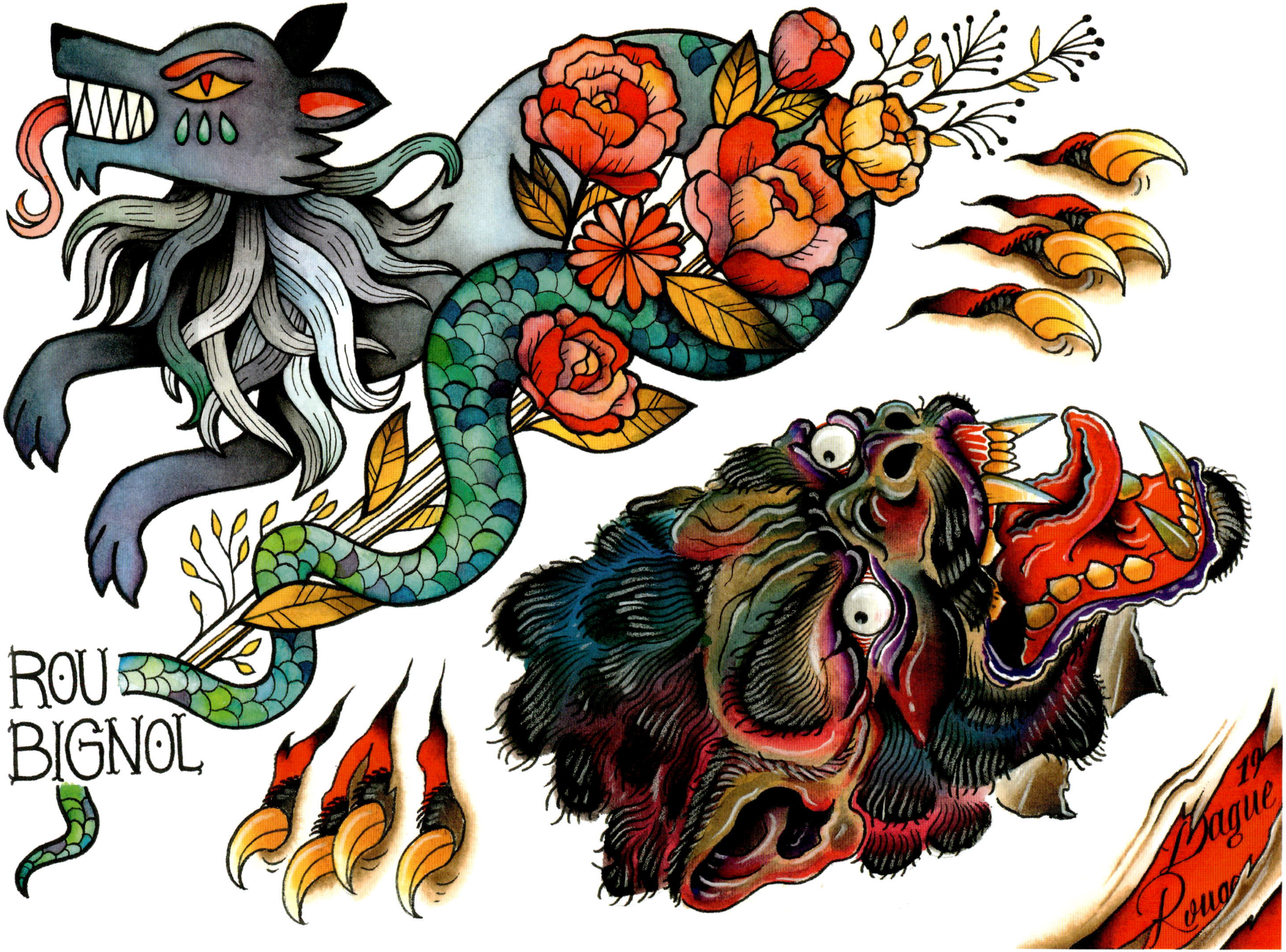
ROU
BIGNOL
19
Dague

Left
The Shok Oner
@the_shok_oner
Strasbourg / France

Right
Niko Mook
@nikomook4real
Dermal Mayhem Tattoo Parlor / Nantes / France

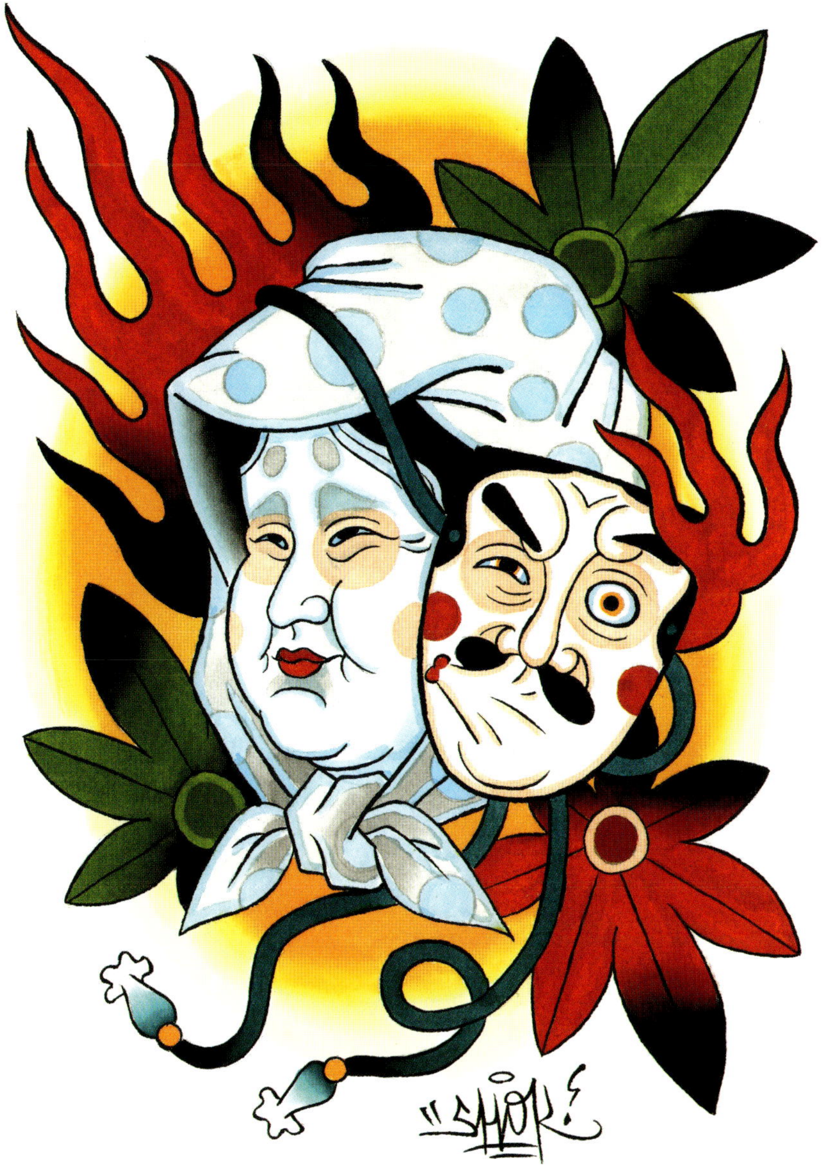

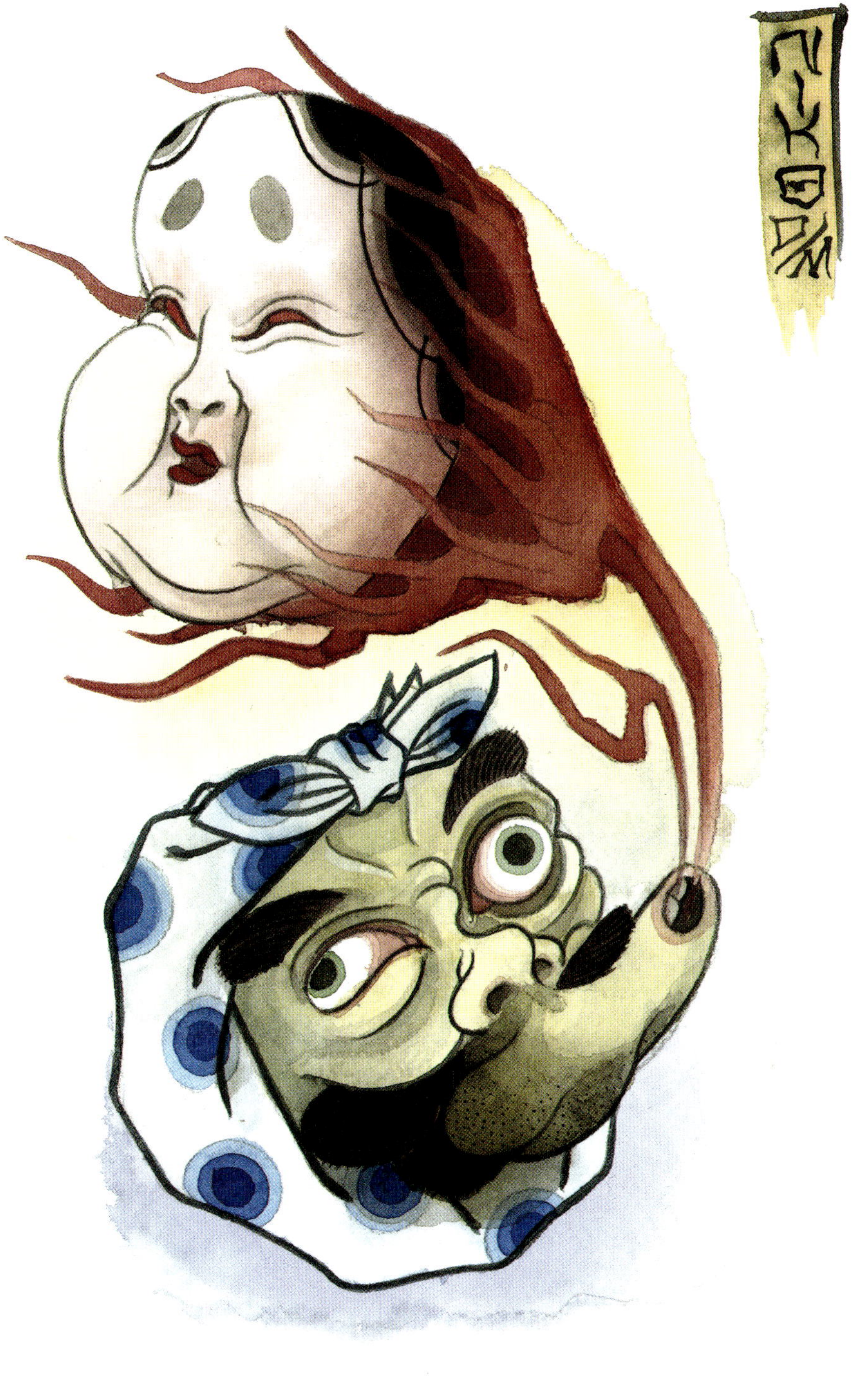

Left
Alberto Sagripanti
@albertosagripanti
Skincraft Tattoo and Piercing / Kirby-in-Ashfield / UK

Right
Marco Coppi
@coppimarco
L'Aquila / Italy

ALBERTO SAGRIPANTI

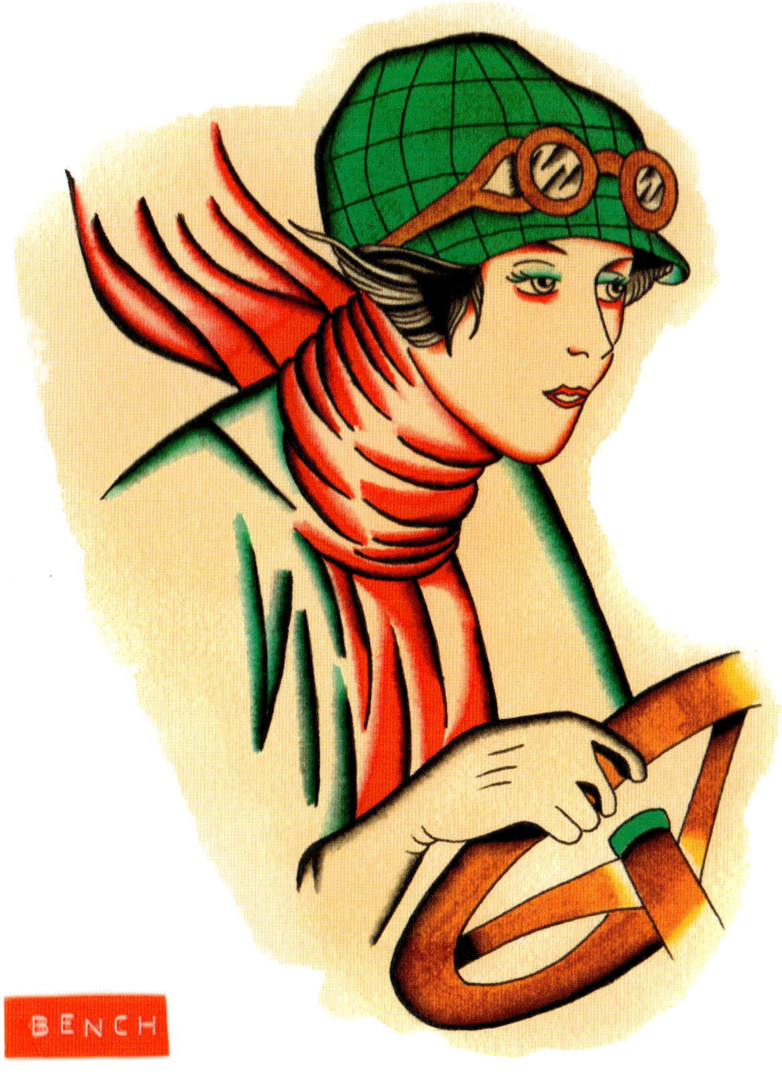

BENCH TO LAST

ITALY

MARCO COPPI

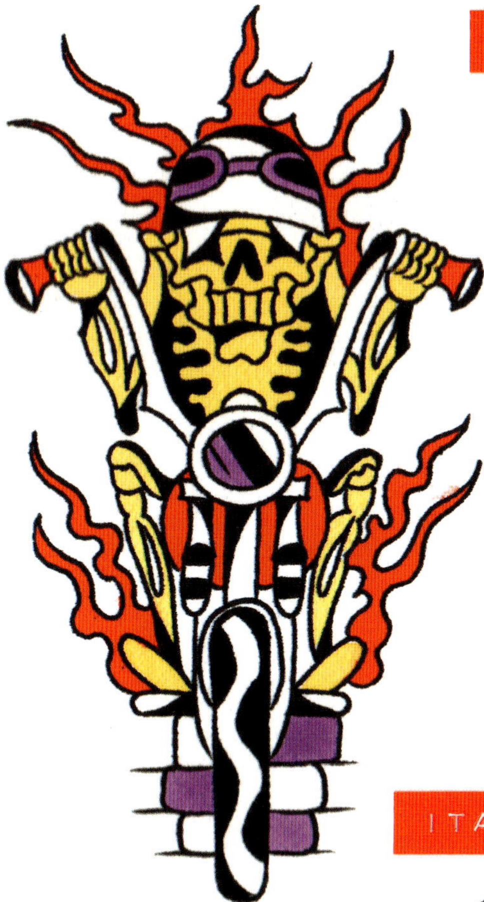

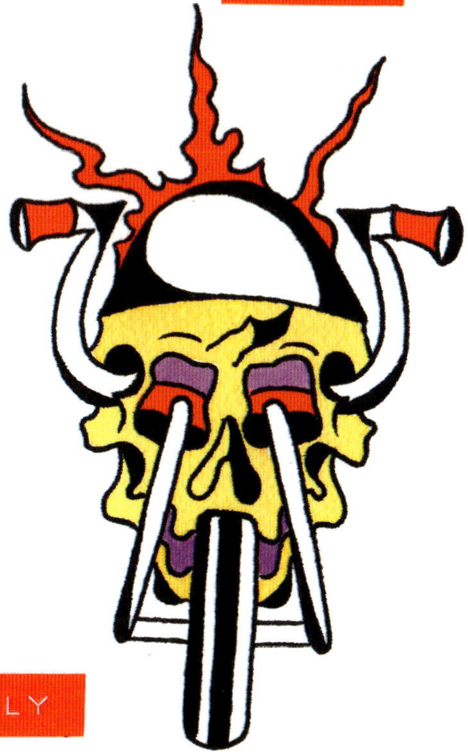

ITALY

BENCH TO LAST

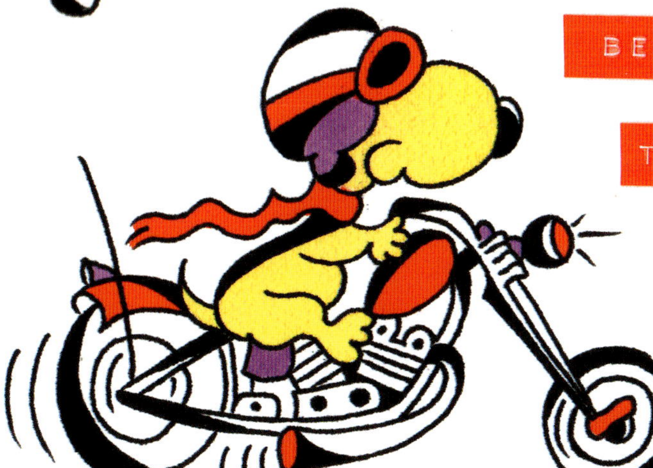

Left
John Stone
@john_stone_tatouage
L'Astrolabe / Dinard / France

Right
Luciano LCN
@luciano_lcn
Black Temple Tattoo Shop / Montpellier / France

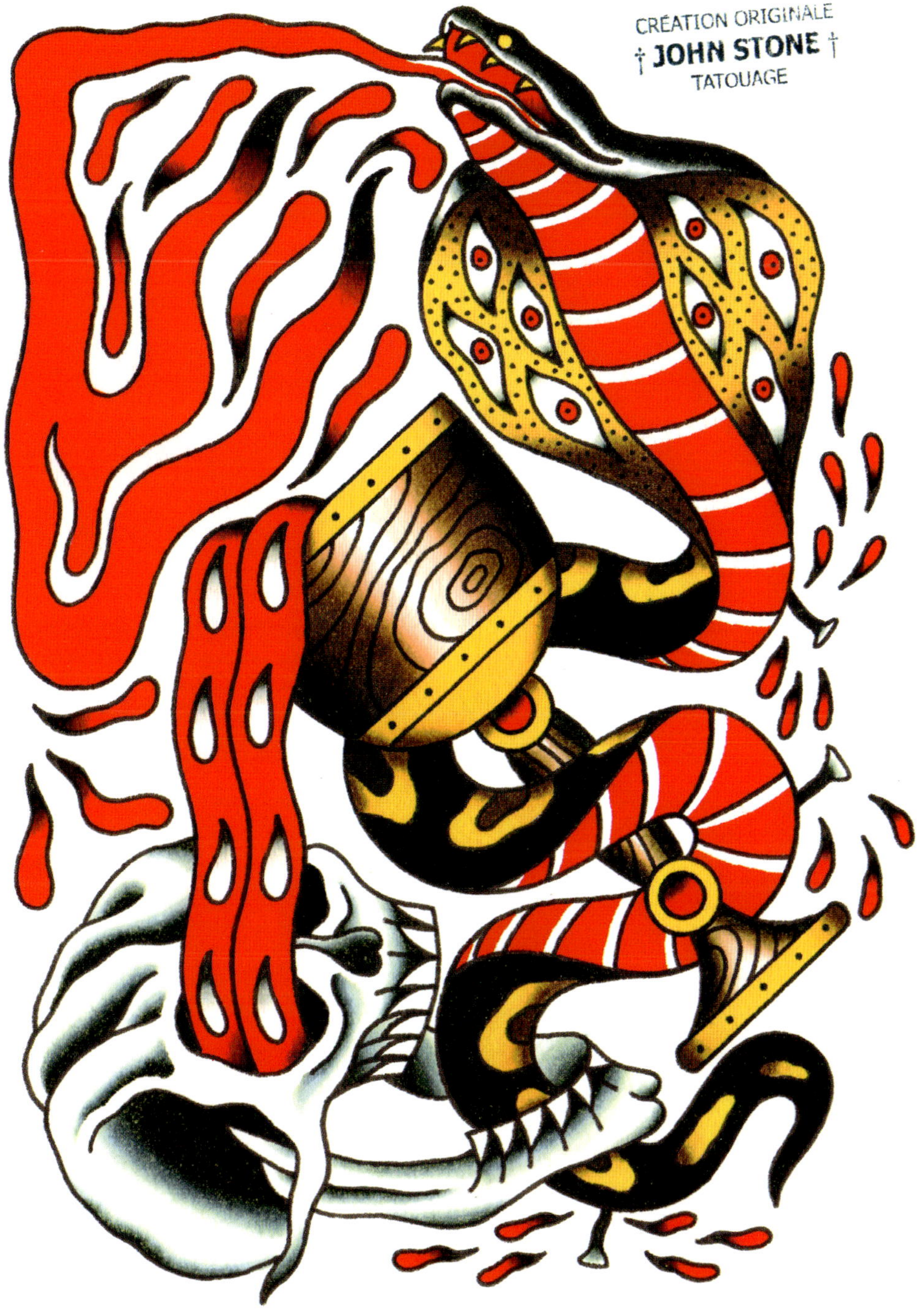
CRÉATION ORIGINALE
† JOHN STONE †
TATOUAGE

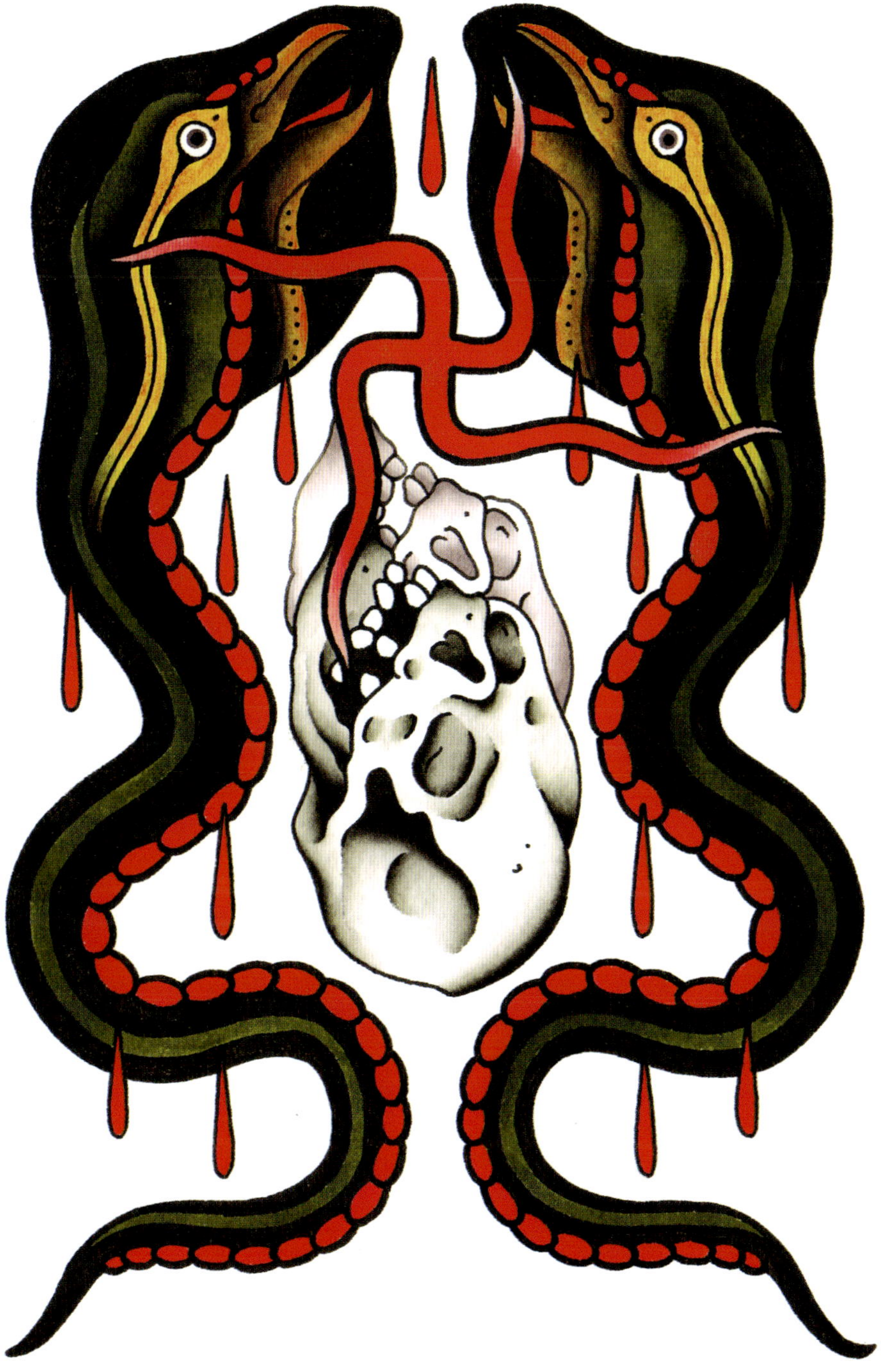

Left
Did-K
@didkvray
Spirit Tattoo Rennes / Rennes / France

Right
Tiwan
@tiwan_tattoo
Spirit Tattoo Rennes / Rennes / France

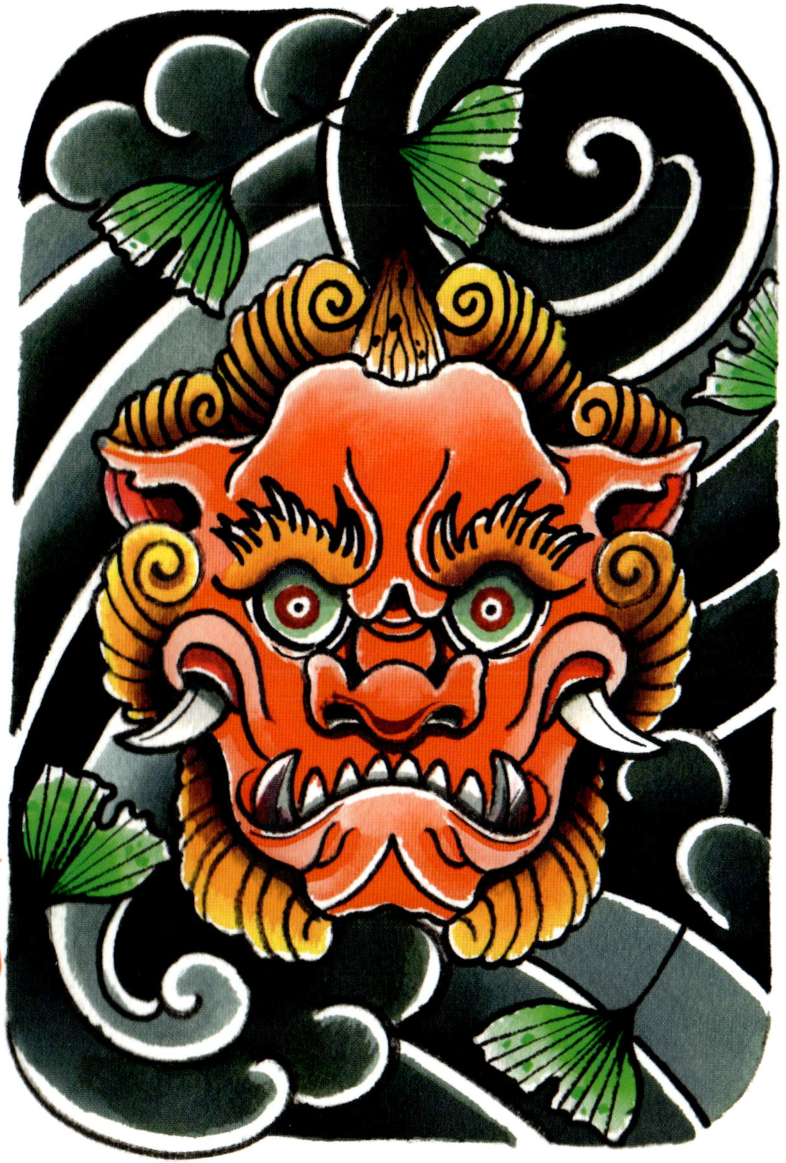

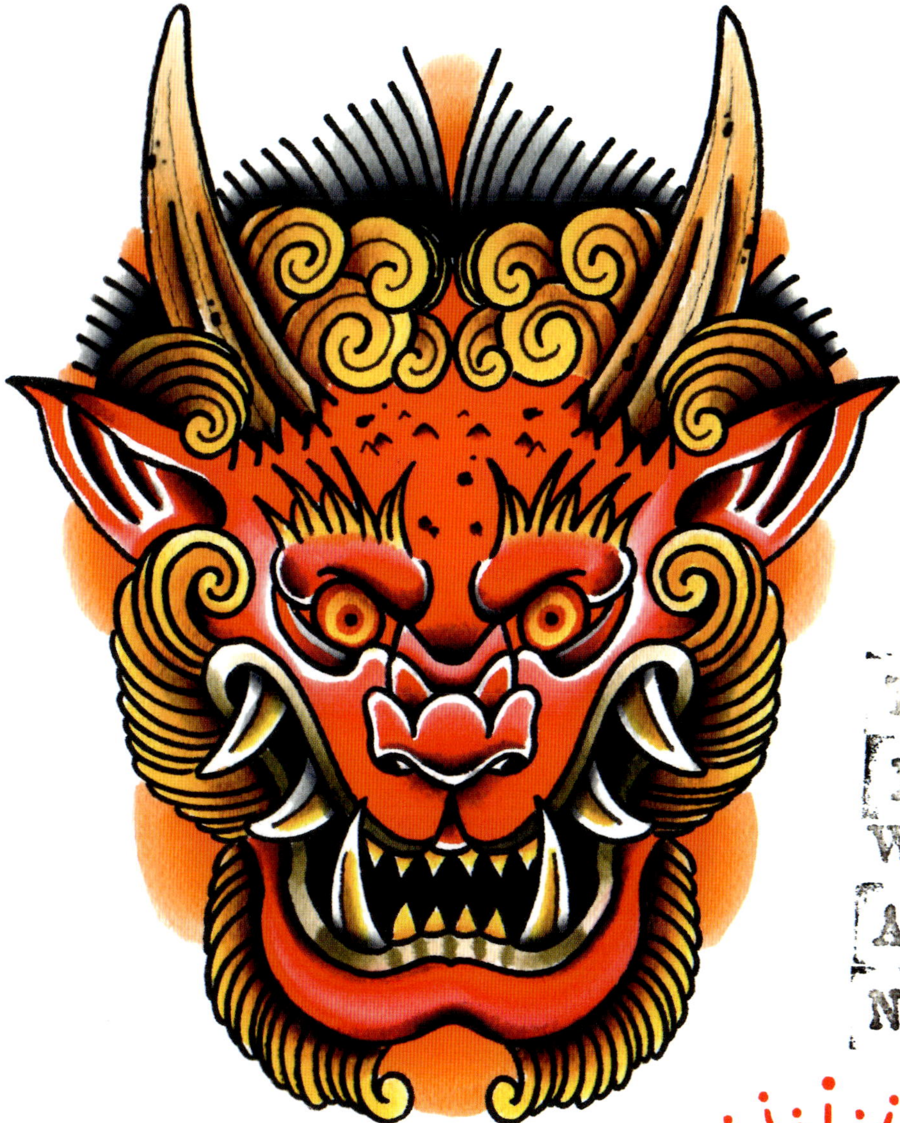

IWAN

Left
Malflore
@malflore
Atelier Triptyque / Montpellier / France

Right
Romain Tattooing
@romaintattooing
Blossom Tattoo Collective / Lyon / France

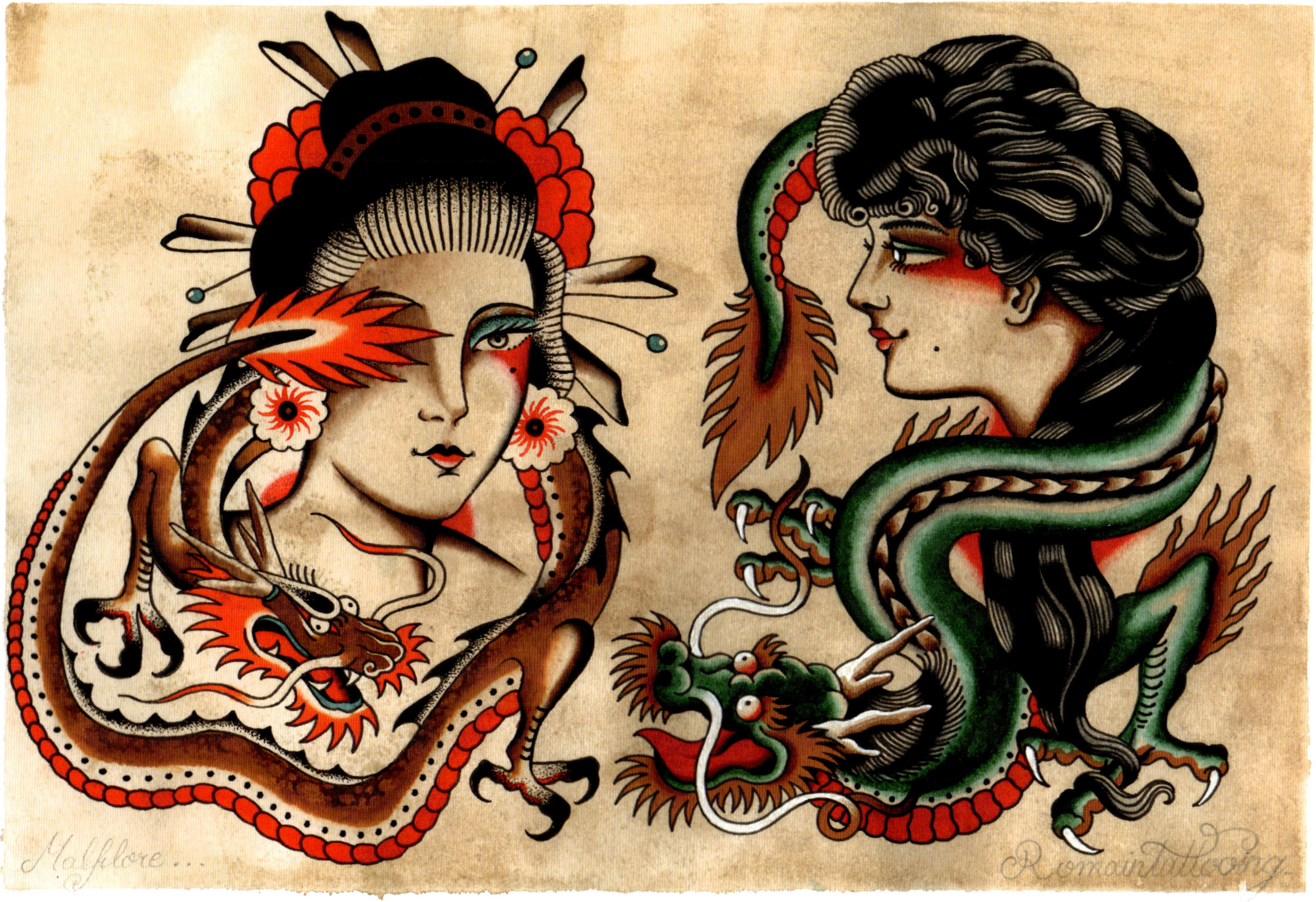
Malfilore...
RomainTattooing.

Left
Iannis Le Tigre
@iannis_letigre
Le Tigre / Annecy / France

Right
John Stone
@john_stone_tatouage
L'Astrolabe / Dinard / France

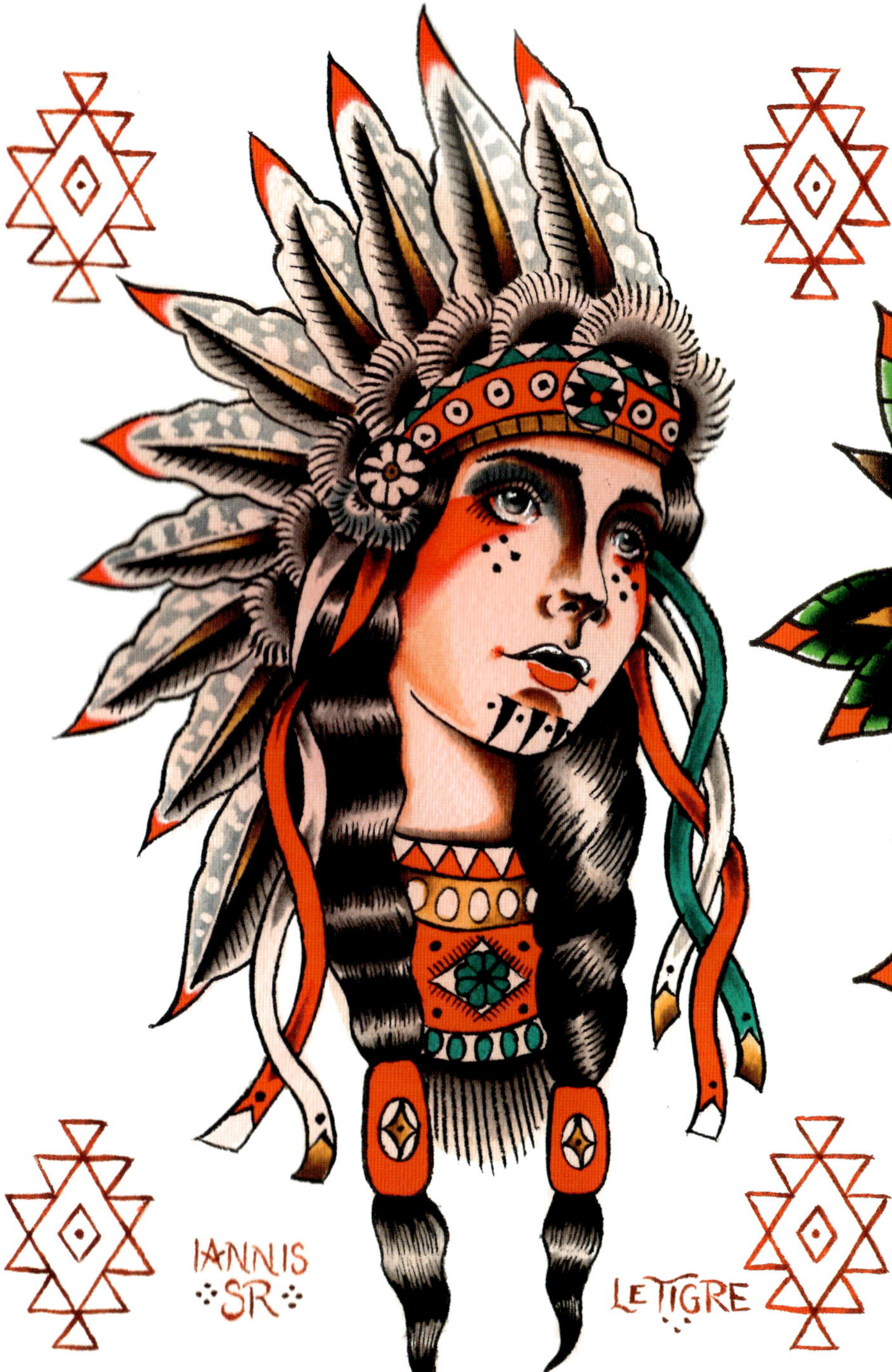
IANNIS
SR
LE TIGRE

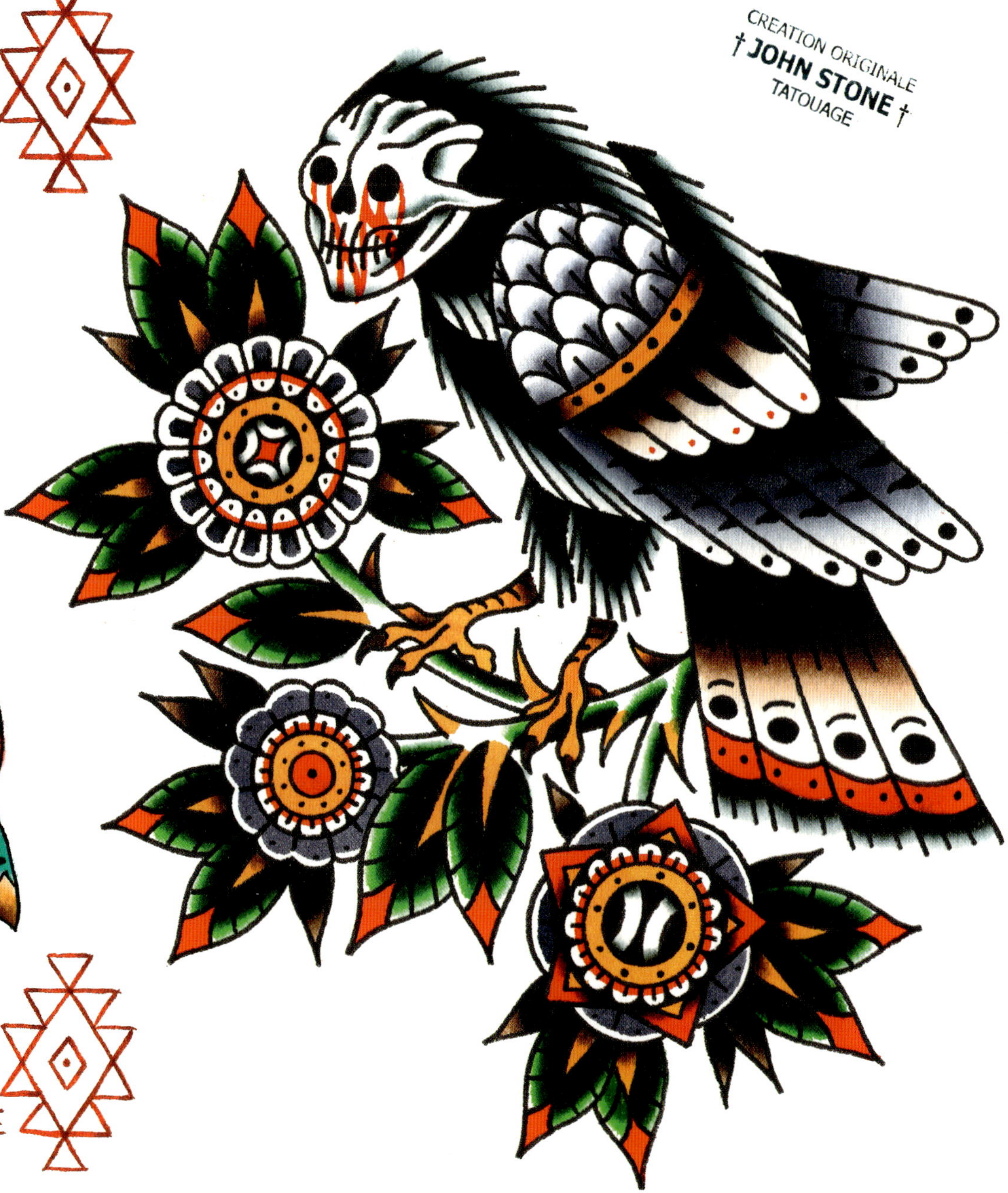
CREATION ORIGINALE
† JOHN STONE †
TATOUAGE

Left
Romain Bonniez
@romainbonniez
Norse Wolf Tattoo / Allos / France

Right
Dorian Blind
@dorianblind_tattoo
La Canne Blanche / Bordeaux / France

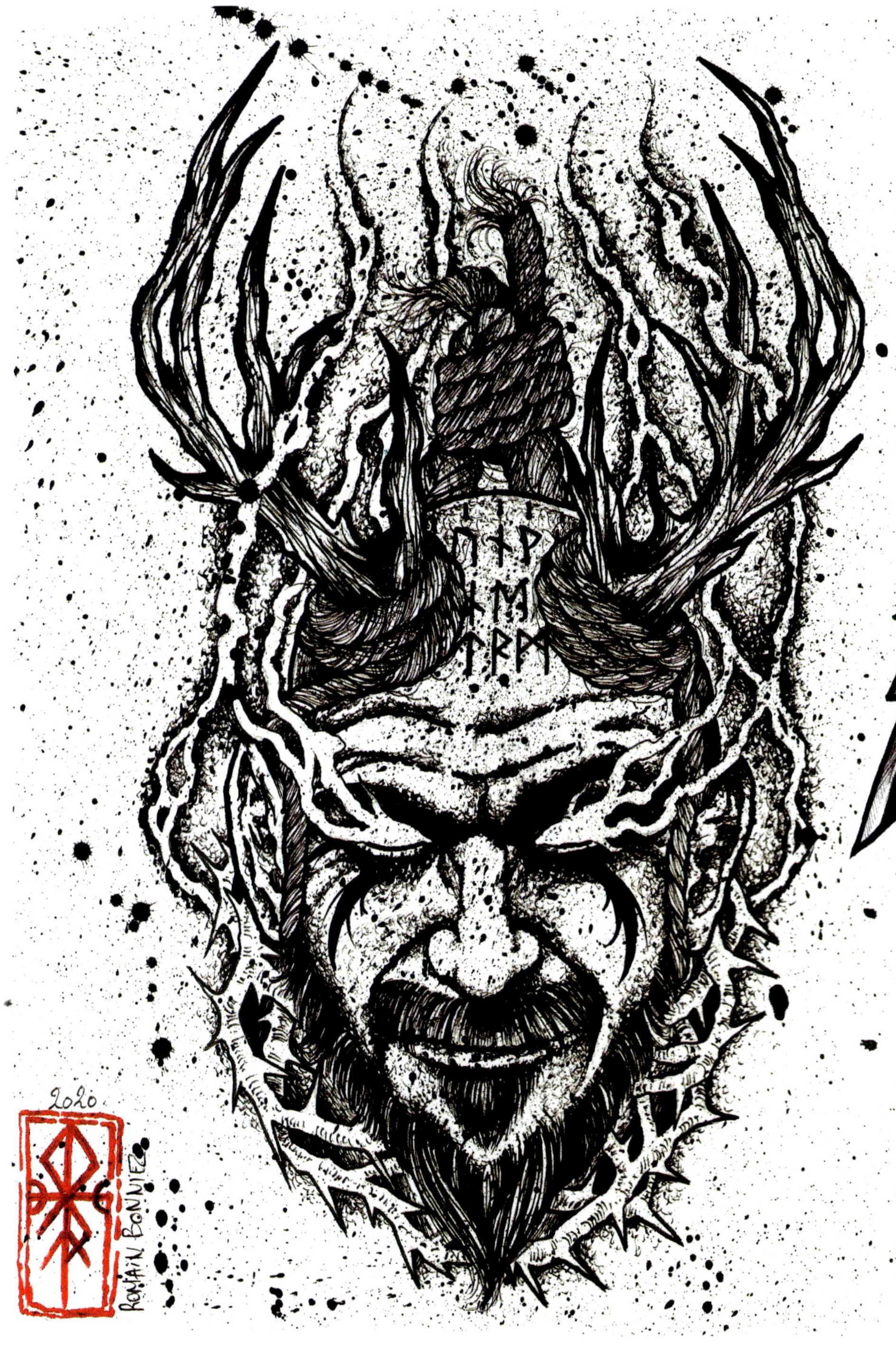
2020
ROMAIN BONNIER

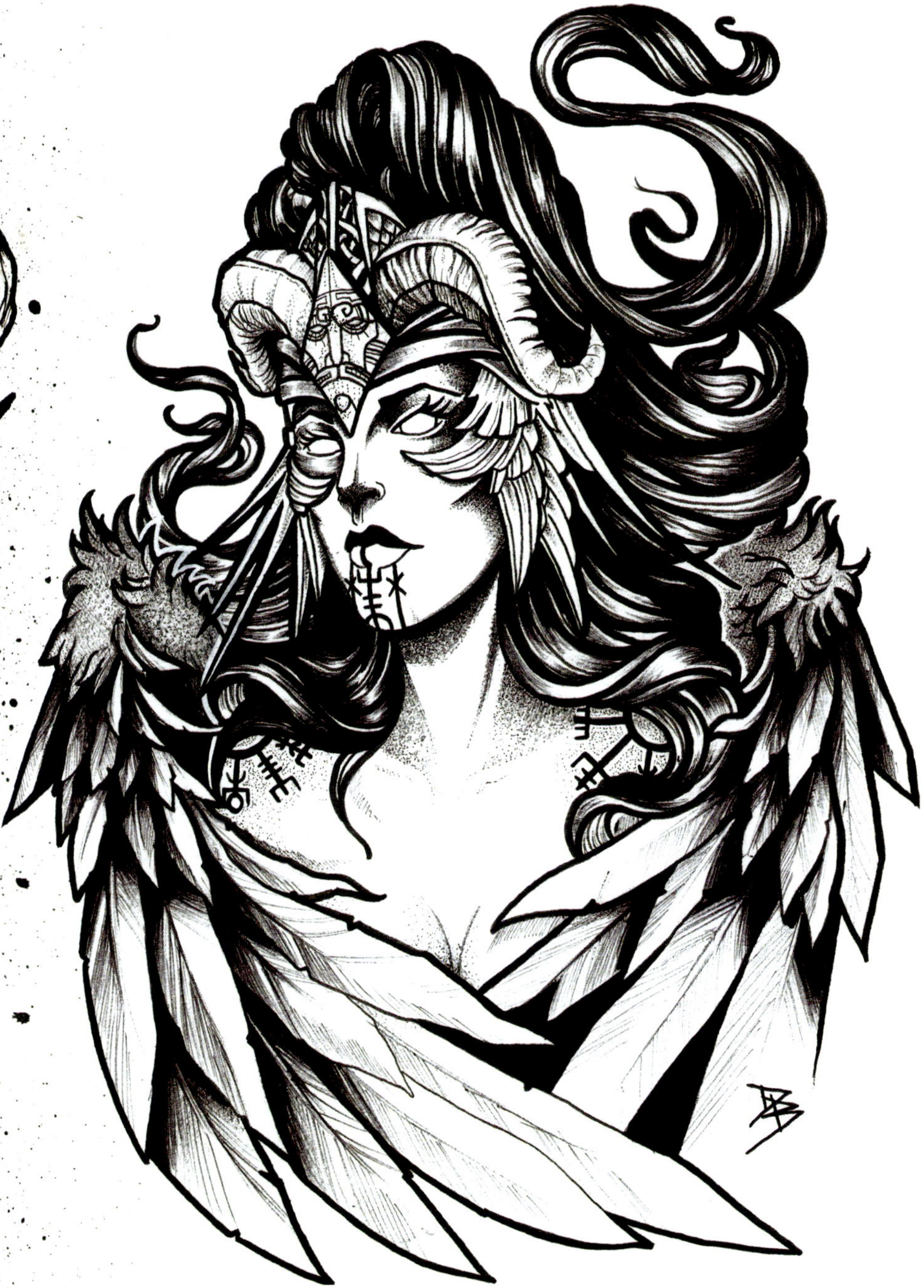

Left
Lorlor
@lorlor_bonne_aventure
Bonne Aventure / Grenoble / France

Right
Odrëy Bonne Aventure
@odrey_bonne_aventure
Bonne Aventure / Grenoble / France

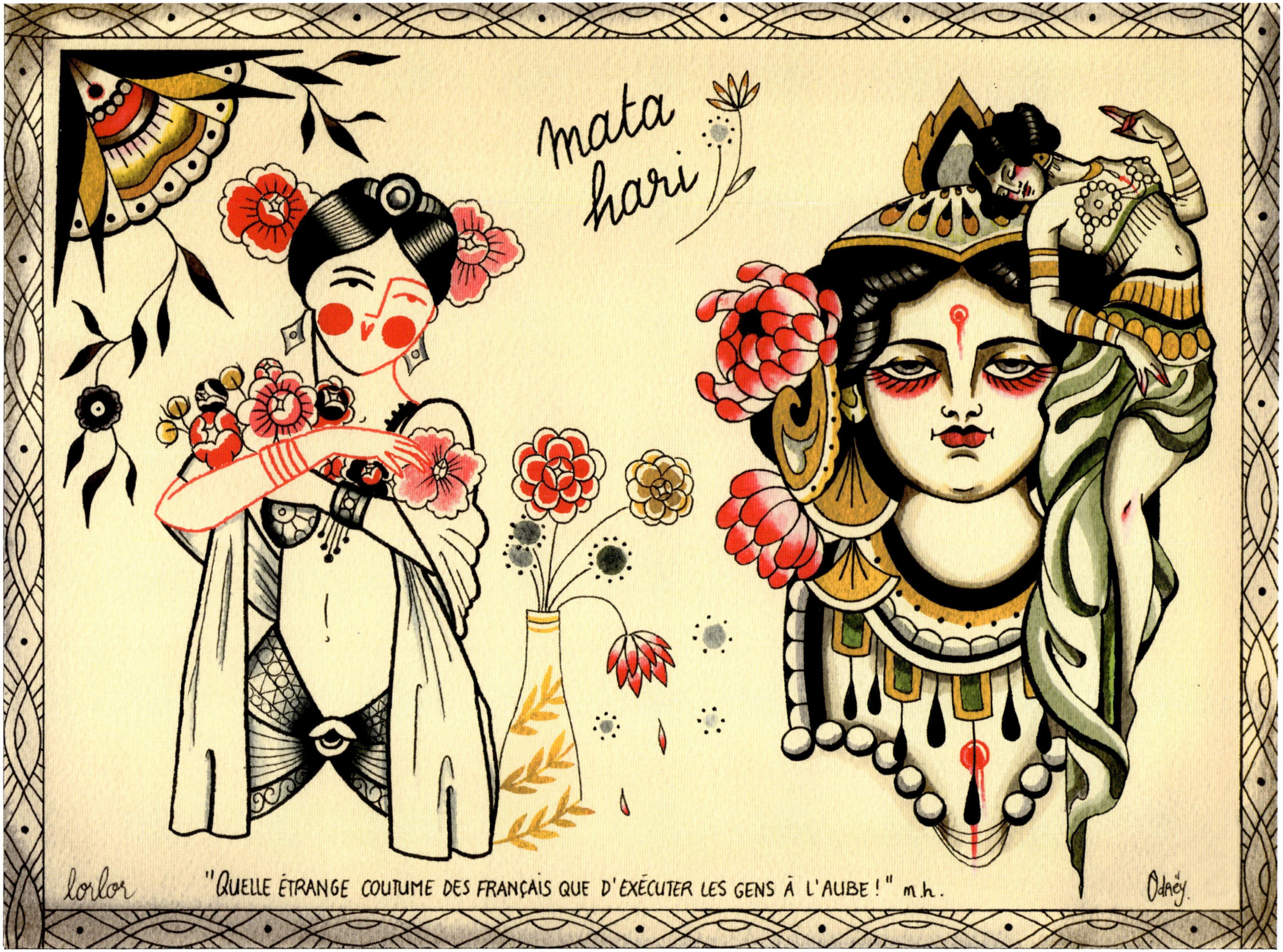
mata
hari
lorlor
"QUELLE ÉTRANGE COUTUME DES FRANÇAIS QUE D'EXÉCUTER LES GENS À L'AUBE !" m.h.
Odaëy.

Left
Toy-Arthur
@toy_arthur_tatouage
FTC Bordeaux / Bordeaux / France

Right
Julien Brunier
@julien.brunier
French Tattoo Connection / Marseille / France

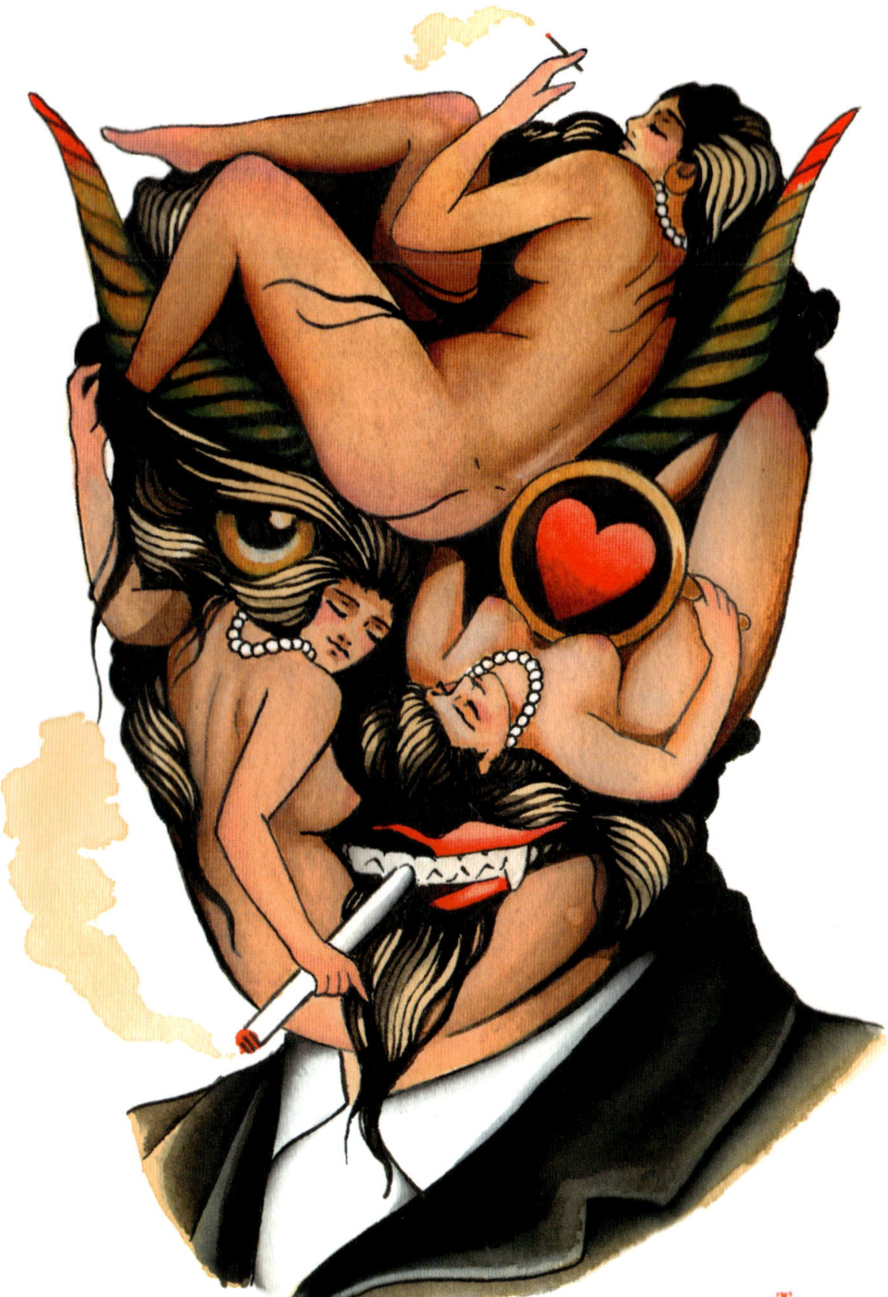

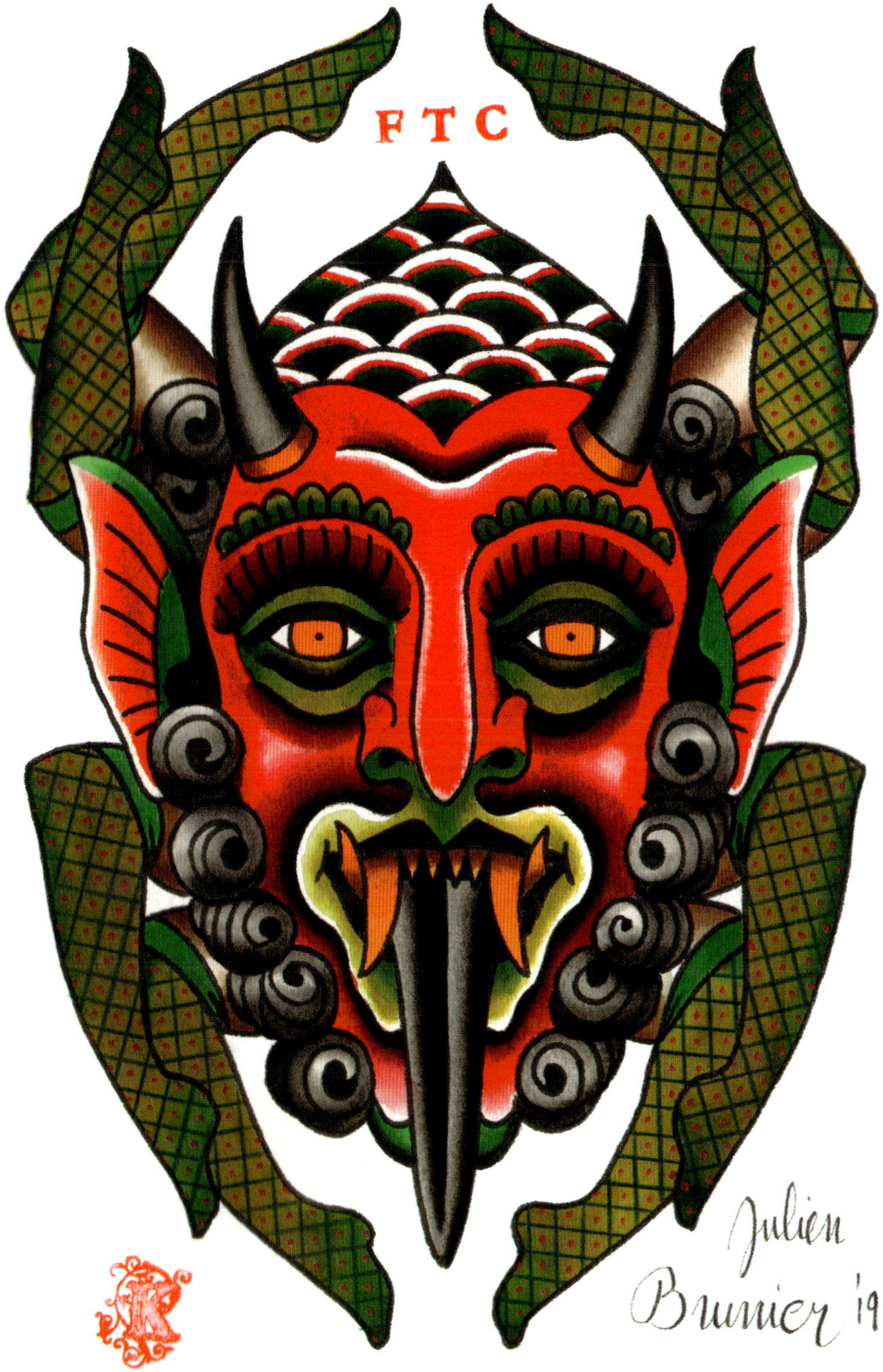
FTC
Julien
Brunier '19

Left
John Stone
@john_stone_tatouage
L'Astrolabe / Dinard / France

Right
Geoff Horn
@geoffhorn_soos
Hole In The Sky Tattoo / Woodland Park / New Jersey / USA

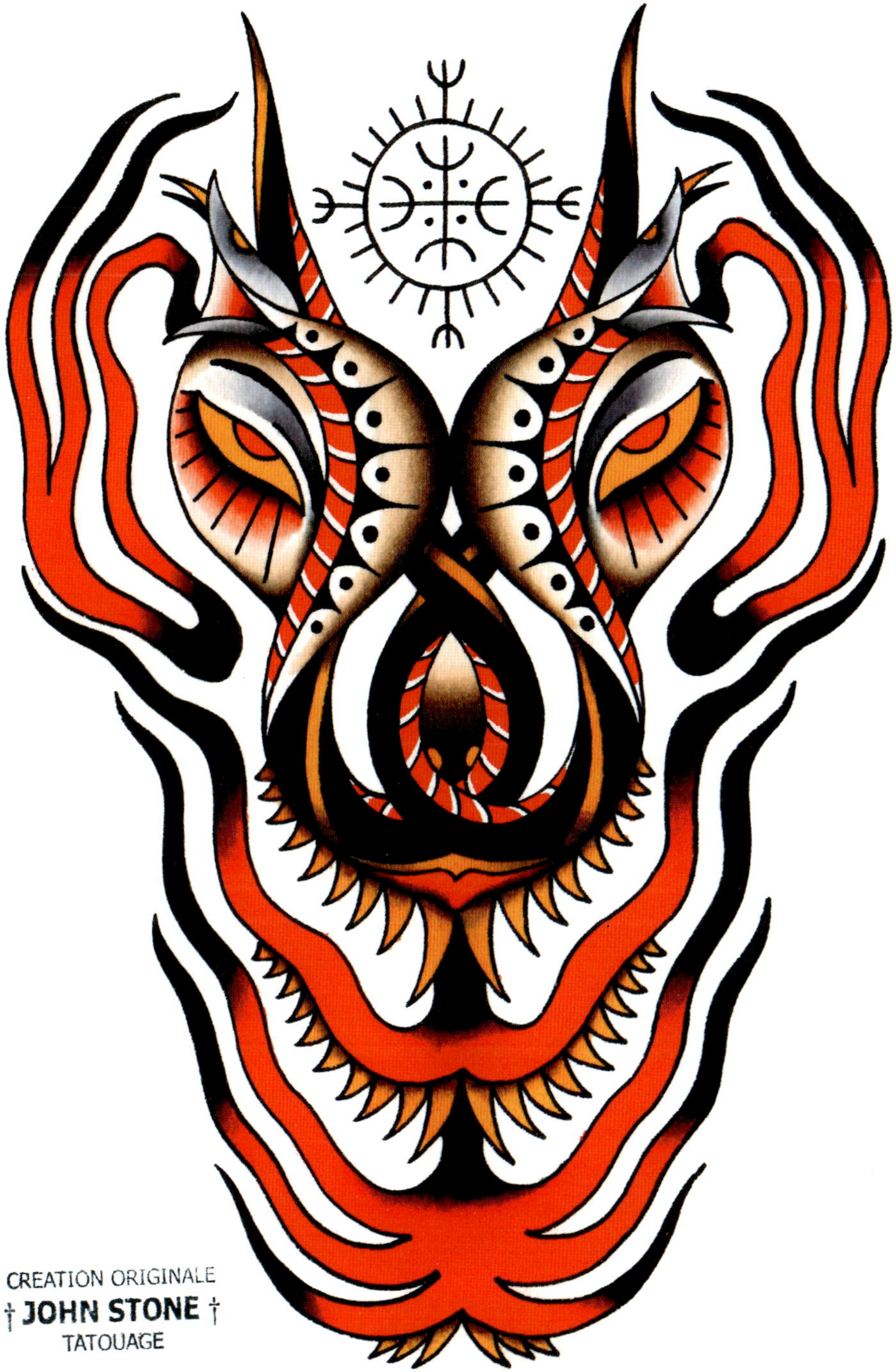
CREATION ORIGINALE
† JOHN STONE †
TATOUAGE

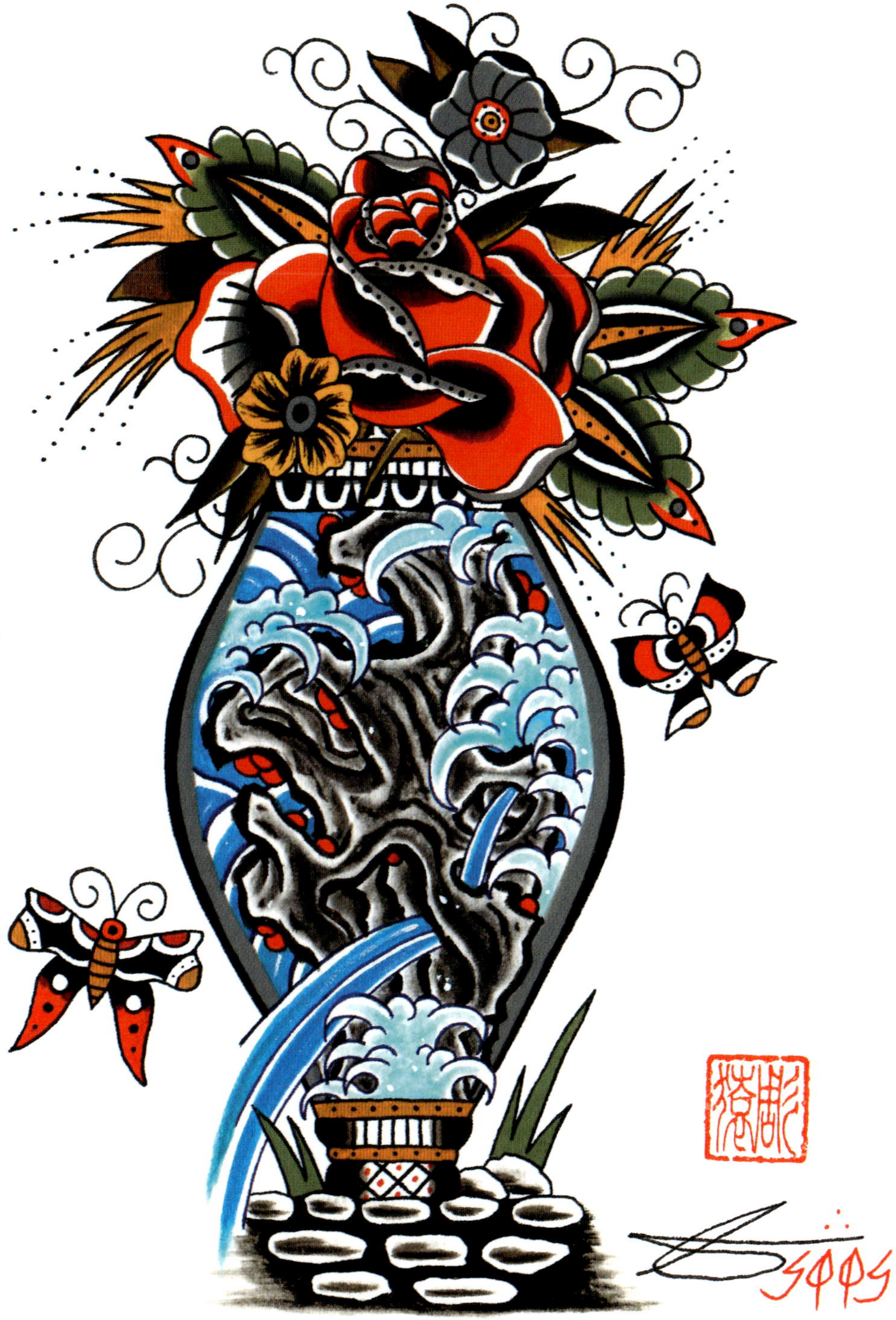

Left
Uncle Ho
@uncle_ho_mitchmalone
Iron Claw / Strasbourg / France

Right
The Shok Oner
@the_shok_oner
Strasbourg / France

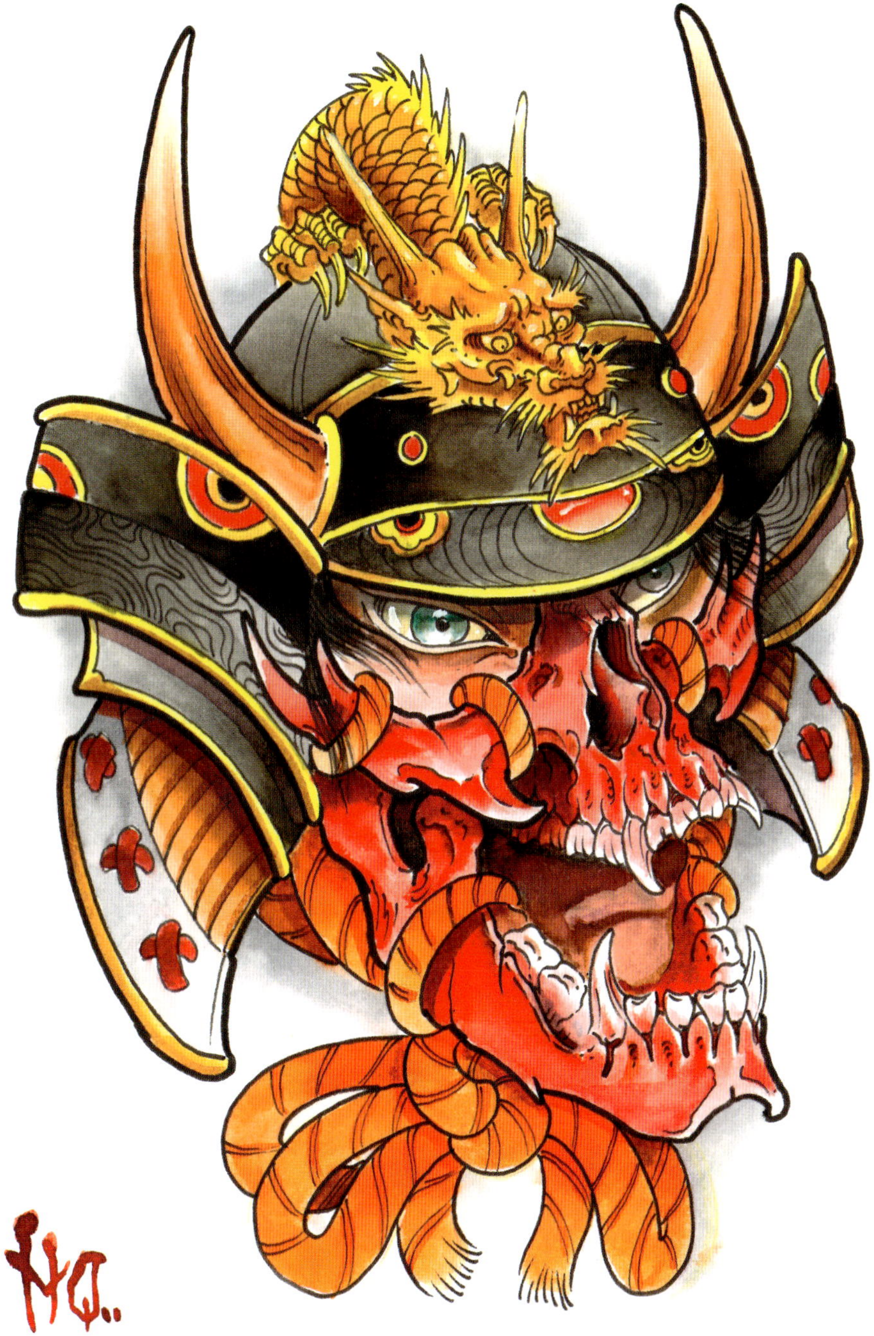

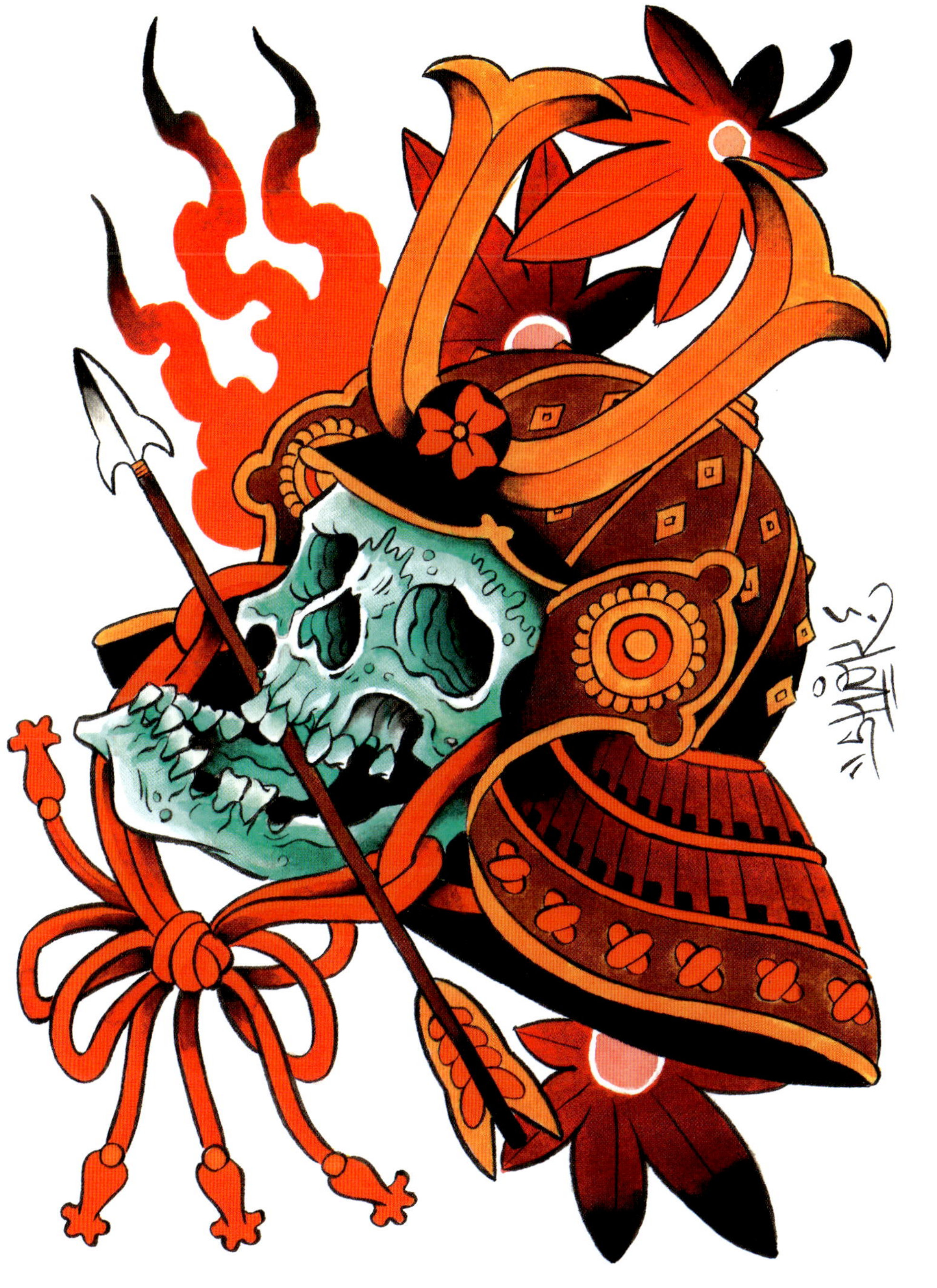

Left and upper center
Josh Dee
@joshdeetattoo
Black Ship Tattoo / Namur / Belgium

Right and bottom center
Max Dem
@maxdemtattoo
Glorybound Tattoo / Antwerp / Belgium

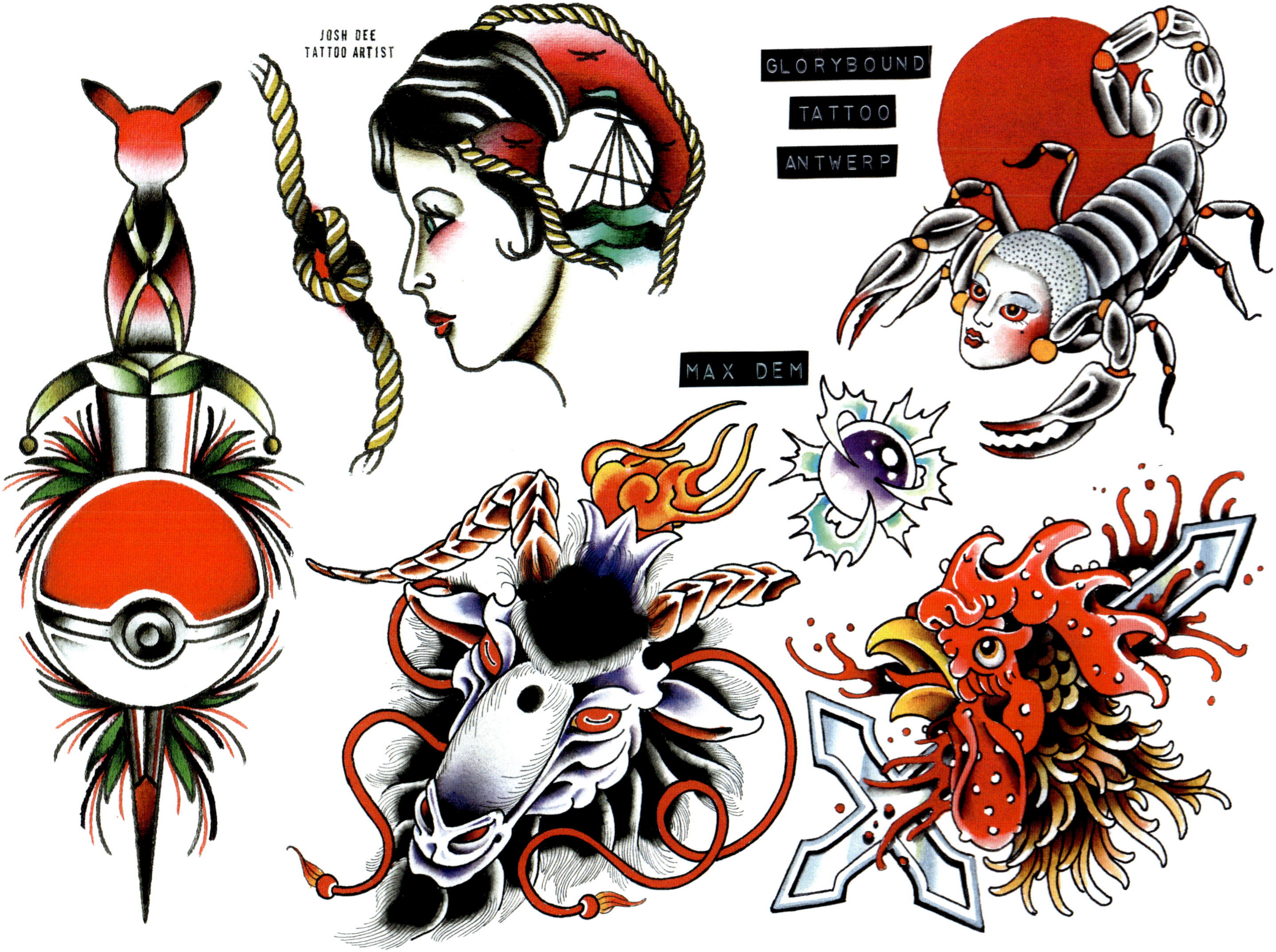
JOSH DEE
TATTOO ARTIST
GLORYBOUND
TATTOO
ANTWERP
MAX DEM

Left
El Bent
@elbenttattoo
True Love / Paris / France

Right
Polo Tattooer
@polotattooer_tgp
The Good Place Tattoo / Toulouse / France

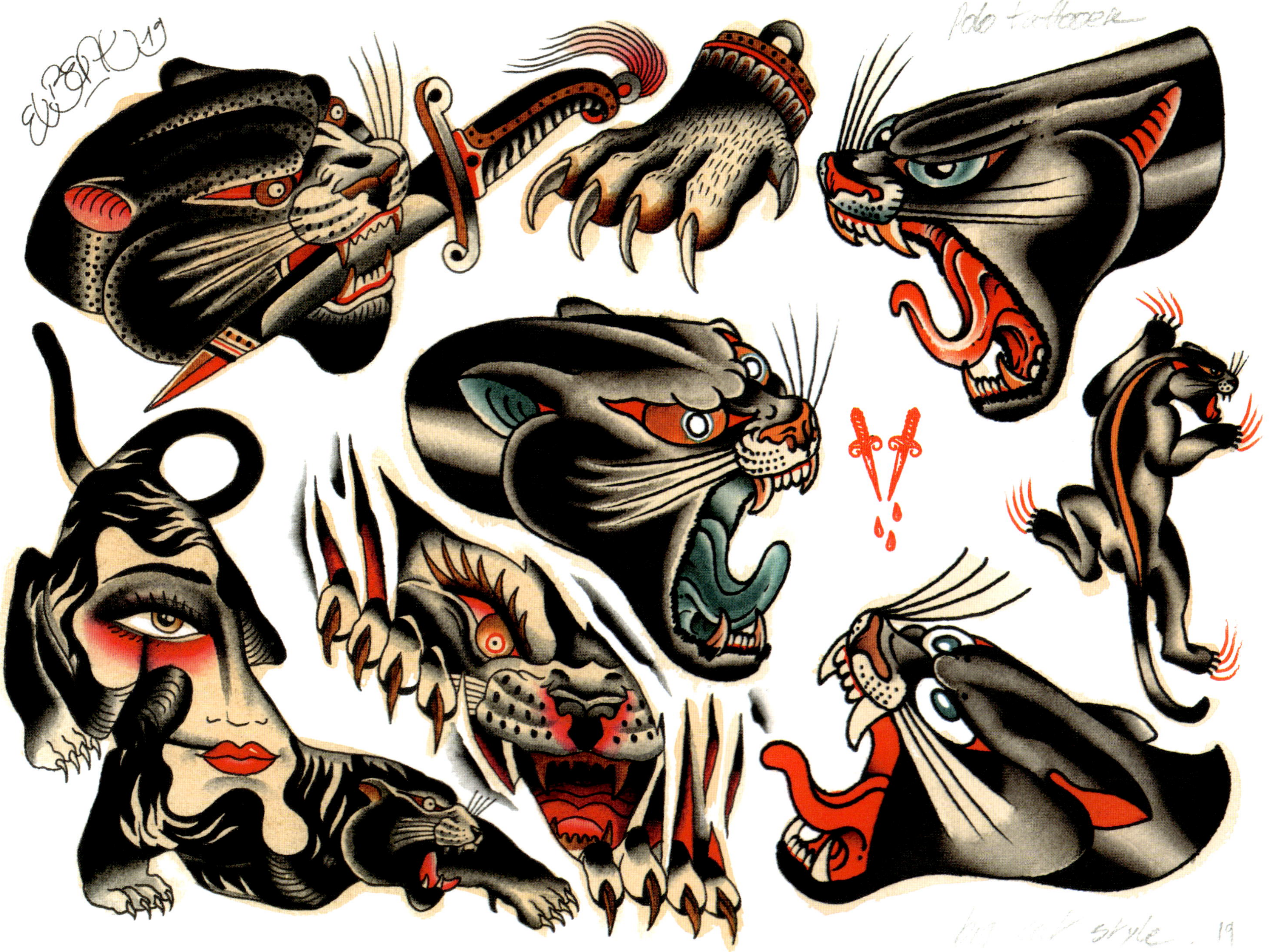
Polo tattooer

Left
Jesus Double Deuce Tattoo
@jesus_double_deuce_tattoo
The Road / Surgères / France

Right
Fat Manu de Tours
@fatmanu_tattoo_de_tours
Coco Bongo Tattoo Club / Tours / France

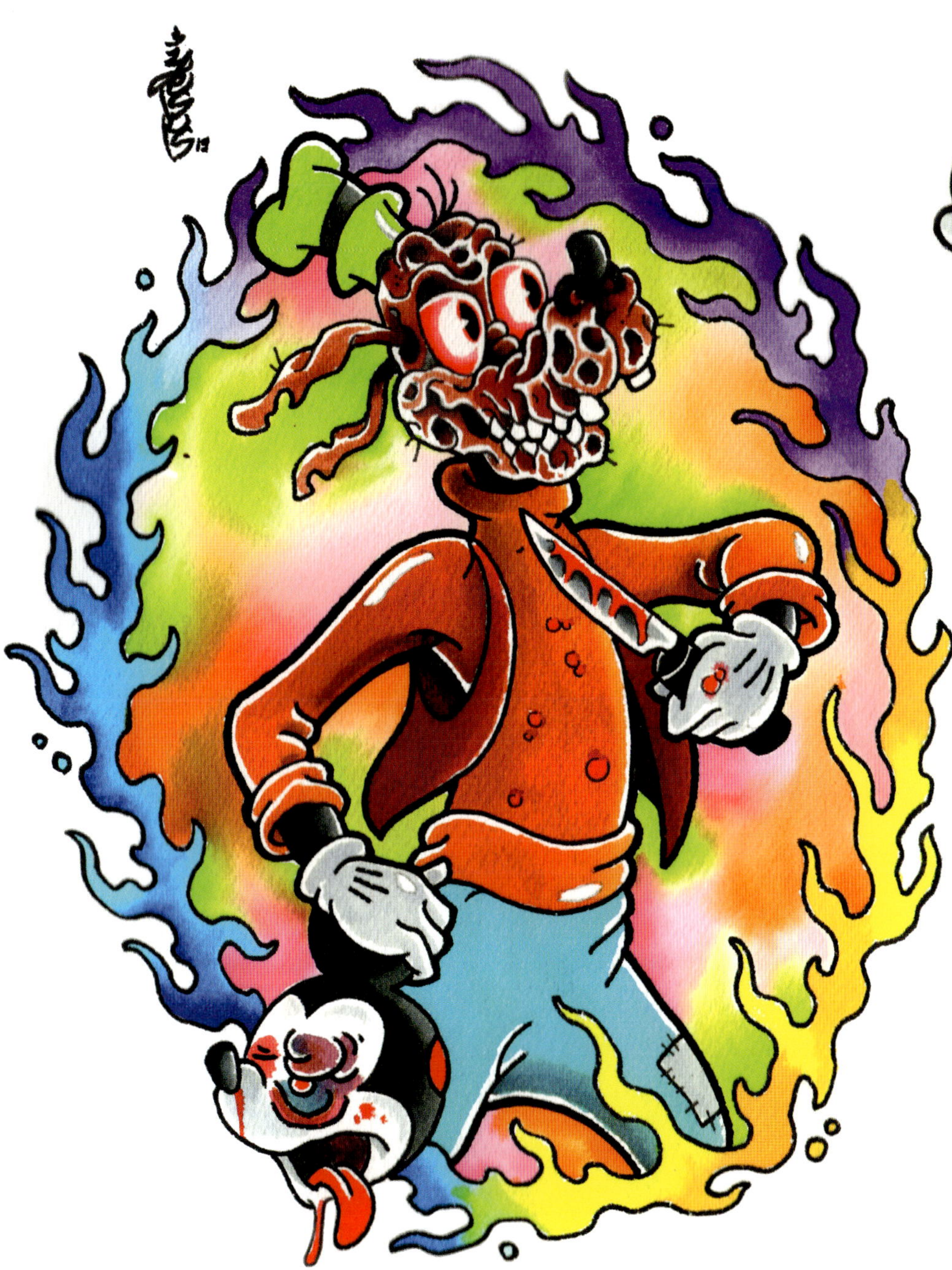

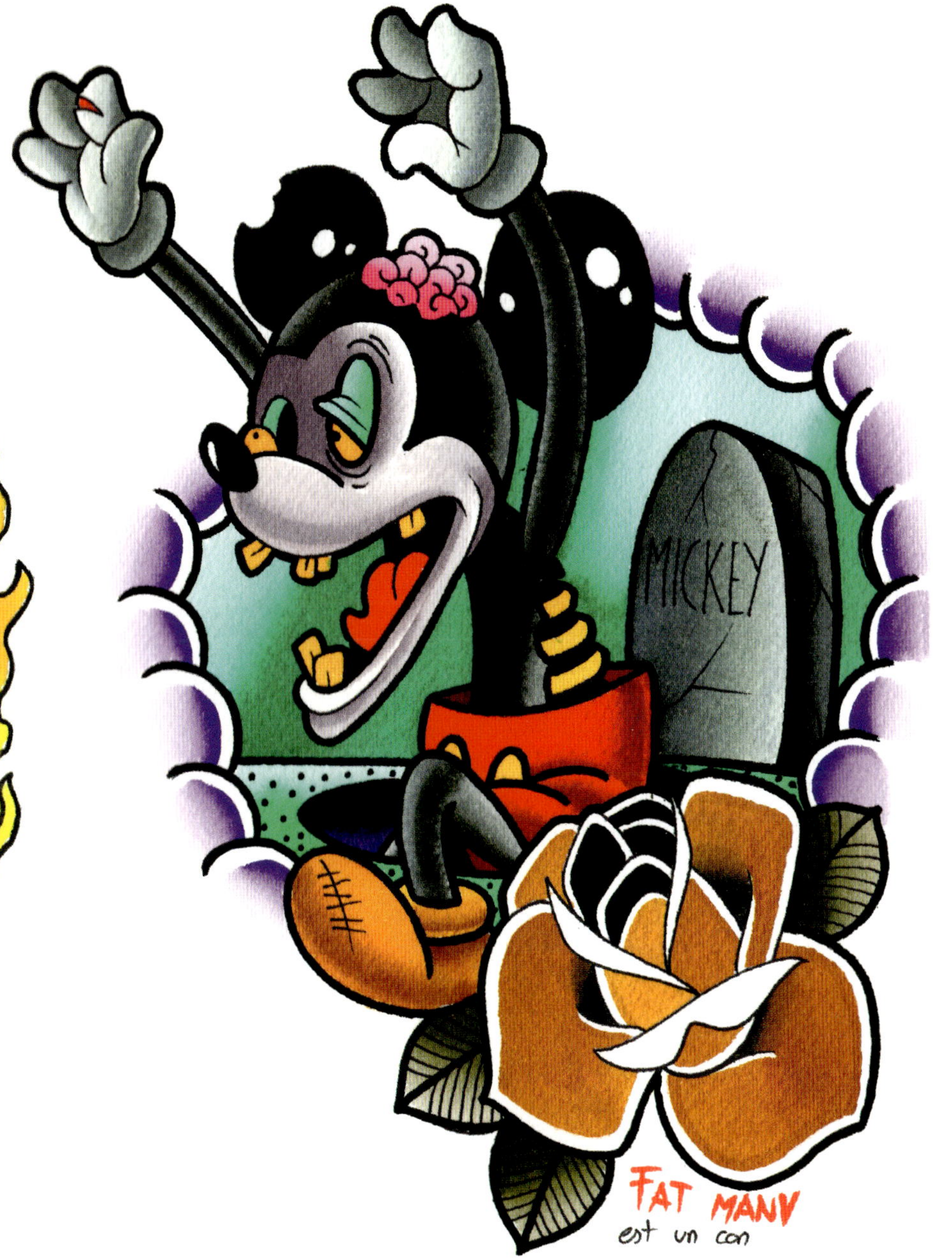
MICKEY
FAT MANU
est un con

Left
Thibaud Rock'a
@thibaud_rcka
BSA Tattoo / Aix-en-Provence / France

Right
Raphaël Masin
@raphael_masin
Ultra Combo Tattoo Club / Aix-en-Provence / France

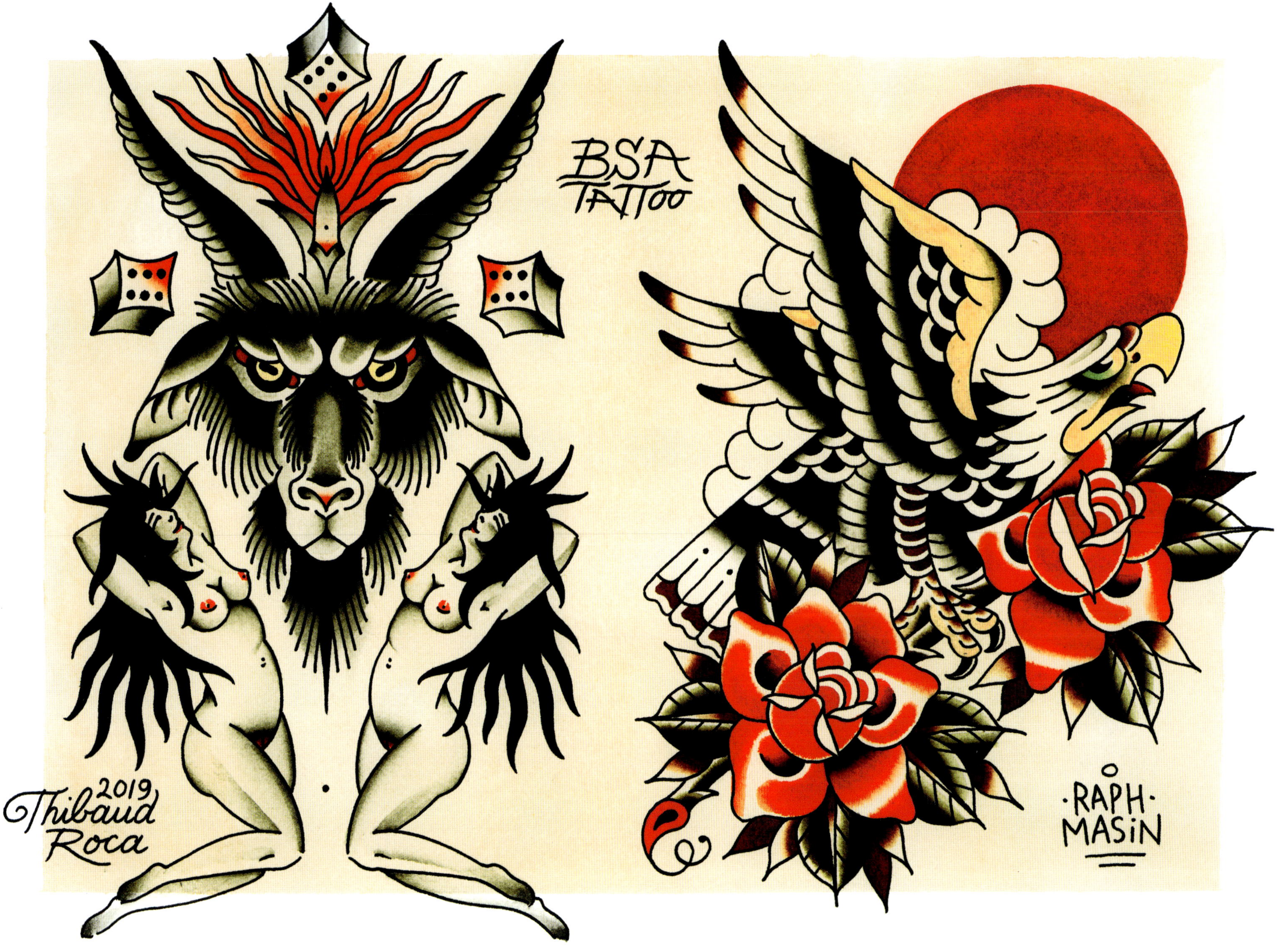
BSA
TATTOO
2019
Thibaud
Roca
RAPH
MASIN

Left
Mosh
@moshtattooer
La Famille Tattoo Club / Grenoble / France

Right
Uncle Ho
@uncle_ho_mitchmalone
Iron Claw / Strasbourg / France

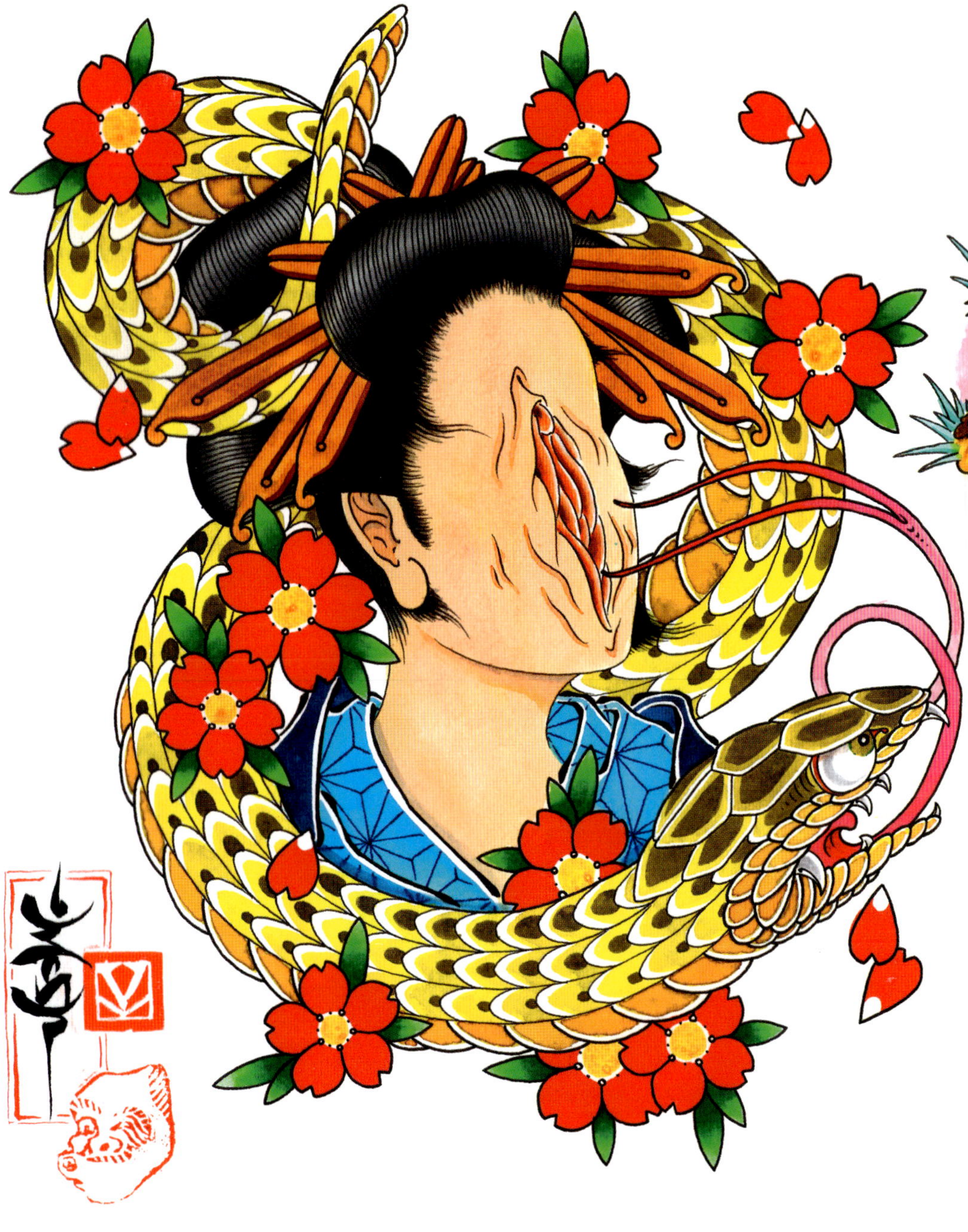

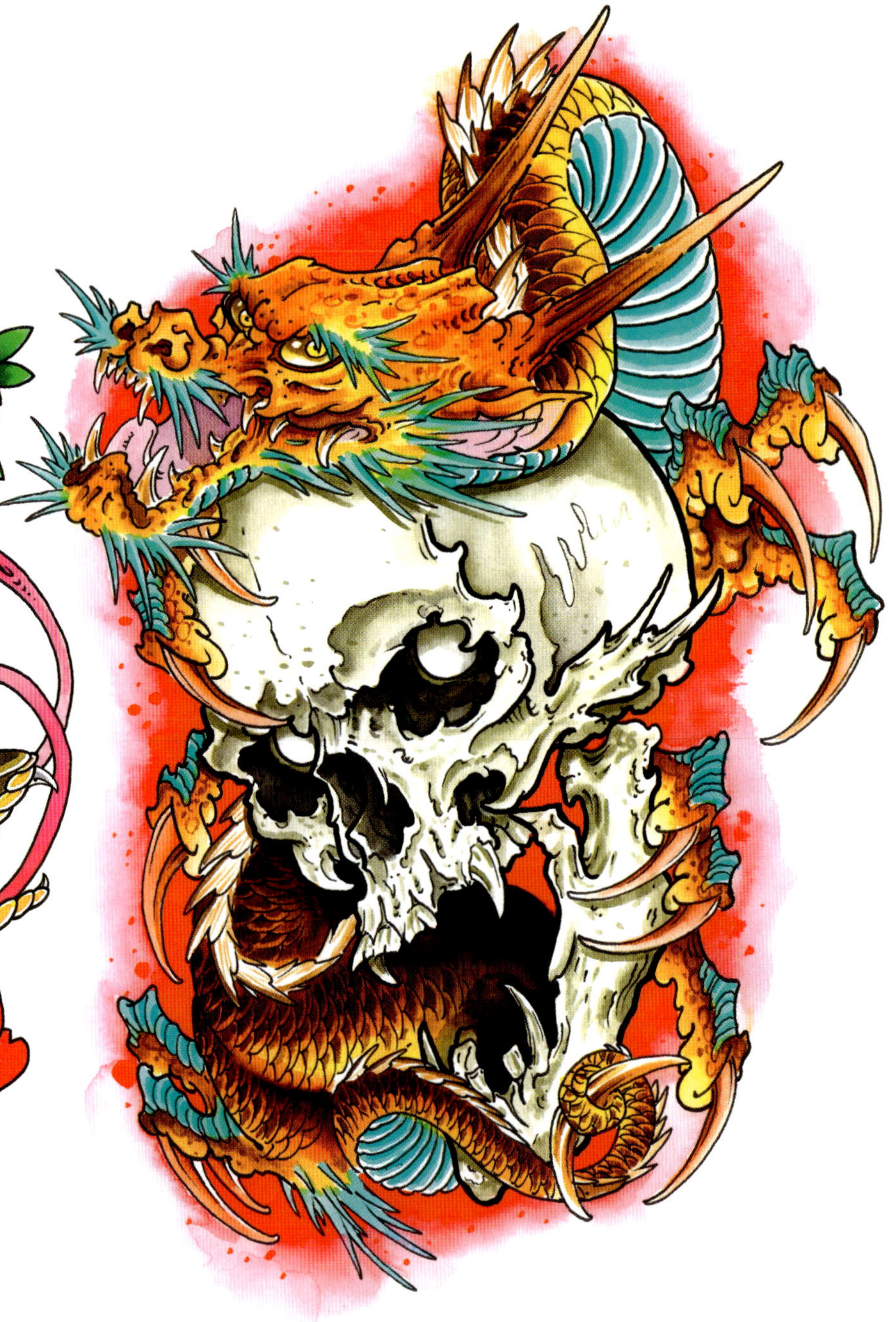

Left
Ju l'Indien
@ju_lindien
Velvet Studio / Grenoble / France

Right
Brice Solana
@bricesolana
Velvet Studio / Grenoble / France

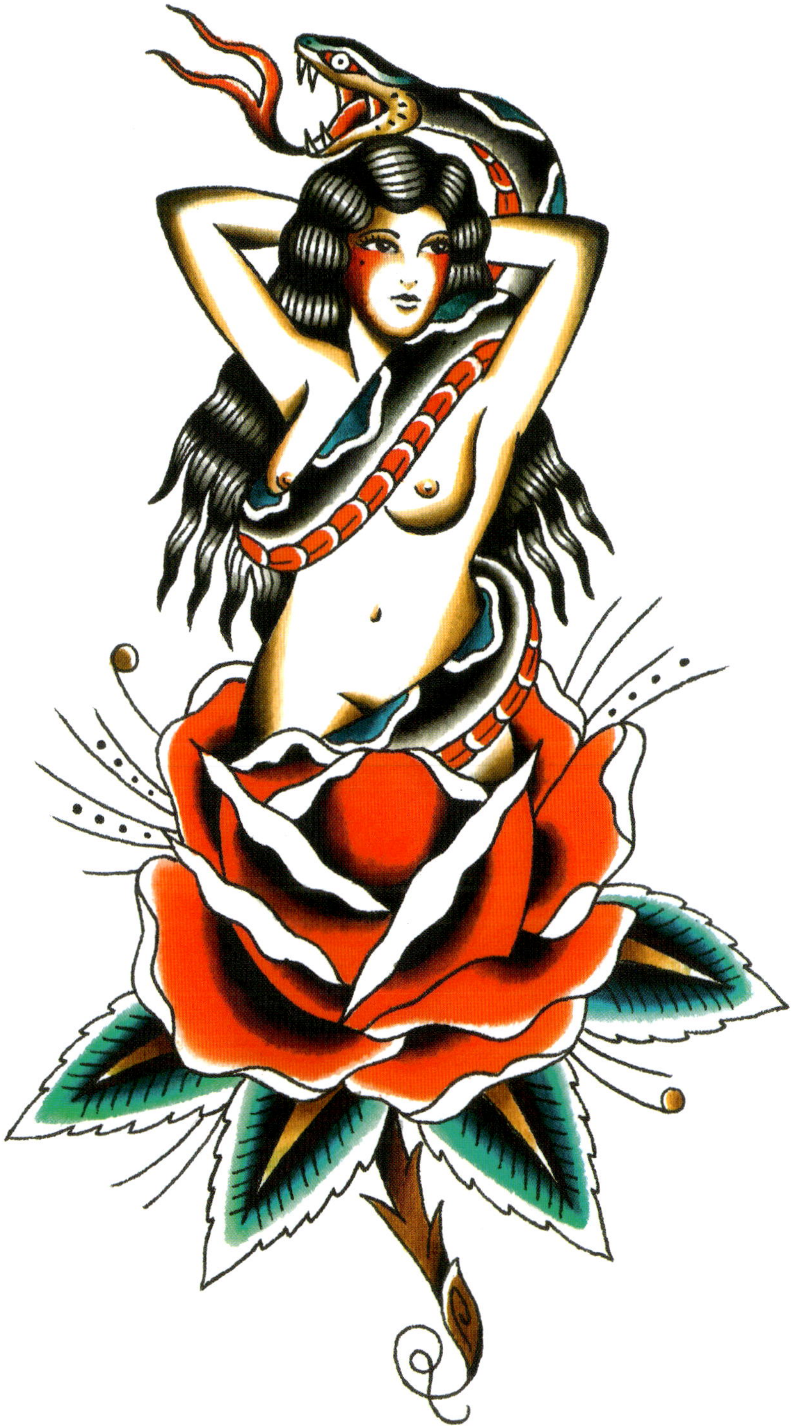

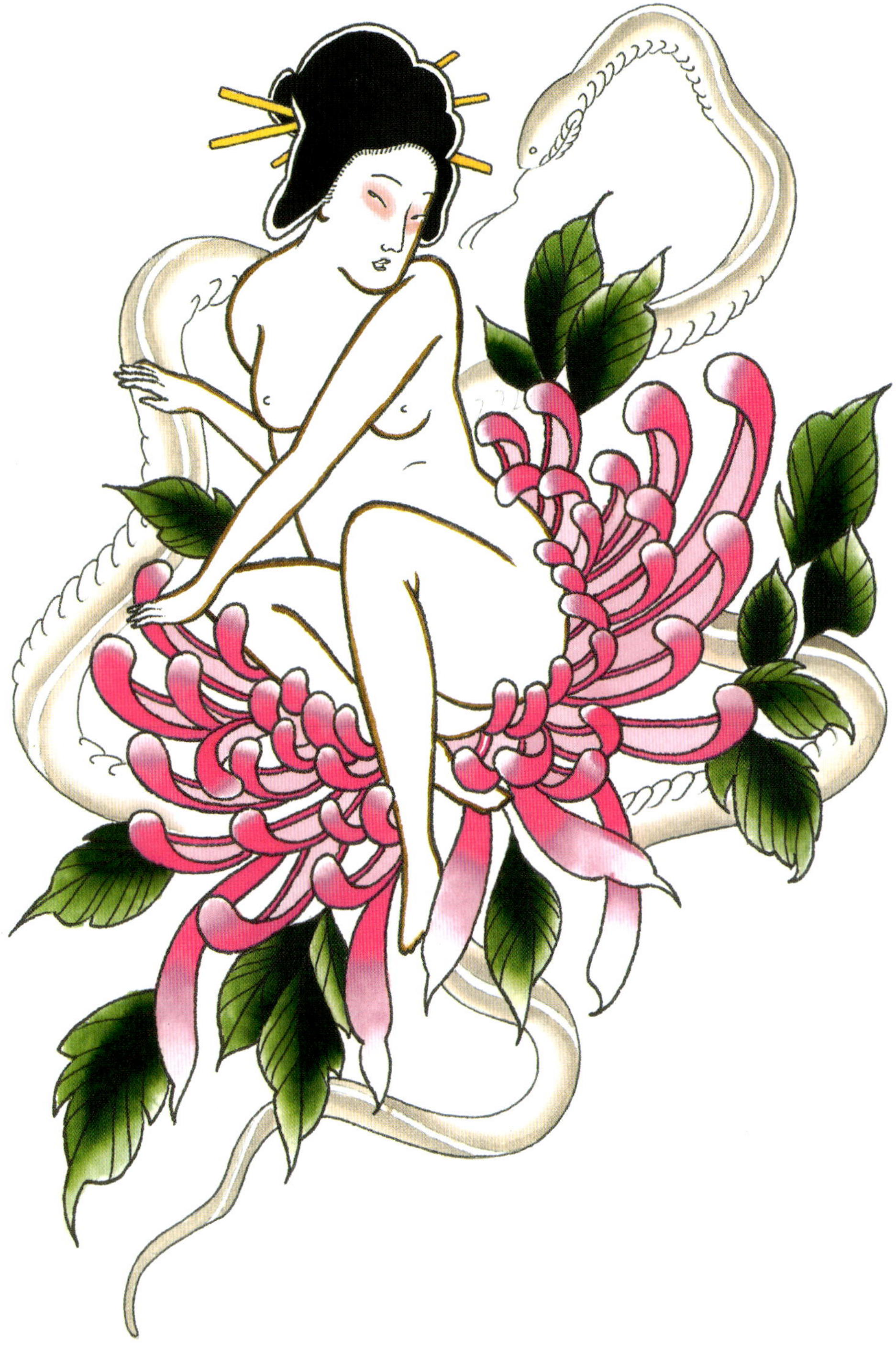

Left
Komar Inkshot
@komarinkshot Café Ink / Le Havre / France

Right
Alice Rigal
@alicetattooer
Matière noire / Paris / France

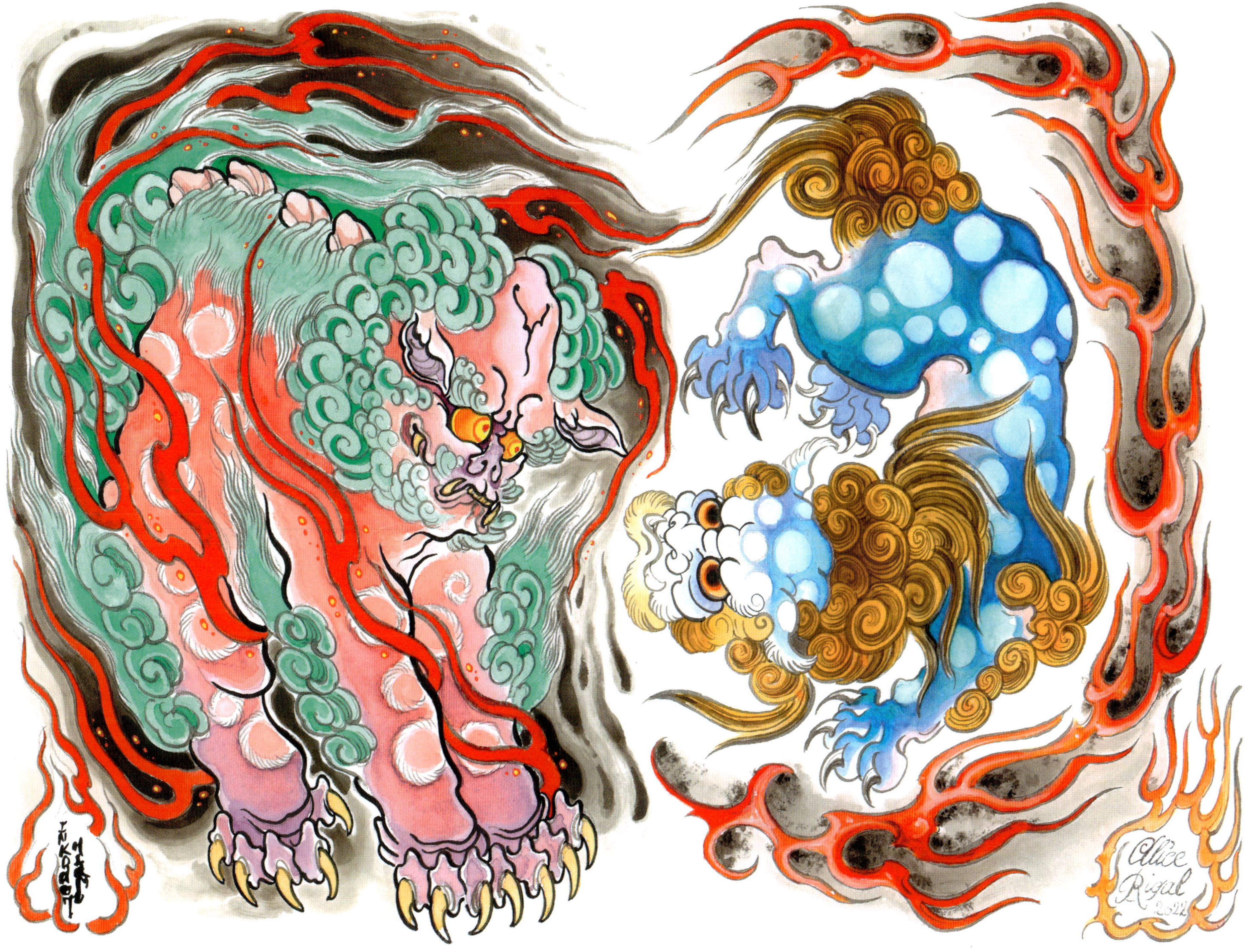
Alice
Rigal
2022

Left
Cris Levil
@cris_le_vil
On the road / France

Right
Yan Lowbrow
@yanlowbrow
Lowbrow / Montpellier / France

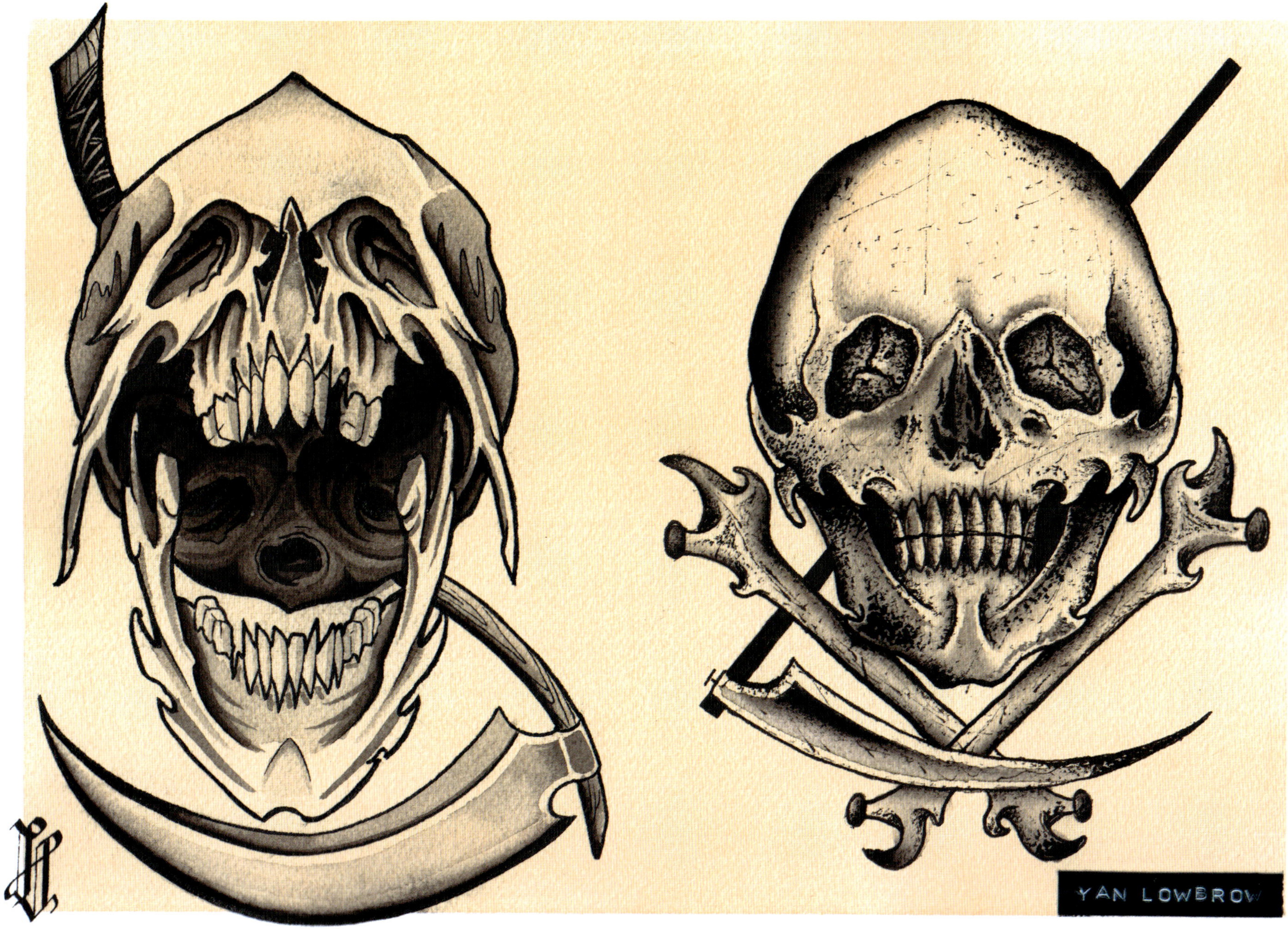

YAN LOWBROW

Left
Monti
@monti_tattooer
Black Door Tattoo / Besançon / France

Right
Loïc Mesot LMT
@loicmesotlmt
LM Tattoo Street Shop / Saint-Mihiel / France

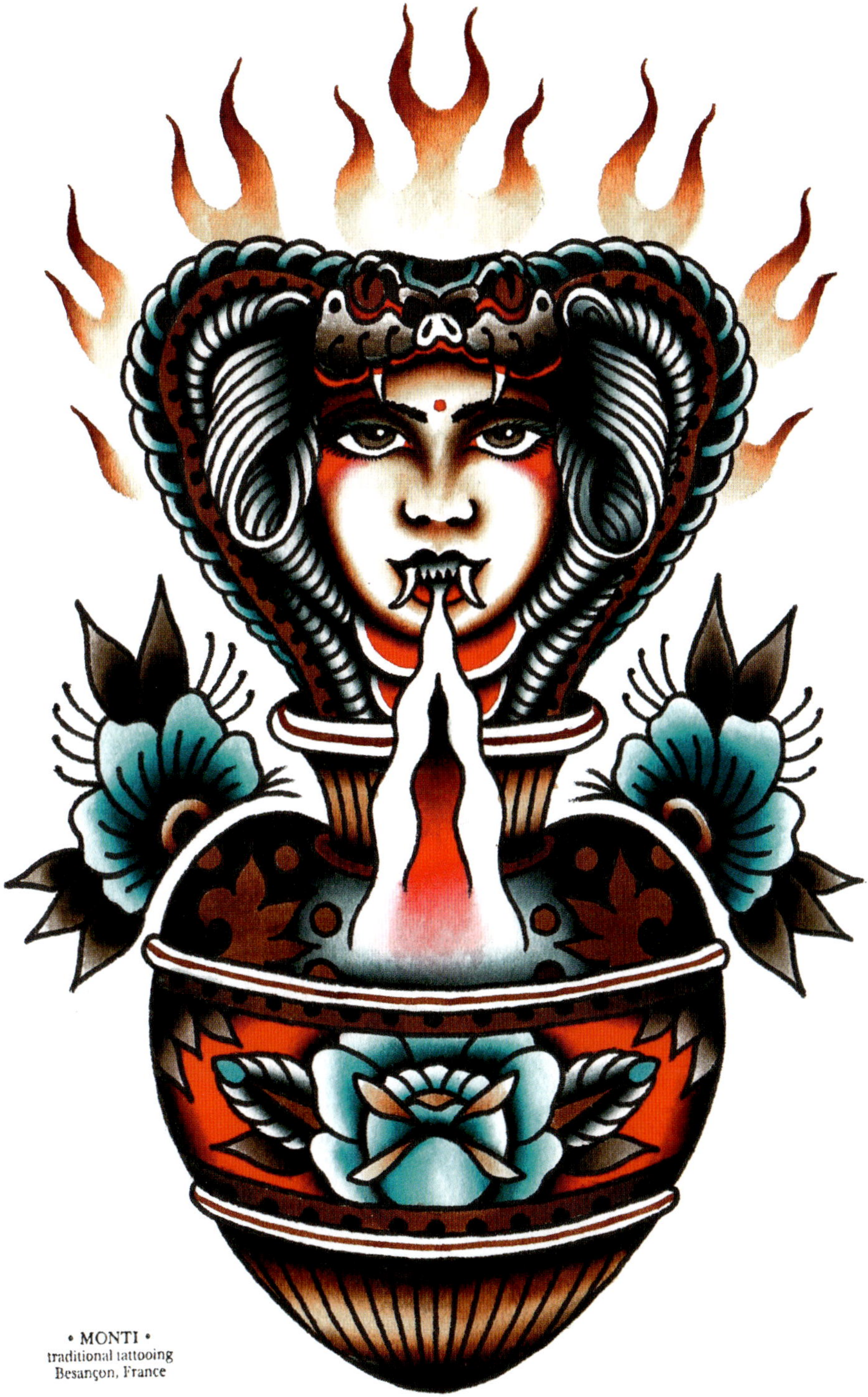
• MONTI •
traditional tattooing
Besançon, France

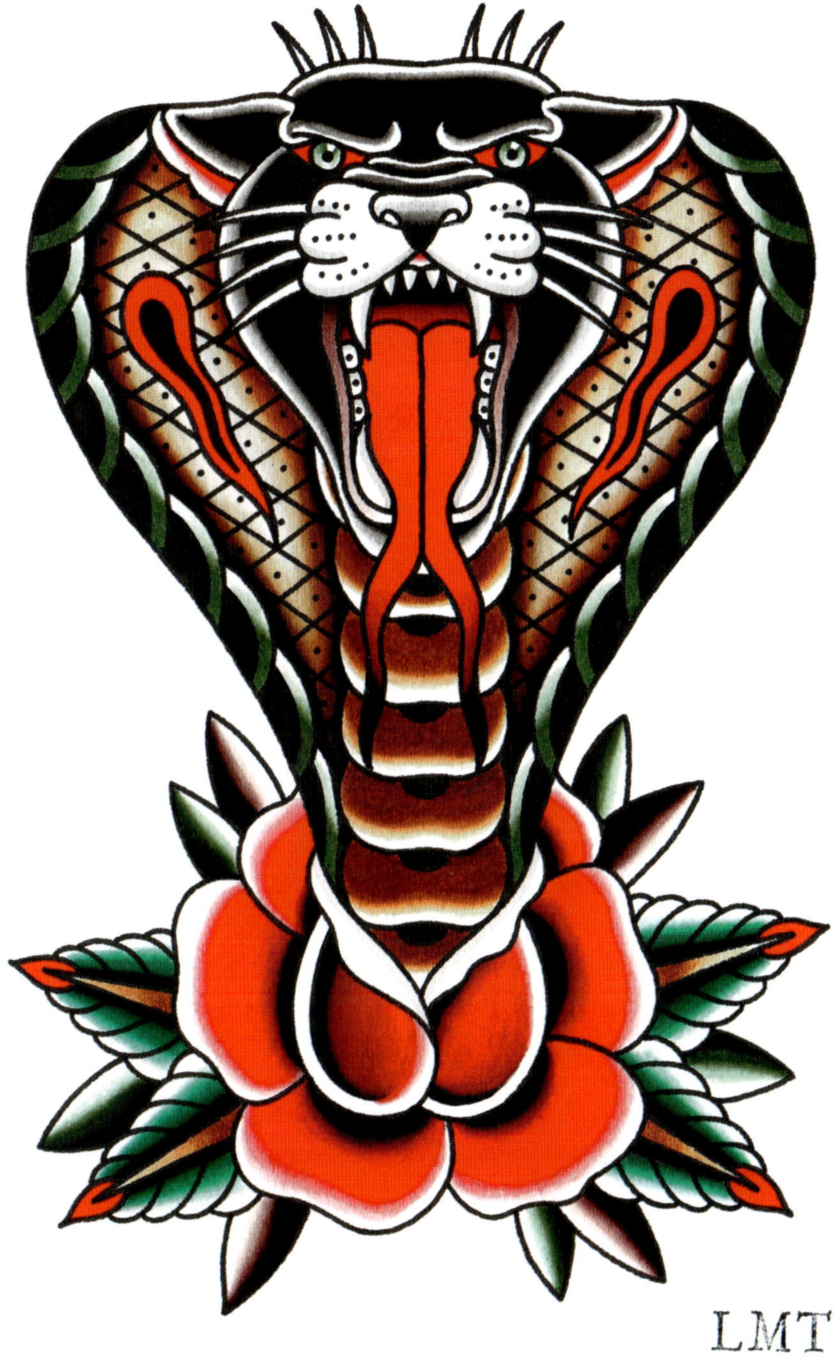
LMT

Left
Ozzy Christ
@ozzy_christ_tattoo
Black Galleon Tattoo Shop / Vire / France

Right
Friedrick Thorsteinn
@friedrick_tattooer
Black Galleon Tattoo Shop / Vire / France

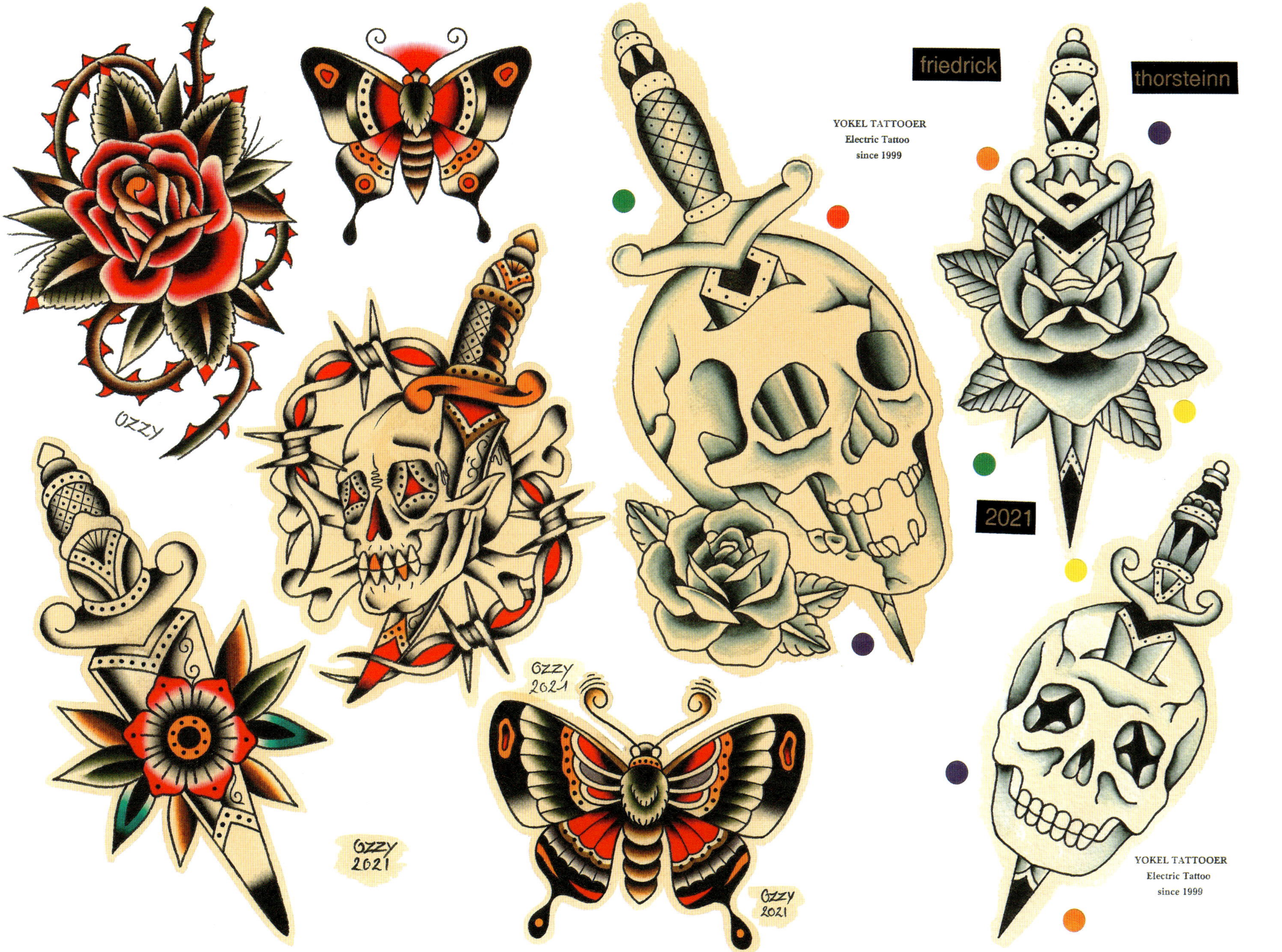
friedrick
thorsteinn
YOKEL TATTOOER
Electric Tattoo
since 1999
2021
OZZY
OZZY 2021
OZZY 2021
OZZY 2021
YOKEL TATTOOER
Electric Tattoo
since 1999

Left
Silvin
@silvin_tattoo
Copa Banana Club / Lille / France

Right
Marto Tattoo
@martotattoo
Copa Banana Club / Lille / France

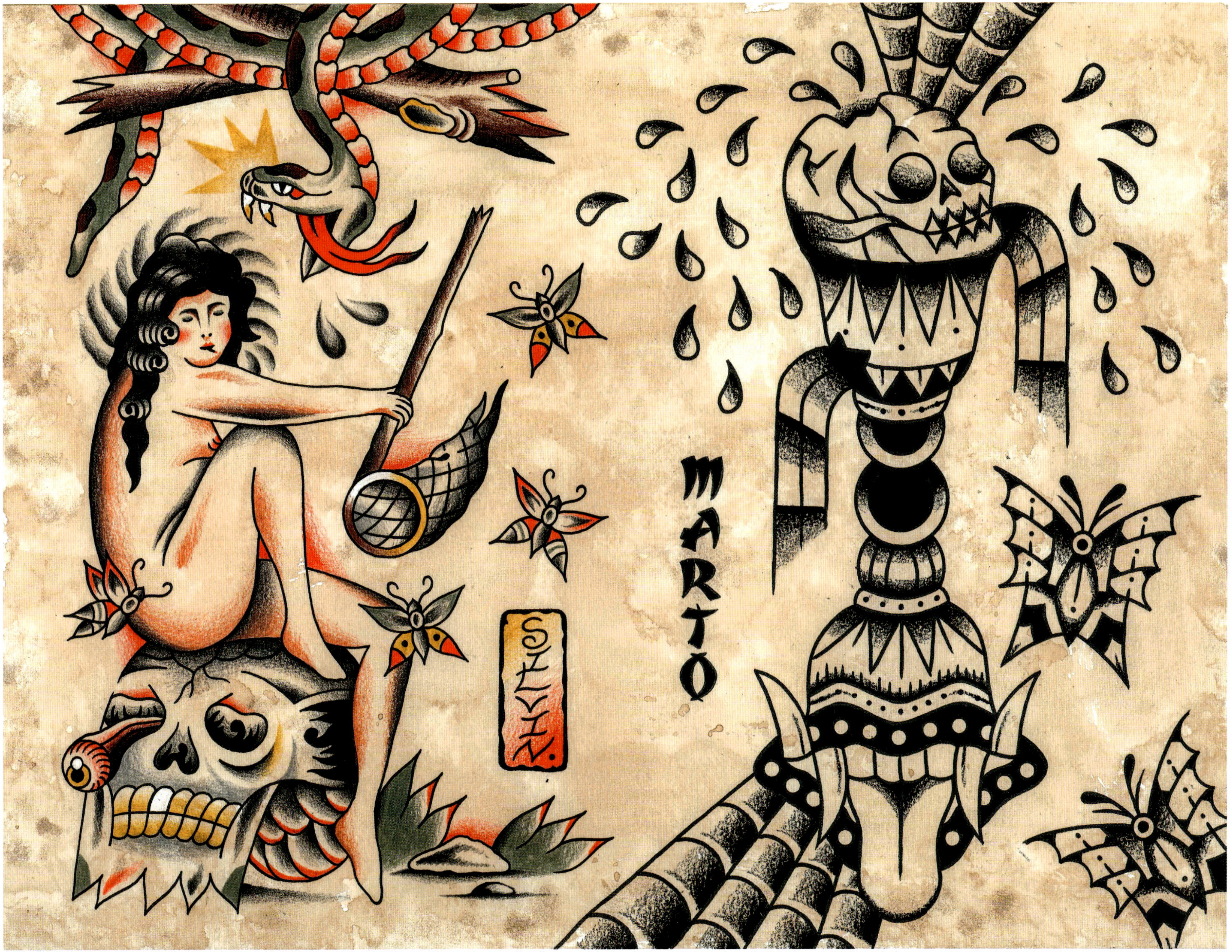

SLEVIN.
MARTO

Left
Yannick Oumouck
@yannickoumouck
Creepy Doll Tattoo Shop / Landivisiaux / France

Right
Uncle Ho
@uncle_ho_mitchmalone
Iron Claw / Strasbourg / France

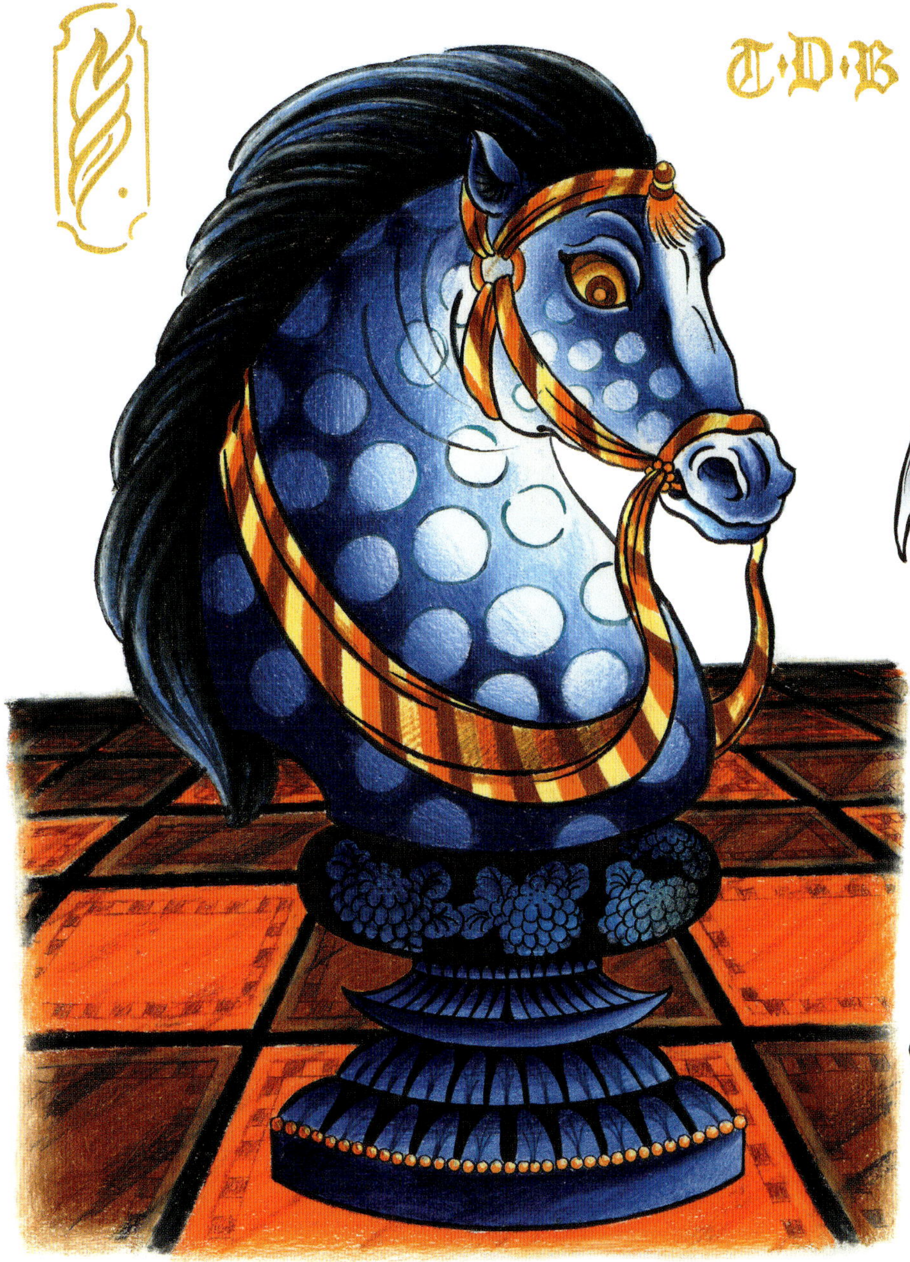
T·D·B

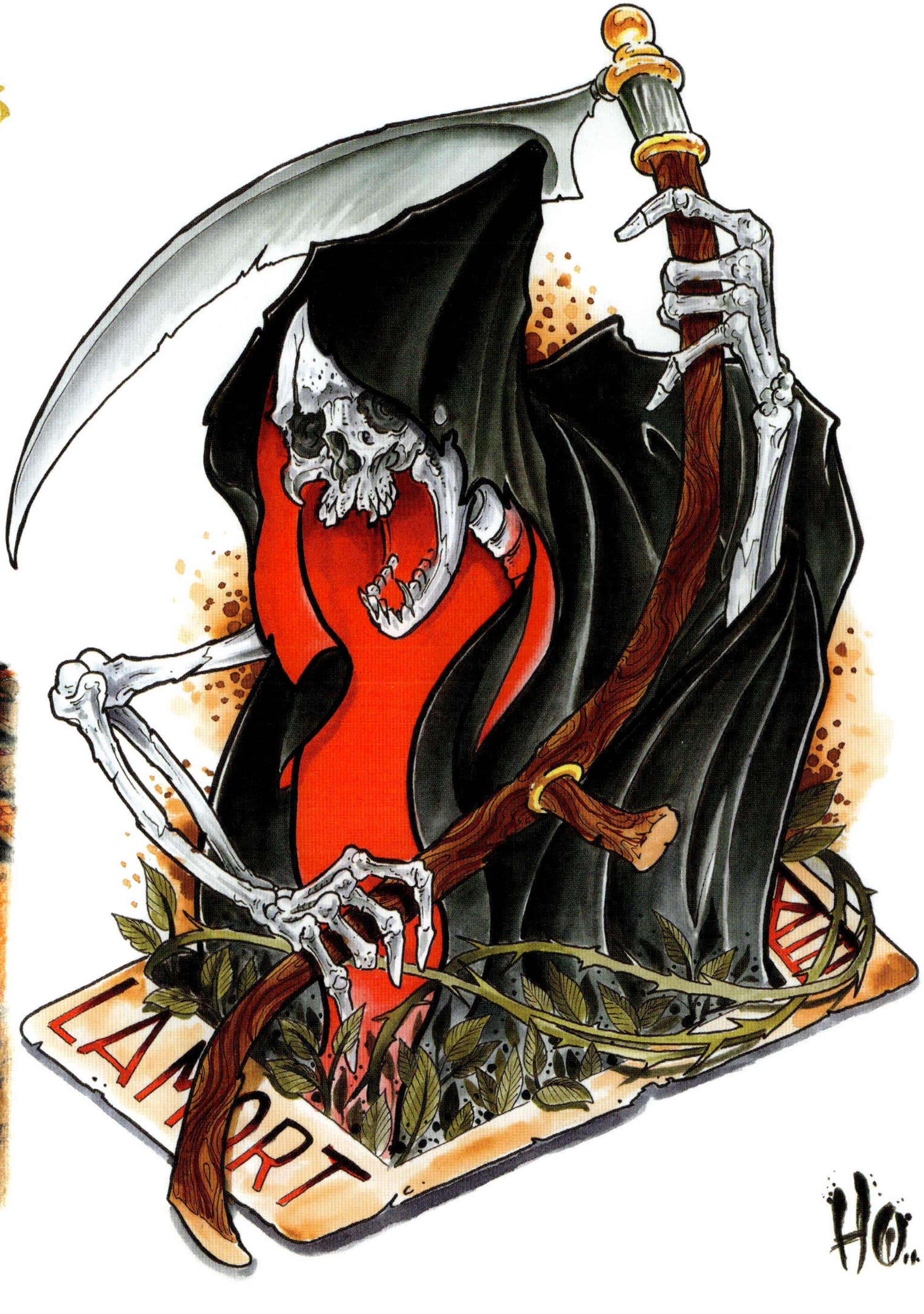
LA MORT
HO.

Left
John Stone
@john_stone_tatouage
L'Astrolabe / Dinard / France

Right
Julien Brunier
@julien.brunier
French Tattoo Connection / Marseille / France

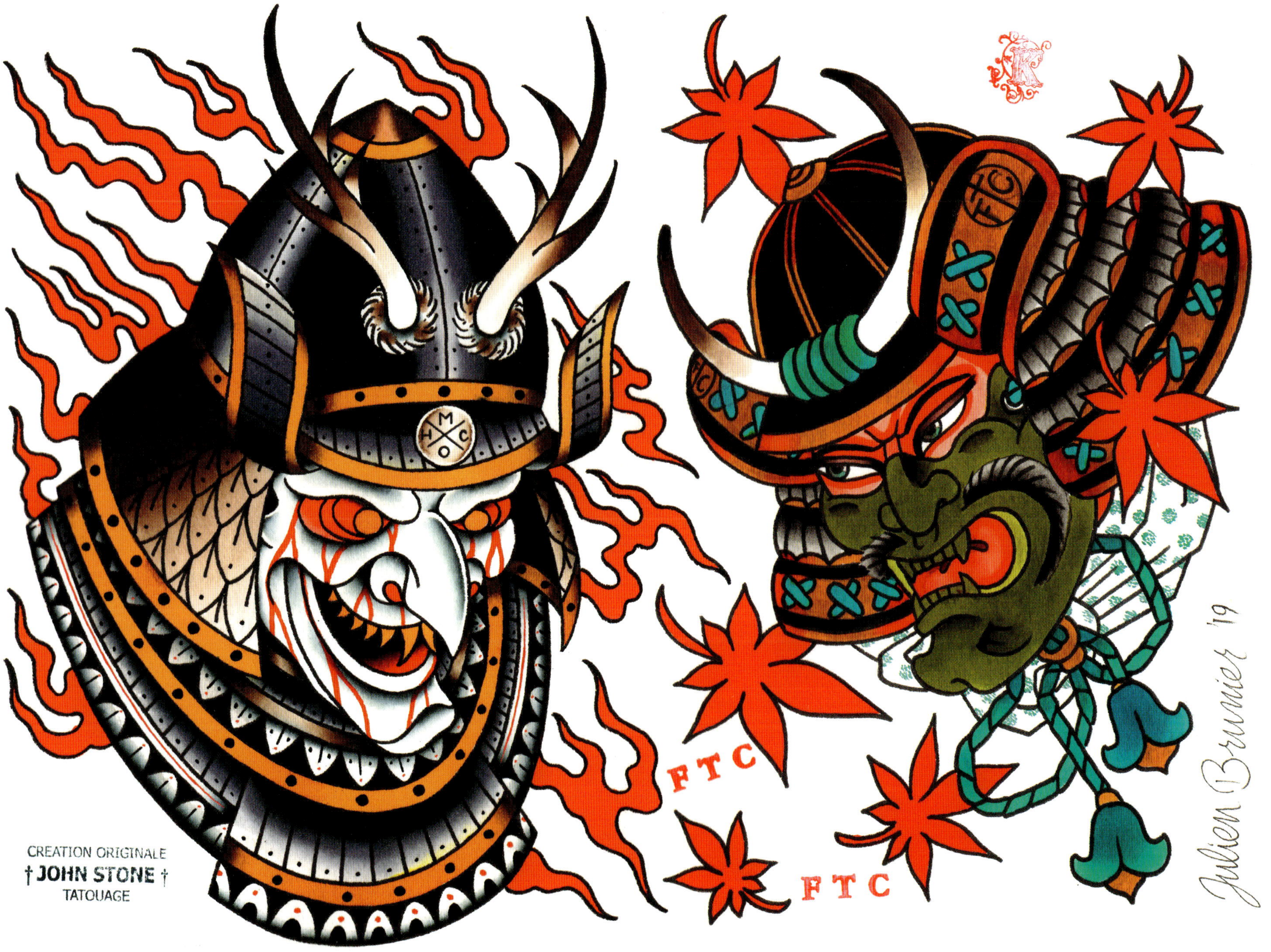
CREATION ORIGINALE
† JOHN STONE †
TATOUAGE
FTC
FTC
Julien Brunier '19

Left and right
Virgulovic
@virgulovic
Artax Tattoo / Lille / France

Center
El Bent
@elbenttattoo
True Love / Paris / France

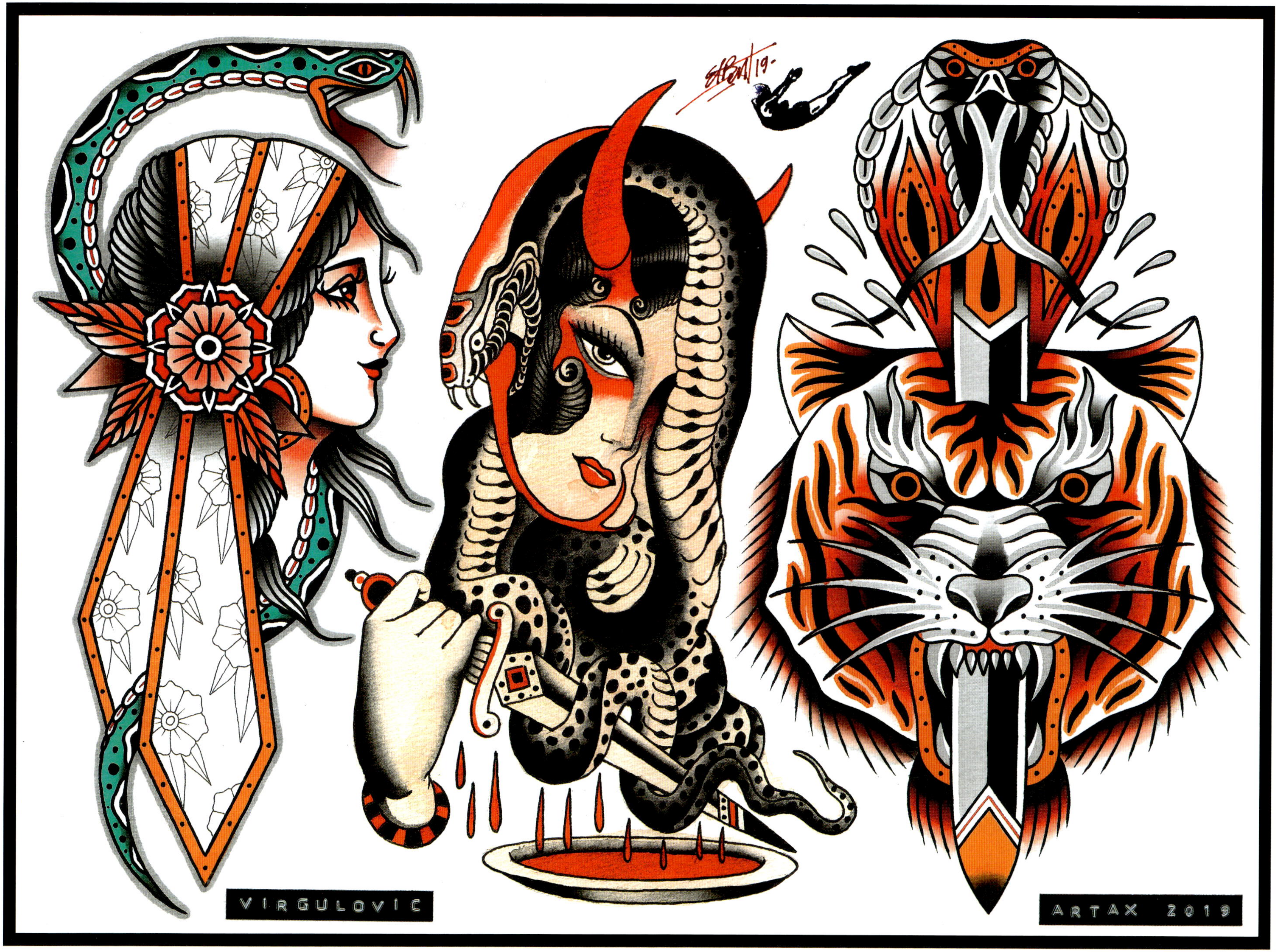
VIRGULOVIC
ARTAX 2019

Left
Neusky
@neuskytattoo
Neusky Tattoo 55 / Saint-Brieuc / France

Right
Romain Bonniez
@romainbonniez
Norse Wolf Tattoo / Allos / France

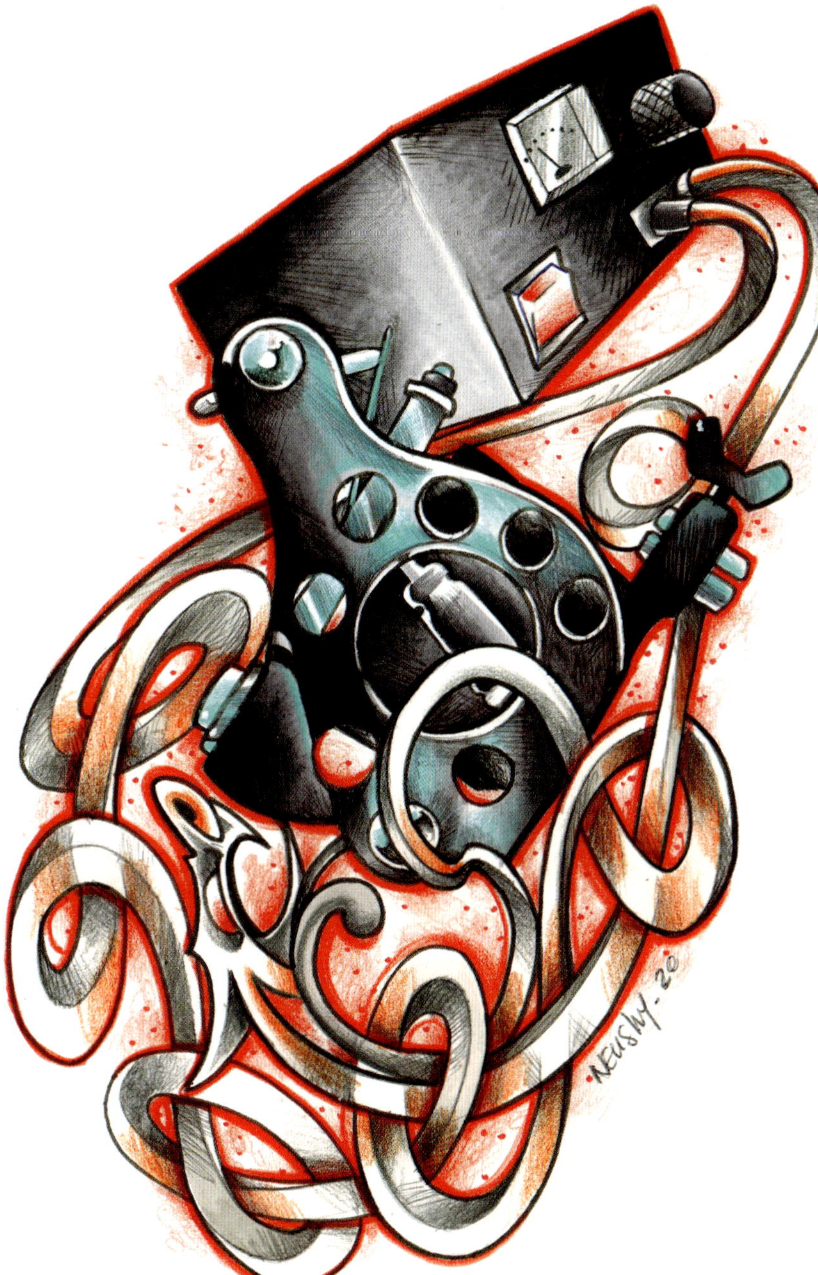
NEUSHY. 20

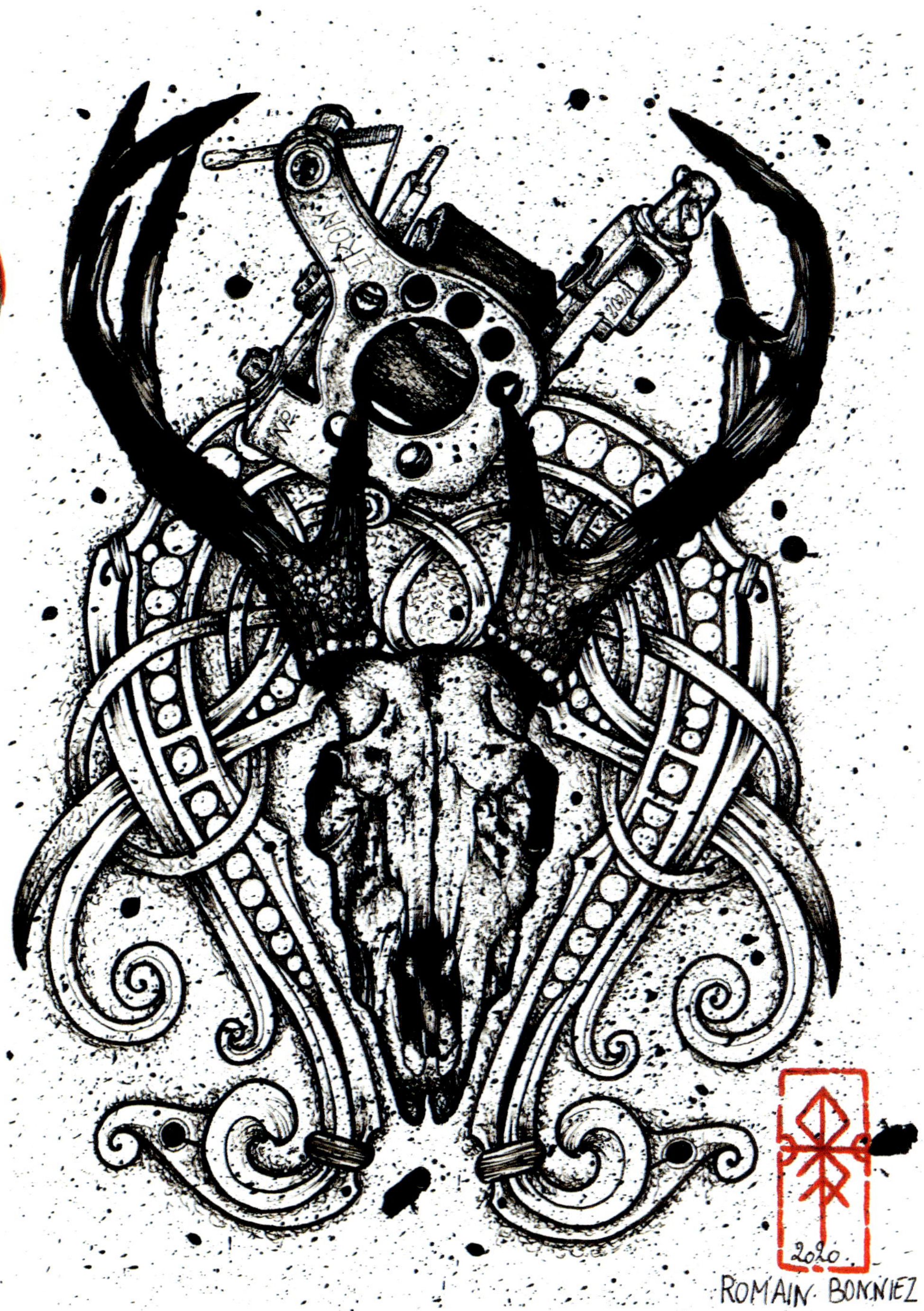
2020.
ROMAIN BONNIEZ

Left
Tiwan
@tiwan_tattoo
Spirit Tattoo Rennes / Rennes / France

Right
Niko Mook
@nikomook4real
Dermal Mayhem Tattoo Parlor / Nantes / France

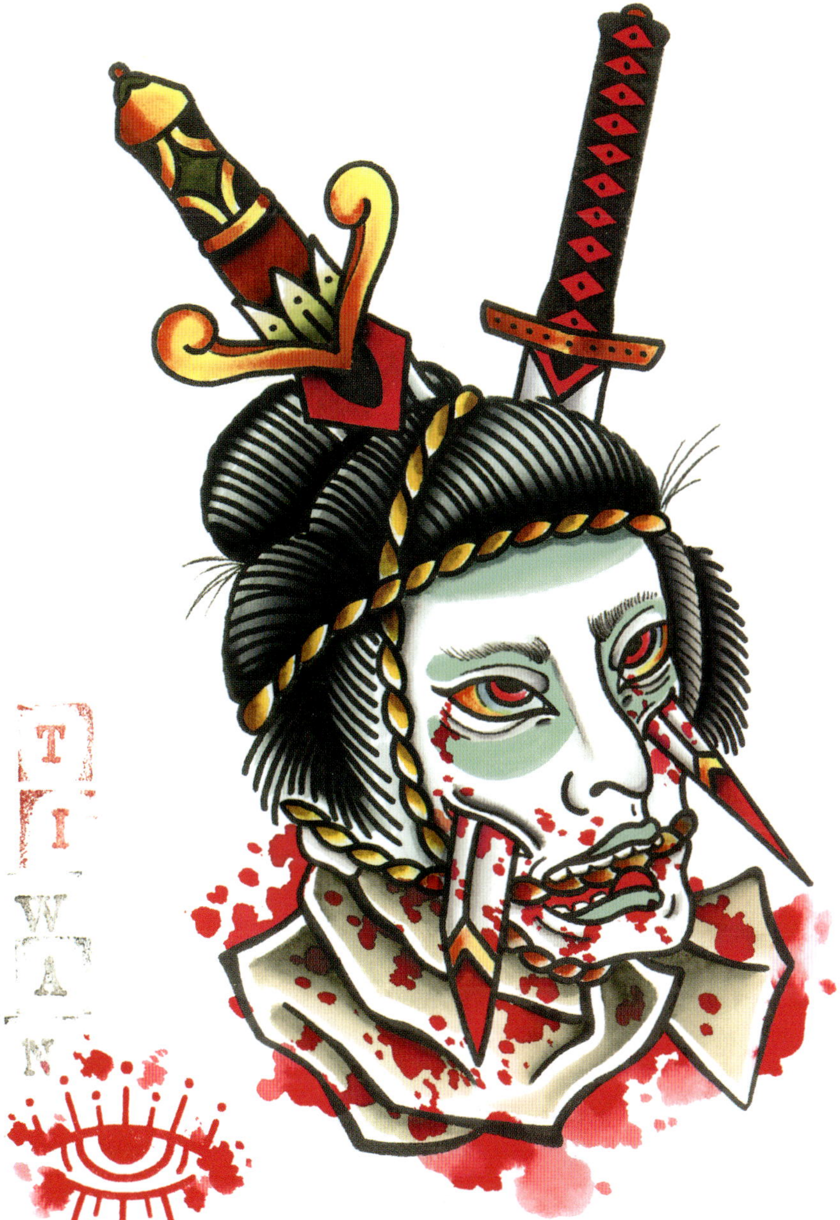
TI WAN

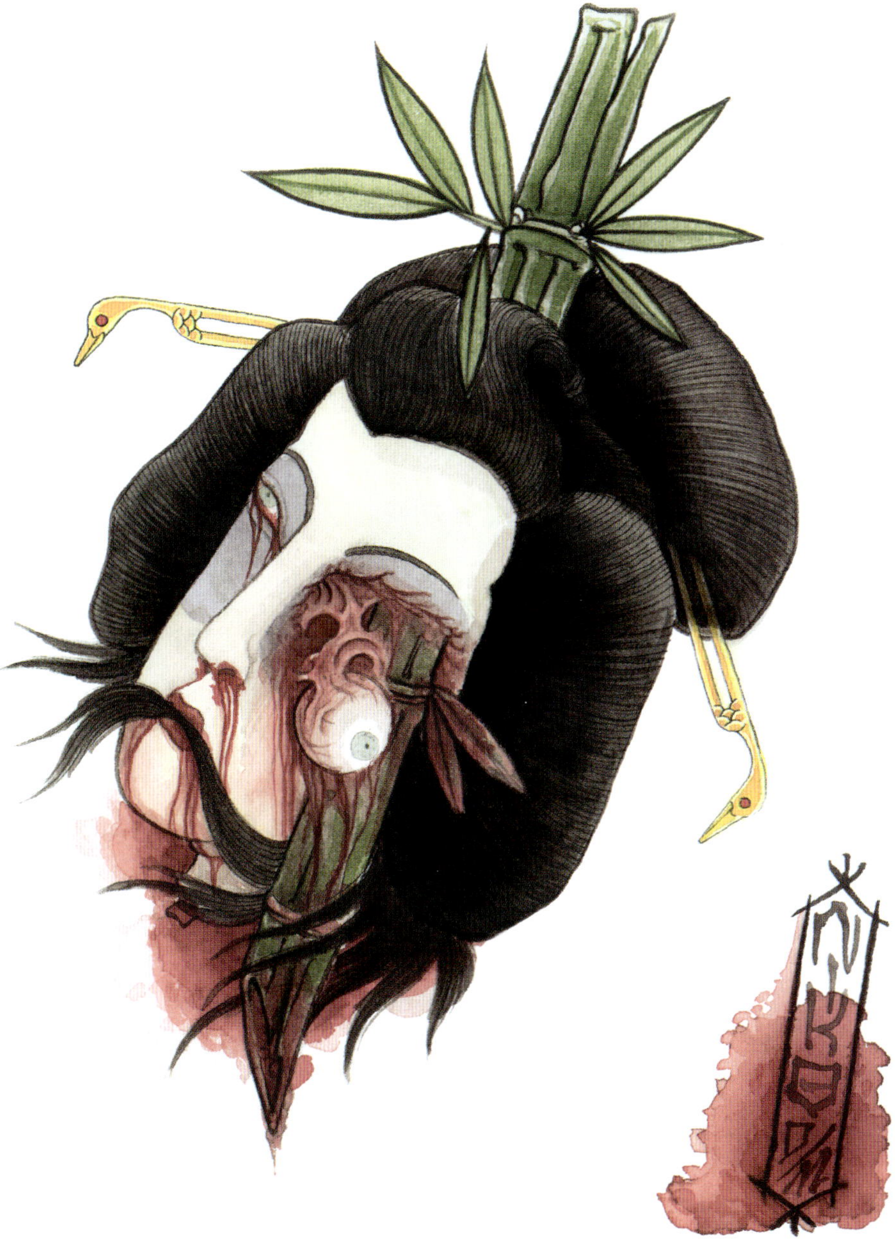

Left
Sylvester Boom
@sylvesterboom
Tribal act / Paris / France

Right
Treiz
@xtreizx
Yoso / Paris / France

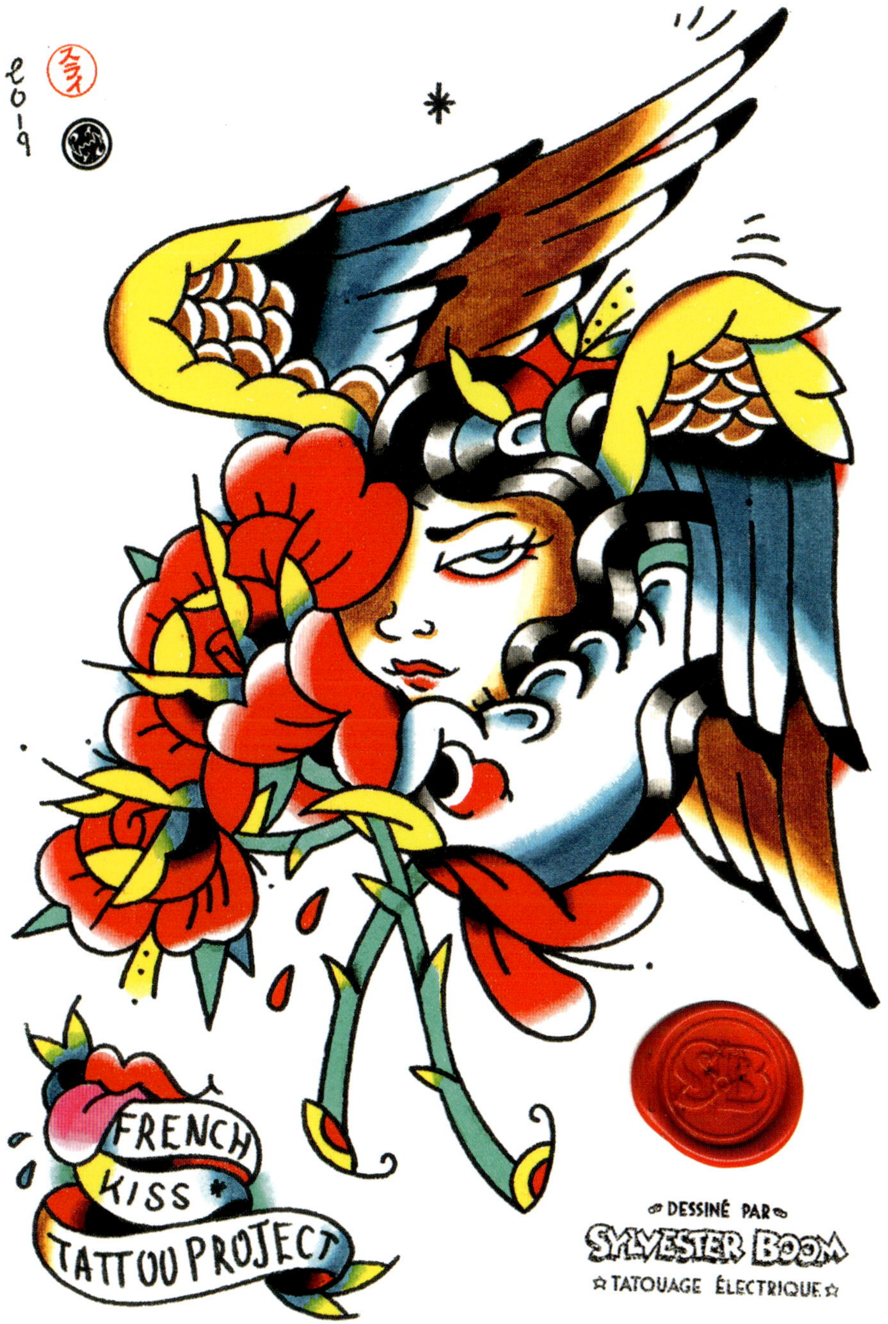
FRENCH
KISS
TATTOU PROJECT
DESSINÉ PAR
SYLVESTER BOOM
☆TATOUAGE ÉLECTRIQUE☆

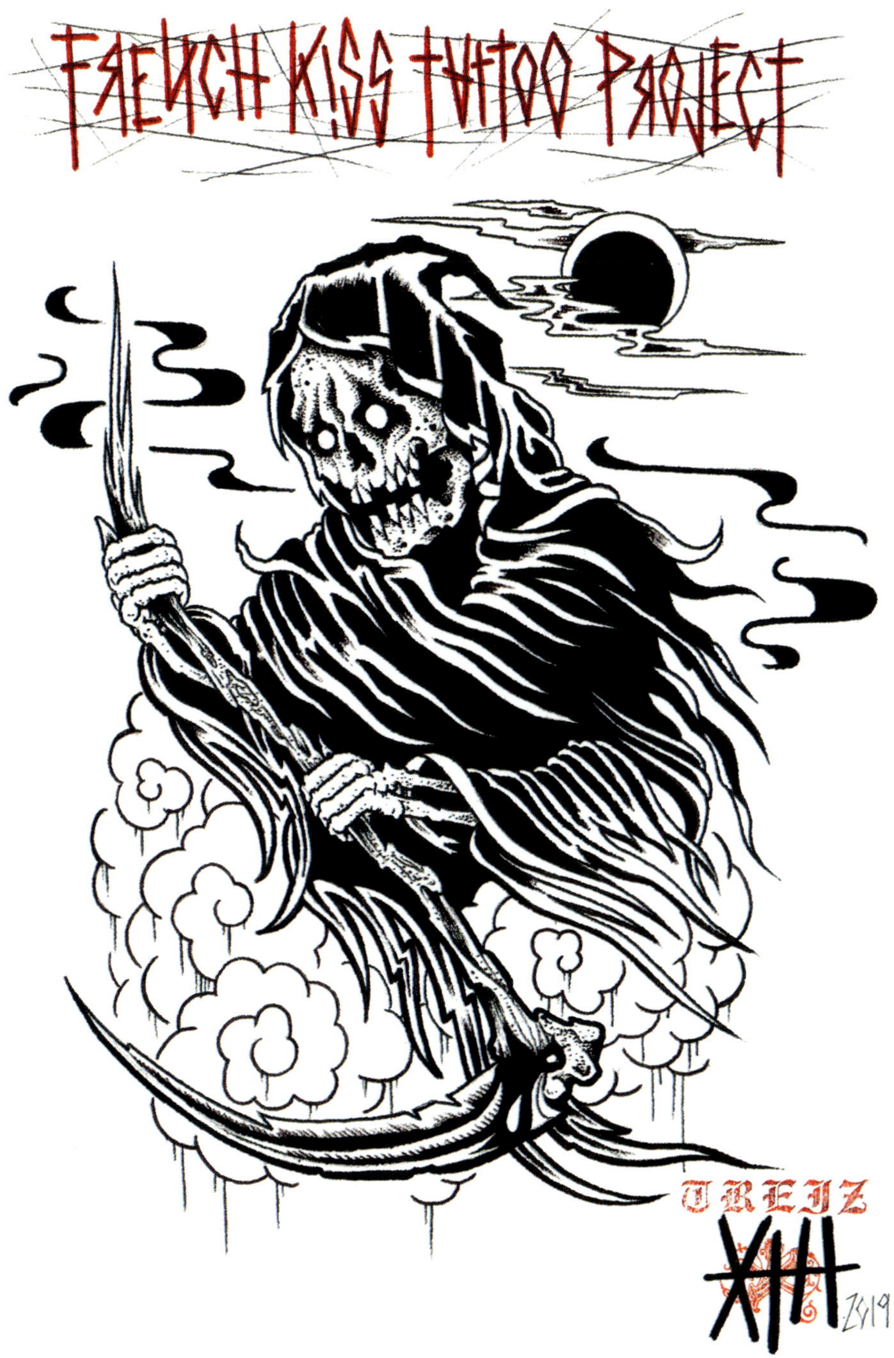
FRENCH KISS TATTOO PROJECT
TREIZ
XIII

Left
Julien Brunier
@julien.brunier
French Tattoo Connection / Marseille / France

Right
Fede Borgia
@fede__borgia
On the road / Germany

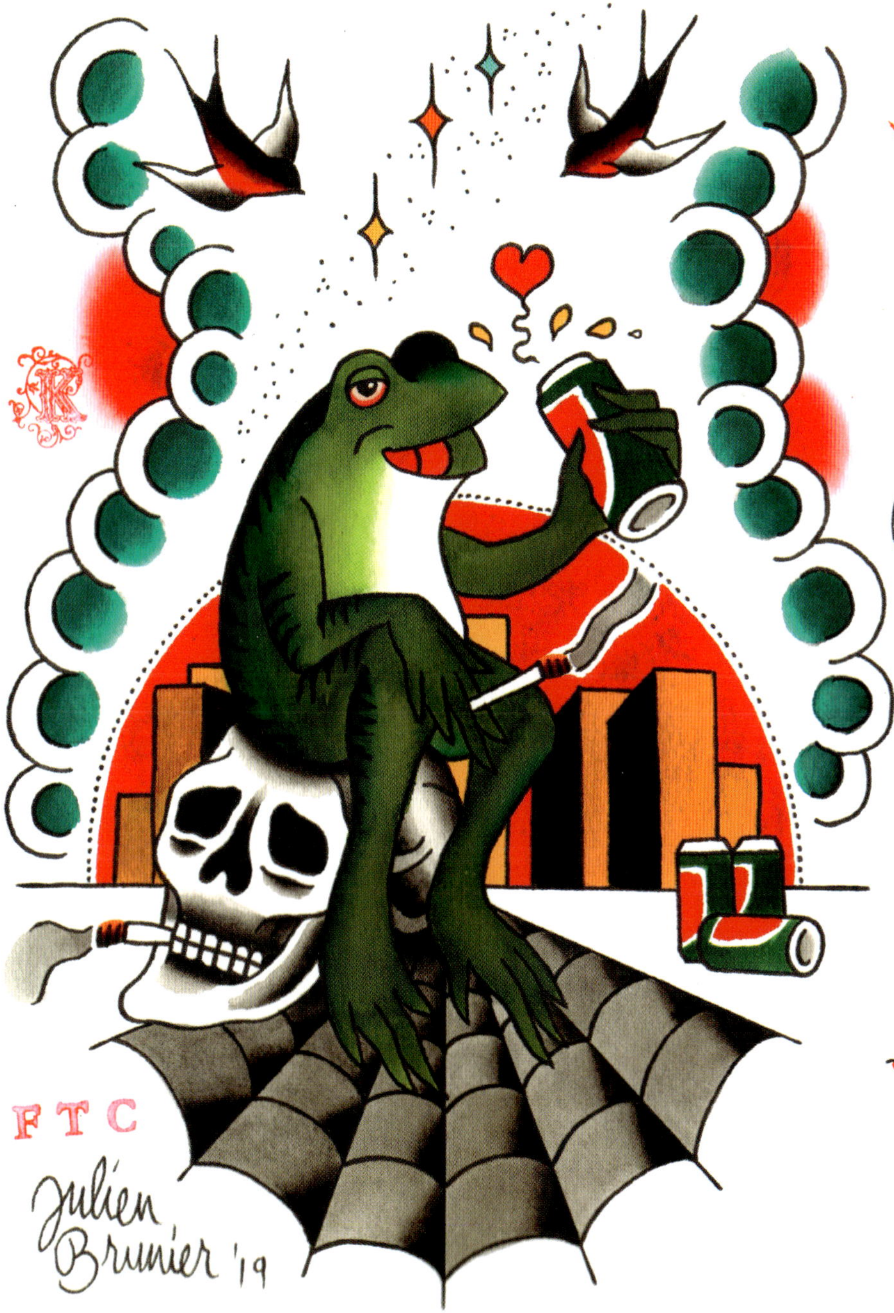
FTC
Julien
Brunier '19

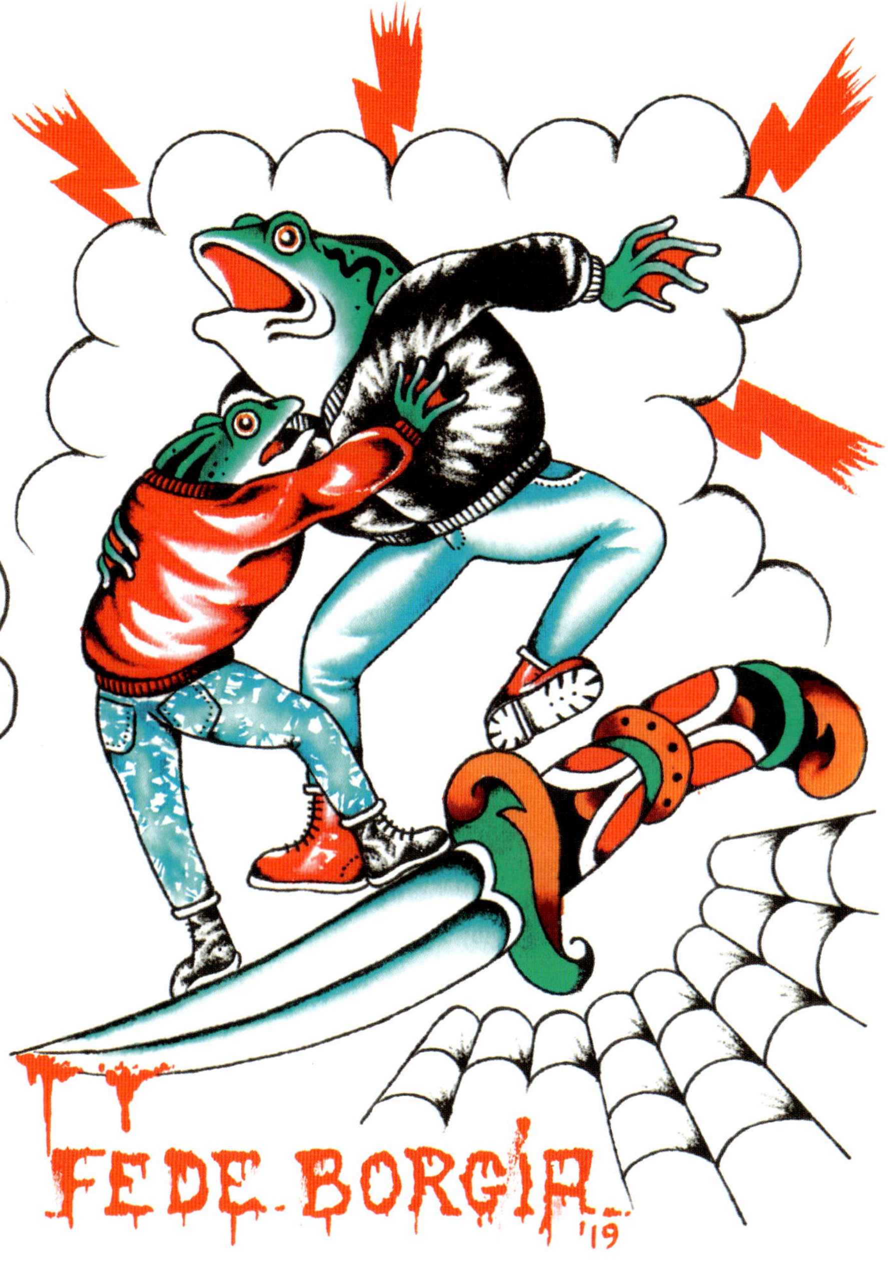
FEDE BORGIR
'19

Left
John Stone
@john_stone_tatouage
L'Astrolabe / Dinard / France

Right
Greg Briko
@greg_briko
Briko Tattoo / Lille / France

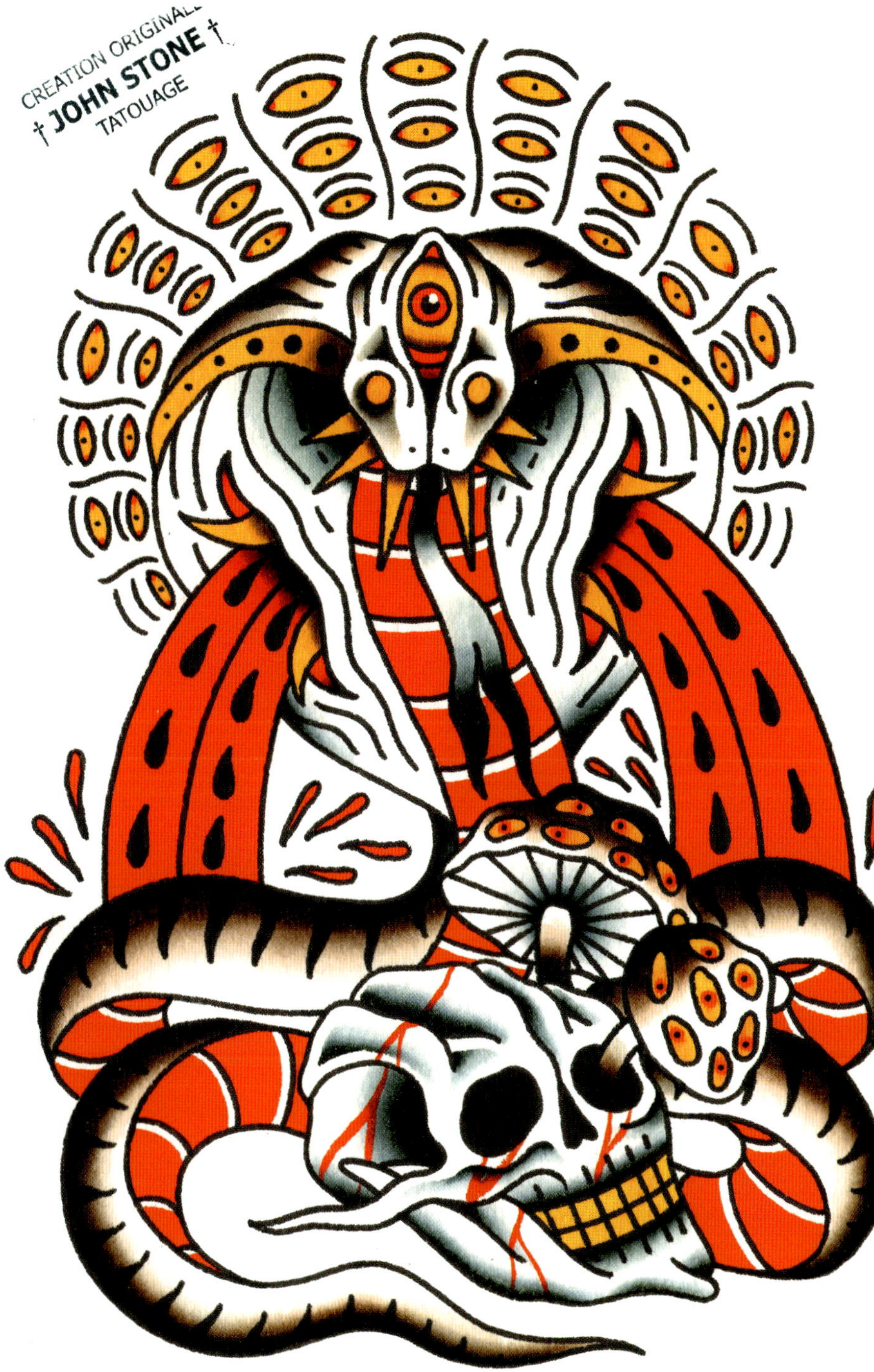
CREATION ORIGINALE
† JOHN STONE †
TATOUAGE

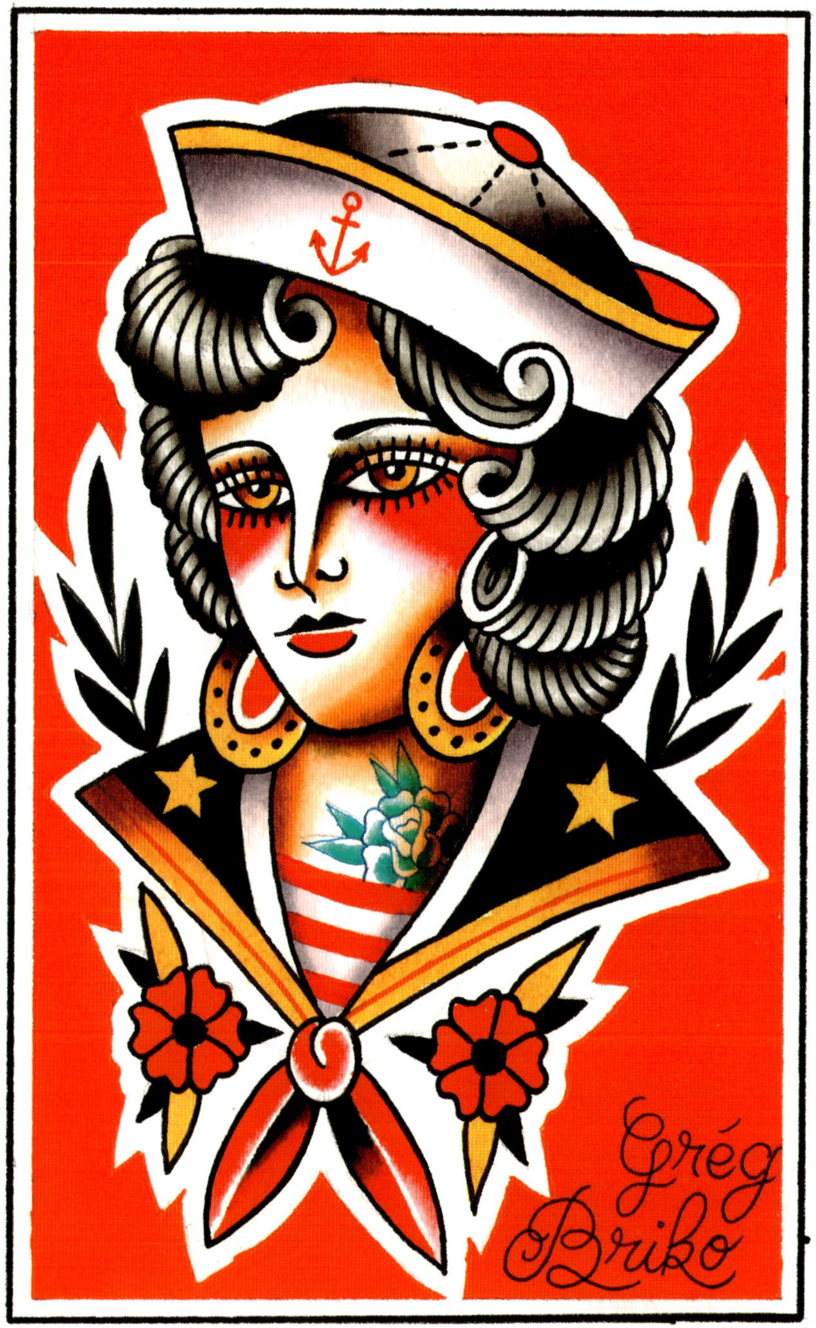
Grég
Briko

Left
Guyguyttt
@guyguyttt
Miséricorde / Sète / France

Right
Jonathan Perle
@jonathan_perle
Turbo Zéro / Nantes / France

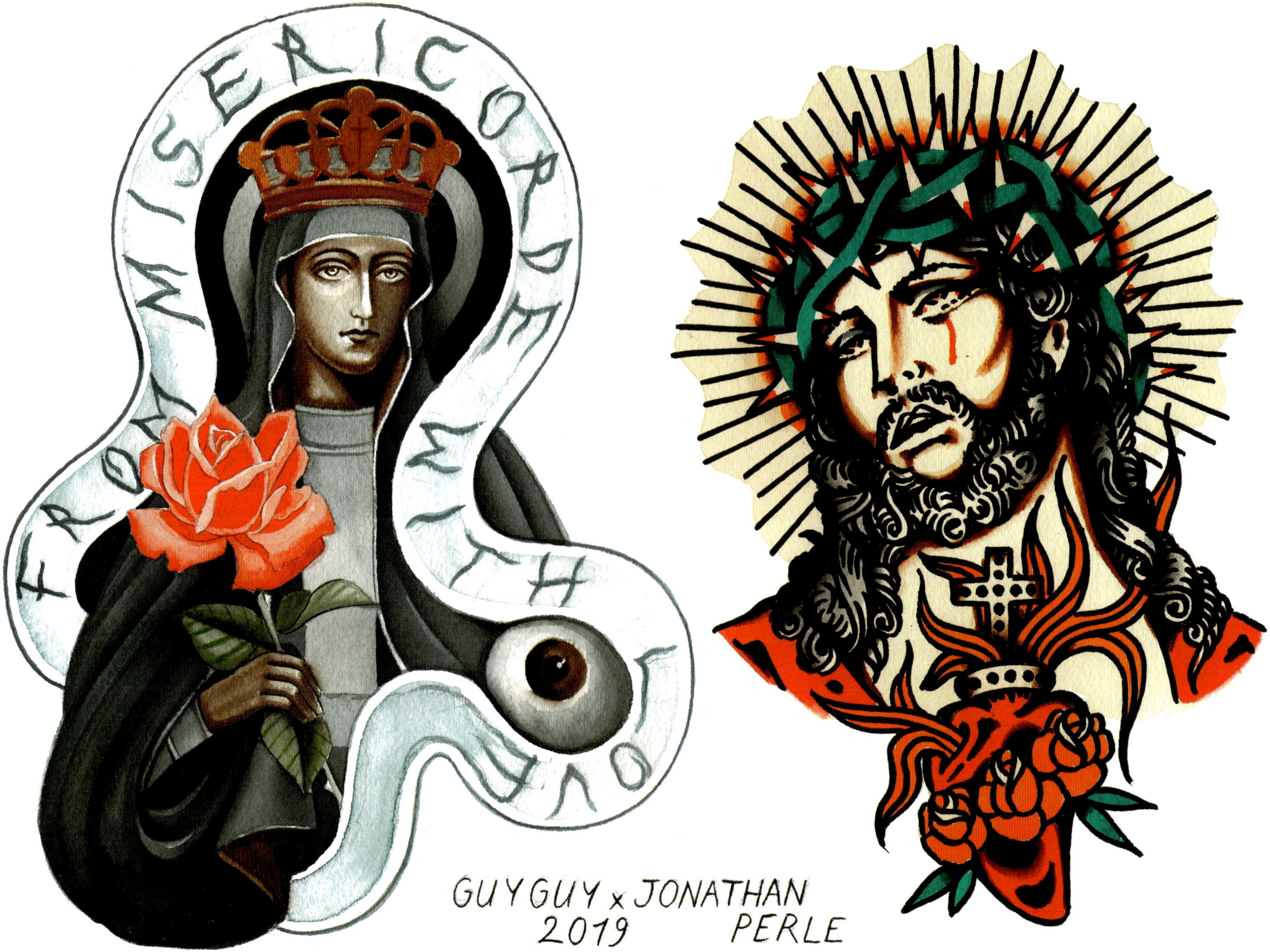
FROM MISERICORDE WITH LOVE
GUYGUY x JONATHAN PERLE
2019

Left
Tiwan
@tiwan_tattoo
Spirit Tattoo Rennes / Rennes / France

Right
Malflore
@malflore
Atelier Triptyque / Montpellier / France

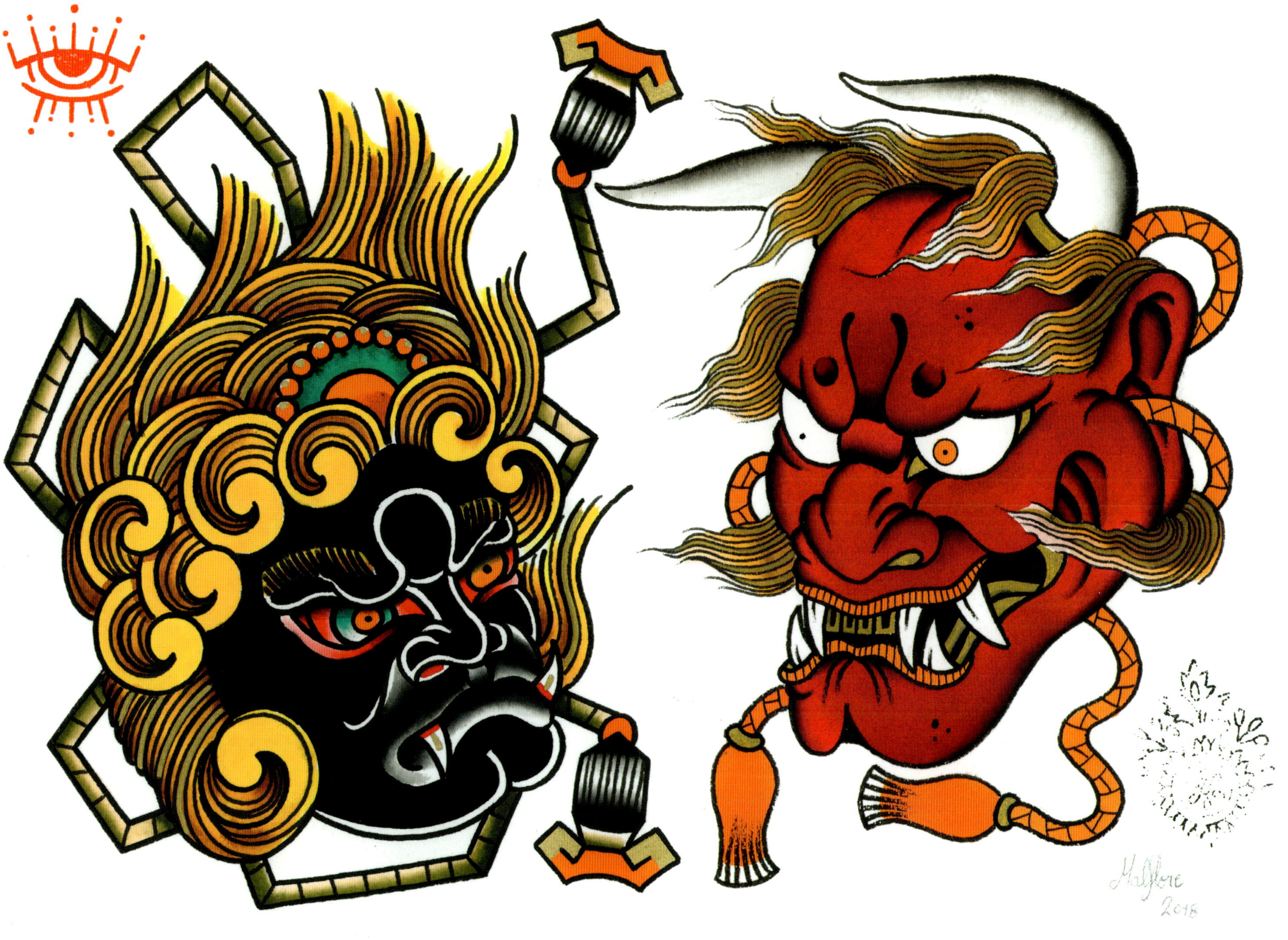
Malfiore
2018

Left
John Stone
@john_stone_tatouage
L'Astrolabe / Dinard / France

Right
Ben Smith
@bensmithtatts
On the road / France

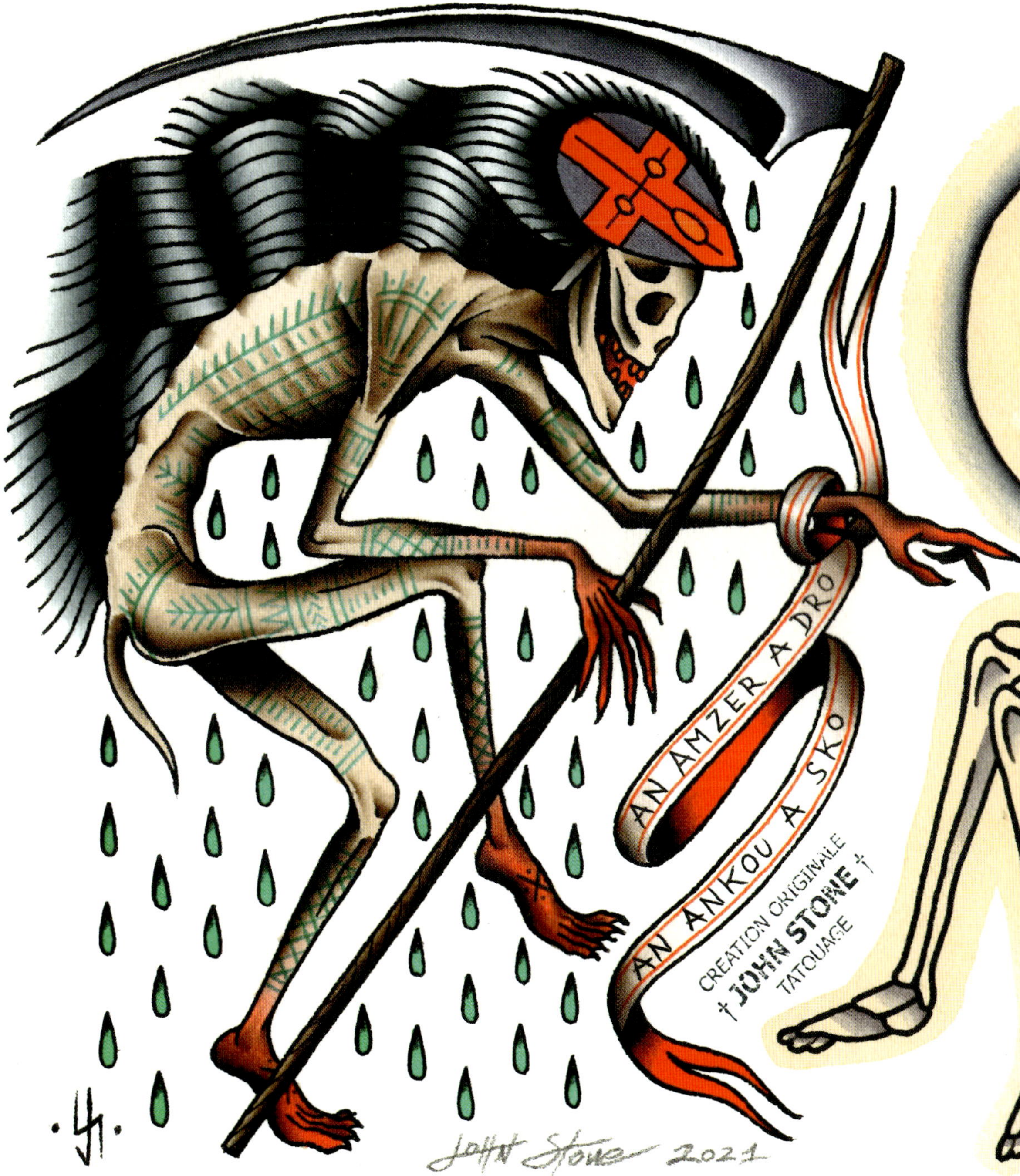
AN AMZER A DRO
AN ANKOU A SKO
CREATION ORIGINALE
† JOHN STONE †
TATOUAGE
John Stone 2021

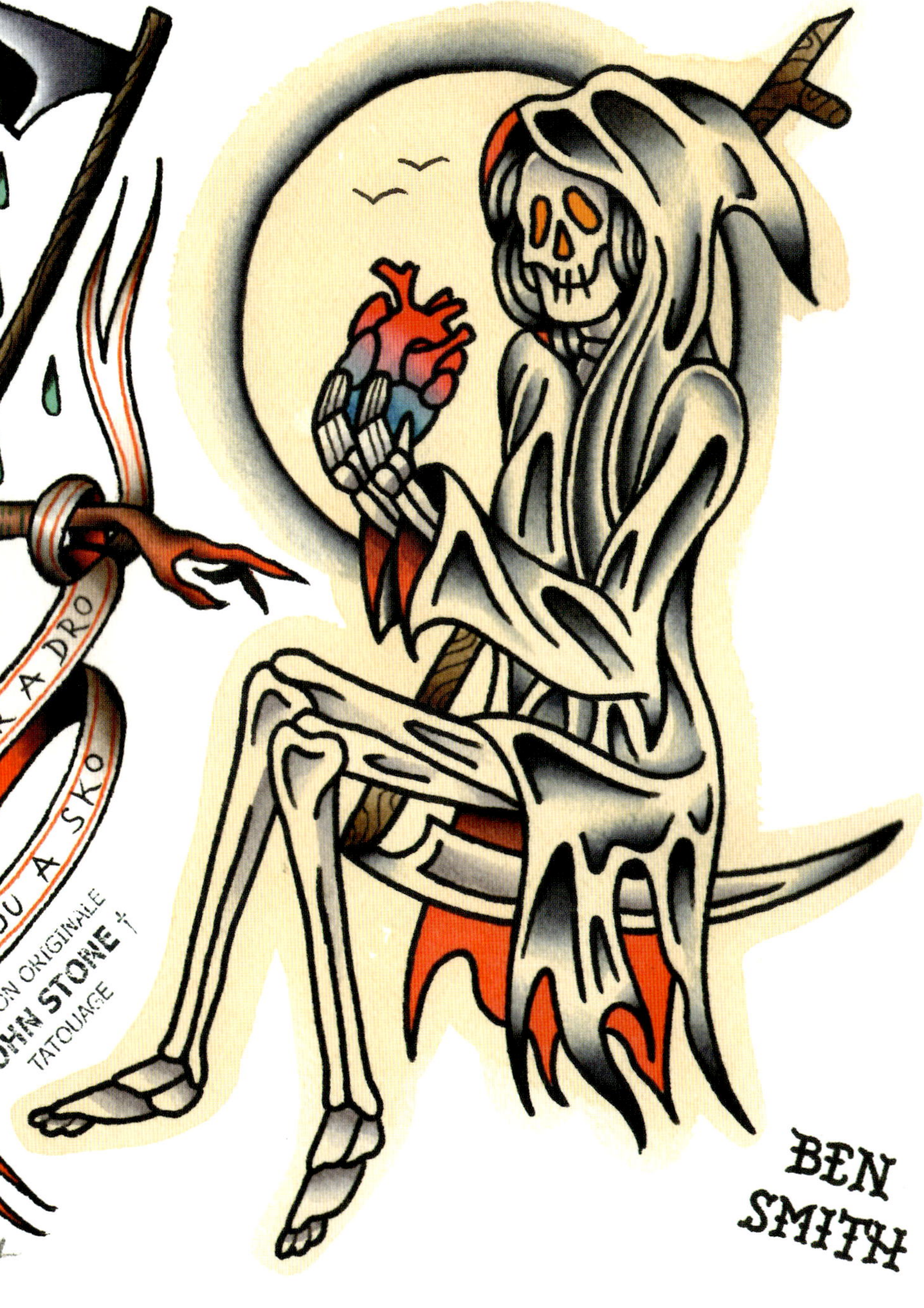
BEN
SMITH

Left
El Bent
@elbenttattoo
True Love / Paris / France

Right
Helena F
@helena__f
Perdu d'Avance Tattoo Club / Paris / France

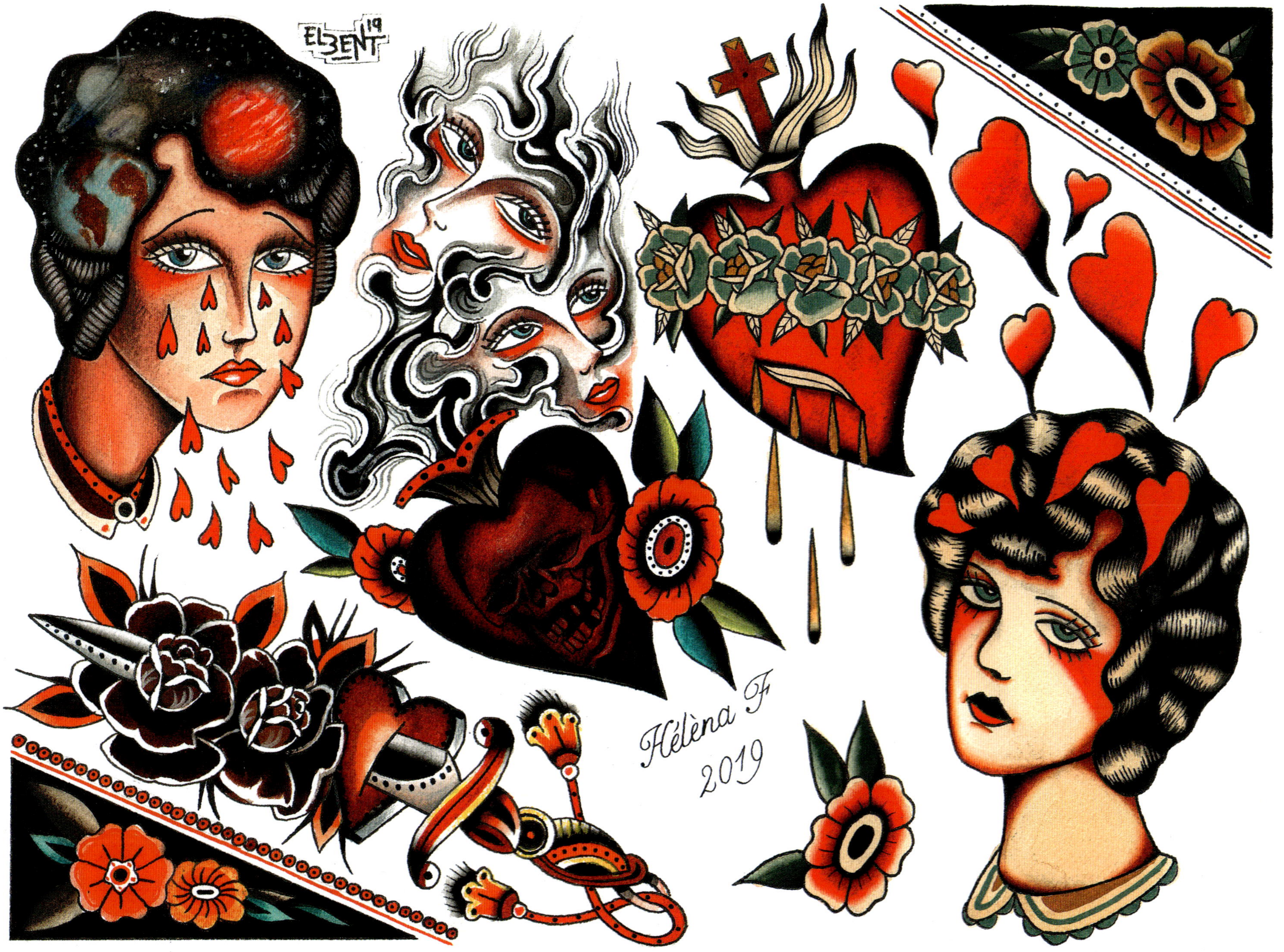
EL3ENT 19
Hélèna F
2019

Left
Tony Grande Truandise
@tonygrandetruandise
L'Ogre Rouge / Pont-Péan / France

Right
Charles
@charlestattoorennes
L'Ogre Rouge / Pont-Péan / France

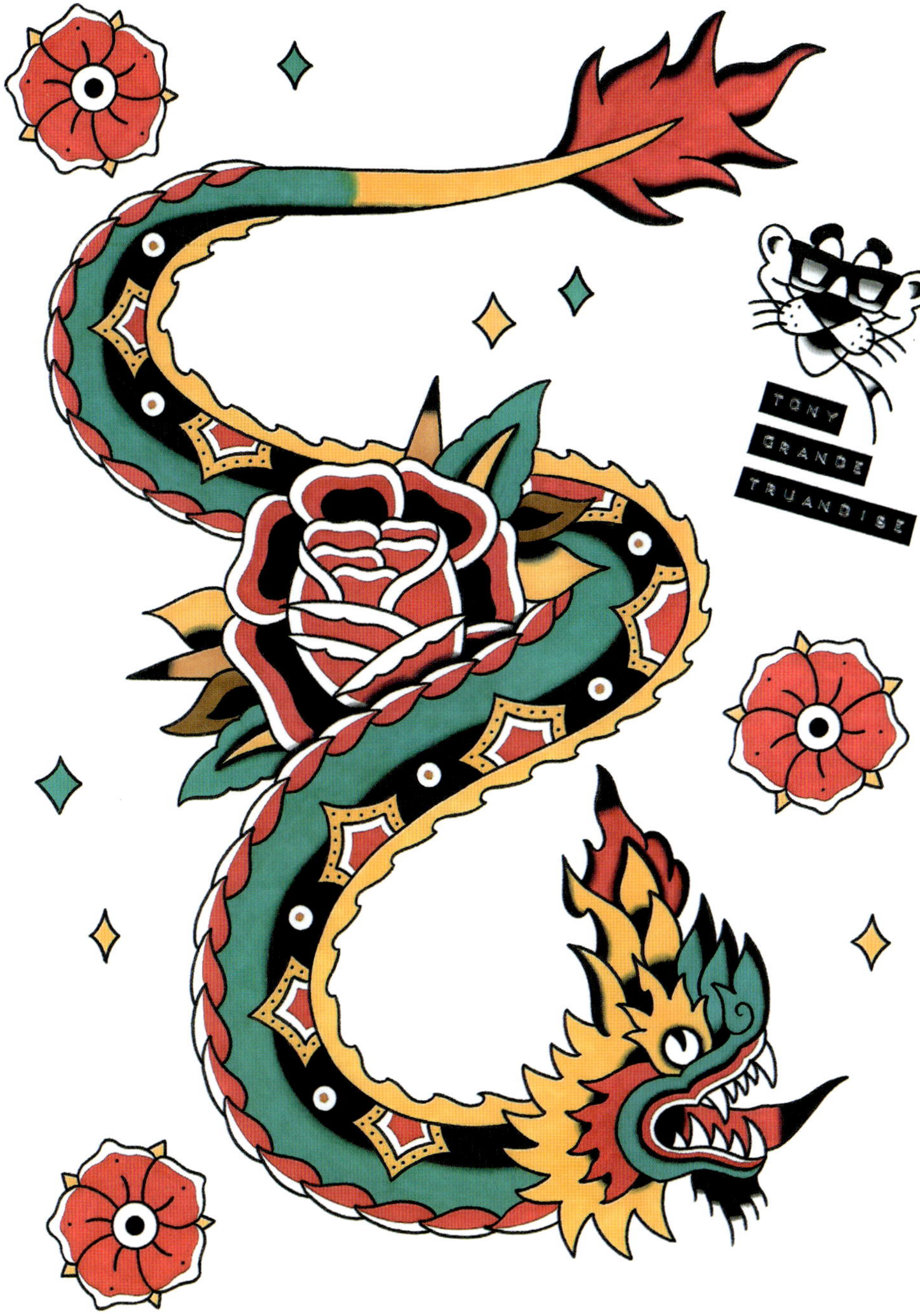
TONY
GRANDE
TRUANDISE

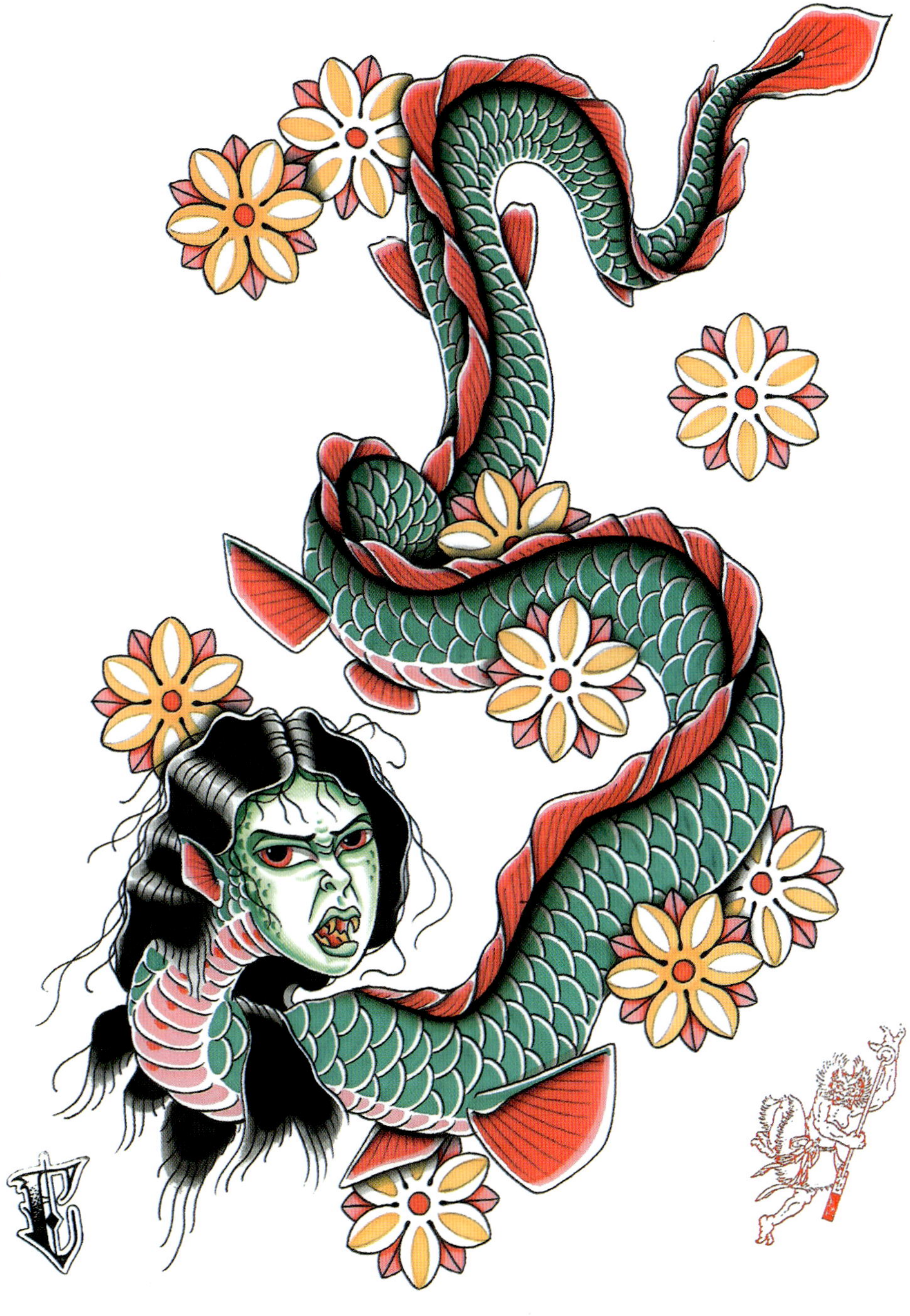

Left
Clément Doineau (Dague Rouge)
@clementdoineau
Grey Bronco Tattoo / Nantes / France

Right
Kim Ai
@kim_ai_tattoo
Kimochi Tattoo Shop / Montpellier / France

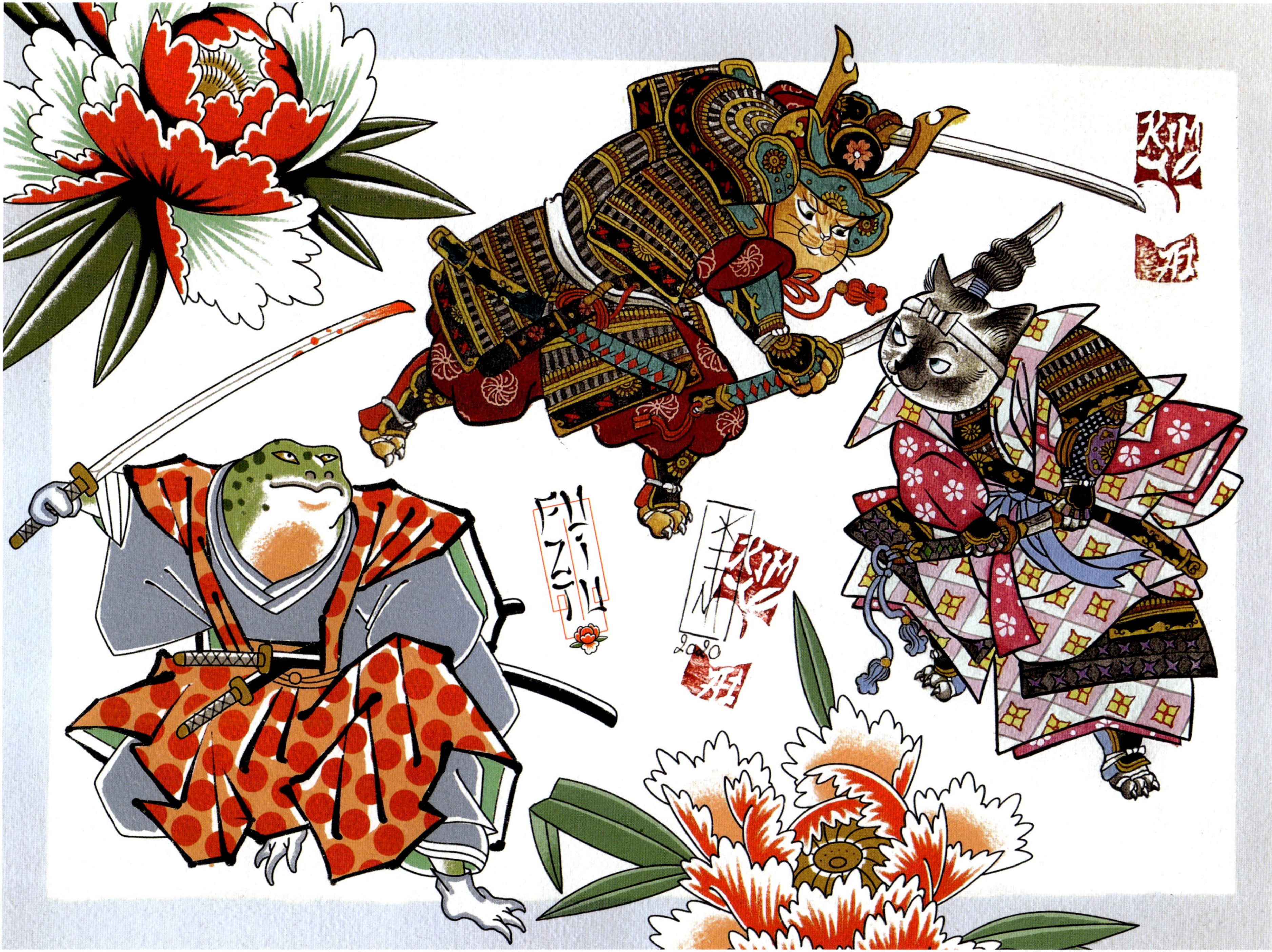
2020

Center
John Stone
@john_stone_tatouage
L'Astrolabe / Dinard / France

Left and right
Just
@classicjustin
Mystery Tattoo Club / Paris / France

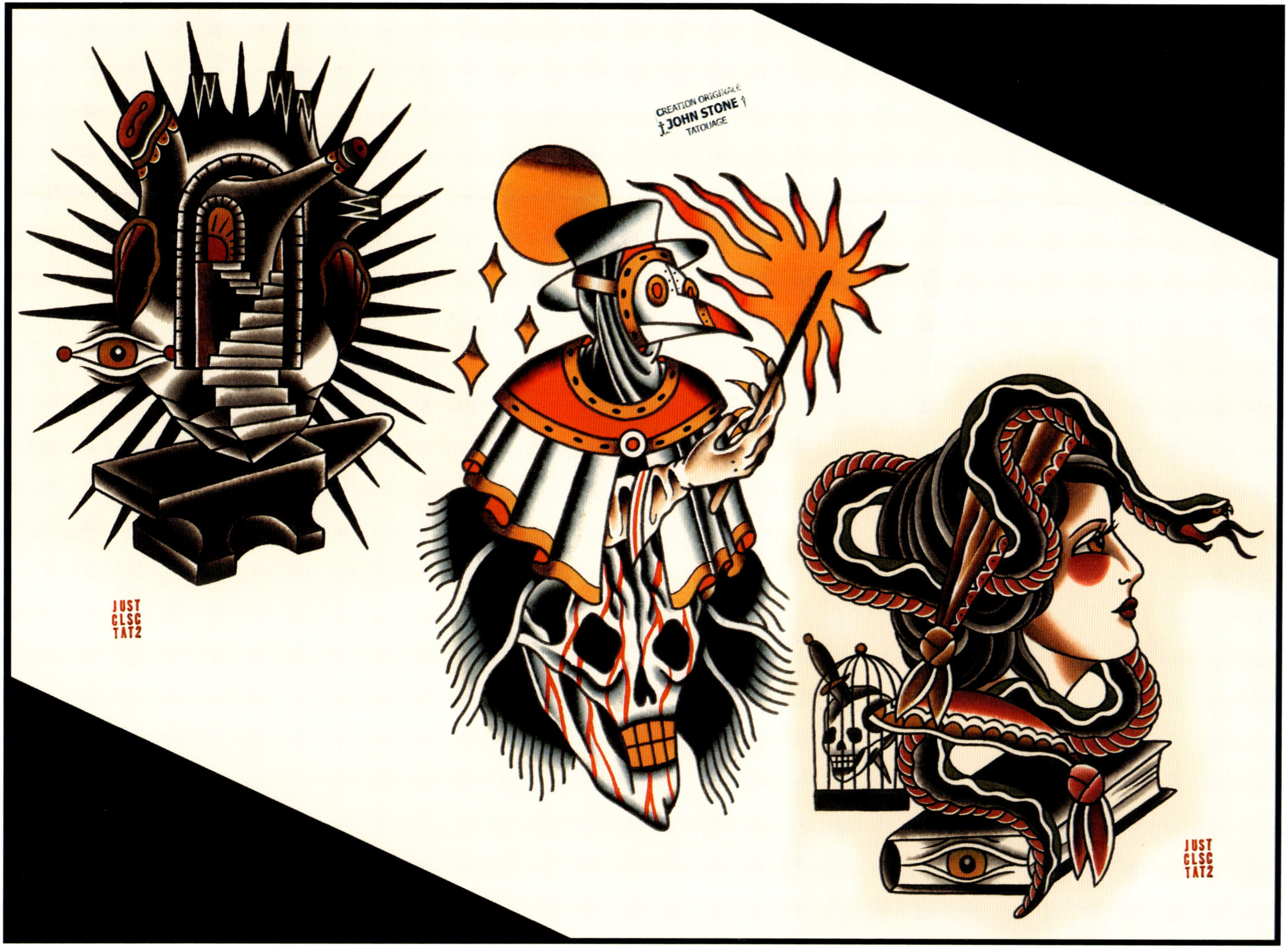
CREATION ORIGINALE
JOHN STONE
TATOUAGE
JUST
CLSC
TAT2
JUST
CLSC
TAT2

Left and bottom center
Max Dem
@maxdemtattoo
Glorybound Tattoo / Antwerp / Belgium

Right and top center
Josh Dee
@joshdeetattoo
Black Ship Tattoo / Namur / Belgium

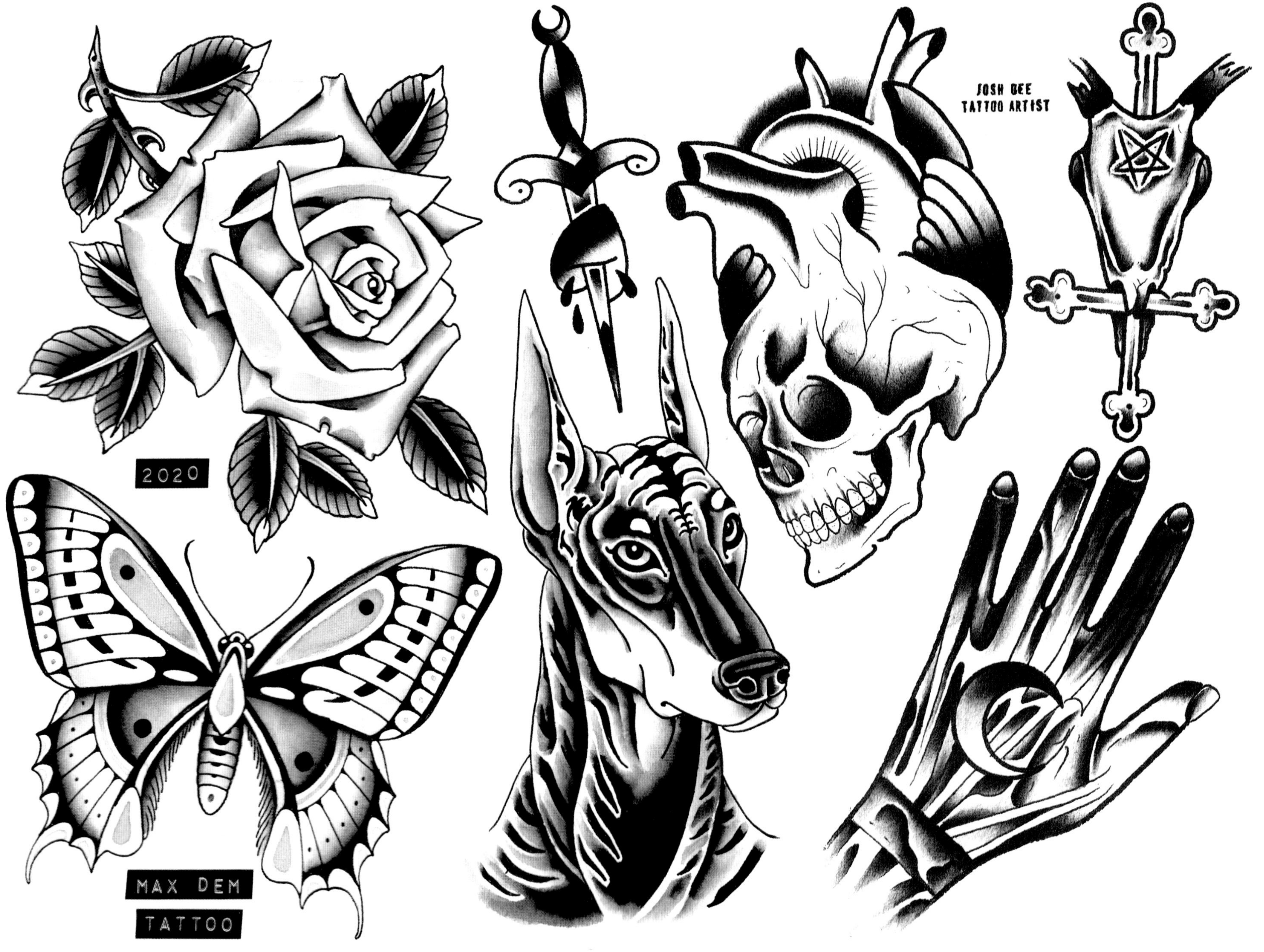

JOSH DEE
TATTOO ARTIST
2020
MAX DEM
TATTOO

Left
John Stone
@john_stone_tatouage
L'Astrolabe / Dinard / France

Right
Phil Kyle
@philkyle
Magnum Opus Tattoo / Pleurtuit / France

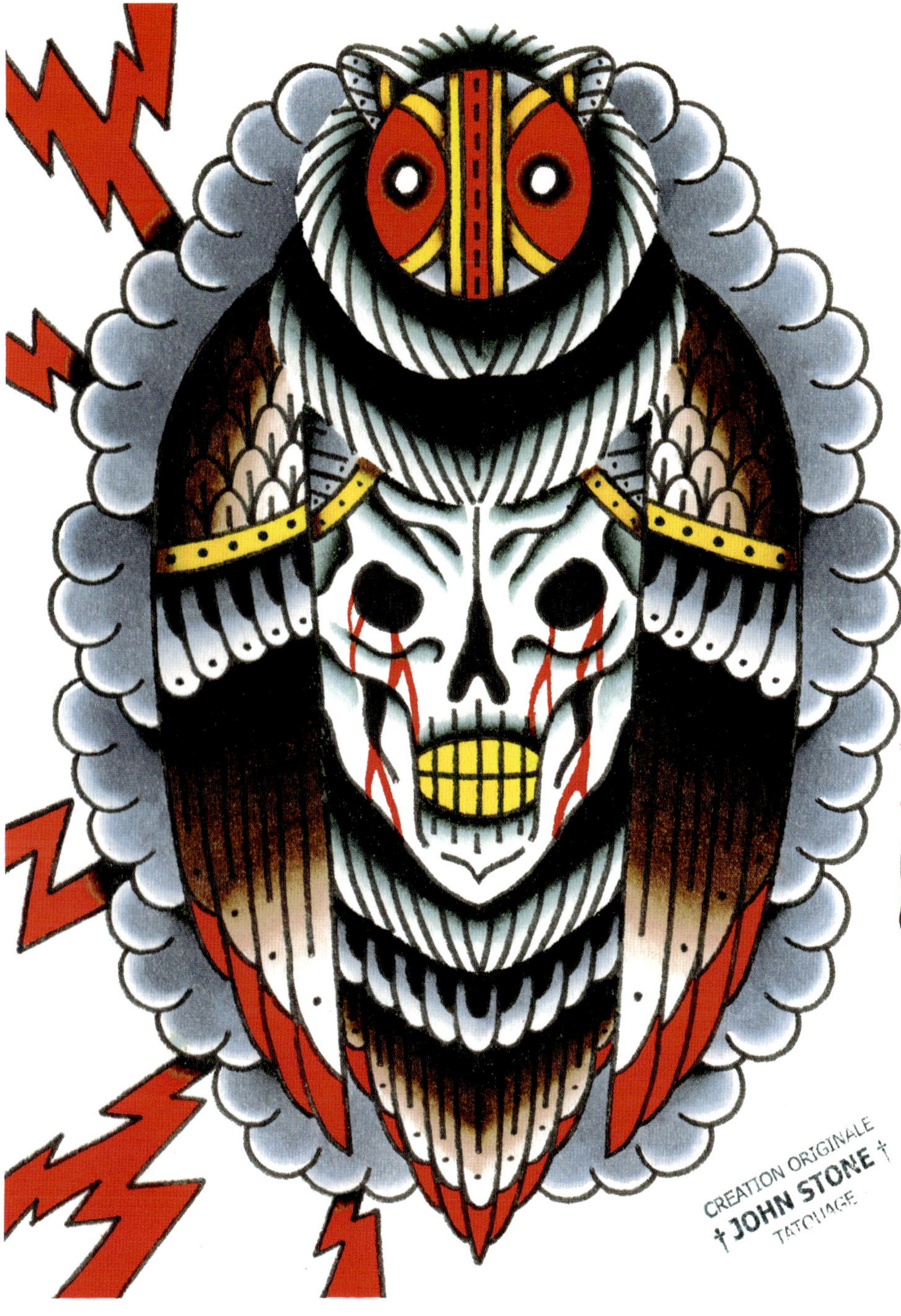
CREATION ORIGINALE
† JOHN STONE †
TATOUAGE

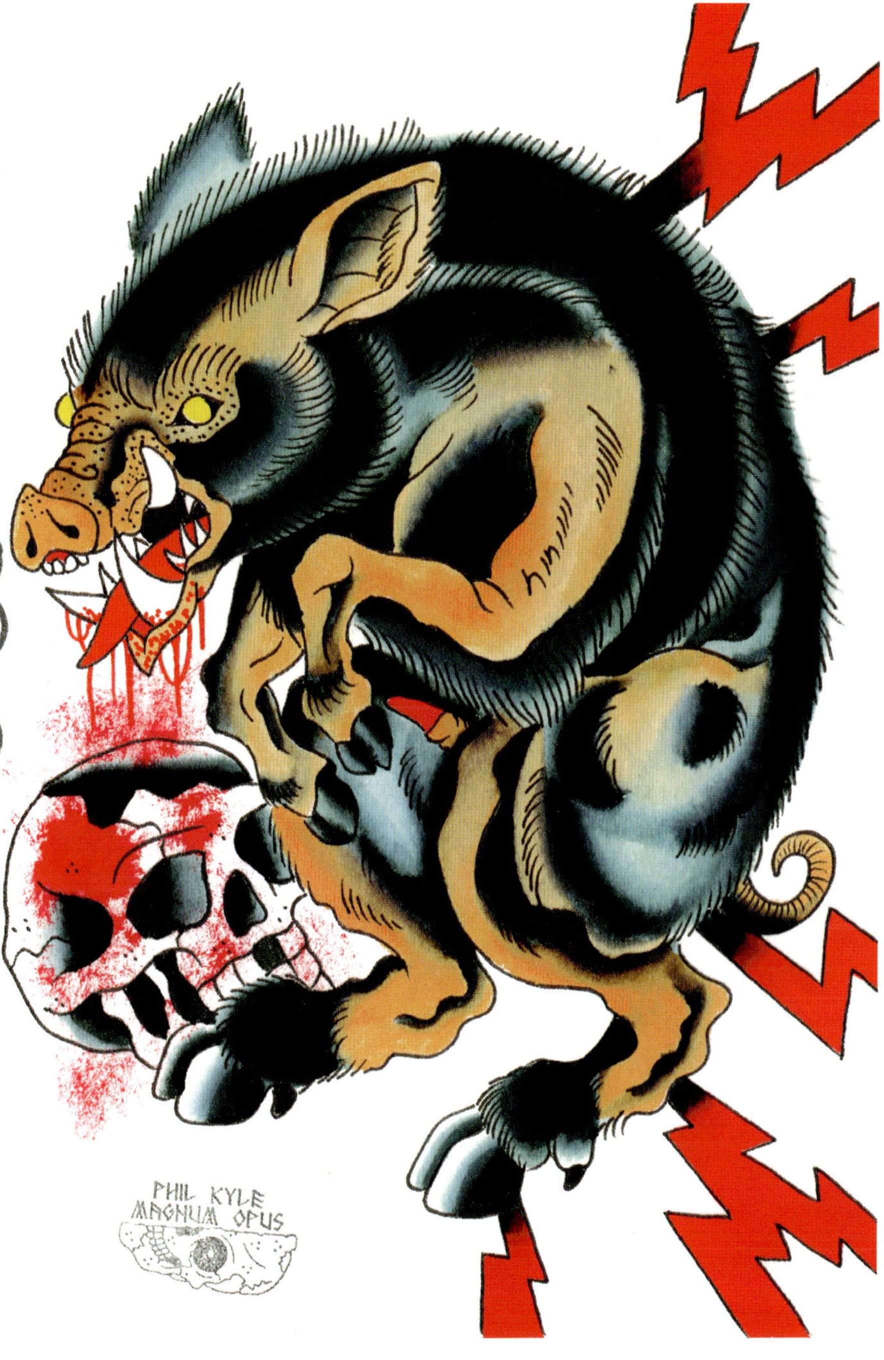
PHIL KYLE
MAGNUM OPUS

Left
Bastien Vandal
@bastienvandal
Balck Hole Tattoo / Quimper / France

Right
Just
@classicjustin
Mystery Tattoo Club / Paris / France

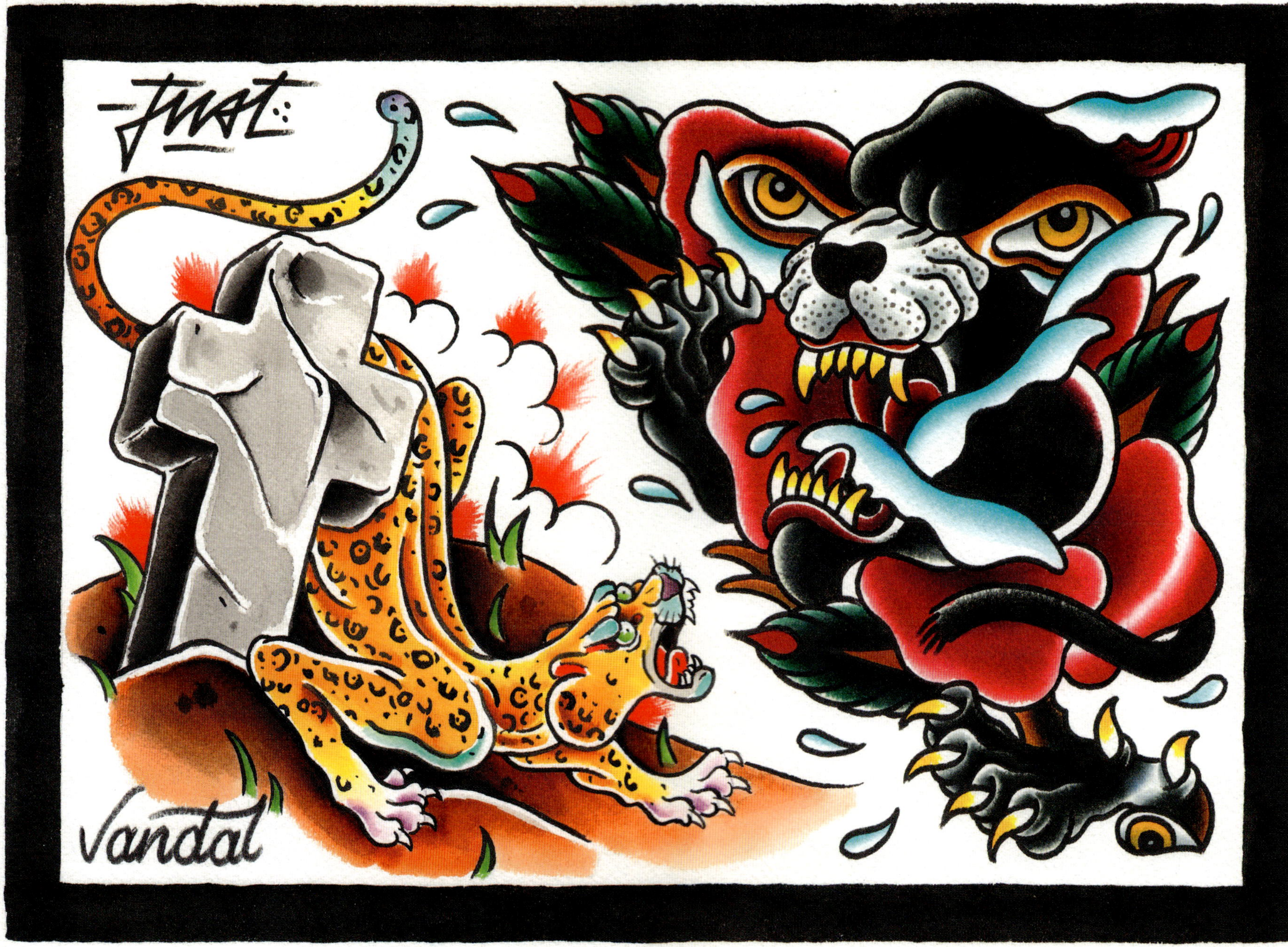
Vandal

Left
Uncle Ho
@uncle_ho_mitchmalone
Iron Claw / Strasbourg / France

Right
Tiwan
@tiwan_tattoo
Spirit Tattoo Rennes / Rennes / France

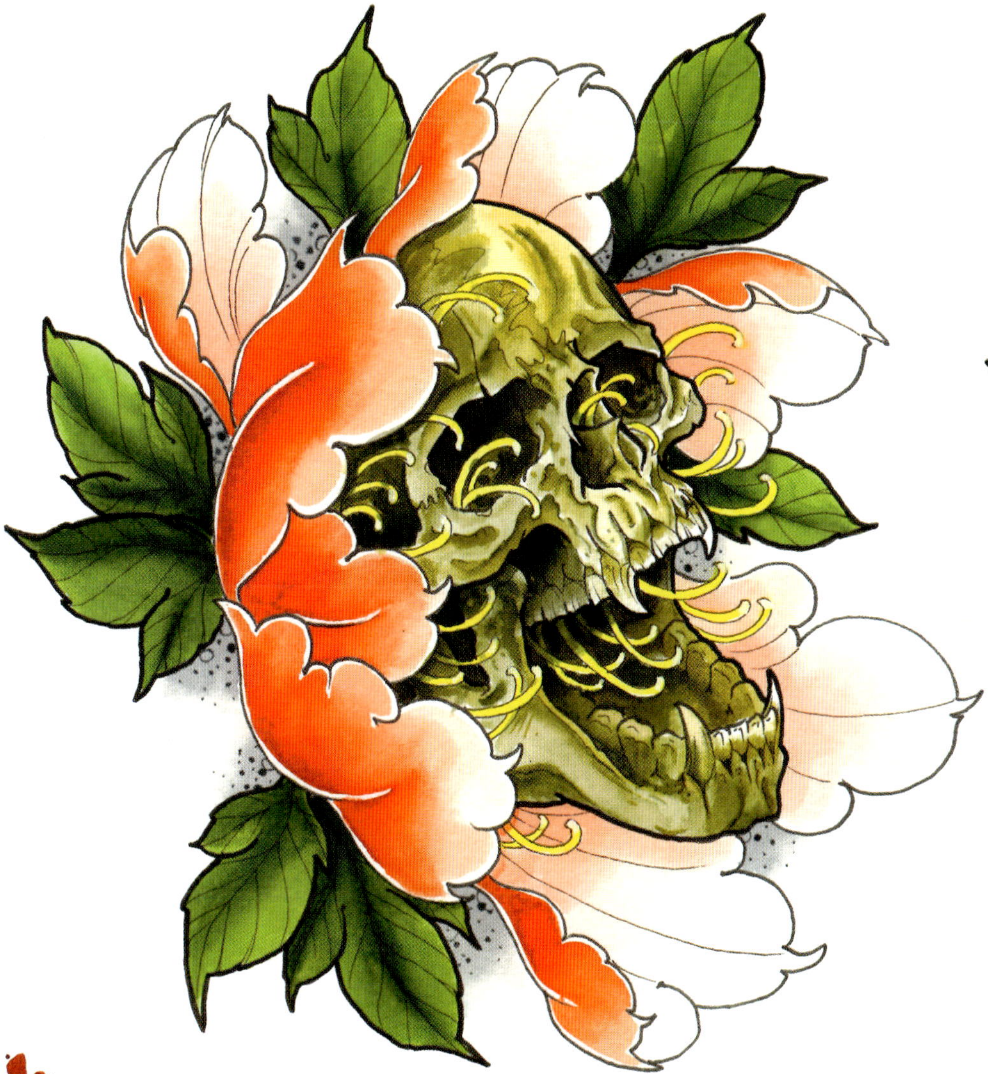

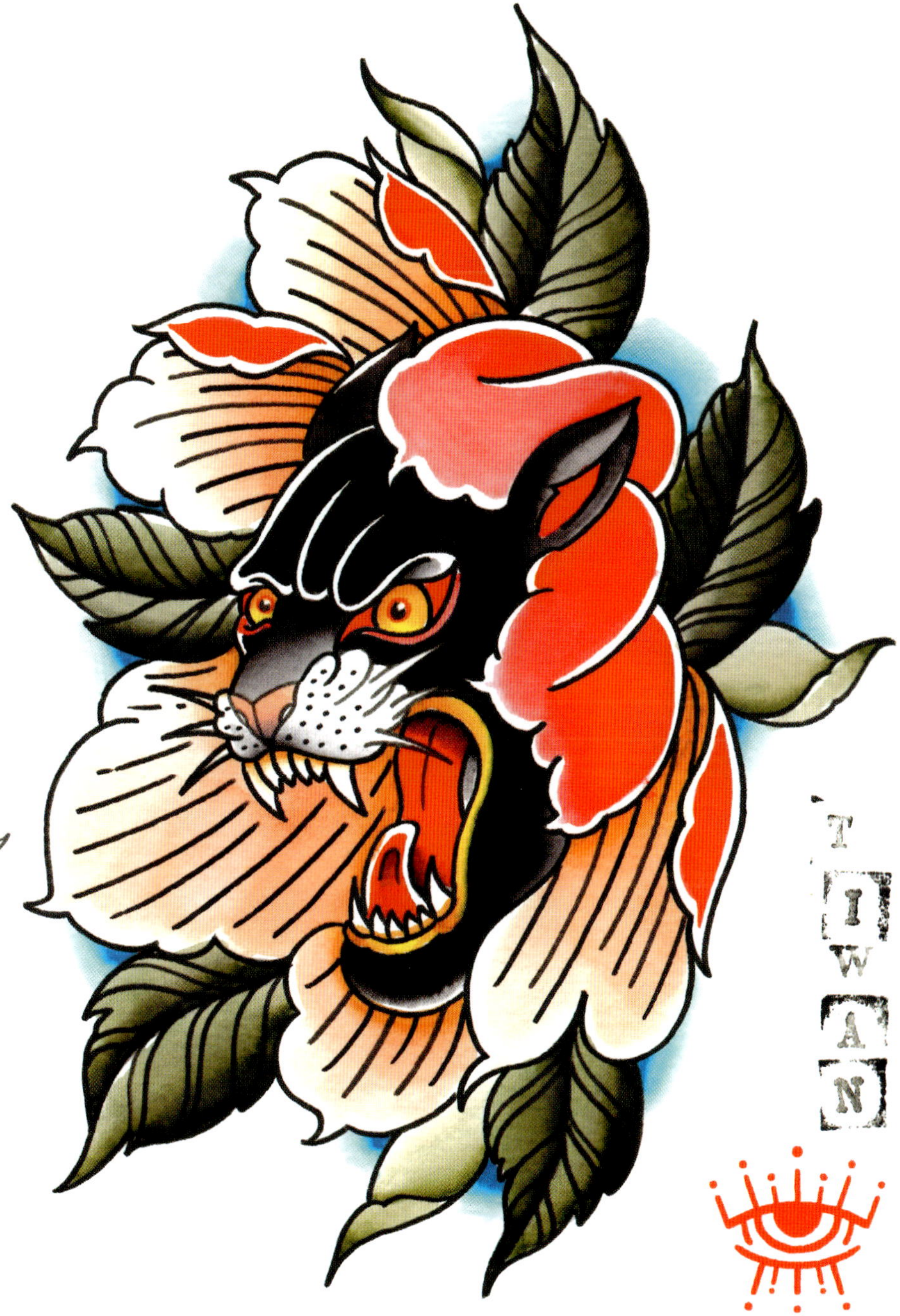
T
I
W
A
N

Left
John Stone
@john_stone_tatouage
L'Astrolabe / Dinard / France

Right
Phil Kyle
@philkyle
Magnum Opus Tattoo / Pleurtuit / France

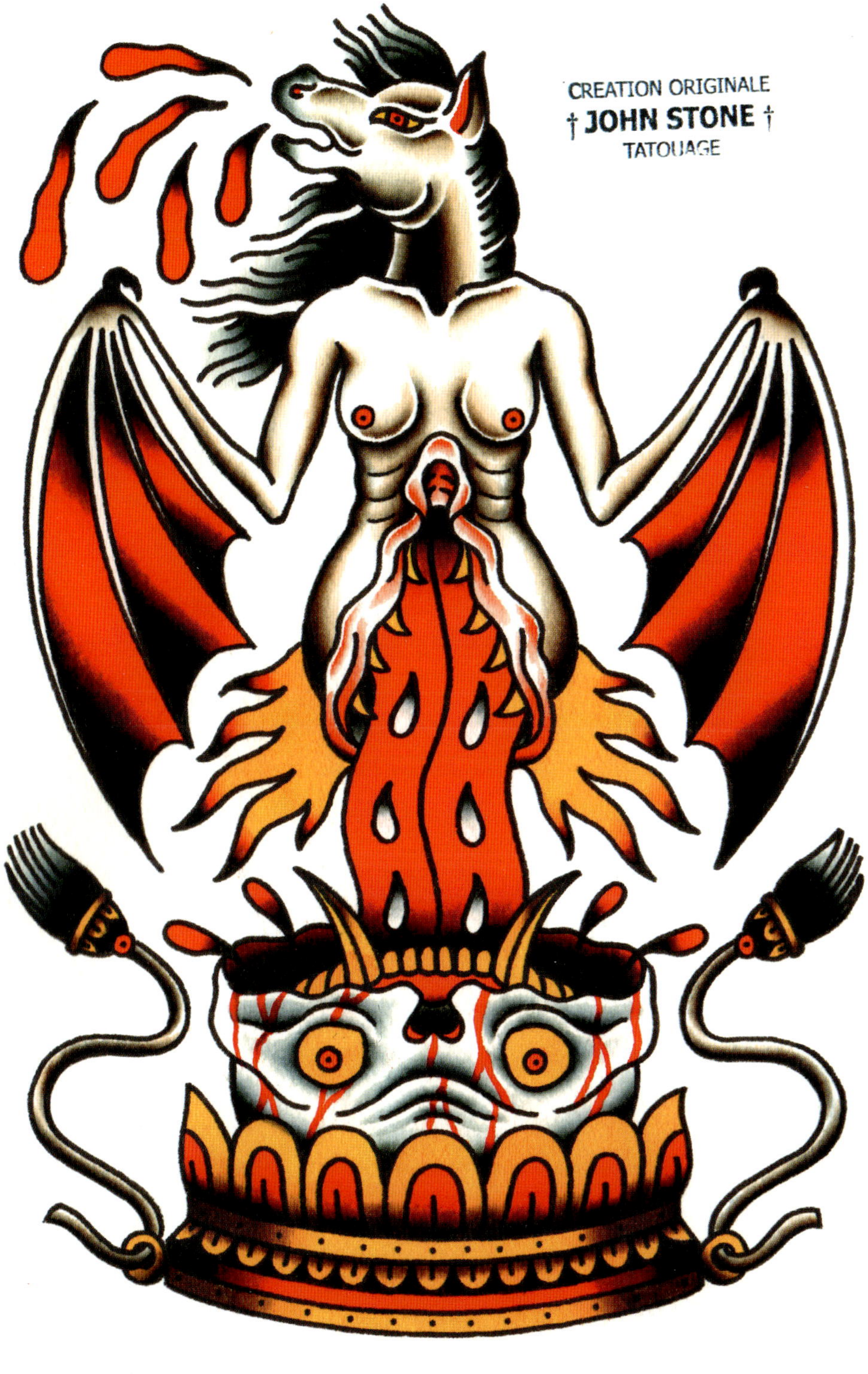
CREATION ORIGINALE
† JOHN STONE †
TATOUAGE

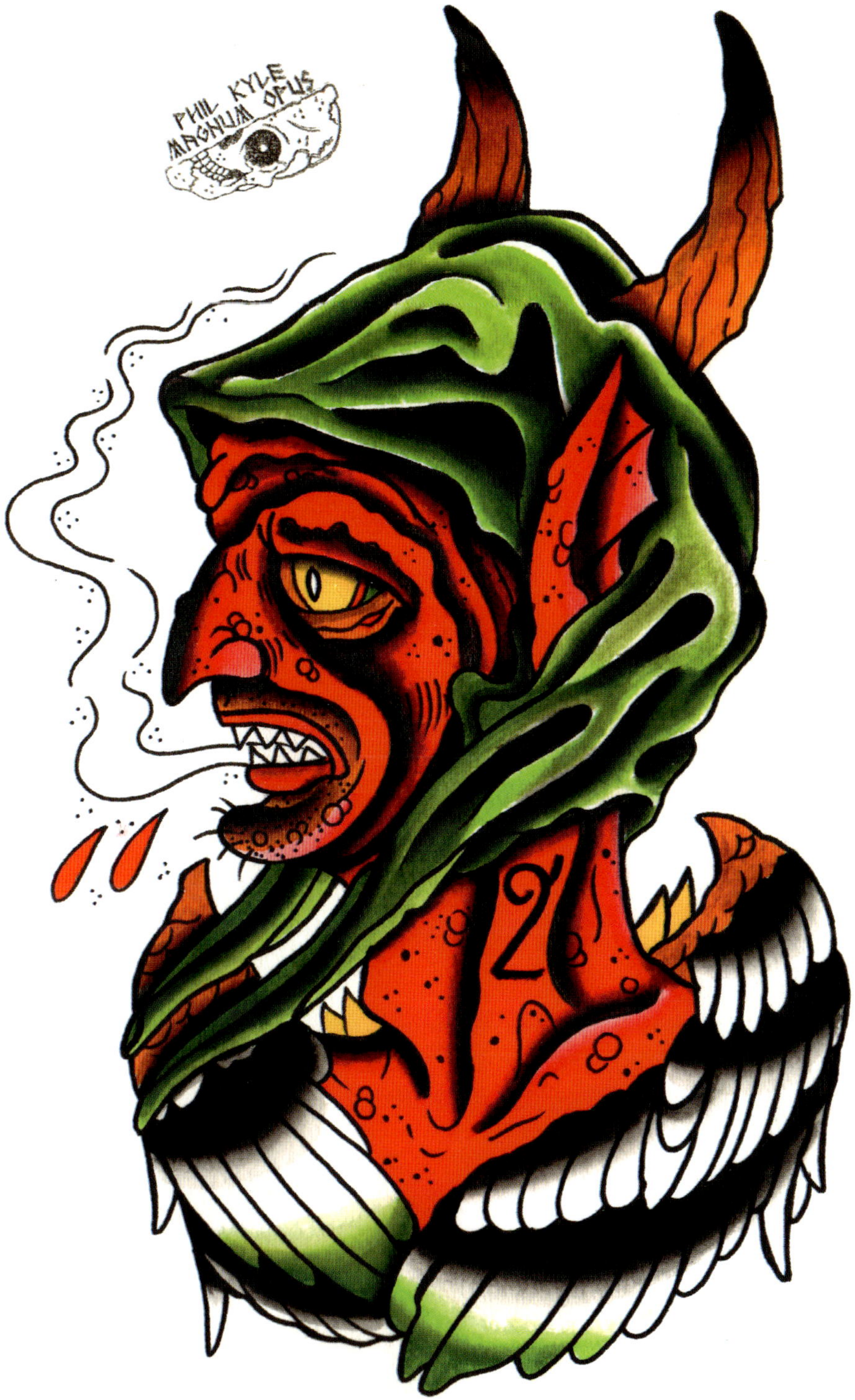
PHIL KYLE
MAGNUM OPUS

Left
El Bent
@elbenttattoo
True Love / Paris / France

Right
Clément Doineau (Dague Rouge)
@clementdoineau
Grey Bronco Tattoo / Nantes / France

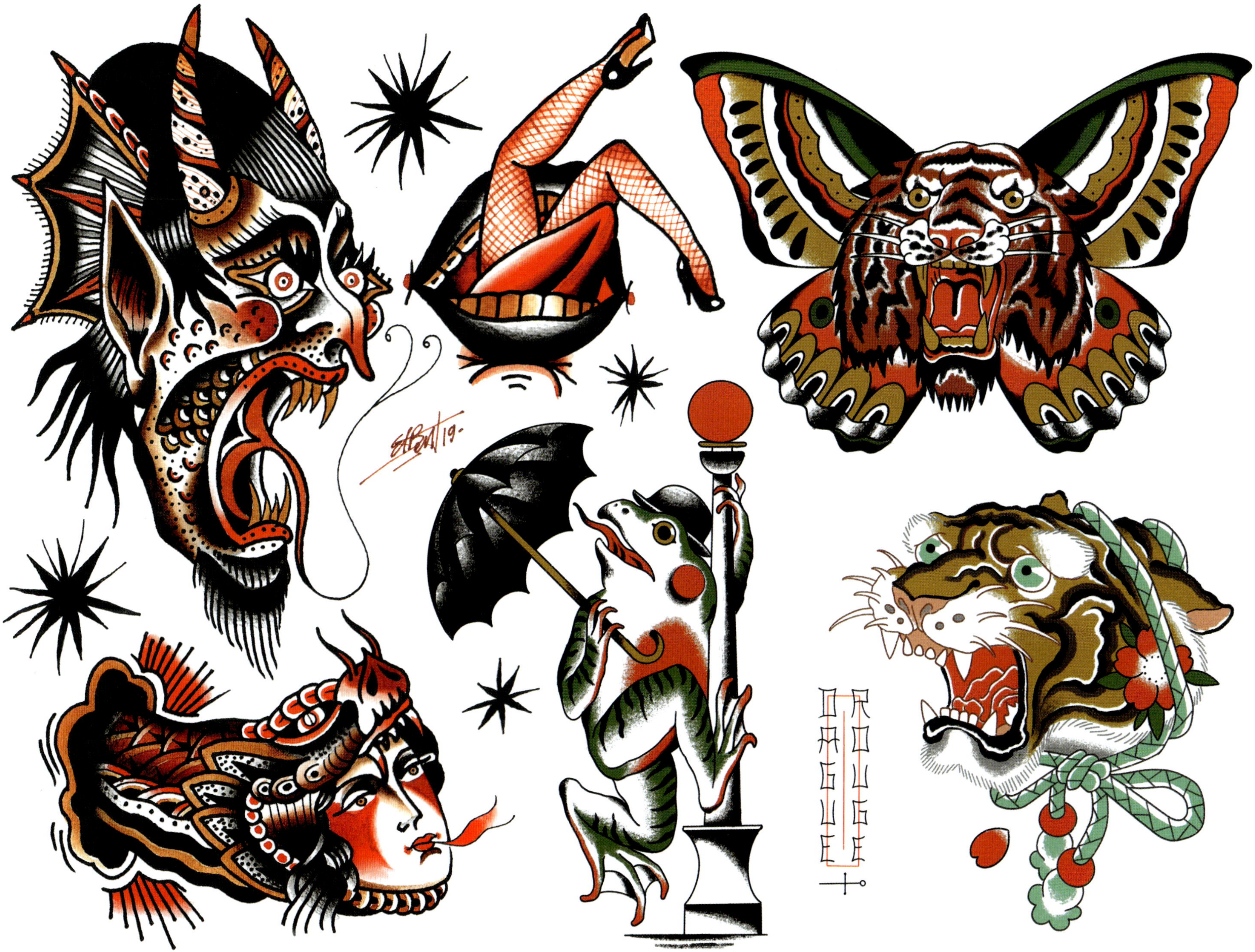
ROUGE
DAGUE

Left
GuiHardside
@guihardside
Par Amour Tatouages / Saint-Brieuc / France

Right
Chocos
@chocosgs
Sheriff Body Art / Serrières / France

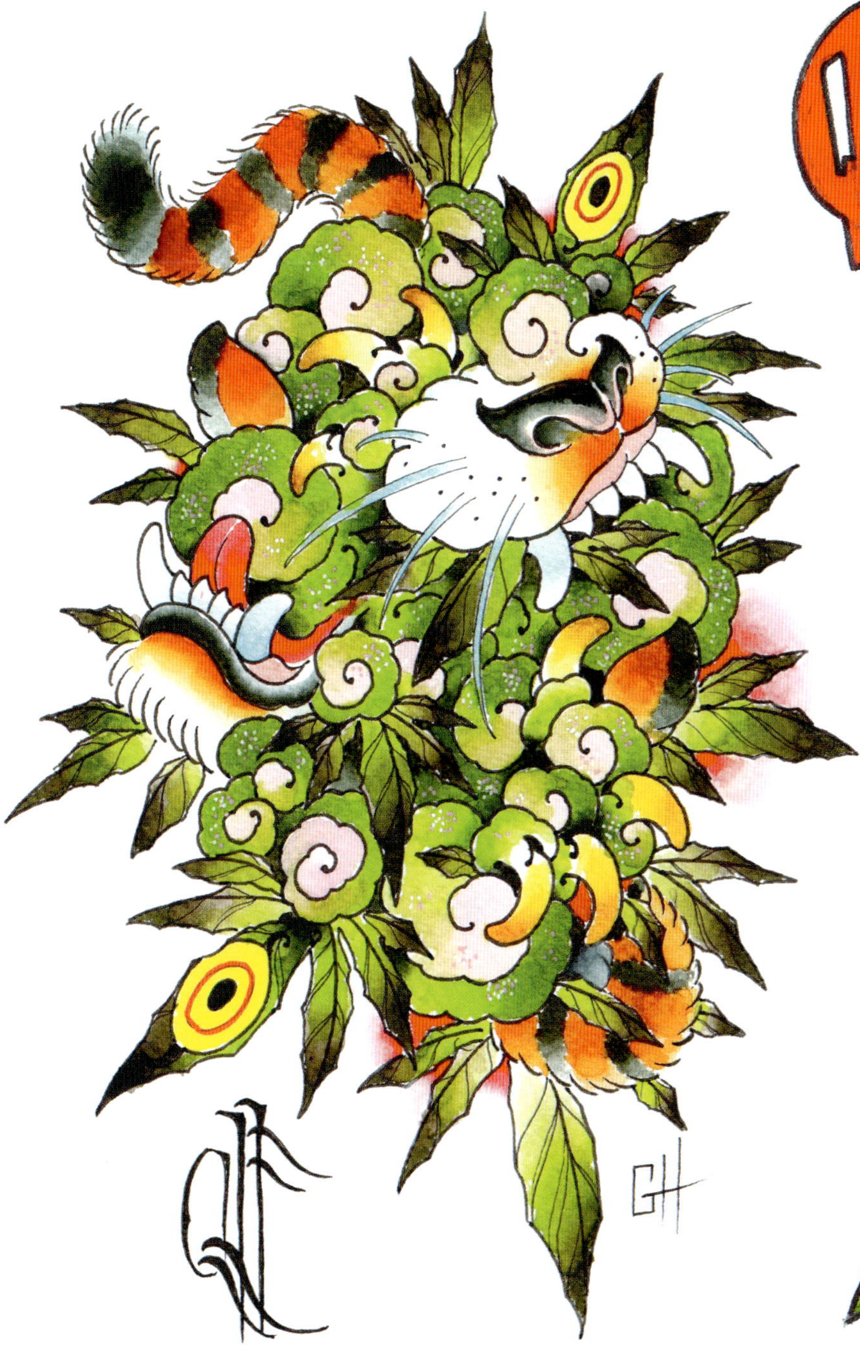

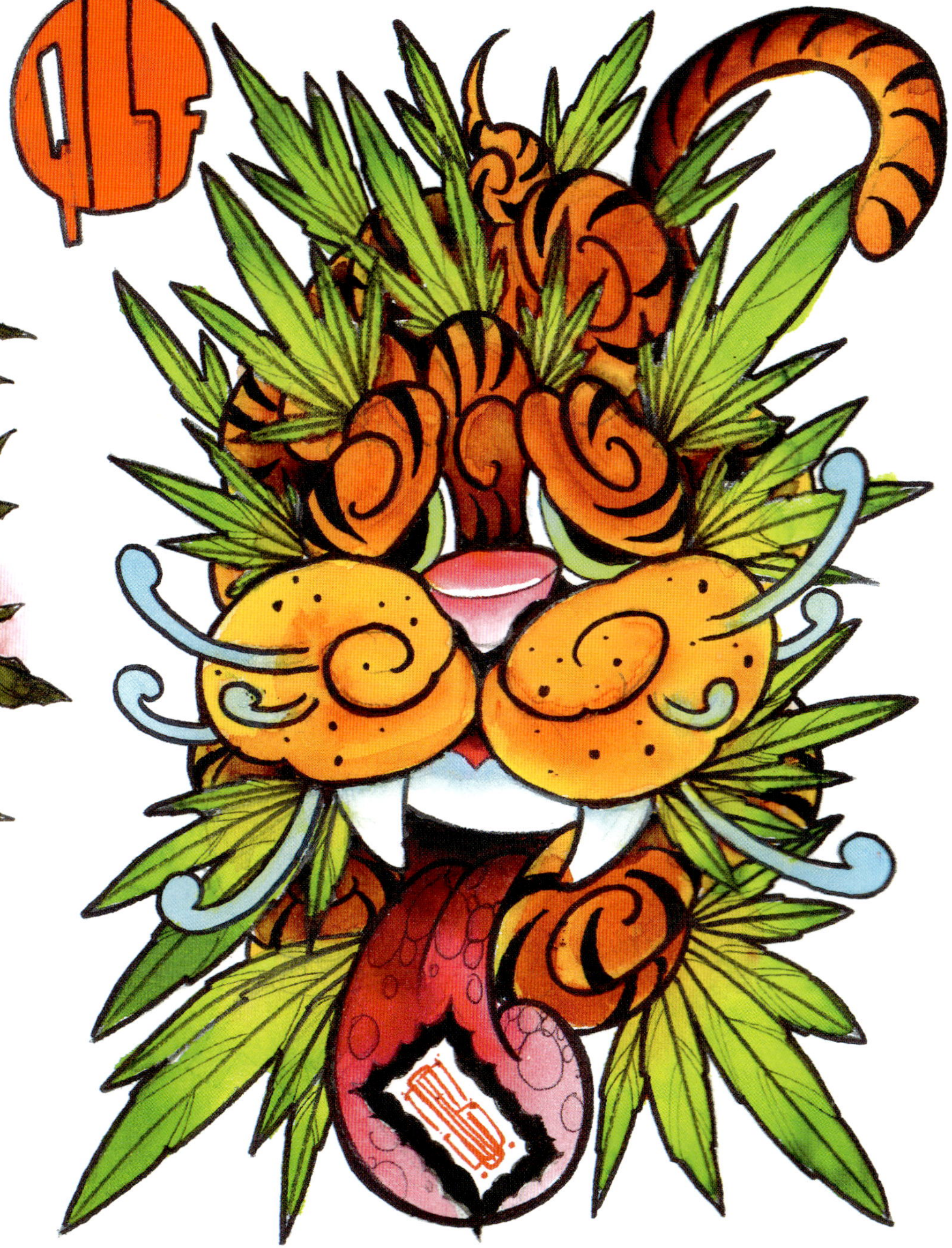

Left
Charles
@charlestattoorennes
L'Ogre Rouge / Pont-Péan / France

Right
Tony Grande Truandise
@tonygrandetruandise
L'Ogre Rouge / Pont-Péan / France

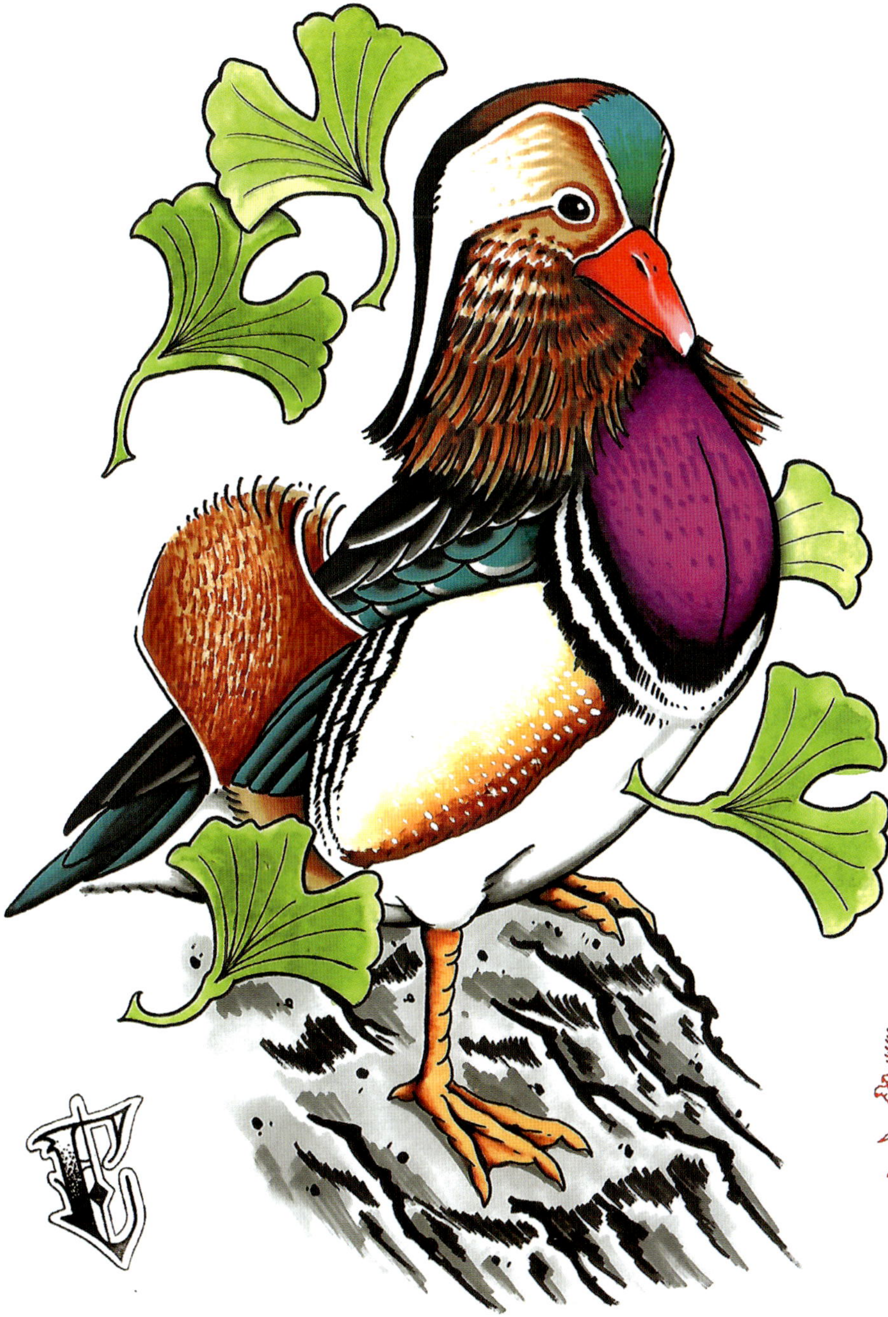

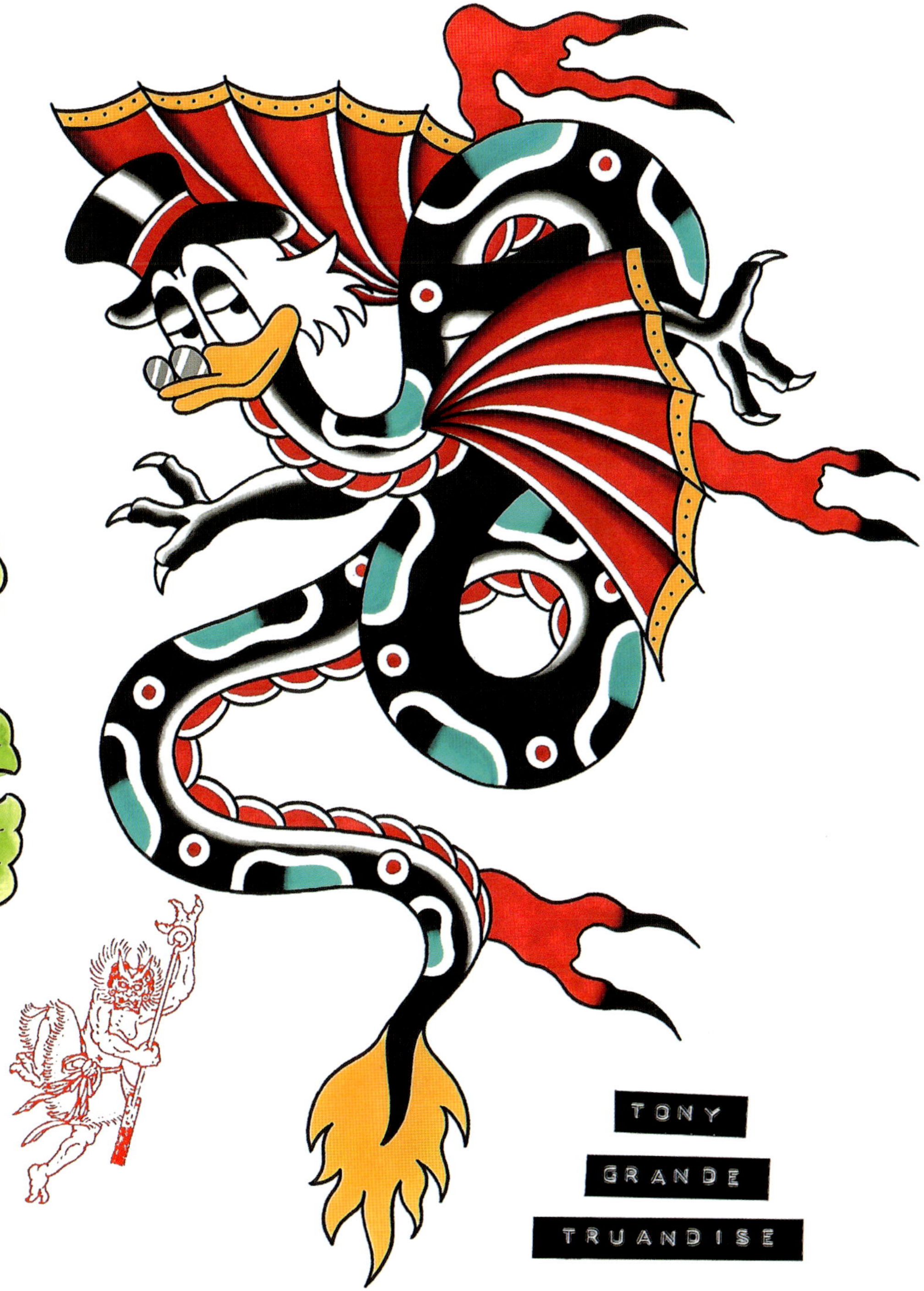

TONY

GRANDE

TRUANDISE

Left
Kim Ai
@kim_ai_tattoo
Kimochi Tattoo Shop / Montpellier / France

Right
Koopa
@koopatattoo
Imperium Electric Tattoo / Biarritz / France

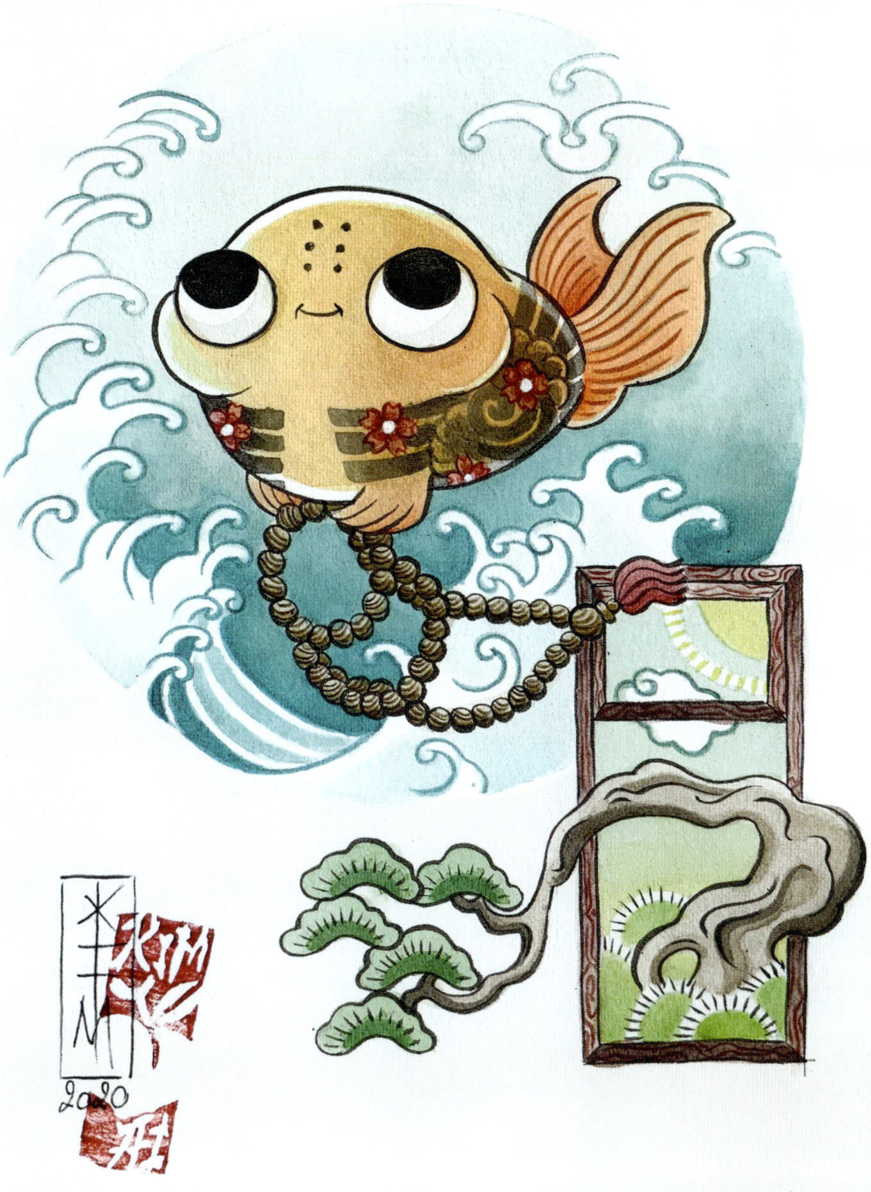
2020

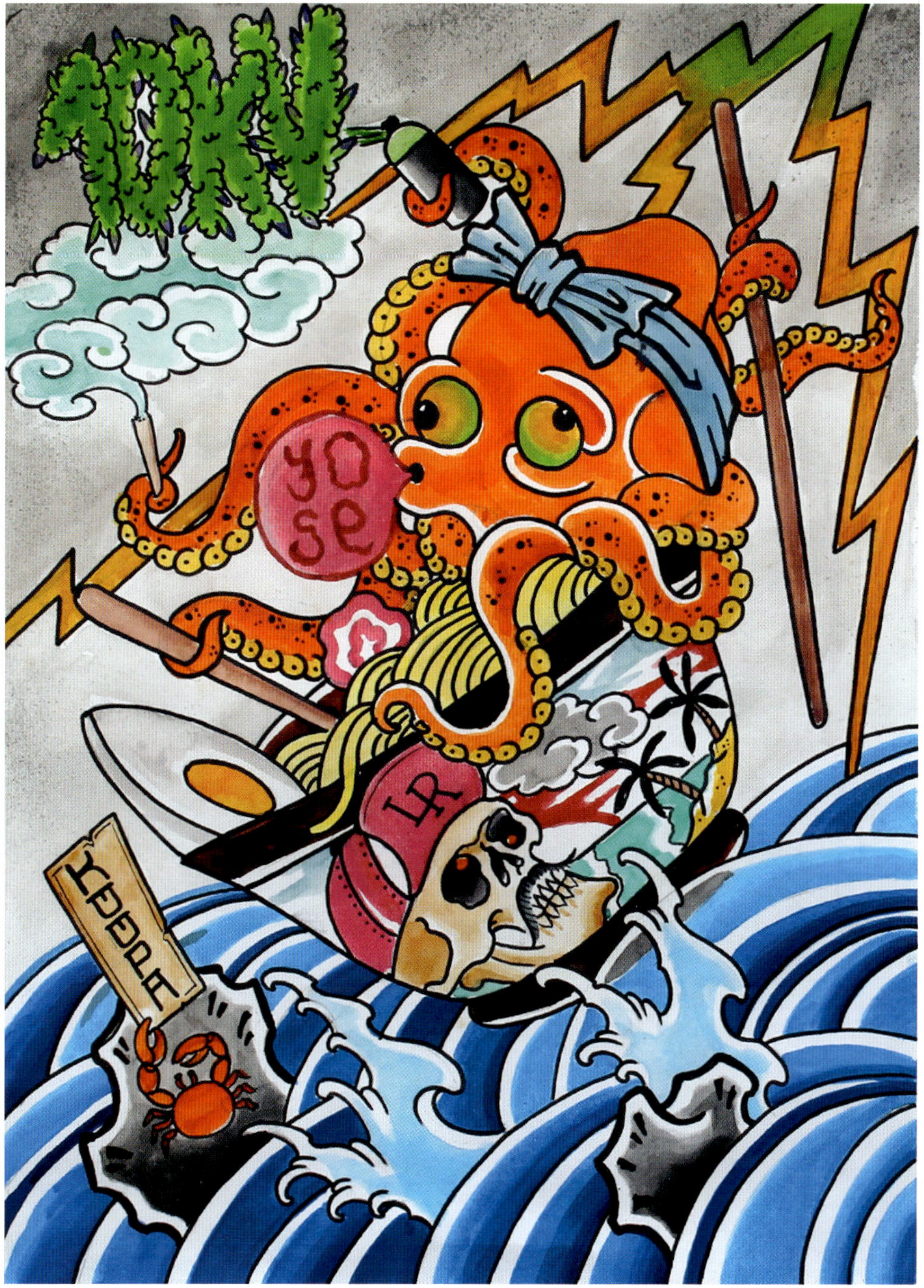
YO
SE
LR

Left
John
@bigdirtyshit
Ponce Tatoueur / Lyon / France

Right
Bandini
@nicobandini
681 Tattoos / Lyon / France

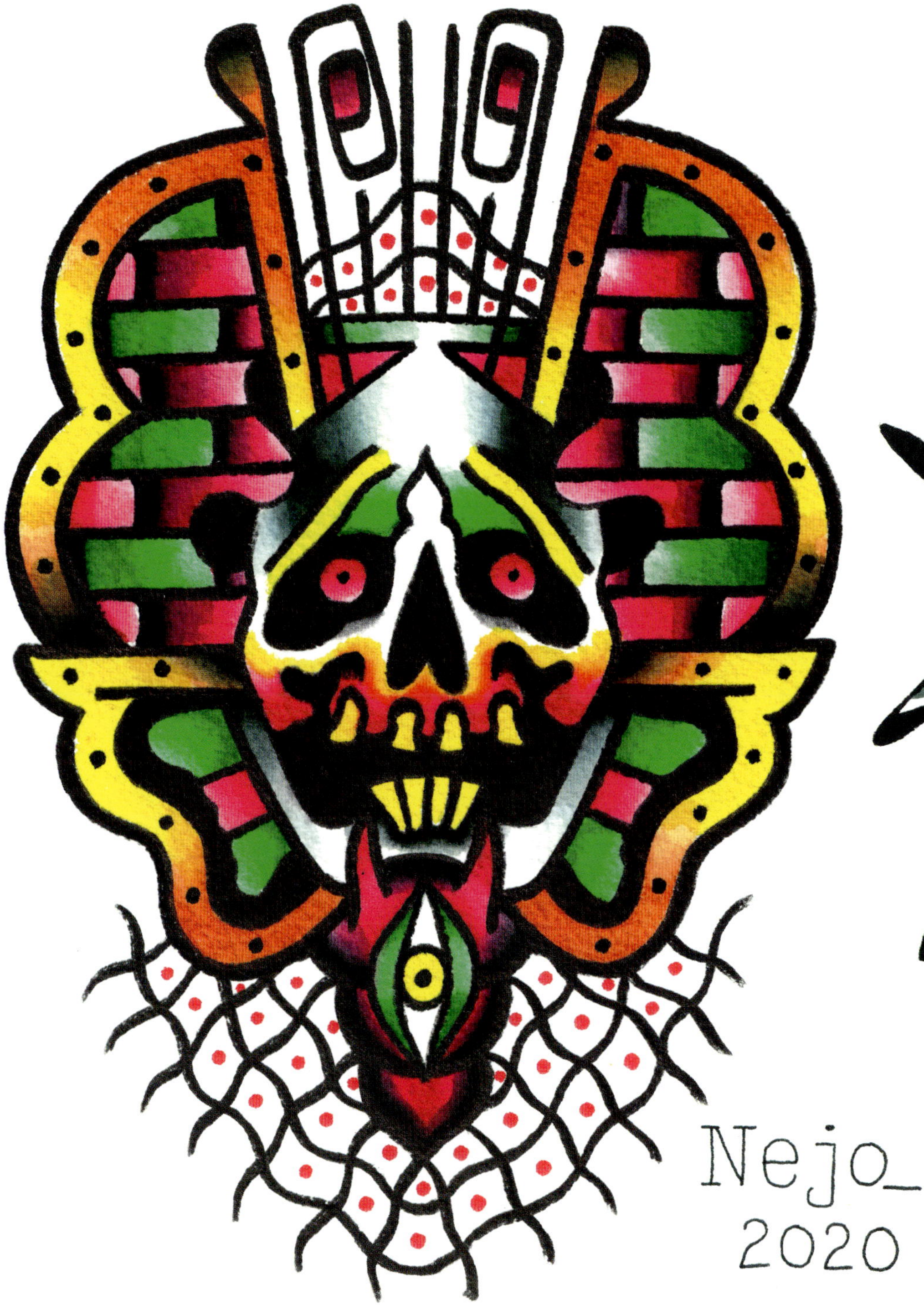
Nejo_
2020

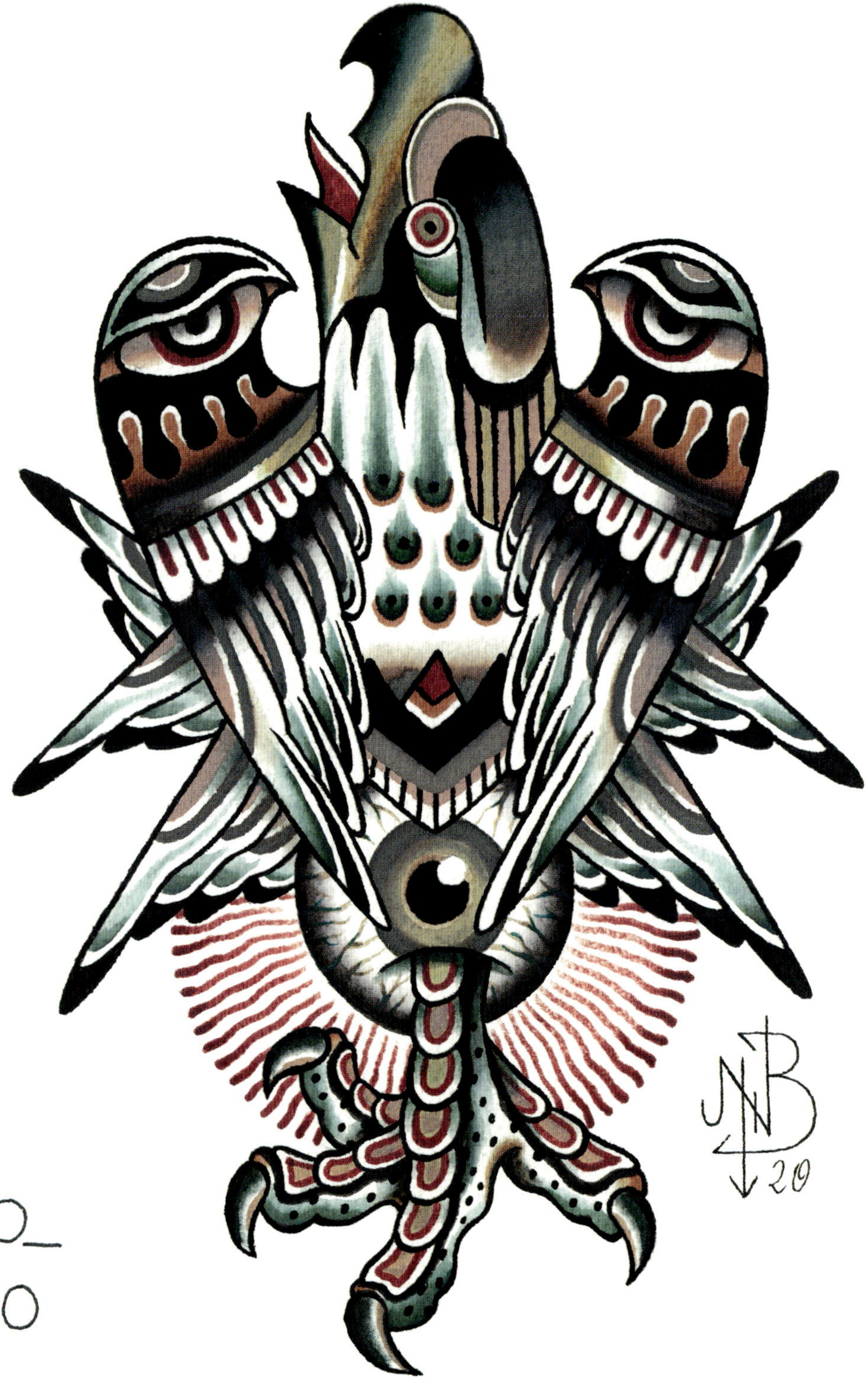

Left
John Stone
@john_stone_tatouage
L'Astrolabe / Dinard / France

Right
Mink Bell
@mink_bell
Electric Funeral Tattoo Craft / Strasbourg / France

CREATION ORIGINALE
† JOHN STONE †
TATOUAGE

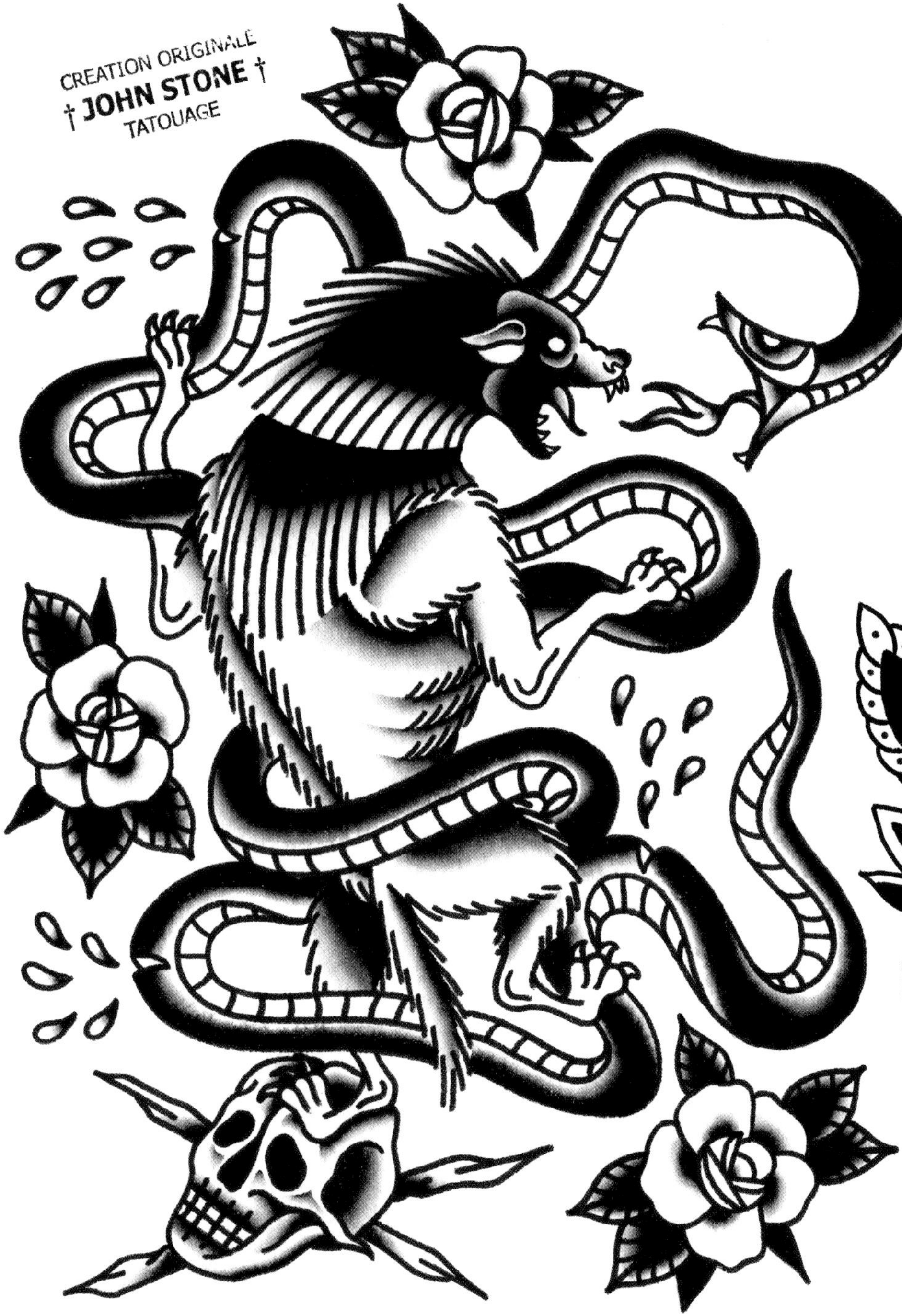

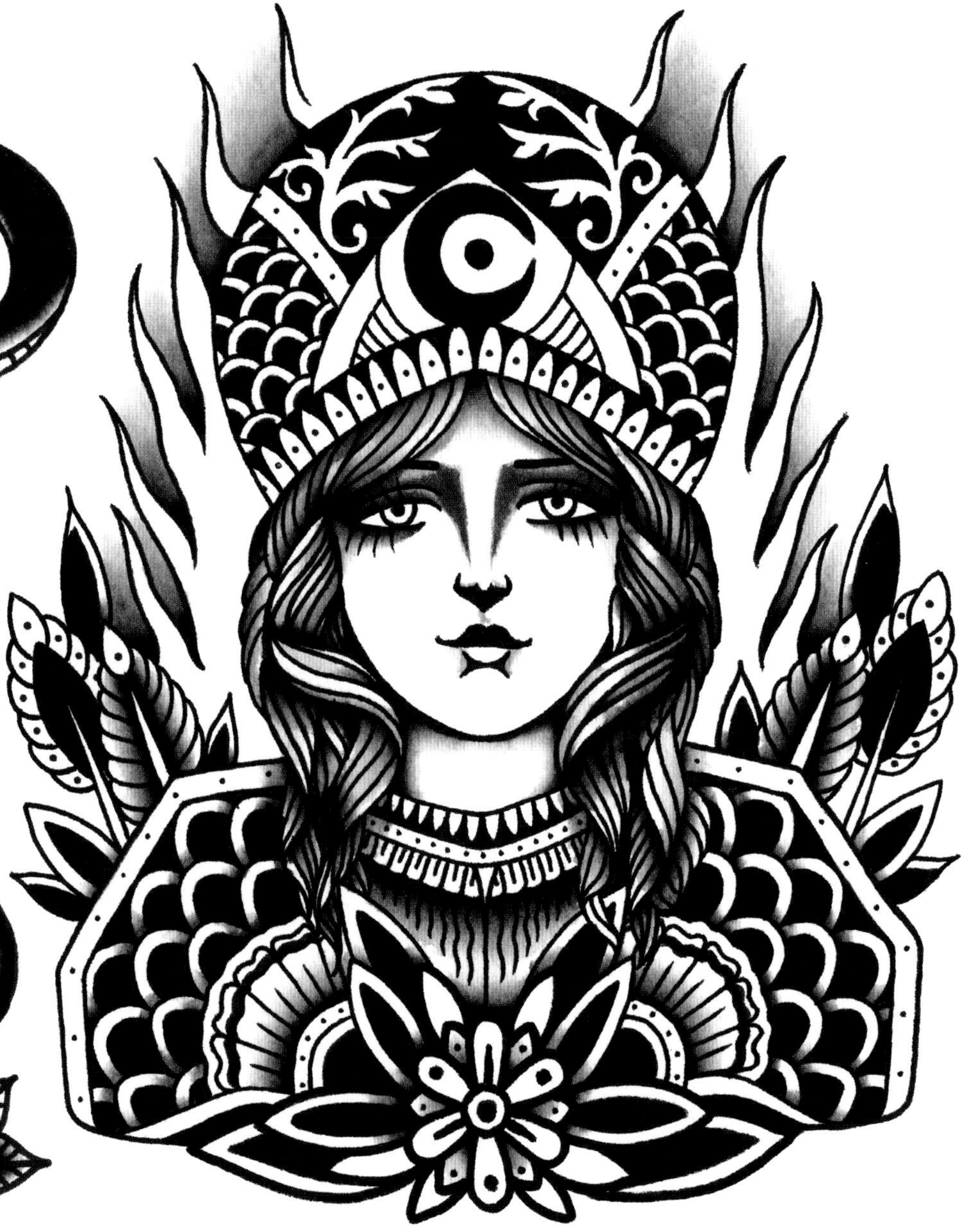

Left
Tony Grande Truandise
@tonygrandetruandise
L'Ogre Rouge / Pont-Péan / France

Right
Pasco
@pasco-octtt
Ocean Child Tattoo / Erstein / France

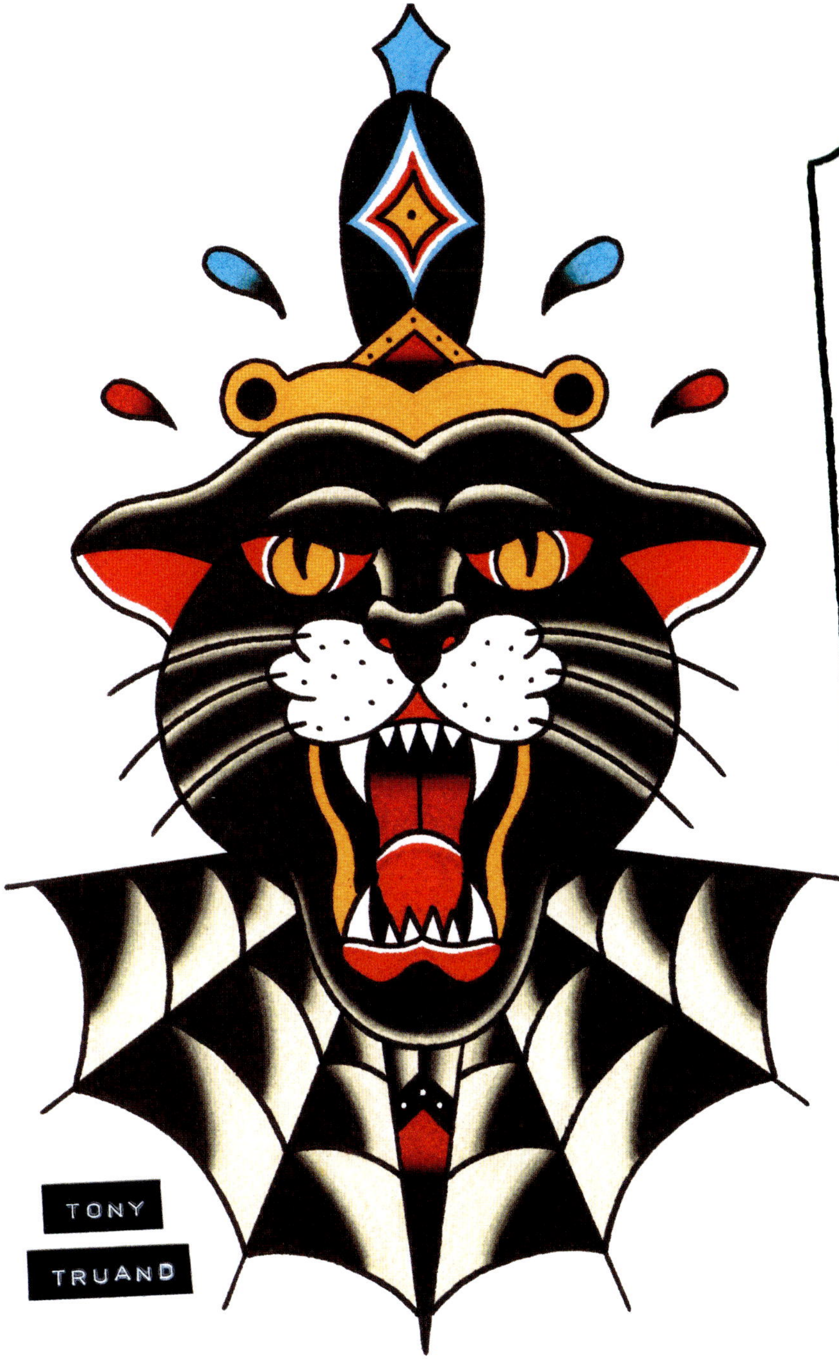

TONY
TRUAND

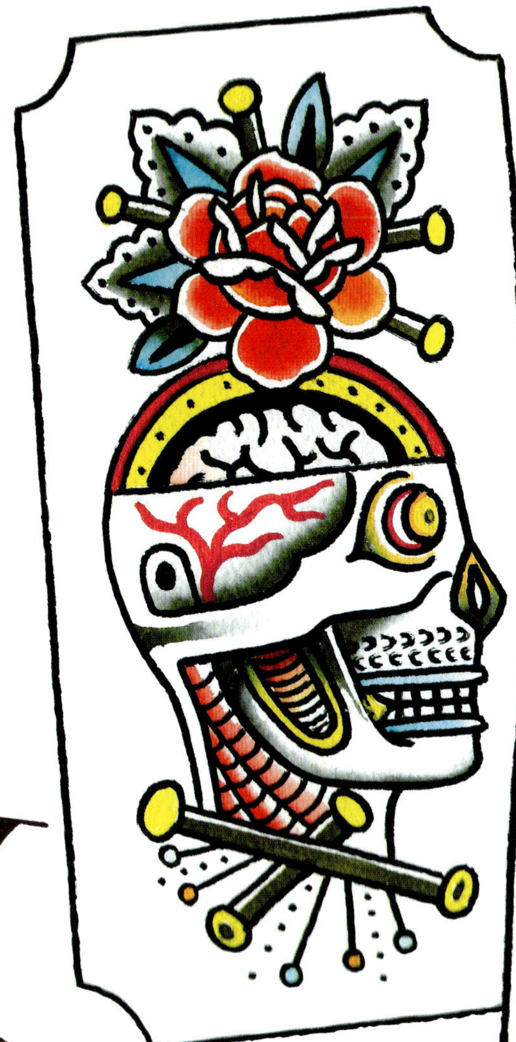

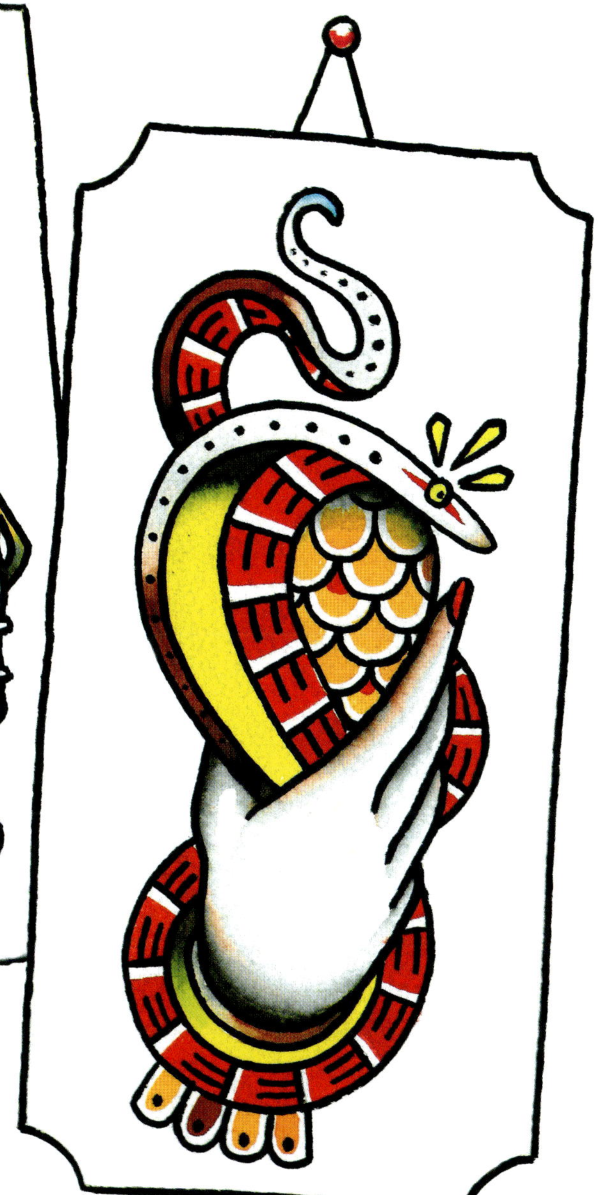

Left
Tiwan
@tiwan_tattoo
Spirit Tattoo Rennes / Rennes / France

Right
El Bent
@elbenttattoo
True Love / Paris / France

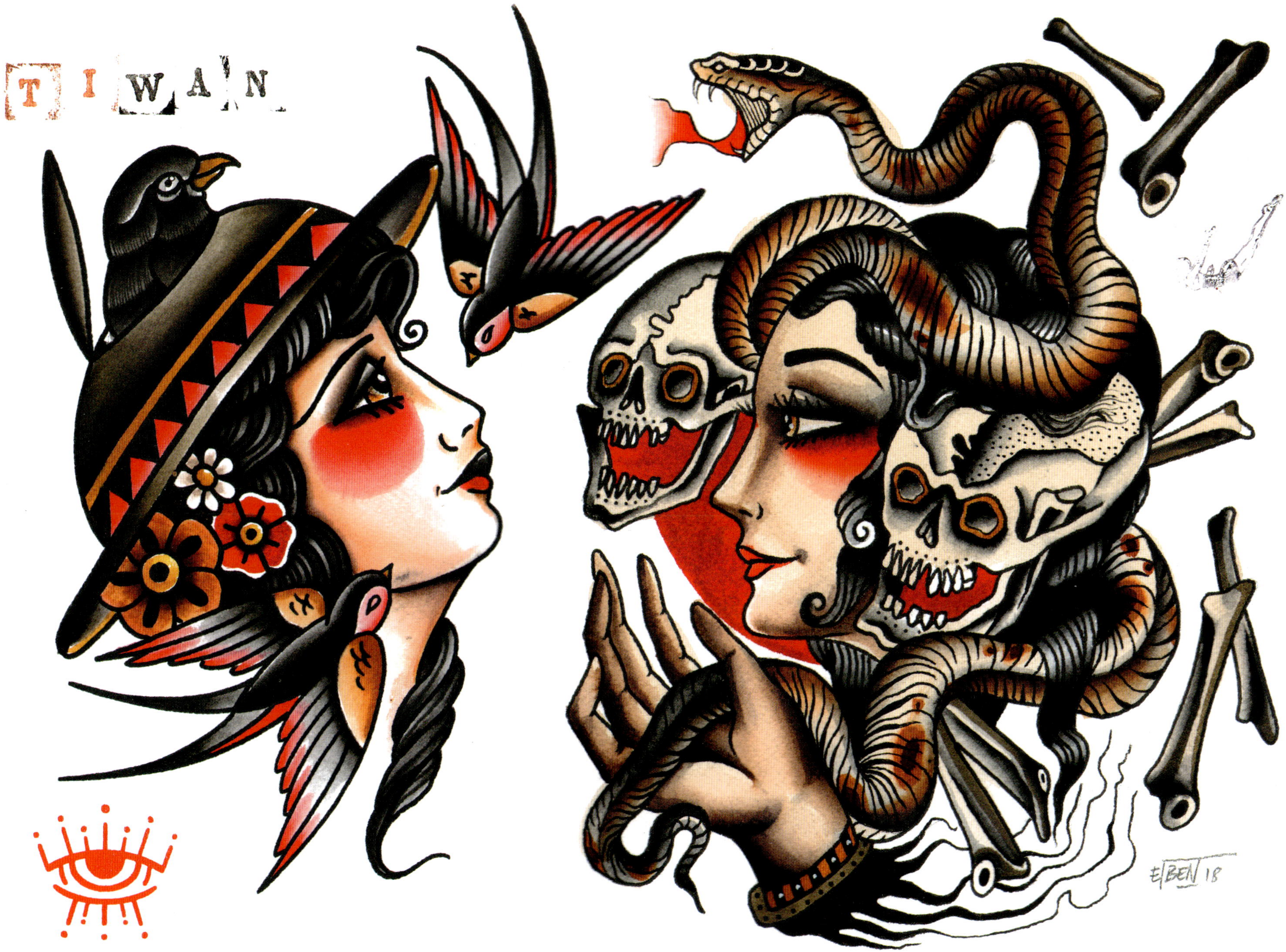

TIWAN
EBEN 18

Left
Max Dem
@maxdemtattoo
Glorybound Tattoo / Antwerp / Belgium

Right and top center
Polo Tattooer
@polotattooer_tgp
The Good Place Tattoo / Toulouse / France

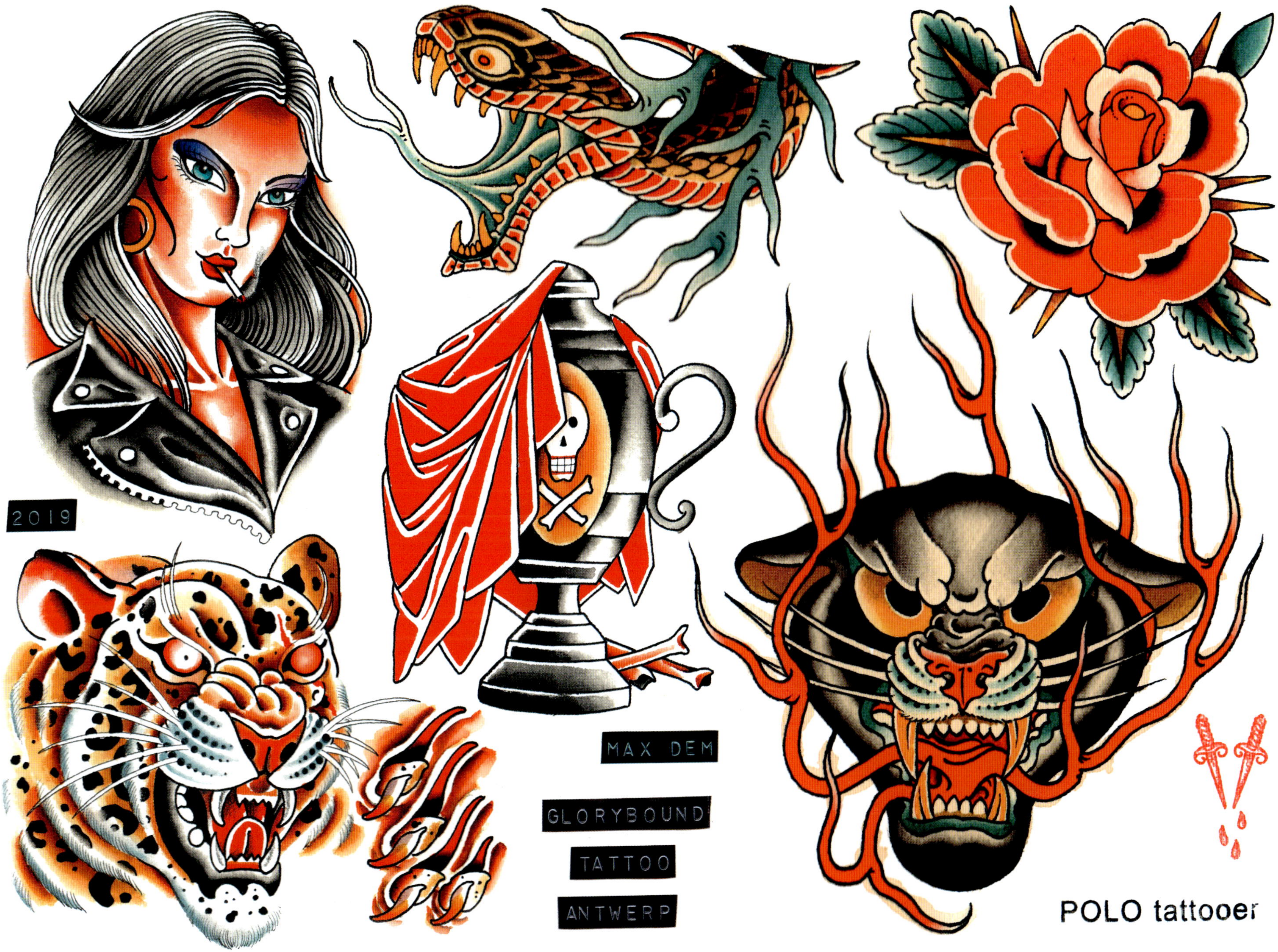
2019
MAX DEM
GLORYBOUND
TATTOO
ANTWERP
POLO tattooer

Left
John Stone
@john_stone_tatouage
L'Astrolabe / Dinard / France

Right
Iannis Le Tigre
@iannis_letigre
Le Tigre / Annecy / France

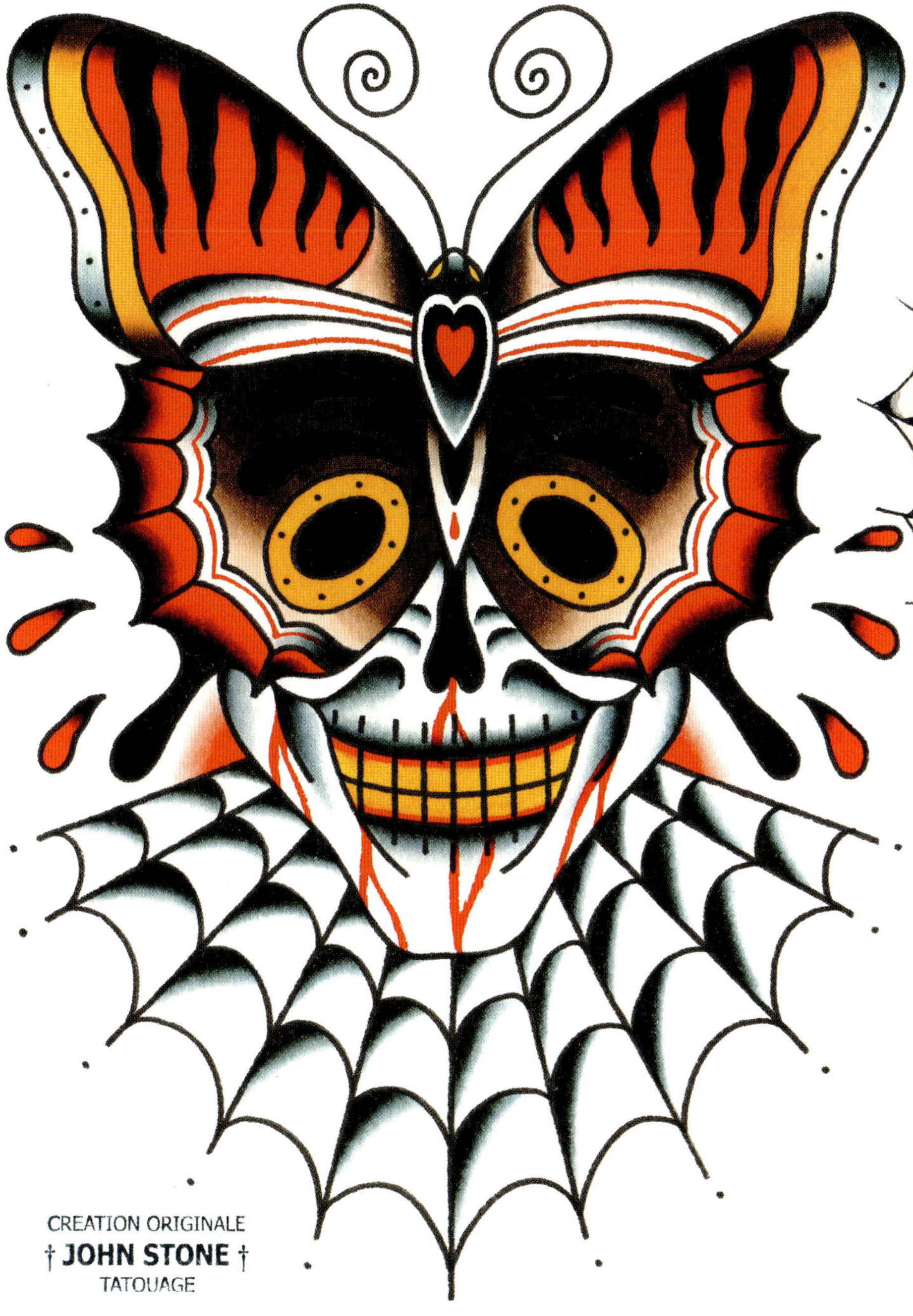

CREATION ORIGINALE
† JOHN STONE †
TATOUAGE

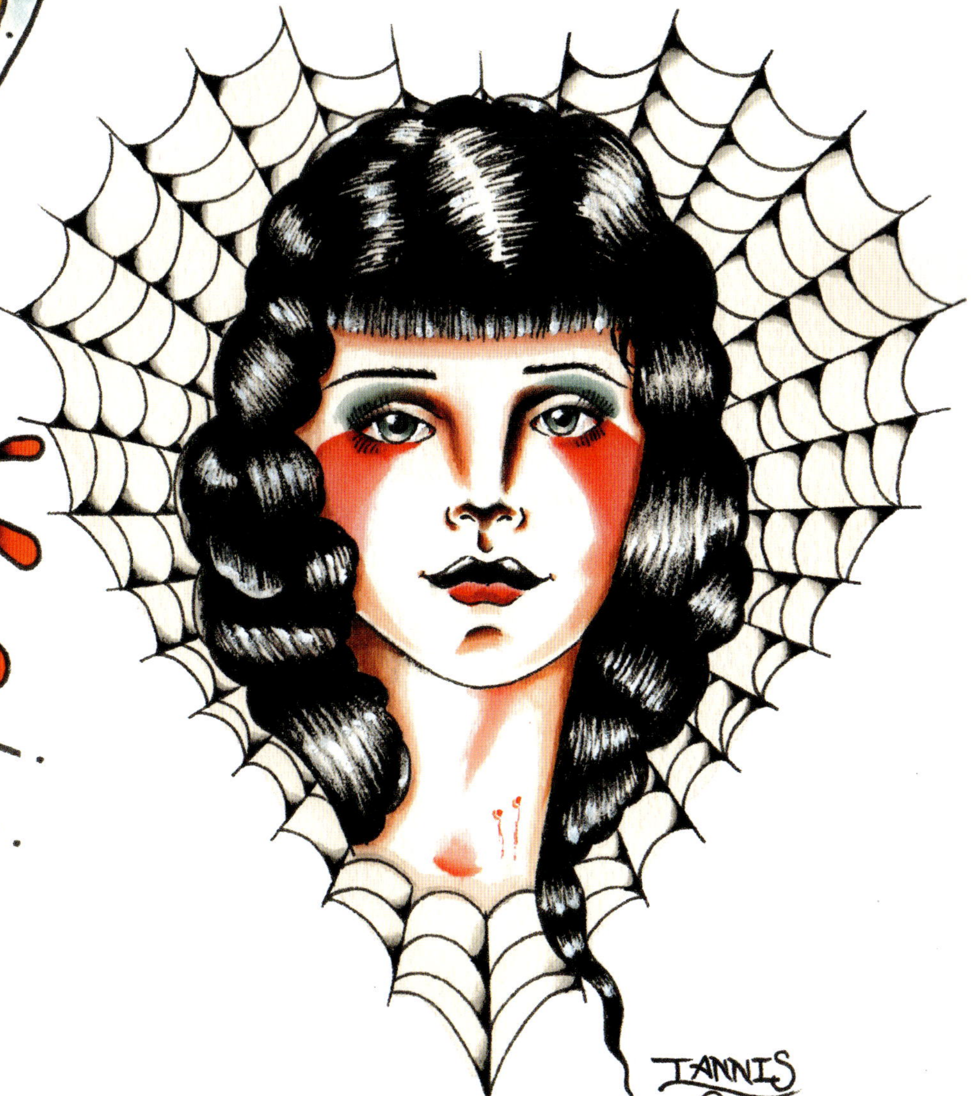

IANNIS
SR
-LETIGRE-

Left
Big Cyrus
@bigcyrus
Casa de Leões / Nantes / France

Right
Chez Nanah!
@cheznanah
On the road / France

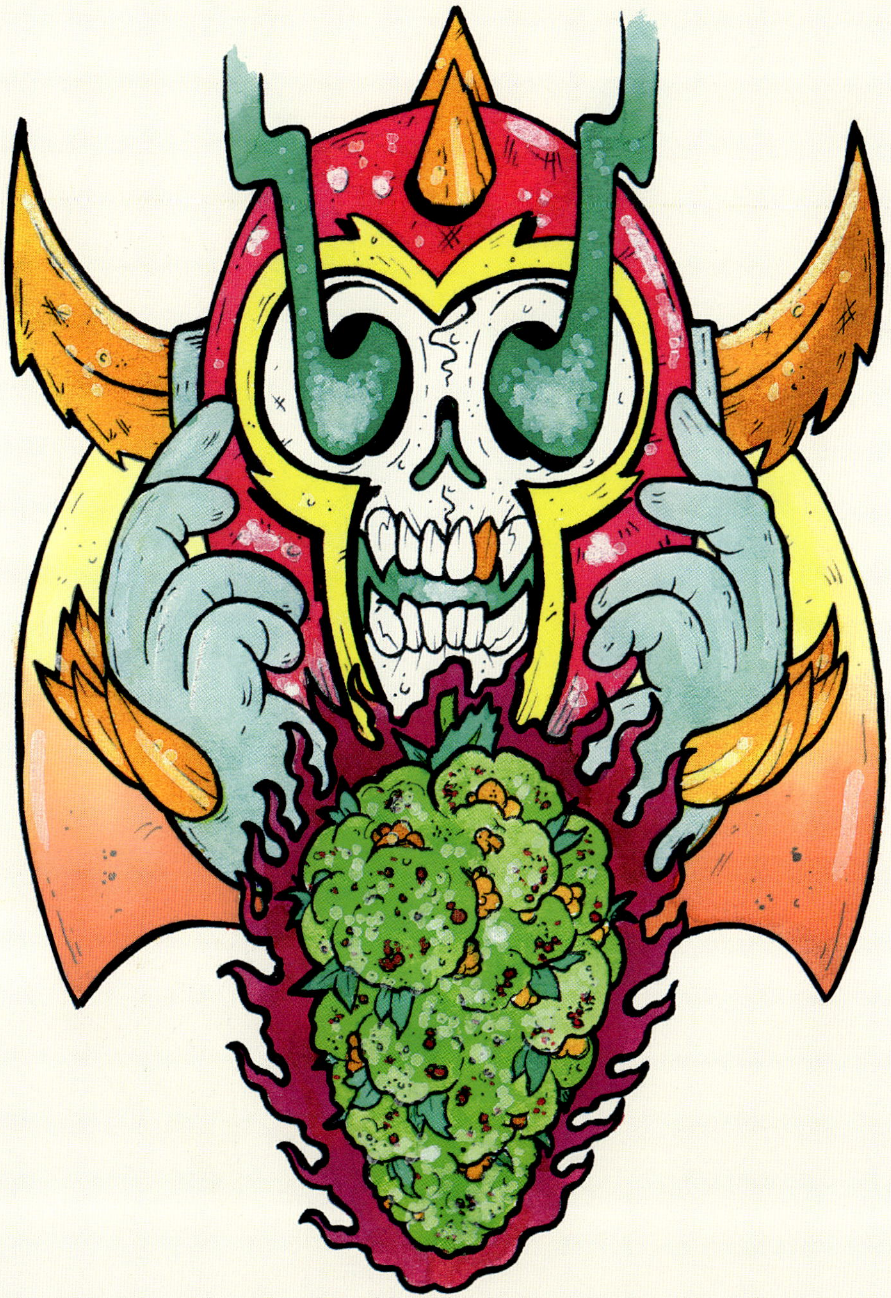

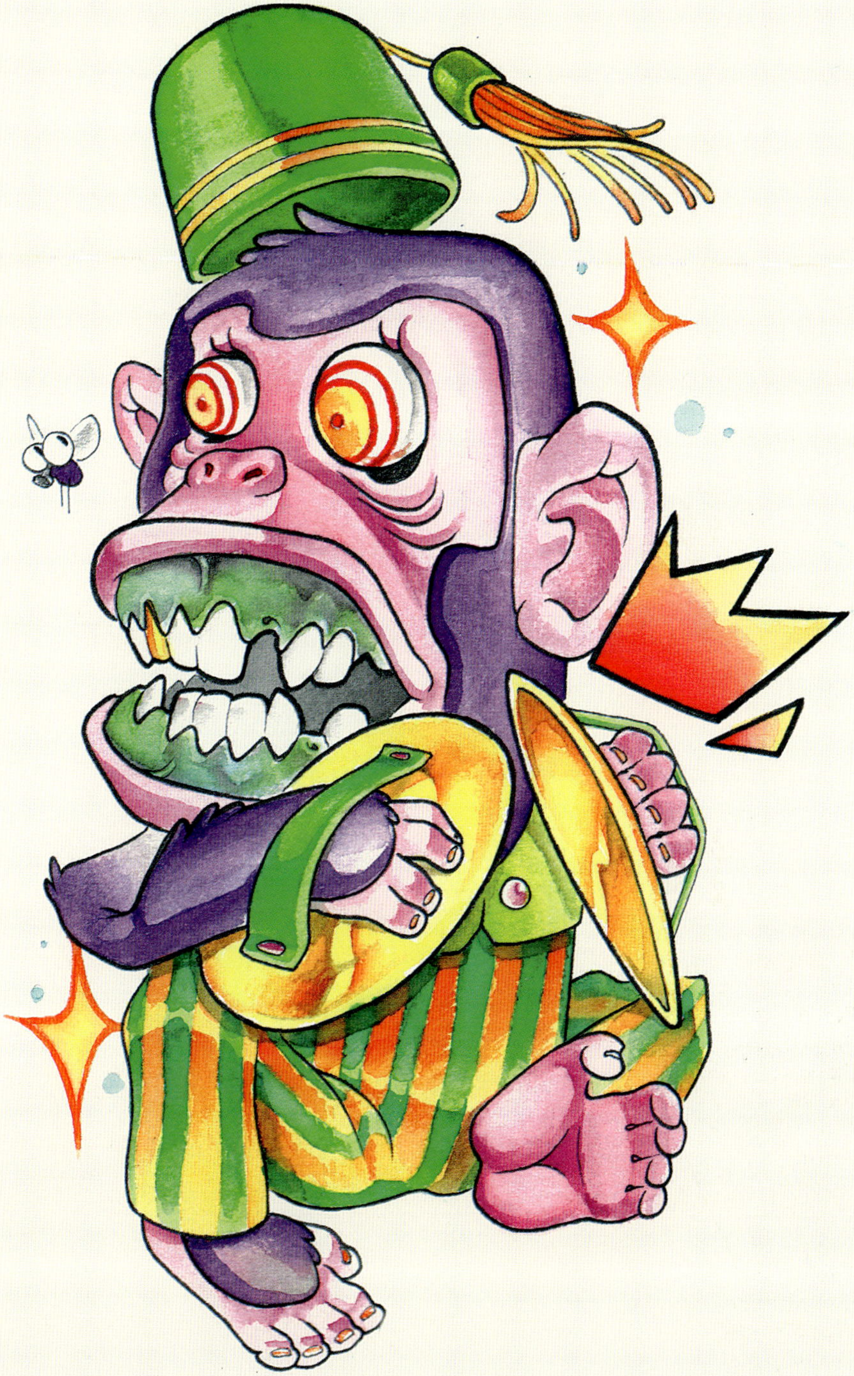

Index of Artists

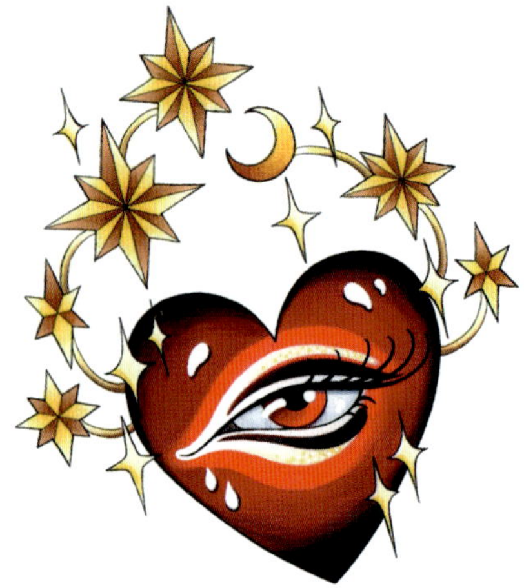

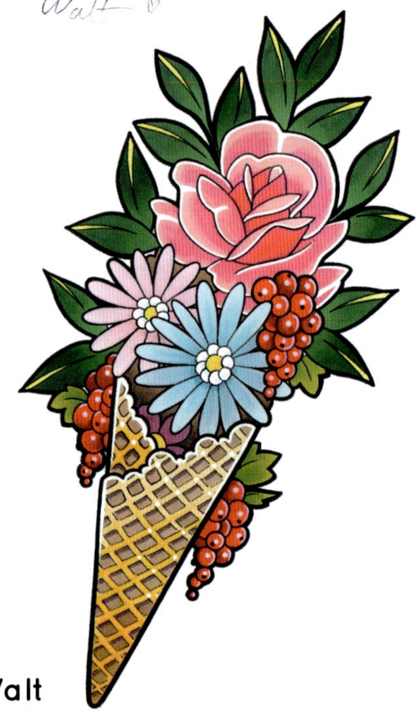

Flash
Mélodie Walt
@melodiewalt
Popink Marseille / Marseille / France